# Lecture Notes in Information Systems and Organisation

Volume 77

AF812789

Lecture Notes in Information Systems and Organization—LNISO—is a series of scientific books that explore the current scenario of information systems, in particular IS and organization. The focus on the relationship between IT, IS and organization is the common thread of this collection, which aspires to provide scholars across the world with a point of reference and comparison in the study and research of information systems and organization. LNISO is the publication forum for the community of scholars investigating behavioral and design aspects of IS and organization. The series offers an integrated publication platform for high-quality conferences, symposia and workshops in this field. Materials are published upon a strictly controlled double blind peer review evaluation made by selected reviewers.

LNISO is abstracted/indexed in Scopus

Bartosz Marcinkowski • Adam Przybyłek •
Aleksander Jarzębowicz • Netta Iivari •
Emilio Insfran • Michael Lang • Henry Linger •
Christoph Schneider
Editors

# Advances in Information Systems Development

## Exploring New Horizons and Opportunities

Springer

*Editors*
Bartosz Marcinkowski
University of Gdańsk
Gdańsk, Poland

Aleksander Jarzębowicz
Department of Software Engineering
Gdańsk University of Technology
Gdańsk, Poland

Emilio Insfran
Universitat Politècnica de València
Valencia, Spain

Henry Linger
Monash University
Clayton, VIC, Australia

Adam Przybyłek
Gdańsk University of Technology
Gdańsk, Poland

Netta Iivari
University of Oulu
Oulu, Finland

Michael Lang
University of Galway
Galway, Ireland

Christoph Schneider
IESE Business School
University of Navarra
Barcelona, Barcelona, Spain

ISSN 2195-4968 ISSN 2195-4976 (electronic)
Lecture Notes in Information Systems and Organisation
ISBN 978-3-031-87879-4 ISBN 978-3-031-87880-0 (eBook)
https://doi.org/10.1007/978-3-031-87880-0



This Springer imprint is published by the registered company Springer Nature Switzerland AG
The registered company address is: Gewerbestrasse 11, 6330 Cham, Switzerland

# Preface: Shaping the Future of Information Systems Development in the Era of Generative AI, Digital Transformation, and New Challenges

Generative AI is not merely a technological advancement; it is a transformative force that redefines the boundaries of human–computer collaboration, creativity, and decision-making. In addition, in the post-pandemic "new normal," remote work has evolved from a temporary necessity into a fundamental shift, transforming industries, reimagining productivity, and reshaping both work–life balance and the modern workplace. These developments underscore an urgent need for interdisciplinary research that bridges technical innovation with societal impact, exploring not only the potential of these technologies but also their ethical implications, governance structures, and long-term sustainability.

Addressing these challenges, this volume of the Lecture Notes in Information Systems and Organization (LNISO) series recognizes the outstanding research originally presented at the 32$^{nd}$ International Conference on Information Systems Development (ISD). It contains extended versions of the 13 best conference papers, as selected by the editors. The selected papers offer valuable insights into the salient challenges and opportunities currently shaping the field of information systems development, particularly in the context of rapidly evolving technologies such as Generative AI and digital transformation.

The ISD conference continues a long tradition that began with the first Polish-Scandinavian Seminar on Current Trends in Information Systems Development Methodologies, held in Gdańsk, Poland, in 1988, which subsequently grew into the International Conference on Information Systems Development. Throughout its history, the conference has been organized at various locations across the globe, fostering international collaboration and knowledge exchange. Thirty-six years after its inception in Gdańsk, the 32$^{nd}$ International Conference on Information Systems Development (ISD'24) returned to its birthplace, hosted by the University of Gdańsk in Sopot/Gdańsk, Poland, on August 26-28, 2024. The theme of ISD'24 was *Harnessing Opportunities: Reshaping ISD in the Post-COVID-19 and Generative AI Era.*

ISD'24 attracted contributions in the general area of information systems development, as well as in specialized areas represented by each track: *Managing IS Development and Operations, Information Systems Modelling, Lean and Agile Soft-*

*ware Development, Data Science and Machine Learning, Digital Transformation, Learning, Education, and Training, New Topics in IS Development, Other topics in IS, and Journal-First Papers.* As an Affiliated Conference of the *Association for Information Systems*, the ISD conference complements the international network of general IS conferences (*ICIS, ECIS, AMCIS, PACIS, HICSS*). All accepted papers were published in the AIS eLibrary (https://doi.org/10.62036/ISD.2024).

The chapters in this volume were selected through a two-stage process. Initially, track chairs nominated the best papers from their tracks for conference awards, resulting in 10 nominations. Authors of these nominated papers were then invited to submit extended versions. Following the conference, invitations were also extended to other outstanding presenters. This collection emphasizes the potential of technology and the synergy between innovative solutions and organizational processes.

Among the contributions, three chapters stand out for their strong alignment with the conference theme:

- In the chapter "Scaling Product Acceptance Analysis Using Annotation Systems Based on Large Language Models," Joseph Januszewicz, Pawel Robert Smolinski, and Jacek Winiarski integrate large language models (LLMs) with the Technology Acceptance Model (TAM), showcasing the transformative potential of LLMs in automating traditional survey-based analyses. This innovative approach demonstrates how LLMs can streamline the evaluation of product acceptance, offering significant efficiency and scalability advantages.
- The chapter "Strategies for Effective Remote Retrospectives: Exploring Retrospective Games, Anonymity, and Continuous Reflection" offers actionable strategies for agile teams grappling with low engagement and hesitancy to provide constructive feedback during remote retrospectives. The study by Yen Ying Ng, Bartosz Leśniewski, Krzysztof Marek, Michael Neumann, and Jacek Trzesicki highlights that incorporating collaborative games enhances meeting engagement and fosters active participation, while anonymity creates a safe space for more comprehensive and honest feedback.
- Finally, in the chapter "Self-Sovereign Identities: Brief History and Survey of the Field," Rodolfo da Silva Costa and Paulo Rupino da Cunha address the growing demand for secure and decentralized digital identity solutions in the post-pandemic digital era. By leveraging blockchain-based Self-Sovereign Identity (SSI) systems, the chapter explores how individuals can regain control of their data. The research underscores the pivotal role of SSI in reshaping ISD practices, with a focus on privacy, security, and regulatory compliance.

The following papers spotlight significant advancements in digital transformation, focusing on organizational, technological, and procedural shifts.

- In the chapter "A Framework for Rigorous Execution and Presentation of Expert Interviews in IS and Digital Transformation Research," Tobias Hassmann and Markus Westner propose a structured methodology to enhance the rigor of expert interviews, validated across multiple digital transformation studies. This framework provides actionable recommendations for conducting and reporting interviews, reinforcing their role in advancing research and practice.

- "Growing Pains of Digital Transformation: Navigating the Challenges in Non-Profits" addresses the unique obstacles faced by non-profit organizations in their digital transformation journeys. By identifying critical barriers and offering insights grounded in both literature and case studies, Alexandra Radu, Gideon Mekonnen Jonathan, and Erik Perjons contribute practical strategies to guide non-profits in achieving digital maturity. This research underscores the multifaceted nature of digital transformation, offering valuable frameworks and perspectives for researchers and practitioners navigating this rapidly evolving landscape.
- "Digital Innovation, Strategic and Lean Management as Success Factors in IT" examines the role of strategic and lean management practices in driving digital innovation within IT organizations. By analyzing industry practices, Elżbieta Wojnicka-Sycz, Jacek Rybicki, and Piotr Sycz identify key success factors that enable companies to navigate the challenges of digital transformation and maintain a competitive edge in a rapidly evolving technological landscape. The findings emphasize the importance of aligning innovation strategies with organizational goals to achieve sustainable growth.
- "A Solution for Developing Corpora for Polish Speech Enhancement in Complex Acoustic Environments" contributes to the technological dimension of digital transformation by addressing challenges in data preparation for speech processing. This chapter by Mariusz Kleć, Krzysztof Szklanny, and Alicja Wieczorkowska introduces innovative methods for generating Polish-language corpora tailored to complex acoustic scenarios, supporting the development of speech enhancement models with improved performance in noisy environments.
- In the chapter "Data-Driven Assessment of Practical Skills in Cybersecurity Challenges," Austėja Bauraitė, Agnė Brilingaitė, and Linas Bukauskas introduce an innovative system for evaluating cybersecurity trainees using secure sandbox environments and automated command-line data analysis. The authors demonstrate the potential of data-driven approaches to transform technical skill assessment, contributing to modernizing cybersecurity education within the scope of digital transformation.

Two chapters explore the innovative use of digital twins to address sustainability challenges.

- In the chapter "A Circular Digital Twin for Climate-Smart Soils Through Community Composting," José Monteiro and João Barata propose a digital twin solution for sustainable soil management, integrating real-time data from sensors to support climate change mitigation through carbon sequestration.
- Relatedly, in the chapter "Design Principles for Food Heritage Digital Twins," Ivo Mendes, José Monteiro, and João Barata apply the concept of digital twins to preserving intangible cultural heritage in traditional cheesemaking, enhancing both sustainability and production efficiency. Together, these two chapters illustrate how digital twins can bridge technological advancement and

societal goals, demonstrating the transformative potential of information systems in addressing environmental and cultural challenges.

The final group of chapters focus on improving foundational practices, tools, and frameworks for information systems development, encompassing operational strategies, methodological advancements, and performance optimization.

- In the chapter "Beyond Agile Methodologies: Exploring the Business Analyst's Role in Agile Software Development," Mateusz Kwiatkowski and Aleksander Jarzębowicz investigate the responsibilities of business analysts within agile teams. Since such a role is not included in any of the most widely used agile methodologies, this chapter explores how it is defined in industry practice. The study provides an understanding of the business analyst's tasks in information systems development processes defined on the basis of an agile approach.
- "Assessing Operational Business-IT Alignment for Architecture Improvement" addresses the persistent challenge of achieving effective business-IT alignment (BITA) in organizations. In this chapter, Pascal André, Ali Benjilany, Hugo Bruneliere, and Dalila Tamzalit introduce a robust methodology combining metrics, consistency rules, and anti-pattern identification to evaluate and improve BITA. By applying this approach in real-world settings, the study offers actionable insights into enhancing architectural design and operational efficiency, reinforcing the strategic value of BITA in modern organizations.
- In the chapter "An EBNF-Based Grammar for Use Case Specification," Marinos Georgiades proposes an innovative framework for formalizing use case specifications using an Extended Backus-Naur Form (EBNF)-based grammar. This framework ensures clarity and consistency in functional requirements specification, enabling semi-automated validation and providing a foundation for potential extensions such as diagram generation and metrics analysis. The chapter demonstrates the practical applicability of the grammar in improving the quality of requirements engineering processes and bridging the gap between stakeholders and technical teams.
- Finally, in the chapter "Changes in Node.js Server-Side Application Performance Characteristics Over Time Under Load," Paweł Kuffel and Bartosz Walter investigate performance dynamics of Node.js frameworks through comprehensive load testing. The study challenges existing performance assumptions, reveals runtime optimization insights, and provides practical recommendations for backend application development. By empirically examining performance characteristics, the research offers valuable guidance for developers seeking to optimize server-side application design.

In summary, this volume presents an extension of the high-quality research showcased at ISD'24, capturing the innovative approaches and solutions to drive forward the field of Information Systems Development. As we look ahead, these contributions will continue to inspire and inform both academic research and practical application, fostering greater synergy between research, industry, and education. We trust that this collection will serve as a significant resource for advancing knowledge and practice in Information Systems Development.

Gdańsk, Poland Bartosz Marcinkowski
Gdańsk, Poland Adam Przybyłek
Gdańsk, Poland Aleksander Jarzębowicz
Oulu, Finland Netta Iivari
Valencia, Spain Emilio Insfran
Galway, Ireland Michael Lang
Clayton, Australia Henry Linger
Barcelona, Spain Christoph Schneider

# Conference Organization

**General Chair**
Bartosz Marcinkowski, University of Gdańsk, Poland
**Program Chair**
Adam Przybyłek, Gdańsk University of Technology, Poland
**Proceedings Chair**
Aleksander Jarzębowicz, Gdańsk University of Technology, Poland
**Publicity Chair**
Yen Ying Ng, Nicolaus Copernicus University, Poland
**Conference Office**
Anna Węsierska, University of Gdańsk, Poland
**Local Arrangement Chairs**
Jacek Winiarski, University of Gdańsk, Poland
Marek Bednarczyk, Polish-Japanese Academy of Information Technology, Poland
**Web Chair**
Dariusz Kralewski, University of Gdańsk, Poland

# International Steering Committee

# Track Chairs

**Managing IS Development and Operations**
Tomas Cerny, University of Arizona, USA
Paulo Rupino da Cunha, University of Coimbra, Portugal
**Information Systems Modelling**
Miguel Mira da Silva, University of Lisbon, Portugal
Geert Poels, Ghent University, Belgium
**Lean and Agile Software Development**
Adam Przybyłek, Gdańsk University of Technology, Poland
Alberto Rodrigues da Silva, University of Lisbon, Portugal
**Data Science and Machine Learning**
Boris Delibašić, University of Belgrade, Serbia
Ivan Luković, University of Belgrade, Serbia
Beata Zielosko, University of Silesia in Katowice, Poland
**Digital Transformation**
Jörg Becker, University of Münster, Germany
Jacek Maślankowski, University of Gdańsk, Poland
**Learning, Education, and Training**
Muhammad Ovais Ahmad, Karlstad University, Sweden
Georgia Kapitsaki, University of Cyprus, Cyprus
**New Topics in IS Development**
Mārīte Kirikova, Riga Technical University, Latvia
Piotr Soja, Cracow University of Economics, Poland
**Journal-First Papers**
Robert Andrei Buchmann, Babes-Bolyai University, Romania
Gheorghe Cosmin Silaghi, Babes-Bolyai University, Romania

# Contents

# Contributors

**Pascal André** Nantes University - CNRS/LS2N, Nantes, France

**João Barata** University of Coimbra, CISUC/LASI, DEI, Coimbra, Portugal

**Austėja Bauraitė** Institute of Computer Science, Vilnius University, Vilnius, Lithuania

**Ali Benjilany** Nantes University - CNRS/LS2N, Nantes, France

**Agnė Brilingaitė** Institute of Computer Science, Vilnius University, Vilnius, Lithuania

**Hugo Bruneliere** IMT Atlantique–CNRS/LS2N, Nantes, France

**Linas Bukauskas** Institute of Computer Science, Vilnius University, Vilnius, Lithuania

**Paulo Rupino Da Cunha** University of Coimbra, CISUC, DEI, Coimbra, Portugal

**Marinos Georgiades** University of Tartu, Tartu, Estonia

**Tobias Hassmann** Munich Business School, Munich, Germany

**Joseph Januszewicz** Geisel School of Medicine at Dartmouth, Hanover, NH, USA

**Aleksander Jarzębowicz** Department of Software Engineering, Gdańsk University of Technology, Gdańsk, Poland

**Gideon Mekonnen Jonathan** Department of Computer and Systems Sciences (DSV), Stockholm University, Kista, Sweden

**Mariusz Kleć** Polish-Japanese Academy of Information Technology, Warsaw, Poland

**Pawel Kuffeł** Poznan University of Technology, Poznan, Poland

**Mateusz Kwiatkowski** Department of Software Engineering, Gdańsk University of Technology, Gdańsk, Poland

**Bartosz Leśniewski** Gdańsk University of Technology, Gdańsk, Poland

**Krzysztof Marek** Warsaw University of Technology, Warsaw, Poland

**Ivo Mendes** University of Coimbra, CISUC/LASI, DEI, Coimbra, Portugal

**José Monteiro** University of Coimbra, CISUC/LASI, DEI, Coimbra, Portugal

**Michael Neumann** University of Applied Sciences and Arts Hannover, Hannover, Germany

**Yen Ying Ng** Nicolaus Copernicus University, Toruń, Poland

**Erik Perjons** Department of Computer and Systems Sciences (DSV), Stockholm University, Kista, Sweden

**Alexandra Radu** Department of Computer and Systems Sciences (DSV), Stockholm University, Kista, Sweden

**Jacek Rybicki** University of Gdańsk, Gdańsk, Poland

**Rodolfo da Silva Costa** University of Coimbra, CISUC, DEI, Coimbra, Portugal

**Pawel Robert Smolinski** University of Gdansk, Gdańsk, Poland

**Piotr Sycz** University of Gdańsk, Gdańsk, Poland

**Krzysztof Szklanny** Polish-Japanese Academy of Information Technology, Warsaw, Poland

**Dalila Tamzalit** Nantes University - CNRS/LS2N, Nantes, France

**Jacek Trzesicki** Warsaw University of Technology, Warsaw, Poland

**Bartosz Walter** Poznan University of Technology, Poznan, Poland

**Markus Westnerm** OTH Regensburg, Regensburg, Germany

**Alicja Wieczorkowska** Polish-Japanese Academy of Information Technology, Warsaw, Poland

**Jacek Winiarski** University of Gdansk/Faculty of Economics, Sopot, Poland

**Elżbieta Wojnicka-Sycz** University of Gdańsk & Gdańsk University of Technology, Gdańsk, Poland

# List of Figures

**Digital Innovation, Strategic and Lean Management as Success Factors in IT**



**A Solution for Developing Corpora for Polish Speech Enhancement in Complex Acoustic Environments**

**Data-Driven Assessment of Practical Skills in Cybersecurity Challenges**



**A Circular Digital Twin for Climate-Smart Soils through Community Composting**

**Design Principles for Food Heritage Digital Twins**



**Beyond Agile Methodologies: Exploring the Business Analyst's Role in Agile Software Development**



**Assessing Operational Business-IT Alignment for Architecture Improvement**



**Changes in Node.js Server-Side Application Performance Characteristics Over Time Under Load**

# List of Tables

**Digital Innovation, Strategic and Lean Management as Success Factors in IT**



**A Solution for Developing Corpora for Polish Speech Enhancement in Complex Acoustic Environments**

**A Circular Digital Twin for Climate-Smart Soils through Community Composting**



**Design Principles for Food Heritage Digital Twins**



**Beyond Agile Methodologies: Exploring the Business Analyst's Role in Agile Software Development**



**Assessing Operational Business-IT Alignment for Architecture Improvement**



**An EBNF-Based Grammar for Use Case Specification**

# Scaling Product Acceptance Analysis Using Annotation Systems Based on Large Language Models

**Joseph Januszewicz, Pawel Robert Smolinski, and Jacek Winiarski**

**Abstract** While Technology Acceptance Models (TAM) are widely used, their practical utility remains in question. Significant challenges to the useful application of TAM include the difficulties in gathering TAM data through traditional methods of surveys and questionnaires and the homogeneity hypothesis for technology predictors, which constrains the usefulness of TAM models in comparing products. This paper addresses both challenges by (1) validating the use of NLP-LLM to incorporate unstructured online data into TAM models rather than surveys and (2) demonstrating and validating a TAM model without homogenous predictors by applying it to the handheld gaming console market. We use Amazon reviews for Nintendo, Steam Deck, Logitech, and Razer consoles, annotating them using Chat GPT NLP-LLM-algorithms to obtain scores for TAM variables. We validate the use of NLP-LLMs by measuring high consistency between LLM runs and strong agreement with scores given by human experts. We then fit separate TAM regressions for each console and compare coefficients, revealing significant heterogeneity with the Steam Deck emerging as a market leader and Nintendo lagging behind its competitors. Altogether, we demonstrate that TAM models with heterogeneous predictors are both useful and applicable, and that NLP-LLM powered models have the ability to provide results highly similar to current more expensive and limited methods.

J. Januszewicz
Geisel School of Medicine at Dartmouth, Hanover, NH, USA
e-mail: joseph.januszewicz.gr@dartmouth.edu

P. R. Smolinski
University of Gdansk, Gdańsk, Poland
e-mail: pawel.smolinski@ug.edu.pl

J. Winiarski (✉)
University of Gdansk/Faculty of Economics, Sopot, Poland
e-mail: jacek.winiarski@ug.edu.pl

 
B. Marcinkowski et al. (eds.), *Advances in Information Systems Development*,
Lecture Notes in Information Systems and Organisation 77,
https://doi.org/10.1007/978-3-031-87880-0_1

## 1 Introduction

The concept of technology acceptance has been a cornerstone in information system research for nearly four decades, igniting a plethora of studies dedicated to its understanding [1–4]. The technology acceptance idea originates with the pioneering work of Fred Davis, who introduced the first Technology Acceptance Model (TAM) in 1985 [5]. Davis's model aimed to understand an individual's willingness to adopt new technologies. Drawing from previous works by Ajzen Icek on social theory of reasoned action [6] and planned behavior [7], Davis identified two main determinants of technology adoption: Perceived Usefulness and Perceived Ease of Use [8].

In the years following Davis's initial model, the field witnessed explosive growth in technology acceptance research accompanied by numerous modifications and expansions of the original model [9–12]. Among these, Venkatesh's Unified Theory of Acceptance and Use of Technology (UTAUT) stands out as a particularly influential development [3, 13]. A simple search on Google Scholar with the keyword "UTAUT" yields over 80,300 entries, underscoring the theory's widespread adoption. Venkatesh expanded upon Davis's model by introducing four predictive variables: Performance Expectancy, Effort Expectancy (parallels of Perceived Usefulness and Ease of Use), Social Influence, and Facilitating Conditions. These variables have been validated by recent meta-analyses and literature reviews as the most reliable predictors of technology acceptance in a broad range of applications [2, 14].

While researchers have generally reached consensus regarding the best technology acceptance model, many scholars have questioned the practical utility of technology acceptance [15–18]. These scholars question what insights the understanding of technology acceptance determinants can provide, beyond the tautological conclusion that users adopt products perceived as useful and easy to use [15]. This lack of practical utility stems from two significant issues: the homogeneity assumption and measurement challenges.

The first issue concerns the long-held assumption of homogeneity in technology acceptance predictors. It posits that the technology acceptance predictors have a consistent effect across all contexts. However, as Salovaara et al. [17, 20] argued, treating the model's predictors as invariant (homogeneous) limits the model's flexibility and applicability. Without heterogeneity in the predictors' effects across different contexts, the model offers little value beyond identifying general factors influencing technology acceptance. Recent meta-analytic results have provided empirical evidence rejecting homogeneity assumption, demonstrating that the model predictors are indeed heterogeneous and have varying effects depending on the context in which they are studied [14, 19, 23].

The second issue relates to the traditional methods of data collection and measurement in technology acceptance research. Technology acceptance data is typically collected through surveys and questionnaires, which present several challenges. These include a lack of standardization across studies [9, 10], difficulties in reaching target demographics and obtaining sufficiently large sample sizes, and the potential for socially desirable responses rather than truthful ones [12]. Moreover, the design and implementation of these surveys often require substantial effort and resources, making it challenging to collect high-quality data on users' attitudes consistently.

These two issues—the homogeneity assumption and measurement challenges—significantly contribute to the lack of practical utility in Technology Acceptance Models. The homogeneity assumption limits the model's ability to provide context-specific insights for improving products or tailoring implementations to specific situations. Meanwhile, the measurement challenges associated with surveys and questionnaires raise questions about the reliability and validity of the data used to construct and validate these models.

To address these limitations, researchers have begun exploring alternative approaches. For the homogeneity issue, scholars like Salovaara and Tamminen [16, 17] have argued for allowing the models' predictors to vary, which could enable practical applications such as product design and comparison. For example, if product A has a greater effect size of Ease of Use (EU) on user adoption than product B, then improvements in design aimed at EU features should lead to greater adoption for product A compared to equivalent changes in product B's design.

Regarding measurement challenges, there has been a move towards leveraging more natural or ecologically valid data sources for inferring attitudes [13]. These include user-generated content such as social media posts, product reviews, and forum discussions. The analysis of such data has been accelerated by the development of Natural Language Processing (NLP) methods and Large Language Models (LLMs), which enable the extraction of user attitudes from vast amounts of unstructured textual content [15, 16].

This paper builds upon research presented at the 32nd International Conference on Information Systems Development (ISD 2024) and the theme of "Harnessing Opportunities: Reshaping ISD in the post-COVID-19 and Generative AI Era". Our paper shows how generative AI can be harnessed to overcome challenges in previous ISD methods. This paper's research includes the previously presented application of TAM to handheld gaming consoles but extends and validates the methodology of using LLMs to create TAM product comparisons.

## 2 Current Study

In this paper, we aim to address these two emerging challenges in technology acceptance research: (1) the limitations of traditional survey-based data collection methods and (2) the homogeneity assumption in acceptance models. Our overarching goal is to validate and apply a novel approach to technology acceptance modeling using Large Language Model (LLM) annotation systems, which we believe can provide more scalable and ecologically valid data for product analysis. To achieve this goal, we conduct two interrelated studies:

## 2.1 Study 1

In the first study, we design and validate an LLM annotation system capable of converting unstructured user reviews into structured annotations measuring key technology acceptance variables. We assess the system's consistency across multiple runs and its accuracy compared to human expert evaluations. We aim to demonstrate that LLM annotation systems can serve as a reliable and scalable alternative to traditional questionnaire-based surveys and expert evaluations in technology acceptance research.

For Study 1, we propose the following hypotheses:

1. **Consistency Hypothesis.** The LLM annotation system will produce consistent results across multiple runs for each technology acceptance variable.

$$\alpha_{LLM} > threshold$$

   Where $\alpha_{LLM}$ represents the agreement of annotations across multiple runs, and the threshold is a predetermined acceptable level of agreement. According to McHugh (2012), these values indicate moderate to strong levels of consistency, where moderate is greater than 0.6 and strong exceeds 0.8 [20].
2. **Validity Hypothesis.** The LLM annotations will show high agreement with human expert annotations.

$$\alpha_{LLM-human} > 0.7$$

   Where $\alpha_{LLM\,-\,human}$ represents agreement coefficient between LLM annotations and human expert annotations, with values above 0.7 indicating substantial agreement.

## 2.2 Study 2

For the second study, we aim to validate the Technology Acceptance Model using the annotated reviews generated by our LLM system in Study 1. We will then investigate the heterogeneity in the TAM by comparing model parameters and variable means across different selected products. This comparative analysis will allow us to test whether acceptance factors vary significantly between products and utilize these differences in product comparison and competitive analysis.

For Study 2, we propose four hypotheses:

3. **Model Validity Hypothesis**. We expect that technology acceptance predictors will demonstrate strong and consistent predictive power across different products, with R-squared values falling within the range of 0.6 to 0.7 [20].

$$R^2_{Nintendo} \approx R^2_{Steam\ Deck} \approx R^2_{Logitech} \approx R^2_{Razer} \approx 0.6 - 0.7 \quad (1)$$

4. **Parameter Significance Hypothesis**. All parameters within our model that predict technology acceptance will be statistically significant across each product analyzed. This hypothesis can be stated that for any model parameter *i* (e.g., EU):

$$\beta_i \neq 0 \quad (2)$$

5. **Heterogeneity Hypothesis**. This hypothesis is an extension of the previous one and a direct verification of Salovaara and Tamminen's [17] and Salovaara et al. [20] claim that the model parameters are heterogeneous. It can be formalized that at least one of the following inequalities is true:

$$\beta_{i\ Nintendo} \neq \beta_{i\ Steam\ Deck} \neq \beta_{i\ Logitech} \neq \beta_{i\ Razer} \quad (3)$$

   If at least one parameter significantly differs, this indicates variation in the effect size of specific model parameters on user acceptance between products. Such variation enables the identification of comparative advantages through differences in these effect sizes.
6. **Mean Differences Hypothesis**. Our last hypothesis is complementary to the previous hypotheses and examines whether there are significant differences in the means of model variables across different products:

$$\overline{X}_{i\ Nintendo} \neq \overline{X}_{i\ Steam\ Deck} \neq \overline{X}_{i\ Logitech} \neq \overline{X}_{i\ Razer} \quad (4)$$

   Mean Differences Hypothesis may appear similar to the Heterogeneity Hypothesis, however they are conceptually distinct. The Heterogeneity Hypothesis explores whether model predictors, such as Perceived Usefulness (PU), have different effects on users' acceptance of different products, questioning whether PU influences acceptance differently across various consoles. In contrast, the Mean Differences Hypothesis focuses on whether there are significant variations in how PU and other model features are perceived across different products.

By conducting these studies, we aim to demonstrate the validity and utility of LLM annotation systems in technology acceptance research while simultaneously addressing the homogeneity assumption. Our approach offers two key advantages: first, it provides a more scalable and ecologically valid method for data collection by leveraging accessible user-generated content. Second, it enhances the practical utility of technology acceptance models by enabling researchers to identify comparative advantages among products through analysis of effect sizes and user sentiment of acceptance factors.

# 3 Methodology

## 3.1 Study 1 Methodology

We designed an LLM annotation system to evaluate customer reviews using a standardized Technology Acceptance Model (TAM) questionnaire format. The system uses a custom prompt instructing the LLM on annotating reviews based on specified acceptance model variables: Perceived usefulness PU, Ease of use EU, Social influence SI, and Facilitating conditions FC. These are rated using a 5-point Likert scale, where 1 indicates a clearly negative perception and 5 indicates a clearly positive perception. If insufficient information is available, the system assigns a 0.

We tested the system's consistency by running multiple annotations on selected Amazon product reviews. The system processes each review individually, extracting annotations related to the TAM variables. The extracted information is then parsed and organized into a data frame with TAM variables as columns, reviews as rows, and LLM annotations as elements.

To measure consistency, we employed the weighted percentage agreement (WPA) metric. This metric calculates the proportion of matching annotations while accounting for the severity of disagreements.

$$WPA = 1 - \frac{\sum_{i=1}^{n} w\left(r_{1i}, r_{2i}\right)}{n \bullet w_{max}} \tag{5}$$

Where:

- $n$ is the total number of items (reviews) being compared.
- $w(r_{1i}, r_{2i})$ represents the penalty weight assigned to the disagreement between the two sets of annotations on the $i$-th item.
- $w_{max}$ is the maximum weight, representing the highest possible penalty for disagreement within the custom weights matrix.

We used a custom penalty matrix where complete agreement has a penalty of 0, and penalties increase quadratically for disagreements, with a maximum penalty of 16 for extreme disagreements. Annotation of 0 is uniquely treated as a "no information" category and is assigned specific penalties: [0, 16, 9, 4, 9, 16]. The rows (representing one annotation with possibilities of 0–5) and columns (representing another such annotation) intersect at the diagonal (where both have the same score) for a penalty of 0. The penalty matrix appears as follows:

$$W = \begin{bmatrix} 0 & 16 & 9 & 4 & 9 & 16 \\ 16 & 0 & 1 & 4 & 9 & 16 \\ 9 & 1 & 0 & 1 & 4 & 9 \\ 4 & 4 & 1 & 0 & 1 & 4 \\ 9 & 9 & 4 & 1 & 0 & 1 \\ 16 & 16 & 9 & 4 & 1 & 0 \end{bmatrix}$$

To validate the system, we compared LLM annotations with those from three independent experts holding PhDs in information systems research, who have published works on Technology Acceptance Models and are not authors of this paper. Experts were given the same prompt and asked to evaluate the same reviews based on the four UTAUT variables using the Likert scale. We then compared their annotations to those generated by LLMs using the WPA metric.

To assess run-to-run consistency, we executed our workflow 50 times on the same set of reviews using GPT-4. We then calculated the weighted percentage agreement (WPA) for every possible pair of runs (e.g., run 1 with run 2, run 1 with run 3, run 2 with run 3, etc.). The weighted percentage agreement quantifies the proportion of similar annotations across two runs, incorporating a penalty for the severity of disagreement. This process was repeated for each TAM variable. Subsequently, we averaged all possible pairwise agreements to determine an average agreement score for each variable, thereby deriving the consistency ratings across 50 workflow runs.

## *3.2 Study 2 Methodology*

For the second study, we needed to select products that met specific criteria. First, the products had to be readily available with a substantial number of user reviews to ensure a robust dataset. Second, they needed to be competing products vying for the same user base, with comparable features and functionalities. Lastly, we focused on technology products, specifically in the handheld gaming console market, as this aligns with our research on technology acceptance.

Based on these criteria, we selected four prominent handheld gaming devices: Nintendo Switch, Steam Deck, Logitech G Cloud, and Razer Kishi. These products compete directly in the portable gaming market, offering similar core functionalities while differentiating themselves through unique features. They also represent a mix of established and newer entrants in the market, providing a diverse range of user experiences and brand perceptions.

We collected a total of 1170 product reviews from official Amazon.com pages of these manufacturers: Nintendo (480 reviews), Logitech G (246 reviews), Razer Kishi (289 reviews), and Steam Deck (155 reviews). We aimed for a balanced representation of all possible star ratings (1 to 5 stars on Amazon) to ensure a diverse range of user experiences and opinions were captured in our dataset.

The reviews were processed using an LLM annotation system developed in Study 1. The annotation process was conducted solely on the review text, without considering the numerical ratings given to products. Reviews lacking adequate information were automatically excluded by the LLM annotation algorithm, resulting in adjusted sample sizes: Nintendo (448 reviews), Logitech (240 reviews), Razer (282 reviews), and Steam Deck (135 reviews).

For analysis, we used regression modeling. We fitted separate regression models for each handheld console product. In these models, the dependent variable was Acceptance, measured by the review's star rating. The independent variables were

Perceived Usefulness (PU) and Perceived Ease of Use (EU), as annotated by the LLM system from the review text.

From these regression models, we examined the R-squared values to assess the total predictive power of the TAM variables. We also analyzed the parameter coefficients, which represent the strength and direction of the relationship between PU and EU ratings and the Acceptance measure.

To test parameter heterogeneity between products, we employed the method described by Ayala Cohen for comparing regression coefficients. This procedure involved using a specialized t-test designed for comparing regression coefficients, yielding a coefficient difference and a p-value indicating statistical significance.

As our Heterogeneity Hypotheses required running multiple beta parameter tests, we applied the Holm-Sidak correction for multiple testing. This correction was chosen as it provides a good balance between maintaining the familywise error rate and preserving statistical power.

To test the Mean Differences Hypothesis in user perceptions of TAM variables across different products, we employed a one-way analysis of variance (ANOVA). We then conducted post-hoc pairwise comparisons using the Tukey method to identify which specific product pairs exhibited the largest differences in user sentiment for each TAM variable.

# 4 Results

## 4.1 *Study 1: LLM Inter-Run Agreement (i.e. Consistency)*

For GPT-4 the WPA scores between runs are: $WPA_{PE} = 0.74$ for Performance Expectancy, $WPA_{EE} = 0.72$ for Effort Expectancy, $WPA_{SI} = 0.86$ for Social Influence, and $WPA_{FC} = 0.76$ for Facilitating Conditions. According to McHugh (2012), these values indicate moderate to strong levels of consistency, where moderate is greater than 0.6 and strong exceeds 0.8 [20]. Such results suggest that while the annotations are generally consistent, there are instances where runs produce divergent annotations. We did test GPT-3.5 to see if it was more consistent but found little difference between GPT-4 and GPT-3.5. The GPT-4 results above are from a model with adjusted temperature (0.25), meaning we have decreased the chance of low-probability answers from being provided by the LLM.

## 4.2 *Study 1: LLM Annotations Compared to Human Experts*

Table 1 presents the agreement between the evaluations of three human experts and mode evaluations generated by GPT-4 model. The average WPA across all pairs (expert and LLM) is highest for Performance Expectancy ($WPA_{PE} = 0.87$) and Effort Expectancy ($WPA_{EE} = 0.73$). The mean WPA scores for Social Influence

**Table 1** Agreement between human experts and GPT-4 annotations

| Variable/Comparison | Agreement Score |
|---|---|
| **Performance expectancy (PE)** | |
| Expert 1 vs expert 2 | 0.6625 |
| Expert 1 vs expert 3 | 0.9542 |
| Expert 1 vs GPT-4 | **0.9458** |
| Expert 2 vs expert 3 | 0.6833 |
| Expert 2 vs GPT-4 | **0.6917** |
| Expert 3 vs GPT-4 | **0.9833** |
| **Effort expectancy (EE)** | |
| Expert 1 vs expert 2 | 0.6625 |
| Expert 1 vs expert 3 | 0.8250 |
| Expert 1 vs GPT-4 | **0.6667** |
| Expert 2 vs expert 3 | 0.6625 |
| Expert 2 vs GPT-4 | **0.6542** |
| Expert 3 vs GPT-4 | **0.8750** |
| **Social influence (SI)** | |
| Expert 1 vs expert 2 | 0.2917 |
| Expert 1 vs expert 3 | 0.8208 |
| Expert 1 vs GPT-4 | **0.9333** |
| Expert 2 vs expert 3 | 0.4208 |
| Expert 2 vs GPT-4 | **0.3250** |
| Expert 3 vs GPT-4 | **0.7542** |
| **Facilitating conditions (FC)** | |
| Expert 1 vs expert 2 | 0.4583 |
| Expert 1 vs expert 3 | 0.4750 |
| Expert 1 vs GPT-4 | **0.3083** |
| Expert 2 vs expert 3 | 0.6750 |
| Expert 2 vs GPT-4 | **0.6500** |
| Expert 3 vs GPT-4 | **0.8417** |

and Facilitating Conditions are on the threshold of moderate and weak, revealing a significantly lower level of consensus among experts when it comes to annotating these factors in reviews ($WPA_{SI} = 0.67$ and $WPA_{FC} = 0.60$).

We can categorize the average WPA for each variable into two groups: the mean agreement amongst human experts alone (comparing expert 1 with expert 2, 2 with 3, and 1 with 3) and the mean agreement between all human experts and LLM model (evaluations of experts 1, 2, and 3 with GPT-4). We will abbreviate agreement between humans as $WPA_H$ with agreement between the human experts and the LLM Model as $WPA_{H\text{-}AI}$. Such categorization allows us to assess if there is a significant difference between the consensus amongst human experts and their agreement with the LLM's evaluations.

For Performance Expectancy, the mean agreement between human experts was $WPA_{H\,(PE)} = 0.77$ while their agreement with GPT-4 evaluations was slightly higher at $WPA_{H\text{-}AI\,(PE)} = 0.87$. Results with $WPA_{H\text{-}AI\,(PE)} > WPA_{H\,(PE)}$ suggest that, on average, the evaluations provided by the LLM more closely matched those of the human experts than human experts agree amongst themselves. A similar pattern is observed for Effort Expectancy, where the agreement between human experts and between humans and the AI does not significantly diverge ($WPA_{H\,(EE)} = 0.72$, $WPA_{H\text{-}AI\,(EE)} = 0.73$) but with $WPA_{H\text{-}AI}$ slightly higher.

The trend holds for Facilitating Conditions as well, with agreements of ($WPA_{H\,(FC)} = 0.54$, $WPA_{H\text{-}AI\,(FC)} = 0.60$). A more notable divergence is found in the case of Social Influence, where the agreement between human experts and the AI ($WPA_{H\text{-}AI\,(SI)} = 0.67$) significantly surpasses the agreement among human experts alone ($WPA_{H\,(SI)} = 0.51$). This implies that, on average, human experts align much more closely with the evaluations provided by LLMs than they do with each other's assessments.

## 4.3 Study 2: LLM Annotation Results

The LLM annotation system produced a data frame containing two columns with annotated Perceived Usefulness (PU) and Perceived Ease of Use (EU) scores on a Likert scale ranging from 1 to 5. These Likert scale annotations aim to mimic questionnaire behavior by annotating the sentiment expressed in the reviews related to each factor. An annotation of 1 indicates that the review clearly expresses negative sentiment toward the factor (e.g., PU), while an annotation of 5 represents a review that clearly expresses positive sentiment toward the factor. Mean sentiment annotations and their standard deviations for each handheld console are presented below in Table 2.

## 4.4 R Squared (Model Fit Hypothesis)

In Table 3, we present the results from fitting TAM regression models for each product. The R-squared values support our Model Fit Hypothesis, which stated that technology acceptance predictors would consistently demonstrate strong predictive power of user acceptance across different products. All models reached the antici-

**Table 2** Descriptive statistics for user star ratings of handheld consoles and mean Large Language Model annotations of Perceived Usefulness and Ease of Use sentiment

| | Rating | | Perceived Usefulness (PU) | | Ease of Use (EU) | |
|---|---|---|---|---|---|---|
| Product | Mean | SD | Mean | SD | Mean | SD |
| Nintendo | 3.03 | 1.43 | 2.86 | 1.40 | 2.51 | 1.05 |
| Steam deck | 3.98 | 1.56 | 3.68 | 1.39 | 3.24 | 1.15 |
| Logitech | 3.47 | 1.61 | 3.40 | 1.36 | 2.96 | 1.01 |
| Razer | 3.46 | 1.48 | 3.27 | 1.37 | 2.73 | 1.04 |

**Table 3** Technology acceptance model regression results

| | Perceived Usefulness (PU) | | Ease of Use (EU) | | $R^2$ |
|---|---|---|---|---|---|
| Product | Coef. (SE) | p-value | Coef. (SE) | p-value | |
| Nintendo | 0.499 (0.049) | < 0.001 | 0.458 (0.065) | < 0.001 | 0.606 |
| Steam deck | 0.458 (0.098) | < 0.001 | 0.593 (0.117) | < 0.001 | 0.647 |
| Logitech | 0.719 (0.078) | < 0.001 | 0.372 (0.105) | < 0.001 | 0.648 |
| Razer | 0.795 (0.059) | < 0.001 | 0.197 (0.078) | 0.012 | 0.725 |

pated R-squared range of approximately 0.6–0.7. For instance, the R-squared value of 0.725 for the Razer console indicates that 72.5% of the variance in user ratings can be explained by the PU and EU scores. These values are typical for TAM and its variants, confirming that TAM is a valid framework for modeling user sentiment towards these products.

## 4.5 Beta Coefficients (Parameter Significance Hypothesis)

As expected, all model coefficients from Table 3 are significant, indicating that PU and EU are important determinants of user acceptance. This is not a surprising result, as pointed out by Barki and Benbasat's [15] critique of TAM: useful and easy-to-use products will always be used by users (and hence these variables will be significant). However, we can also observe that the parameter coefficients have different effect sizes, and despite all being significant, some products have larger coefficients than others. These differences suggest underlying heterogeneity in TAM parameter estimates across products. They indicate that the strength of the relationships between the independent variables and user acceptance may vary among different handheld console offerings.

## 4.6 Effect Size Differences (Heterogeneity Hypothesis)

The analysis of model coefficient differences using the Cohen procedure (Table 4) suggests significant variability in coefficients across different technology products. This coefficient heterogeneity points to differing product-specific influences on user acceptance. For instance, in the case of Nintendo versus Razer, the comparison indicates statistically significant differences across all TAM coefficients. For Razer, the effect of PU on user acceptance is significantly larger, implying that PU has a stronger positive impact on user acceptance compared to Nintendo. However, Nintendo holds a significant advantage in the importance of EU which exerts a comparatively larger effect on user acceptance. This suggests that users place greater emphasis on the ease-of-use features when evaluating Nintendo products, as opposed to the Razer.

**Table 4** Summary of effect size comparisons across products (Cohen procedure with Holm-Sidak correction)

| Comparison | Variable | Coef. Difference | p-adj | Significant |
|---|---|---|---|---|
| Logitech vs razer | PU | −0.075 | 0.995 | No |
| | EU | 0.174 | 0.150 | No |
| Nintendo vs Logitech | PU | −0.219 | 0.018 | Yes |
| | EU | 0.086 | 0.897 | No |
| Nintendo vs razer | PU | −0.295 | < 0.001 | Yes |
| | EU | 0.260 | 0.001 | Yes |
| Nintendo vs steam deck | PU | 0.041 | 1.000 | No |
| | EU | −0.135 | 0.600 | No |
| Steam deck vs Logitech | PU | −0.261 | 0.049 | Yes |
| | EU | 0.221 | 0.142 | No |
| Steam deck vs razer | PU | −0.336 | 0.003 | Yes |
| | EU | 0.395 | < 0.001 | Yes |

**Note.** The magnitude represents the strength of the difference between groups, with larger absolute values indicating a more substantial difference. The sign (positive or negative) indicates the direction of the difference, where positive means the first product has a higher value compared to the second product, while a negative value means the opposite

**Table 5** Tukey's HSD for user star ratings

| Comparison | Mean Difference | Lower | Upper | p-adj | Significant |
|---|---|---|---|---|---|
| Logitech vs. Nintendo | −0.444 | −0.753 | −0.135 | <0.001 | Yes |
| Logitech vs. razer | −0.0098 | −0.349 | 0.329 | 0.999 | No |
| Logitech vs. steam deck | 0.5069 | 0.091 | 0.922 | 0.009 | Yes |
| Nintendo vs. razer | 0.4342 | 0.140 | 0.727 | <0.001 | Yes |
| Nintendo vs. steam deck | 0.951 | 0.571 | 1.330 | <0.001 | Yes |
| Razer vs. steam deck | 0.5168 | 0.112 | 0.921 | 0.005 | Yes |

Guided by the recommendations of Salovaara et al. [20], we contend that once the differences between technology products are identified within technology acceptance models, this heterogeneity can be leveraged for product design and comparison. We discuss that in greater detail in the subsequent discussion section.

## 4.7 *Mean Differences (Mean Differences Hypothesis)*

The results of one-way ANOVA showed a statistically significant difference in the average user star ratings ($F(3, 1101) = 15.82$, $p < 0.001$), average Perceived Usefulness ($F(3, 1101) = 16.31$, $p < 0.001$), and average Ease of Use ($F(3, 1101) = 20.57$, $p < 0.001$). Tables 5, 6, and 7 contain the post-hoc comparisons using the Tukey HSD test for user star ratings, PU annotations and EU annotations, respectively.

**Table 6** Tukey's HSD for Perceived Usefulness scores (LLM annotations)

| Comparison | Mean Difference | Lower | Upper | p-adj | Significant |
|---|---|---|---|---|---|
| Logitech vs. Nintendo | −0.5384 | −0.822 | −0.254 | <0.001 | Yes |
| Logitech vs. razer | −0.1305 | −0.442 | 0.181 | 0.718 | No |
| Logitech vs. steam deck | 0.2815 | −0.100 | 0.663 | 0.190 | No |
| Nintendo vs. razer | 0.4079 | 0.137 | 0.677 | <0.001 | Yes |
| Nintendo vs. steam deck | 0.8199 | 0.471 | 1.168 | <0.001 | Yes |
| Razer vs. steam deck | 0.412 | 0.040 | 0.783 | 0.018 | Yes |

**Table 7** Tukey's HSD for Ease of Use scores (LLM annotations)

| Comparison | Mean Difference | Lower | Upper | p-adj | Significant |
|---|---|---|---|---|---|
| Logitech vs. Nintendo | −0.426 | −0.663 | −0.231 | <0.001 | Yes |
| Logitech vs. razer | −0.207 | −0.468 | 0.006 | 0.115 | No |
| Logitech vs. steam deck | 0.253 | −0.012 | 0.569 | 0.112 | No |
| Nintendo vs. razer | 0.219 | 0.010 | 0.421 | 0.033 | Yes |
| Nintendo vs. steam deck | 0.679 | 0.460 | 0.991 | <0.001 | Yes |
| Razer vs. steam deck | 0.460 | 0.2271 | 0.7931 | <0.001 | Yes |

The analysis of user ratings and LLM annotations for PU and EU amongst the various handheld consoles highlights significant disparities in user sentiment, particularly disadvantaging Nintendo. According to the results in Table 2, Nintendo registers the lowest means in both star ratings and annotations for PU and EU. This is reinforced by the post-hoc comparisons in Tables 5, 6, and 7, where Nintendo's ratings are significantly lower than those of its competitors, indicating a less favorable user perception.

In contrast, Steam Deck emerges as the favorite amongst users in all variables analyzed. It has significantly higher user ratings than all other products. According to Tables 6 and 7, Steam Deck outperforms its competitors in PU and EU annotations, with the exception of Logitech, where the differences are not statistically significant, indicating a similar level of user sentiment.

Logitech and Razer find themselves in a balanced position among competitors in this product category. An analysis of user sentiment reveals that they slightly outperform Nintendo in terms of user perception while trailing Steam Deck by a small margin.

# 5 Discussion

## *5.1 Validation of LLM-NLP Annotations (Study 1)*

Technology acceptance is a useful measure that helps companies design and target their products effectively. While consumer data has become increasingly accessible, the opportunity for analysis of consumer trends was previously limited by the reliance on traditional surveys and human expert annotations. The development of Natural Language Processing (NLP) with Large Language Model (LLM) annotation systems has provided researchers and companies with a powerful new tool for measuring technology acceptance in a scalable and cost-effective manner.

In study 1, we demonstrate the success of LLMs, specifically GPT-4, in this field. With a lowered temperature, GPT-4 provides consistent results over many runs. Furthermore, we find that LLM's reliability and agreement with human experts are largely sufficient for current analysis tasks. Furthermore, as shown by the agreement scores (see Table 1), LLMs can be as effective as human experts when it comes to annotating attitudes in customer data. In our study, LLMs performed exceptionally well, with agreement scores between the AI and human experts coming very close to or even surpassing the agreement between human experts themselves. For example, we found that for Performance Expectancy, Facilitating Conditions, and Social Influence, the agreement is higher between the experts and the LLM than between the experts themselves. For the remaining category, Effort Expectancy, the agreement scores are almost identical. Statistically, higher agreement of the LLMs and experts (i.e. $WPA_{H\text{-}AI}$) means that annotation scores generated by the LLM are more closely clustered around the mean of the human experts than the human experts themselves. Such a result suggests that LLMs can be reliably and accurately used to analyze and annotate consumer data.

The use of LLM annotation systems offers several advantages over traditional survey methods, including cost-effectiveness, scalability, and the ability to leverage existing user-generated data from various online sources. Of these advantages, the most significant is the nearly unlimited LLM capacity to analyze reviews. For example, our analysis was limited by the time constraints of human experts with 15 reviews an acceptable middle ground between statistical power and feasibility per human expert. While the comparatively lower number of reviews does limit our analysis, it also shows the increased/superior capabilities of LLM analysis compared to traditional methods. However, it is important to note several potential limitations and challenges associated with LLM annotation systems, such as the need for prompt engineering, the closed source nature of many popular LLMs, and the trade-off between consistency and flexibility.

### *5.2 Product TAM Comparative Analysis (Study 2)*

The comparative analysis of handheld gaming consoles using the Technology Acceptance Model (TAM) revealed distinct performance metrics across the products, underscoring how variations in Perceived Usefulness PU and Ease of Use EU impact consumer acceptance. By examining the user data for Nintendo, Steam Deck, Logitech, and Razer, notable trends emerged in the factors that drive user adoption and satisfaction.

Firstly, Steam Deck leads in both PU and EU scores, positioning it as the top choice amongst users who value both high functionality and usability. Its superior PU ratings suggest that users perceive it as a powerful gaming device, likely due to its advanced processing capabilities, graphics quality, and comprehensive game library. The high EU scores reinforce their user-friendly interface and ergonomic design, both critical for sustained user engagement. Steam Deck's balance in both PU and EU positions it as a market benchmark for competitors [21].

Nintendo, by contrast, has relatively low PU scores, indicating that users see room for improvement in its functional capabilities, such as processing speed and graphics. Nintendo's EU scores, however, are somewhat stronger, suggesting that while users find it easy to use, the console's functional limitations may deter consumers from focusing on performance. This insight can help Nintendo prioritize technical enhancements, particularly in areas that enhance perceived utility, to better align with user expectations.

Logitech and Razer consoles, while not outperforming Steam Deck, hold competitive PU scores, reflecting user satisfaction with their performance-related features. Both brands, however, show moderate EU scores, indicating potential areas for interface and design improvements to facilitate ease of use. Logitech's and Razer's higher PU relative to EU implies that while these devices are appreciated for their core functionality, users may find certain aspects of the user interface or ergonomics less intuitive than they would prefer. For Logitech and Razer, increasing the intuitiveness and accessibility of the interface could result in improved user satisfaction and market position.

The Heterogeneity Hypothesis posited in TAM studies is thus supported by this analysis, showing that TAM parameters vary not only across product types but also in their influence on user satisfaction and adoption rates. The differentiation in TAM coefficients between consoles indicates that companies should not assume a one-size-fits-all approach to product design. Instead, manufacturers can strategically focus on specific TAM variables—PU or EU—depending on their target market's preferences.

This product-specific heterogeneity also provides valuable market intelligence for product improvement. For example, Nintendo's relatively lower PU coefficient highlights efforts to improve core gaming features, such as performance upgrades or exclusive game content, could significantly enhance user satisfaction. In contrast, for Steam Deck, with high satisfaction already reported across both PU and EU, maintaining this balance with incremental upgrades may be a viable strategy to reinforce its position as the preferred console [22].

Products appealing to a user base prioritizing functionality (e.g., professional gamers) should emphasize PU improvements, while products targeting casual gamers may benefit from enhancing EU-related features, such as simplified interfaces and ease of access. This segmentation aligns product enhancements with distinct user needs, fostering more focused and effective innovation within the competitive landscape of handheld gaming.

### 5.3 Example of Actionable Insights for Handheld Gaming Consoles

The TAM analysis provides targeted insights for enhancing user adoption and satisfaction in handheld gaming consoles by aligning product improvements with specific user expectations for Perceived Usefulness PU and Ease of Use EU. Each console examined—Steam Deck, Nintendo, Logitech, and Razer—has distinct strengths and areas for improvement that can guide actionable strategies for product development, marketing, and user engagement. Nintendo is well-positioned to capitalize on its reputation for ease of use, which resonates with casual and family-oriented gamers. However, its lower PU scores suggest that functional enhancements could enhance its competitiveness. For Nintendo, actionable improvements could include [22]:

- Hardware upgrades—investing in faster processors, better graphics, and extended battery life could attract more performance-oriented users without compromising Nintendo's accessibility.
- Exclusive content and feature expansion—offering exclusive games, downloadable content (DLC), or unique gameplay features, such as improved controller functionality, could boost PU by enhancing the console's overall entertainment value.
- Customization and flexibility—adding modular accessories or customizable features (e.g., adaptable controls, additional storage) would increase the appeal to users looking for more functional flexibility, thus improving PU scores.

For Steam Deck, which currently leads in both PU and EU scores, actionable insights focus on maintaining its high standards while innovating in niche areas to solidify user loyalty. Specific actions could involve [21]:

- Feature-rich updates—maintaining Steam Deck's competitive edge by enhancing cloud gaming options, improving load times, and integrating advanced graphics support will help retain its top PU score.
- Personalization and advanced user settings—offering more personalized settings for graphics, controls, and interface design would cater to experienced users, aligning with the high EU rating Steam Deck users currently value.
- Community-driven enhancements—leveraging user feedback to continuously improve hardware and software updates could keep Steam Deck at the forefront, making it a go-to choice for gamers seeking both power and usability.

Logitech and Razer, which show competitive PU ratings, may find that focusing on EU enhancements could better address user needs, especially for users who prefer intuitive, easy-to-navigate interfaces. Actionable improvements for these brands include [22]:

- Enhanced user interface UI and ergonomics—updating the console's UI for a more streamlined, intuitive experience could significantly increase EU. Improve-

ments such as simplified menu navigation, larger, responsive touchscreens, or ergonomic controller design can make the device more accessible and comfortable for extended use.
- Software ecosystem integration—adding seamless integration with popular gaming platforms (e.g., cross-platform play, cloud saves) and user-friendly software ecosystems would cater to users looking for both utility and convenience.
- Collaborations with game developers—building partnerships with game developers to release optimized games for their consoles could boost PU by enhancing the perceived performance and exclusive game experience.

These insights underscore the benefit of product differentiation within the handheld gaming console market. Nintendo could enhance PU by focusing on functional versatility and exclusive content, aligning with its base of casual gamers. Steam Deck's top scores suggest it should emphasize maintaining and refining its balance of PU and EU through incremental, user-driven enhancements. Logitech and Razer, meanwhile, could benefit from improving EU through ergonomic and UI advancements, aligning with the needs of users seeking both functionality and ease of use.

By focusing on these targeted improvements, each brand can better meet its user base's expectations, building stronger brand loyalty and enhancing its market position. Through these specific TAM-driven actions, manufacturers can create products that not only resonate with user preferences but also respond proactively to the competitive dynamics of the handheld gaming industry.

### *5.4 Perceived Usefulness and Ease of Use Product Features*

In this study, PU features reflect aspects like console performance, graphics quality, and exclusive game offerings, directly affecting the perceived utility. EU features, such as intuitive menu navigation and ergonomic design, impact the ease of interaction with the product. The findings suggest that while all consoles could benefit from a balance of PU and EU enhancements, Steam Deck and Logitech could prioritize advanced functionality PU, whereas Nintendo could improve user accessibility EU to elevate the overall user experience and acceptance.

## 6 Limitations and Future Studies

This study offers valuable insights into the use of the Technology Acceptance Model (TAM) for evaluating handheld gaming consoles, yet several limitations should be considered in interpreting the findings and guiding future research. The analysis relied exclusively on online user reviews from Amazon, which, while rich in user-generated content, may not fully represent the broader population of console users.

Amazon reviews typically capture opinions from individuals motivated to share their experiences, which can introduce biases, such as emphasizing extreme satisfaction or dissatisfaction. Additionally, reviews on a commercial platform may not reflect the diversity of demographics, gaming preferences, and gaming experiences across various regions and cultures. Indeed, while Amazon forbids the creation of fake reviews, these still often occur. While we have chosen products which enjoy significant adoption, and thusly have a lower motivation and need for fake reviews, the challenge still exists. Future studies could address these limitations by gathering data from multiple sources, such as social media platforms, gaming forums, and dedicated gaming review sites, to better capture a more comprehensive and diverse set of user sentiments. Other LLMs could also be used to detect fake reviews.

While the Large Language Model (LLM) annotation system used in this study was validated for reliability and accuracy, it is still an emerging tool in sentiment analysis. LLMs may have limitations in interpreting nuanced user sentiments, especially when reviews contain sarcasm, slang, or complex gaming jargon. Additionally, although LLMs provide a scalable alternative to traditional surveys, they may inadvertently introduce biases due to the training data or annotation guidelines. Future research could explore hybrid methods, combining human and LLM annotations, or employ alternative sentiment analysis models to cross-validate and refine sentiment scores, ensuring they align closely with actual user experiences and attitudes.

This study analyzed user sentiment and TAM parameters for a single generation of each console. However, handheld gaming consoles frequently undergo updates and improvements, which may significantly impact user perceptions of Perceived Usefulness PU and Ease of Use EU. For example, software updates or hardware revisions can alter user experience, and new gaming titles can shift user expectations. A longitudinal approach, tracking TAM parameters and user sentiment over time, could provide more nuanced insights into how user acceptance evolves in response to product changes, competitor developments, and shifts in market trends. Longitudinal studies would also allow researchers to observe if user priorities change as technologies mature, providing manufacturers with actionable intelligence for iterative design and marketing strategies.

The study did not explicitly consider geographical or cultural variations in technology acceptance, which can impact PU and EU differently across regions. Cultural differences in gaming preferences, such as a preference for specific types of games or console features, may affect how users perceive the usefulness and ease of use of these consoles. Future studies could include cross-cultural analyses, comparing TAM parameters across regions to understand how cultural factors influence user acceptance. This would allow manufacturers to tailor features and marketing strategies to specific regions, enhancing the relevance of the product to diverse user groups.

While TAM provides a robust foundation for understanding technology acceptance, it may overlook other psychological and social factors influencing user adoption, such as perceived enjoyment, habit, or social influence. Expanding the analysis by integrating models like the Unified Theory of Acceptance and Use of Technology (UTAUT) or including additional variables, such as enjoyment or perceived value, could provide a more holistic view of the factors driving user acceptance. Future research could explore extended models that incorporate these variables to gain a deeper understanding of the factors influencing handheld gaming console adoption.

Finally, as the market for handheld gaming consoles grows and diversifies, user expectations and priorities may shift. Emerging competitors, technological advancements (such as cloud gaming capabilities or VR integration), and changes in gaming content availability can redefine what users consider useful or easy to use. Future studies could investigate how external factors, such as competitive shifts or technological innovations, impact TAM parameters for handheld consoles. This could involve examining how emerging features or competitor innovations influence users' perceived usefulness and ease of use, allowing manufacturers to stay ahead in a dynamic market.

Addressing these limitations in future research could enhance the generalizability and depth of insights provided by TAM analysis, helping manufacturers better understand and respond to the evolving landscape of user needs and expectations in the handheld gaming industry.

## 7 Conclusions

This paper addresses two emerging challenges in technology acceptance research, namely the limitations of traditional data collection and the homogeneity assumptions. We show that using Large Language Models (LLM) annotations can provide more scalable and data that is consistent between LLM runs and is in significant agreement with human expert consensus.

Our study also demonstrates the value of the Technology Acceptance Model (TAM) without homogenous assumptions, allowing for greater comparison between products and therefore greater applicability. In comparing handheld gaming consoles, this TAM provides useful and actionable insights for product development and marketing strategies. By analyzing TAM variables—Perceived Usefulness PU and Ease of Use EU—across consoles like Steam Deck, Nintendo, Logitech, and Razer, we reveal significant differences in user preferences that can guide targeted improvements. The heterogeneity in TAM parameters indicates that no single approach fits all consoles; instead, manufacturers can focus on specific areas aligned with their users' priorities.

Steam Deck's balanced strength in both PU and EU establishes it as a market leader, where maintaining and refining its current features will likely sustain its popularity. Nintendo, with lower PU scores, could benefit from enhancements in performance-oriented features, which are increasingly valued by users. Logitech and Razer, competitive in PU but trailing in EU, may improve their user satisfaction by making the interface and overall user experience more accessible.

Our findings confirm TAM's effectiveness in identifying distinct consumer preferences, thus enabling manufacturers to prioritize feature development which resonates with target audiences. Our study highlights TAM's potential to move beyond confirming that users prefer products that are useful and easy to use; instead, it demonstrates how TAM can be strategically applied to diagnose product strengths and weaknesses, guiding data-driven design and marketing decisions in the competitive handheld gaming market.

**Supplementary Materials:** Additional details including datasets and Python scripts are available in the supplementary materials at https://osf.io/v43km/.

## References


1. Marangunić, N., & Granić, A. (2015). Technology acceptance model: A literature review from 1986 to 2013. *Universal Access in the Information Society, 14*, 81–95. https://doi.org/10.1007/s10209-014-0348-1
2. Williams, M. D., Rana, N. P., & Dwivedi, Y. K. (2015). The unified theory of acceptance and use of technology (UTAUT): A literature review. *Journal of Enterprise Information Management, 28*, 443–488. https://doi.org/10.1108/JEIM-09-2014-0088
3. Venkatesh, V., Thong, J.Y.L., Xu, X., (2016). Unified theory of acceptance and use of technology: A synthesis and the road ahead. Accessed Dec 18, 2023, from https://papers.ssrn.com/abstract=2800121
4. Enu-Kwesi, F., & Opoku, M. O. (2020). Relevance of the technology acceptance model (TAM) in information management research: A review of selected empirical evidence. *Pressacademia, 7*, 34–44. https://doi.org/10.17261/Pressacademia.2020.1186
5. Davis, F. D. (1985). *A technology acceptance model for empirically testing new end-user information systems: Theory and results, Thesis*. Massachusetts Institute of Technology. Accessed Dec 21, 2023, from https://dspace.mit.edu/handle/1721.1/15192
6. Ajzen, I. (1980). Understanding attitudes and Predictiing social behavior. *Englewood Cliffs*. Accessed Dec 21, 2023, from https://cir.nii.ac.jp/crid/1572543024551612928
7. Ajzen, I. (1991). The theory of planned behavior. *Organizational Behavior and Human Decision Processes, 50*, 179–211. https://doi.org/10.1016/0749-5978(91)90020-T
8. Davis, F. D. (1989). Perceived usefulness, perceived ease of use, and user acceptance of information technology. *MIS Quarterly, 13*, 319–340. https://doi.org/10.2307/249008
9. Gefen, D., & Straub, D. (1997). Gender differences in the perception and use of E-mail: An extension to the technology acceptance model. *MIS Quarterly, 21*, 389–400. https://doi.org/10.2307/249720
10. Dishaw, M. T., & Strong, D. M. (1999). Extending the technology acceptance model with task–technology fit constructs. *Information & Management, 36*, 9–21. https://doi.org/10.1016/S0378-7206(98)00101-3
11. Venkatesh, V., & Davis, F. (2000). A theoretical extension of the technology acceptance model: Four longitudinal field studies. *Management Science, 46*, 186–204. https://doi.org/10.1287/mnsc.46.2.186.11926
12. Venkatesh, V., Thong, J. Y. L., & Xu, X. (2012). Consumer acceptance and use of information technology: Extending the unified theory of acceptance and use of technology. *MIS Quarterly, 36*, 157–178. https://doi.org/10.2307/41410412
13. Venkatesh, V., Morris, M. G., Davis, G. B., & Davis, F. D. (2003). User acceptance of information technology: Toward a unified view. *MIS Quarterly, 27*, 425–478. https://doi.org/10.2307/30036540

14. Blut, M., Chong, A., Tsigna, Z., & Venkatesh, V. (2022). Meta-analysis of the unified theory of acceptance and use of technology (UTAUT): Challenging its validity and charting a research agenda in the Red Ocean. *Journal of the Association for Information Systems, 23*, 13–95. https://doi.org/10.17705/1jais.00719
15. Barki, H., & Benbasat, I. (2007). Quo vadis, TAM? *Journal of the Association for Information Systems, 8*, 211–218.
16. Hirschheim, R. (2007). Introduction to the special issue on "Quo Vadis TAM—issues and reflections on technology acceptance research". *Journal of the Association for Information Systems, 8*. https://doi.org/10.17705/1jais.00128
17. Salovaara, A., & Tamminen, S. (2009). Acceptance or appropriation? *A Design-Oriented Critique of Technology Acceptance Models, in: Future Interaction Design, II*, 157–173. https://doi.org/10.1007/978-1-84800-385-9_8
18. Malatji, W., van Eck, R., & Zuva, T. (2020). Understanding the usage, modifications, limitations and criticisms of technology acceptance model (TAM). *Advances in Science, Technology and Engineering Systems Journal, 5*, 113–117. https://doi.org/10.25046/aj050612
19. Smolinski, P., Szostakowski, M., & Winiarski, J. (2023). E-learning software: Comparing the use behavior among academicians and schoolteachers. *Electronic Journal of E-Learning, 21*, 98–109. https://doi.org/10.34190/ejel.21.2.2736
20. Salovaara, A., Öörni, A., & Sokura, B. (2013). *Heterogeneous use for multiple purposes: A point of concern to IS use models' validity, ICIS 2013 proceedings*. https://aisel.aisnet.org/icis2013/proceedings/HumanBehavior/24
21. Smolinski, P. R., Januszewicz, J. & Winiarski, J. (2024). Scaling technology acceptance analysis with Large Language Model (LLM) annotation systems: A validation study. In B. Marcinkowski, A. Przybylek, A. Jarzębowicz, N. Iivari, E. Insfran, M. Lang, H. Linger, & C. Schneider (Eds.), *Harnessing opportunities: Reshaping ISD in the post-COVID-19 and generative AI Era (ISD2024 Proceedings)*. Gdańsk: University of Gdańsk. ISBN: 978-83-972632-0-8. https://doi.org/10.62036/ISD.2024.95
22. Smolinski, P. R., Januszewicz, J. & Winiarski, J. (2024). From information systems theory to market intelligence: Heterogeneous technology acceptance models as a tool for product analysis. In B. Marcinkowski, A. Przybylek, A. Jarzębowicz, N. Iivari, E. Insfran, M. Lang, H. Linger, & C. Schneider (Eds.), *Harnessing Opportunities: Reshaping ISD in the post-COVID-19 and Generative AI Era (ISD2024 Proceedings)*. Gdańsk: University of Gdańsk. ISBN: 978-83-972632-0-8. https://doi.org/10.62036/ISD.2024.58
23. Scherer, R., Siddiq, F., & Tondeur, J. (2019). The technology acceptance model (TAM): A meta-analytic structural equation modeling approach to explaining teachers' adoption of digital technology in education, Computers & Education 128, 13–35. https://doi.org/10.1016/j.compedu.2018.09.009

# Strategies for Effective Remote Retrospectives: Exploring Retrospective Games, Anonymity, and Continuous Reflection

**Yen Ying Ng, Bartosz Leśniewski, Krzysztof Marek, Michael Neumann, and Jacek Trzesicki**

**Abstract** **Context:** The shift to remote work during the COVID-19 pandemic has exacerbated the long-standing challenge of conducting engaging and productive sprint retrospectives. This transition has introduced new complexities, including decreased team trust, the loss of valuable non-verbal communication, and reduced brainstorming effectiveness. **Objective:** Our research investigates strategies to improve remote retrospectives for Scrum teams experiencing low engagement and reluctance to provide constructive feedback. **Method:** Through three Action Research cycles, we sequentially introduced and evaluated retrospective games, anonymous feedback, and continuous issue documentation throughout the sprint. **Results:** The introduction of games demonstrably increased meeting engagement and active participation, while anonymity created a more secure environment for more comprehensive and honest feedback. Furthermore, continuous reflection helped ensure that critical issues were not overlooked and promoted proactive, real-time problem-solving. A replication study with a Kanban team at a different company supported the positive impact of games and anonymity but showed mixed results regarding continuous issue documentation. **Conclusion:** This research adds to the existing knowledge on agile software development in remote settings, offering actionable strategies for agile practitioners to improve their continuous

Y. Y. Ng (✉)
Nicolaus Copernicus University, Toruń, Poland
e-mail: nyysang@hotmail.com

B. Leśniewski
Gdańsk University of Technology, Gdańsk, Poland
e-mail: b.lesniewski0@gmail.com

K. Marek · J. Trzesicki
Warsaw University of Technology, Warsaw, Poland
e-mail: Krzysztof.Marek@pw.edu.pl; jacektrzesicki@gmail.com

M. Neumann
University of Applied Sciences and Arts Hannover, Hannover, Germany
e-mail: michael.neumann@hs-hannover.de



B. Marcinkowski et al. (eds.), *Advances in Information Systems Development*, Lecture Notes in Information Systems and Organisation 77,
https://doi.org/10.1007/978-3-031-87880-0_2

improvement practices. Our results underscore that remote retrospectives can be effective but require adaptations to address the inherent challenges of virtual environments, such as lower engagement and trust. These adaptations should be tailored to the unique context and needs of each team.

## 1 Introduction

The widespread adoption of agile methods has transformed the landscape of software project management. While the foundational principles of agile methods are straightforward, their practical implementation frequently presents challenges [1, 10, 16, 18, 19, 21, 28, 37, 40, 44, 48]. A recurring theme in the literature pertains to the difficulty in maintaining engaging and productive sprint retrospectives [12, 24, 26, 29, 31, 34, 36, 38, 50]. Strict adherence to the format outlined in the Scrum Guide can make retrospectives tedious, potentially leading to disengagement among team members and diminishing the impact of this vital agile practice. Additionally, common pitfalls, such as a lack of structure, the dominance of vocal individuals, and the absence of time or authority to implement action items, further erode the efficacy of retrospectives [2, 36].

Recognizing the critical role of sprint retrospectives in promoting continuous improvement, researchers have advocated the adoption of collaborative games in the retrospective process to mitigate these challenges. Indeed, several research studies have reported that introducing games to retrospectives breaks the monotony and boosts their productivity [26, 29, 36, 38, 51].

However, the COVID-19 pandemic posed an unprecedented challenge for agile teams that traditionally relied on collocation and face-to-face interactions [3, 37]. The pandemic forced agile teams to rapidly adapt their work processes and practices to accommodate a work-from-home (WFH) setup [46]. While the direct virtualization of agile practices enabled teams to sustain the delivery of product increments, it was insufficient to replicate the dynamics and effectiveness of in-person collaboration [3, 37].

Our research aligns with the conference theme [22], "Harnessing Opportunities: Reshaping ISD in the Post-COVID-19 and Generative AI Era" by exploring how sprint retrospectives need to adapt to stay effective in the remote work environment. The shift to remote work has adversely affected sprint retrospectives for three main reasons. Firstly, remote teams lack opportunities to foster team morale and build trust through in-person interactions and personal connections [11, 24, 49]. A deficit of mutual trust within a team can lead to reluctance in openly discussing issues, resulting in unresolved problems [2, 27]. Secondly, in face-to-face communication, feedback is accompanied by body language, facial expressions, and tone of voice, which help in conveying the intent clearly and ensuring that criticism is taken constructively [2, 3, 47]. This nuanced interaction, crucial during retrospectives, is lost in remote environments. The absence of these non-verbal cues can lead to misunderstandings and perceptions of feedback being more critical or personal than intended. This can exacerbate feelings of discomfort and resistance to openly discuss and resolve issues. Thirdly, conducting brainstorming activities online has been reported as much less effective than in-person sessions, leading to reduced engagement and productivity [23].

In light of these challenges, this work proposes and explores strategies to enhance sprint retrospectives in remote settings. Insights are drawn from an Action Research project conducted at a multinational corporation, where members of remote Scrum teams hesitated to provide critical feedback to each other due to concerns over potential conflicts and harm to interpersonal relationships. This project was driven by two research questions: (1) What challenges do remote Scrum teams face during sprint retrospectives?; and (2) What strategies can be implemented to address these challenges?

The primary contributions of our research are twofold: firstly, we provide validated strategies that enhance the effectiveness of sprint retrospectives in remote settings; and secondly, we enrich the existing knowledge base regarding remote retrospectives.

## 2 Related Work

### *2.1 Challenges in Agile Retrospectives*

Despite their potential benefits, retrospectives often face significant challenges. A primary root cause is a lack of understanding and appreciation for the value of this ceremony [36]. When retrospectives are conducted mechanically, they can demotivate team members and negatively affect outcomes. Without a clear agenda or effective facilitation, discussions may become unfocused [15, 36].

Furthermore, agile teams frequently struggle to propose effective solutions to identified issues or to implement agreed-upon action items [30, 36, 38]. The dominance of a few vocal participants can silence others, preventing the team from benefiting from diverse perspectives [30, 36, 38]. Additionally, when discussions become complaint-driven rather than solution-oriented, retrospectives can become unproductive [38].

As a result of the aforementioned issues, team members might begin to view retrospectives as a waste of time and stop attending them altogether [15]. Given that agile teams typically work under intense time pressure, the temptation to skip unproductive retrospectives is even stronger [36, 39].

Gaikwad et al. [14] pointed out additional challenges in agile retrospectives: the lack of anonymity and the time-consuming nature of the meetings. These issues have long been identified in face-to-face idea generation sessions [8]. Participants may fear negative evaluation from others [35] and feel anxious about potential social consequences when sharing ideas that contradict those of higher-status team members [6]. This apprehension can inhibit participation, leading to the loss of valuable ideas [6]. Our prior research [26] confirmed these issues, showing that senior team members often dominate retrospectives despite the use of games, as junior members hesitate to challenge them.

Furthermore, in face-to-face groups, participants cannot express themselves simultaneously and must take turns to share their thoughts–a phenomenon known as production blocking [8, 35]. Nunamaker et al. [17] found that these inhibitory factors can be reduced through electronic idea generation sessions, where participants are anonymous (mitigating evaluation apprehension) and participation is asynchronous (mitigating production blocking). Similar findings were reported by Davis et al. [6], suggesting that leveraging electronic tools can enhance the effectiveness of retrospectives by encouraging broader participation and more diverse idea generation.

## *2.2 Retrospective Games*

Retrospective games are a type of collaborative games specifically designed for agile retrospectives. These structured social activities draw inspiration from gameplay to facilitate knowledge sharing, experience reflection, and problem-solving within agile teams. They encourage exploration of ideas in ways that might not emerge in standard discussions, help identify hidden assumptions, develop a shared understanding of challenges, and generate innovative solutions [29, 36, 38, 50]. These activities encourage participation from less vocal team members, help overcome inhibitions, and foster creative thinking by engaging alternative cognitive processes [31, 36, 38]

Moreover, retrospective games align with the principles of collaborative learning, where team members co-construct knowledge through social interaction [9]. This approach promotes collective reflection and continuous improvement, which are core tenets of agile methods.

The use of collaborative games to revitalize sprint retrospectives has attracted considerable attention. Przybylek and Kotecka [38] pioneered this approach, adapting and evaluating five retrospective games within a real-world environment at Intel. Their goal was to support more effective and enjoyable retrospective meetings. They found that game-based retrospectives fostered creativity, involvement, and communication among participants, yielding better results than traditional retrospectives. This study spurred further research, with replications in diverse contexts and companies, incorporating additional retrospective games [29, 31, 39, 50]. Notably, Przybylek and his team conducted a follow-up study [36] across three companies, replicating the original study with enhanced scientific rigor. Feedback consistently indicates that retrospective games effectively mitigate common "accidental difficulties" associated with sprint retrospectives, such as lack of structure, monotony, excessive complaints, or uneven participation, ultimately leading to more productive meetings.

Below, we provide an overview of three retrospective games utilized in this study. The *Sailboat* game uses a nautical metaphor to facilitate the identification of factors influencing a team's progression. The sailboat represents the team itself. The goal is to reach the island, symbolizing the team's objectives or desired outcomes. The wind propelling the sailboat forward represents the elements and actions that drive the team's success. Conversely, the anchors symbolize the impediments or obstacles that slow the team down. Additionally, the rocks in the water represent potential risks and challenges that could derail the team's progress if not addressed. By visualizing these elements, the team can collaboratively focus on strategies to enhance their journey towards achieving their goals [15].

The *Starfish* game expands on the typical three questions used in retrospectives. It prompts reflection on five aspects: Stop Doing (wasteful activities), Less Doing (high-effort, low-benefit tasks), Keep Doing (effective practices), More Doing (activities to increase), and Start Doing (new ideas to implement). This comprehensive approach provides a holistic view of the team's practices and areas for improvement [15].

The *5L's* game—standing for Liked, Learned, Lacked, Longed for, and Loathed—prompts participants to reflect on what they liked about the past sprint, what they learned, what they felt was lacking, what they longed for or wished had happened, and what things they disliked. This structure encourages both positive and negative feedback, giving the team a well-rounded perspective [38].

### *2.3 Research Gap*

While previous studies have demonstrated the effectiveness of retrospective games in enhancing face-to-face sprint retrospectives [36, 38], there is a notable gap in the literature regarding their application in a remote work environment. The shift to remote settings has introduced new challenges, including reduced trust among team members and the loss of non-verbal cues [11, 24, 49]. Consequently, this study also explores anonymous feedback mechanisms. This direction is informed by insights from Gaikwad et al. [14] and our prior research [26], which suggest that the non-anonymous nature of retrospectives can hinder open communication due to potential social repercussions.

Finally, this study incorporates insights on constructive feedback from management science. The most effective feedback is delivered immediately after an event [33, 42], enabling a clear understanding of what is working well and what areas require improvement. Therefore, feedback should be a continuous process [20, 43].

## 3 Research Methodology

### *3.1 Research Method*

As we aimed "to address real-world problems and improve organizational performance by combining scholarly observations with practical interventions" [7],

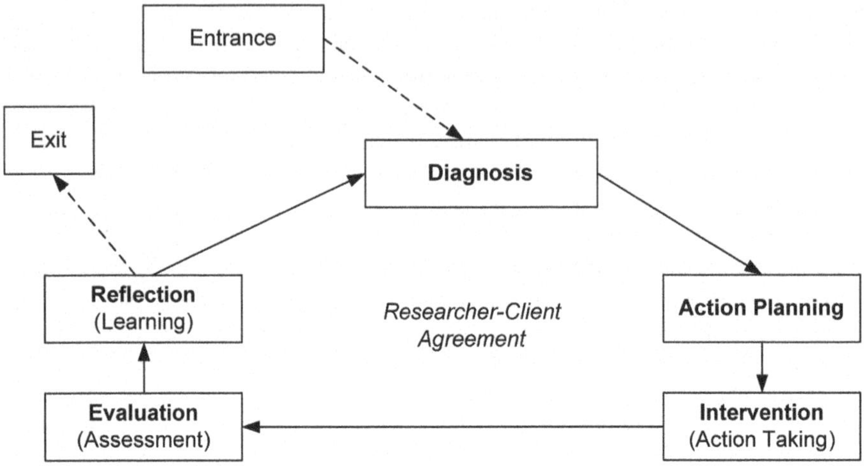


**Fig. 1** CAR process model (source: [7])

we employed Action Research (AR) as our research approach. With a strong foundation in Information Systems [5, 7], AR has recently attracted growing interest in Software Engineering [3, 18, 19, 36]. This method involves a collaborative process between researchers and practitioners to solve real-world problems while simultaneously generating new knowledge [4]. Our study employs Canonical Action Research [45] as shown in Fig. 1, informed by its successful application in a related contexts [31, 36].

AR can be initiated by practitioners (problem-driven) or researchers (research-driven) [41]. In problem-driven initiation, practitioners face a complex problem and seek academic help. In research-driven initiation, researchers seek real-world settings to apply their ideas, needing to convince practitioners of the potential benefits.

In this study, we incorporate both approaches. Initially, we adopted a problem-driven initiation, assisting three remote Scrum teams struggling with low engagement and reluctance in providing critical feedback during retrospectives [30]. Following the successful implementation and positive outcomes of our proposed interventions, we then applied them in another company to evaluate their applicability in a different context and setting, adopting a research-driven initiation. This dual approach allowed us to mitigate a key limitation of AR—the generalization of findings [25].

## 3.2 Data Collection

Our data collection strategy was multi-faceted to thoroughly explore the phenomena under study. We began by conducting unstructured interviews to identify and understand the problematic areas. Subsequently, participant observation, with field notes documenting our observations, was used to closely monitor the implementation of interventions in practice. Finally, the evaluation of our interventions incorporated two complementary methods. Firstly, we gathered feedback via a questionnaire distributed after each AR cycle to capture the immediate perceptions and experiences. This questionnaire contained an identical set of questions across all cycles, ensuring consistency in data collection and enabling direct comparisons between interventions. Secondly, at the conclusion of the project, we organized a focus group to facilitate in-depth discussion and qualitative feedback from the participants. The focus group discussion was guided by the following questions:

- Did the interventions we implemented address any of the issues your team previously experienced with retrospective meetings?
- What are the advantages and disadvantages of game-based retrospectives?
- What are your thoughts on the use of anonymous idea generation in retrospectives?
- What do you think about the practice of continuously documenting significant issues throughout the sprint?
- What are your comments on the questionnaire results? Why do you think 5Ls was rated lower than the other games?
- From your experience with this research, can you offer any further insights?

Employing the dual approach of quantitative and qualitative data collection enabled us to triangulate the data, thereby enhancing the reliability and validity of our findings.

Due to regulatory restrictions within the participating organizations and concerns about participant comfort, we did not record the interviews or focus group sessions. Instead, responses were documented through note-taking.

### *3.3 Data Analysis*

We employed a deductive content analysis to interpret the qualitative data, which included notes from the interviews and focus group sessions, field notes from participant observations, and responses to the open-ended questions in the questionnaires. Grounded theory coding techniques were used, beginning with open coding to identify key categories. Axial coding was then applied to refine these categories and establish relationships between them, helping to uncover underlying patterns within the data. Microsoft Excel was used to facilitate the coding process.

### *3.4 Research Context*

The original project was carried out in a multinational corporation recognized as one of the world's largest semiconductor chip manufacturers. Among the five

**Table 1** Participating teams and their compositions

| | Team_A | Team_B | Team_C | Team_D |
|---|---|---|---|---|
| Team lead | ×1 | ×1 | ×1 | ×1 |
| Product owner | ×1 | ×1 | ×1 | |
| Scrum master | ×1 | ×1 | ×1 | |
| Developer | ×5 | ×2 | ×9 | ×4 |
| Intern | | ×2 | ×2 | |

qualifying Scrum teams, a survey was conducted to assess interest in research participation. Ultimately, we onboarded three teams—denoted as *Team_A*, *Team_A*, and *Team_A*—where every member enthusiastically agreed to participate in the study. The composition of each team is presented in Table 1.

All teams operated remotely, working in two-week sprints and conducting meetings via Microsoft Teams. Each sprint concluded with a retrospective, during which, among other activities, action items were assigned to specific team members. The subsequent retro began with a review of the previous iteration's action items, scrutinizing their success and evaluating the intended impact against the actual outcome. However, each team used a different format for conducting their retrospective meetings.

In *Team_A*, members filled out a table provided by the Scrum Master with two columns: "What we did well" and "What we could have done better". The team then discussed the items and formulated corrective actions. Their retrospectives often concluded earlier than scheduled, due to a lack of substantial insights for discussion. Typically, only two or three points were noted, resulting in one or two action items to be addressed.

*Team_B* took an unconventional approach to collecting issues for discussion during the retrospective—they documented them continuously throughout the sprint in a shared document. At the beginning of the retrospective, team members had time to supplement the list of observations, and then the meeting proceeded in a standard manner. The collected insights were categorized into three themes: "What we should stop doing", "What we should start doing", and "What we should continue doing".

*Team_C* followed the same process as *Team_A*, but their columns were labeled differently: "Stop doing", "Keep doing", and "Start doing".

The replication study was conducted in a medium-sized cybersecurity organisation, involving a remote Kanban team (referred to as *Team_D*), consisting of five members. In *Team_D*, members documented reflections in a shared digital workspace using Miro, where they organised their observations into three columns: "What helped us move forward", "What held us back" and "How could we do things differently". During the retrospective, the team collaboratively reviewed and discussed each item, identifying key areas for improvement and defining specific actions to address them. *Team_D*'s retrospectives were not conducted with consistent timing, allowing flexibility to accommodate the team's workflow.

# 4 The First Action Research Cycle: Game-Based Retrospectives

## 4.1 Diagnosing

The key issue identified across *Team_A*, *Team_B*, and *Team_C* was the lack of active participation in retrospective meetings, leading to minimal outcomes and a sense of wasted time among team members. This perception further reduced their enthusiasm for future retrospectives. Scrum Masters facilitating these meetings encountered difficulties in eliciting insights and encouraging dialogue among their teams.

Our investigation revealed several underlying causes for this lack of engagement. A common sentiment, exemplified by a team member's remark—*"Team members do not feel comfortable openly expressing their opinions, and for newcomers, it may be difficult to identify issues and initiate discussions for improvements"*—highlights broader challenges. These include timidity, discomfort in offering criticism, particularly towards more experienced colleagues or superiors, and difficulties in identifying issues and proposing solutions.

## 4.2 Action Planning and Taking

We chose to incorporate three retrospective games namely *Sailboat*, *Starfish*, and *5L's*, which have been effective in mitigating similar issues in related studies [26, 29, 31, 36, 38, 50].

Each game was introduced to the team by the Scrum Master and utilized during a distinct retrospective. Accordingly, the AR cycle spanned over three sprints. The retros were conducted directly in the Microsoft Teams environment. The Scrum Master provided an interactive board on which participants placed their "sticky notes" in chosen categories. Once a participant had placed all their observations, they raised a virtual hand to signal that they were ready for discussion. Once all participants were prepared, the team discussed each category in turn.

## 4.3 Evaluating and Specifying Learning

The evaluation results (Fig. 2) show that *Sailboat* and *Starfish* were generally well-received by all teams. However, most members of *Team_B* expressed a neutral stance towards *Starfish*. They reasoned that the categories "Stop doing" and "Do less of" were less relevant for mature teams like theirs, where long-term process optimization had already minimized areas for further improvement. As for the *5L's* game, it was not received positively, with the exception of one-third of *Team_B* members.

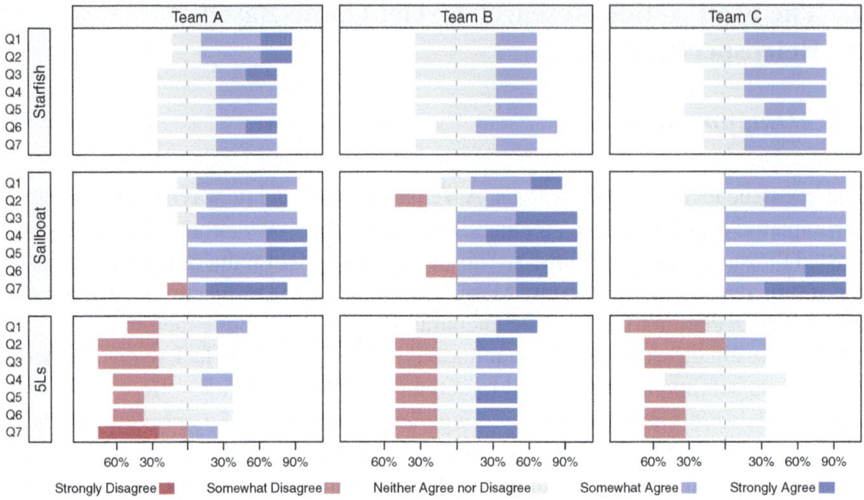


Q1. The game yields better outcomes compared to our standard approach.
Q2. The game should be permanently adopted by our team.
Q3. The game is a valuable complement to our standard approach.
Q4. The game enhances participants' creativity.
Q5. The game increases participants' involvement.
Q6. The game enhances communication among team members.
Q7. The game is easy to understand and play.

**Fig. 2** Results of evaluating the intervention in the first AR cycle

During the focus group session, participants highlighted several advantages of the game-based retrospectives, including the structured approach to collecting insights, and the opportunity to reflect on the sprint from different perspectives. One participant encapsulated this sentiment by stating, *"retro games establish a systematic approach for conveying feedback, organizing issues into distinct categories, and ensuring that various viewpoints are heard"*. Additionally, many participants recognized that the retro games also stimulated creativity. Nonetheless, some voiced concerns about potential drawbacks, such as the difficulty in conducting a root cause analysis of the problems encountered and the possibility of becoming bored with using only *Sailboat* and *Starfish* in the long term.

## 5 The Second Action Research Cycle: Anonymity in Retrospectives

### *5.1 Diagnosing*

After mitigating the issues related to the team's lack of proactive participation and low engagement, a notable absence of discussion about serious issues during the retrospectives became apparent. This situation could have been a result of either the absence of such issues or a lack of trust within the team, consequently leading to a reluctance to provide critical feedback.

## *5.2 Action Planning and Taking*

In the absence of established best practices for building trust in remote settings beyond what had already been established within the participating teams, we decided to explore an alternative solution. Drawing from our previous study [26], we decided to introduce anonymity in the idea-generation phase of the game-based retrospectives. Although the 5L's game had not gained traction in the first AR cycle, we opted to give it a second chance, this time in an anonymous version. By allowing team members to contribute their thoughts anonymously, we aimed to create a safe space for sharing critical feedback and discussing more serious issues that may have been overlooked in previous retrospectives.

Despite the wide range of web apps available for conducting anonymous game-based retrospectives, we were unable to leverage these platforms due to the company's policy requiring the protection of data discussed in retrospective sessions. To overcome this limitation, we developed a custom in-house tool that allowed team members to submit their ideas anonymously during the retrospective meeting.

This cycle also spanned three sprints, employing the same trio of games but with added anonymity. During the retrospectives, held via Microsoft Teams, the Scrum Master provided a link to our custom tool, enabling team members to anonymously share their thoughts relevant to the game in play. Participants quickly adapted to the new tool. In the case of *Team_A* and *Team_B*, the Scrum Master occasionally prompted participants to provide more detailed entries. This was done to ensure the clarity of ideas for other team members and to minimize the need for authors to offer explanations during the discussion.

## *5.3 Evaluating and Specifying Learning*

The evaluation results (Fig. 3) show that the ratings for the *Starfish* game improved even further compared to the non-anonymous version, whereas the *Sailboat* game received slightly lower ratings than in the previous cycle. Additionally, the *5L's* game did not manage to gain traction.

During the focus group discussion, participants acknowledged the benefits of anonymity in creating a safe space for constructive feedback, particularly in teams prone to conflict or where members feel uncomfortable expressing negative opinions. However, a challenge emerged in ensuring that anonymous comments

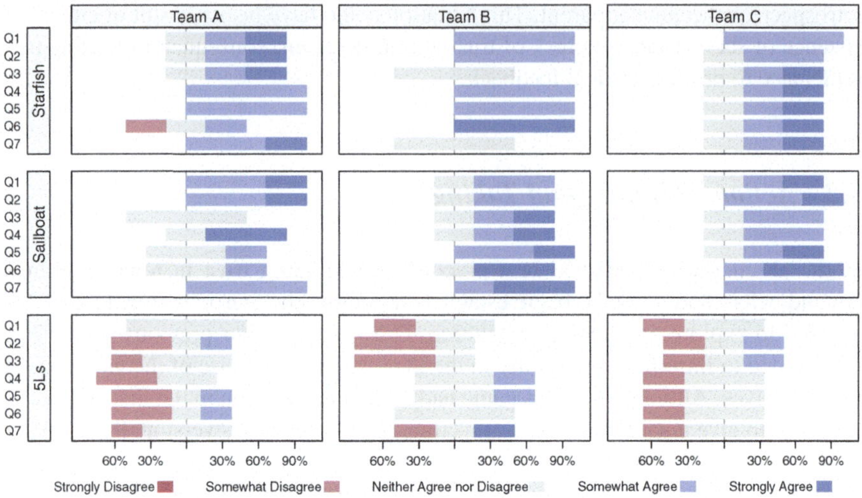


**Fig. 3** Results of evaluating the intervention in the second AR cycle

were detailed enough for the team to grasp their meaning without additional clarification from the author.

Moreover, participants suggested that the use of anonymous inputs may serve as an insightful tool for gauging the level of trust within the team. By comparing the nature of the feedback received in both transparent and anonymous settings, the team could observe the impact of anonymity on the openness and honesty of the feedback provided.

Lastly, when probed about the continued low ratings for the *5L's* game, participants explained that the game's categories did not resonate with them, finding them ambiguous and not always applicable. They elaborated, *"not every sprint leads to a learning opportunity, and it's often challenging to identify what we liked or loathed"*. Conversely, they appreciated that *"Starfish offers well-defined categories that assist in pinpointing critical issues"* and highlighted that *"Sailboat is also straightforward and uniquely integrates the sprint goal and team vision into the discussion, which are aspects frequently overlooked"*.

## 6 The Third Action Research Cycle: Ongoing Anonymous Feedback

### *6.1 Diagnosing*

Although the anonymous approach was recognized as a beneficial measure in promoting constructive criticism within the teams, the challenge of not all relevant matters being brought up during the retrospectives remained. This situation could potentially arise from certain issues being unintentionally overlooked.

## 6.2 Action Planning and Taking

Inspired by *Team_B*'s initial retrospective approach, we resolved to introduce a practice of ongoing documentation of significant issues throughout the sprint. These documented issues would then be discussed in the following retrospective session. At the beginning of the sprint, the Scrum Master for each team set up a new instance of the retrospective game in the tool developed in the previous cycle. The game chosen was the team's preferred option from the three introduced earlier. The Scrum Master provided team members with a link and an access code to join this instance. Team members were encouraged to populate the game board whenever they encountered a situation worth noting, ensuring that it would be discussed in the retrospective.

## 6.3 Evaluating and Specifying Learning

*Team_A*, which used the *Starfish* game, observed no significant change compared to the previous cycle. For the other teams, *Sailboat* was the game of choice, and documenting events throughout the sprint led to slightly improved outcomes. The results from the questionnaire assessing this latest cycle are depicted in Fig. 4.

During the focus group, participants were unable to conclusively determine whether this approach was superior to the one used in the previous cycle. One individual expressed concern that continuous documentation might lead to gathering irrelevant information, though this concern was not supported by any observable outcomes.

Conversely, another participant highlighted that this approach helped ensure that crucial matters were not overlooked. Echoing this sentiment, another member remarked, *"although it appears more time-intensive, this approach leads to improved results and enhances communication during the retrospective meeting"*.

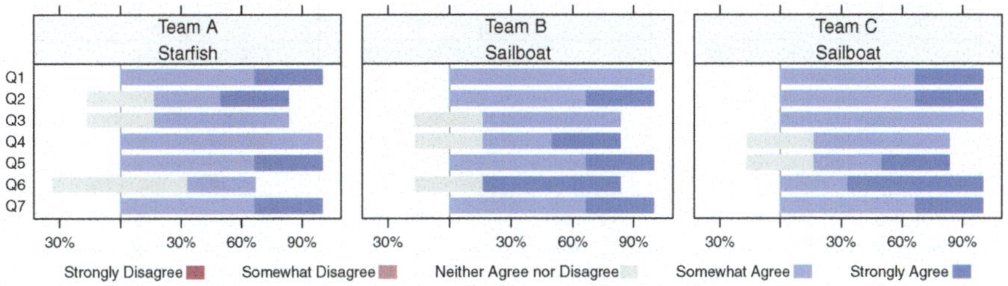


**Fig. 4** Results of evaluating the intervention in the third AR cycle

In addition, participants acknowledged that the ongoing documentation of issues promoted timely, ad-hoc communication. Documented observations sometimes triggered requests for clarification, leading to clearer communication of problematic issues. Furthermore, this approach enabled some problems to be resolved well before the scheduled retrospective meeting.

## 7 Insights from a Replication Study

We conducted a reduced-scale replication study, testing our strategies across three retrospective meetings using the *Sailboat* and *Starfish* games. Figure 5. presents the aggregated results from these sessions.

The responses from *Team_D* closely mirrored those of the original teams regarding the effectiveness of the game-based format and the use of anonymous feedback. However, the approach of continuous issue documentation received mixed feedback, with lower scores than in the original study, indicating a less pronounced impact in this replication setting.

One participant, who accounted for many of the neutral responses, remarked, *"I don't feel any major change compared to past retros. All retros have been good. The lack of them was the issue."* Another participant noted, *"I think it's always fun to shake up the retro format a little anyways, so I would be open to trying different boards or styles."*

During the focus group session with *Team_D*, participants emphasized that game-based retrospectives enhanced engagement and helped break down feedback into clearer action items. They also noted that using a variety of formats helps keep the discussions fresh and engaging.

Regarding anonymity, *Team_D* proposed an interesting variation they termed "semi-anonymous format". In this approach, participants would add post-its anonymously in real time, allowing others to react immediately, while giving authors the option to reveal their identity and provide additional context if they felt comfortable doing so.

Despite the lower quantitative scores, the focus group with *Team_D* revealed that documenting issues as they arise throughout the sprint is still a valuable practice.

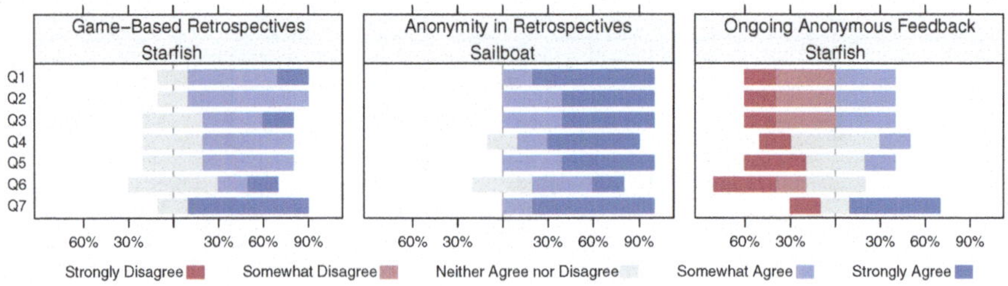


**Fig. 5** Evaluating intervention effectiveness in *Team_D*

This approach helps ensure important points aren't forgotten by the time of the retrospective and provides a fuller picture for discussing and resolving recurring problems.

# 8 Threats to Validity

## *8.1 Construct Validity*

The main limitation of our study is the reliance on subjective evaluations—perceptions, feelings, experiences, and memories of participants—rather than objective measures like the number of valuable ideas generated. However, objective measurements might not fully capture the unique context of each sprint, as even retrospectives conducted using the same method would yield different results due to the distinct nature of each sprint.

Relying on human input introduces social threats to construct validity. Participants were pre-informed about the intervention's aims and expected improvements, potentially leading to response bias or socially desirable answers. To mitigate this, we emphasized the importance of honest feedback to figured out useful practices.

Researcher expectancy bias is another potential threat, where we might interpret evidence in line with our preconceptions. To mitigate this, we employed multiple researchers to analyze the data independently, and discrepancies in interpretation were discussed and resolved through consensus.

## *8.2 Internal Validity*

Research conducted in real-world industry settings inherently involves uncontrollable variables. Factors other than our intervention could have influenced the results. Retrospective outputs depend not only on the format employed, but also on the richness of sprint events and team dynamics. Additionally, the diagnosing phase might have biased participants as we inquired about issues with their retrospectives, potentially indicating a need for improvement.

## *8.3 External Validity*

The generalizability of findings from AR is contingent upon contextual similarity, often referred to as transferability. To facilitate transferability, we have provided a comprehensive account of our AR project, including the specific context, challenges, and interventions employed. We believe that remote agile teams facing similar challenges may benefit from adapting our approach, but encourage further research to explore its broader applicability across diverse team settings.

# 9 Discussion

Drawing from insights gathered through three AR cycles, we have distilled four lessons learned to enhance the effectiveness of sprint retrospectives, particularly in promoting active participation among team members and constructive criticism.

**Lesson 1: Experiment with Different Retrospective Formats**
Our findings support existing research, confirming that the integration of retrospective games enhances session dynamics and promotes active participation [36, 50]. This approach not only broadens the range of viewpoints brought to the table but also allows team members to reflect on the past through diverse lenses.

**Lesson 2: Monitor the Effectiveness of Different Retrospective Formats**
While *Starfish* and *Sailboat* were well-received, *5L's* did not gain as much traction. This observation aligns with previous research findings and highlights the importance of monitoring team responses to different formats [36]. Mindfully selecting games that align with the team's specific context and maturity level is crucial for successful retrospective sessions.

**Lesson 3: Embrace Anonymity for Constructive Criticism**
Creating a safe and comfortable environment is crucial for team members to feel free to share their thoughts and feelings openly. Our implementation of anonymous feedback mechanisms proved beneficial in fostering a space for constructive criticism, leading to more in-depth and honest feedback. Yet, the necessity for detailed explanations when providing anonymous input was time-consuming, posing a disadvantage by requiring additional effort and extending the duration of the sessions.

It is critical to recognize that anonymity is ideally a transitional tool rather than a permanent fixture. In an open feedback culture, the ultimate goal is to build trust and psychological safety within the team, enabling members to provide constructive criticism without the need for anonymity [13]. To this end, we advocate for continued research into strategies that cultivate a culture of trust, respect, and open communication, especially within the context of remote work.

**Lesson 4: Experiment with Continuous Reflection**
Ongoing population of the game board with significant issues throughout the sprint, while a potentially controversial idea, showed promise in ensuring crucial matters were not overlooked during the retrospective. This proactive approach also triggered ongoing reflection and communication, facilitating immediate resolution of some issues. This continuous reflection adds another valuable layer to the retrospective process and embodies Schön's concept of "reflection-in-action" [42]. Rather than

relegating reflection to a dedicated retrospective meeting, this approach encourages team members to engage in a continuous process of thinking about their experiences during the sprint itself. This "knowing-in-action" allows for real-time adjustments and problem-solving, preventing issues from escalating.

Furthermore, London [20] emphasizes the importance of timely and ongoing feedback for continuous improvement and skill development, reinforcing the value of this approach.

## 10 Conclusions

This study explored various strategies to enhance retrospectives in remote Scrum teams. The initial lack of engagement and proactive participation underscored the need to move beyond traditional, rigid retrospective formats. Introducing retrospective games, such as *Starfish* and *Sailboat*, proved highly effective in revitalizing the process, fostering active participation and promoting diverse perspectives. This is in line with findings from prior research in collocated teams, where game-based retrospectives also improved active participation and led to positive societal outcomes [29, 31, 36, 38].

While games can encourage participation, a safe environment is paramount for honest and constructive feedback [13]. Embracing anonymity for feedback proved instrumental in fostering psychological safety, leading to more honest and richer contributions.

Finally, ongoing population of the game board with significant issues throughout the sprint not only ensured that all relevant matters were not forgotten, but some of them were addressed immediately before the retrospective meeting. However, a replication study with a Kanban team did not yield the same positive results, emphasizing the need to tailor strategies to the unique context and needs of each team.

This study highlights the importance of flexibility and innovation in conducting sprint retrospectives. Future research should continue exploring innovative ways to unlock the full potential of this vital Scrum practice, potentially with the assistance of Generative AI. AI-driven tools could analyze retrospective data to identify recurring patterns and suggest improvement actions [32]. Ultimately, cultivating a culture of continuous improvement and experimentation will empower teams to overcome any challenge.

## References

1. Ahmad, M. O., Dennehy, D., Conboy, K., & Oivo, M. (2018). Kanban in software engineering: A systematic mapping study. *Journal of Systems and Software, 137*, 96–113.

2. Ahmad, M. O., & Gustavsson, T. (2024). Nexus between psychological safety and non-technical debt in large-scale agile enterprise resource planning systems development. In A. Jarzębowicz, I. Luković, A. Przybyłek, M. Staroń, M. O. Ahmad, & M. Ochodek (Eds.), *Software, system, and service engineering* (pp. 63–81). Springer.
3. Bablo, J., Marcinkowski, B., & Przybylek, A. (2023) Overcoming challenges of virtual scrum teams: Lessons learned through an action research study. In C. J. Stettina, J. Garbajosa, & P. Kruchten (Eds.), *Agile processes in software engineering and extreme programming* (pp. 34–49). Springer.
4. Baskerville, R. L. (1999). Investigating information systems with action research. In *Communications of the Association for Information Systems, 2*(1), 19.
5. Baskerville, R., & Myers, M. D. (2004). Special issue on action research in information systems: Making IS research relevant to practice: Foreword. *MIS Quarterly, 28*(3), 329–335.
6. Davis, J., Zaner, M., Farnham, S., Marcjan, C., & McCarthy, B. (2003). Wireless brainstorming: Overcoming status effects in small group decisions. In *36th Annual Hawaii International Conference on System Sciences*.
7. Davison, R., Martinsons, M., & Ou, C. (2012). The roles of theory in canonical action research. English. *MIS Quarterly, 36*(3), 763–786.
8. Diehl, M., & Stroebe, W. (1987). Productivity loss in brainstorming groups: Toward the solution of a riddle. *Journal of Personality and Social Psychology, 53*(3), 497.
9. Dillenbourg, P. (1999). What do you mean by collaborative learning? In P. Dillenbourg (Ed.), *Collaborative-learning: Cognitive and computational approaches* (pp. 1–19). Elsevier.
10. Dolezel, M., Buchalcevova, A., & Mencik, M. (2019). The state of agile software development in the Czech Republic: Preliminary findings indicate the dominance of "Abridged" scrum. In P. Doucek, J. Basl, A. M. Tjoa, M. Raffai, A. Pavlicek, & K. Detter (Eds.), *Research and practical issues of enterprise information systems* (pp. 43–54). Springer.
11. Dorairaj, S., & Noble, J. (2013). Agile software development with distributed teams: Agility, distribution and trust. In *2013 Agile Conference* (pp. 1–10).
12. Fabian, K., & Holger, G. (2021). Chatbot-supported retrospective. In *Project management development–practice and perspectives* (p. 7).
13. Fowler, F. M. (2019). The sprint retrospective. In *Navigating hybrid scrum environments: Understanding the essentials, avoiding the pitfalls*. Apress.
14. Gaikwad, P. K., Jayakumar, C. T., Tilve, E., Bohra, N., Yu, W., & Spichkova, M. (2019). Voiceactivated solutions for agile retrospective sessions. *Procedia Computer Science, 159*, 2414–2423.
15. Gonçalves, L., & Linders, B. (2015). *Getting value out of agile retrospectives: A toolbox of retrospective exercises*. Ben Linders.
16. Jarzębowicz, A., & Ślesiński, W. (2019). What is troubling IT analysts? A survey report from poland on requirements-related problems. In *Engineering software systems: Research and praxis. KKIO 2018. Advances in intelligent systems and computing* (vol. 830, pp. 3–19). Springer.
17. Jay F. Nunamaker, L. M. A., Jr., & Konsynski, B. R. (1987). Facilitating group creativity: Experience with a group decision support system. *Journal of Management Information Systems, 3*(4), 5–19.
18. Joskowski, A., Przybylek, A., & Marcinkowski, B. (2023). Scaling scrum with a customized nexus framework: A report from a joint industry-academia research project. *Software: Practice and Experience, 53*(7), 1525–1542.
19. Kowalczyk, M., Marcinkowski, B., & Przybylek, A. (2022). Scaled agile framework. Dealing with software process-related challenges of a financial group with the action research approach. *Journal of Software: Evolution and Process, 34*(6), e2455.
20. London, M. (2014). *The power of feedback: Giving, seeking, and using feedback for performance improvement*. Routledge.
21. Marciniak, P., & Jarzębowicz, A. (2017). An industrial survey on business analysis problems and solutions. In *Software engineering: Challenges and solutions. KKIO 2016. Advances in intelligent systems and computing* (vol. 504, pp. 163–176). Springer.

22. Marcinkowski, B., Przybyłek, A., Jarzębowicz, A., Livari, N., Insfran, E., Lang, M., Linger, H., & Schneider, C. (Eds.). (2024). *Harnessing Opportunities: Reshaping ISD in the Post-COVID-19 and Generative AI Era (ISD2024 Proceedings)*. University of Gdańsk.
23. Masood, Z., Blincoe, K., & Damian, D. (2023). What have we learned? A conceptual framework on New Zealand software professionals and companies' response to COVID-19. *EMSE, 28*(5), 109.
24. McHugh, O., Conboy, K., & Lang, M. (2012). Agile practices: The impact on trust in software project teams. *IEEE Software, 29*(3), 71–76.
25. McKay, J., & Marshall, P. (2001). The dual imperatives of action research. *Information Technology & People, 14*(1), 46–59.
26. Mich, D., & Ng, Y. Y. (2020). Retrospective games in intel technology Poland. In *15th Conference on Computer Science and Information Systems* (pp. 705–708).
27. Moe, N. B., & Dingsoyr, T. (2008). Scrum and team effectiveness: Theory and practice. In P. Abrahamsson, R. Baskerville, K. Conboy, B. Fitzgerald, L. Morgan, & X. Wang (Eds.), *Agile processes in software engineering and extreme programming* (pp. 11–20). Springer.
28. Neumann, M., Kuchel, T., Diebold, P., & Schön, E.-M. (2024). Agile culture clash: Unveiling challenges in cultivating an agile mindset in organizations. *Computer Science and Information Systems, 21*, 1013–1031.
29. Ng, Y. Y., & Kuduk, R. (2024). Implementing action items over improving the format of retros. In *Symposium on applied computing SAC'24* (pp. 853–855). ACM.
30. Ng, Y. Y., Leśniewski, B., Marek, K., Neumann, M., & Trzesicki, J. (2024). Unlocking feedback in remote retrospectives: Games, anonymity, and continuous reflection in action. In B. Marcinkowski, A. Przybyłek, A. Jarzębowicz, N. Iivari, E. Insfran, M. Lang, H. Linger, & C. Schneider (Eds.), *Harnessing opportunities: Reshaping ISD in the post-COVID-19 and generative AI era*. University of Gdańsk.
31. Ng, Y. Y., Skrodzki, J., & Wawryk, M.: Playing the sprint retrospective: A replication study. In A. Przybylek & M. Morales-Trujillo (Eds.), *Advances in agile and user-centred software engineering* (pp. 133–141). Springer.
32. Nguyen-Duc, A., Cabrero-Daniel, B., Przybylek, A., Arora, C., Khanna, D., Herda, T., Rafiq, U., Melegati, J., Guerra, E., Kemell, K.-K., Zhang, Z., Le, H., & Abrahamsson, P. (2023). Generative artificial intelligence for software engineering–A research agenda. arXiv:2310.18648
33. Nowostawski, M. (2016). *Make them grow: Giving feedback people apply*. CreateSpace Independent Publishing Platform.
34. Östman, N., & Hallmén, S. (2023). *Exploring development team dialogues through Game-Based Sprint Retrospectives*. Uppsala University.
35. Paulus, P. B., & Dzindolet, M. (2008). Social influence, creativity and innovation. *Social Influence, 3*(4), 228–247.
36. Przybylek, A., Albecka, M., Springer, O., & Kowalski, W. (2022). Game-based Sprint retrospectives: Multiple action research. *Empirical Software Engineering, 27*(1), 1–56.
37. Przybyłek, A., Belter, D., & Conboy, K. (2025). A study of Scrum @ S&P global in the post-COVID-19 era: Unsuitable for remote work or just flawed implementation? *Information and Software Technology*, 107728. ISSN 0950-5849. https://doi.org/10.1016/j.infsof.2025.107728. https://www.sciencedirect.com/science/article/pii/S0950584925000679
38. Przybylek, A., & Kotecka, D. (2017). Making agile retrospectives more awesome. In *2017 Federated Conference on Computer Science and Information Systems (FedCSIS)* (pp. 1211–1216).
39. Przybylek, A., & Kowalski, W. (2018). Utilizing online collaborative games to facilitate agile software development. In *2018 Federated Conference on Computer Science and Information Systems (FedCSIS)* (pp. 811–815).
40. Przybylek, A., & Olszewski, M. K. (2016). Adopting collaborative games into Open Kanban. In *2016 Federated Conference on Computer Science and Information Systems (FedCSIS)* (pp. 1539–1543).

41. Root-Bernstein, R. S. (1989). *Discovering: Inventing solving problems at the frontiers of scientific knowledge*. Harvard University Press.
42. Schön, D. A. (2017). *The reflective practitioner: How professionals think in action*. Routledge.
43. Seitsamo-Räsänen, S. (2021). *Building an Agile Approach to Individual Feedback*. Master's Thesis. Haaga-Helia University of Applied Sciences.
44. Sosnowski, M., Bereza, M., & Ng, Y. Y. (2021). Business-oriented approach to requirements elicitation in a scrum project. In A. Przybyłek, J. Miler, A. Poth, & A. Riel (Eds.), *Lean and agile software development* (pp. 185–191). Springer.
45. Susman, G. I. (1983). Action research: A sociotechnical systems perspective. In G. Morgan (Ed.), *Beyond method: Strategies for social research* (pp. 95–113). Sage.
46. Topp, J., Hille, J.-H., Neumann, M., & Mötefindt, D. (2022). How a 4-day work week and remote work affect agile software development teams. *Lean and Agile Software Development, 438*, 61–77.
47. Tripathy, M. (2021). Constructive criticism: Creating positive behaviour at work places. *Revista Gestão & Tecnologia, 21*(4), 76–92.
48. Trzesicki, J., Marek, K., & Przybylek, A. (2024). Impact of the kanban maturity model on a team's agile transformation: Tripling throughput and elevating quality in three months. In D. Šmite, E. Guerra, X. Wang, M. Marchesi, & P. Gregory (Eds.), *Agile processes in software engineering and extreme programming* (pp. 107–116). Springer.
49. Tyagi, S., Sibal, R., & Suri, B. (2022). Empirically developed framework for building trust in distributed agile teams. *Information and Software Technology, 145*, 106828.
50. Wawryk, M., & Ng, Y. Y. (2019). Playing the sprint retrospective. In *2019 Federated Conference on Computer Science and Information Systems* (pp. 871–874).
51. Zakrzewski, M., Kotecka, D., Ng, Y. Y., & Przybylek, A. (2019). Adopting collaborative games into agile software development. In E. Damiani, G. Spanoudakis, & L. Maciaszek (Eds.), *Evaluation of novel approaches to software engineering* (pp. 119–136). Springer.

# Self-Sovereign Identities: Brief History and Survey of the Field

**Rodolfo da Silva Costa and Paulo Rupino Da Cunha**

**Abstract** Self-Sovereign Identity (SSI) is a paradigm shift in digital identity management, empowering individuals with control over their personal data. Blockchain technology, with its decentralized and tamper-proof nature, provides a robust foundation for SSI systems. This paper presents a comprehensive systematic literature review (SLR) of 94 research articles on blockchain-based SSI, published in eight different academic databases. The SLR analyzes the current state-of-the-art, categorizes research into six major groups, and identifies 18 distinct areas of interest. Additionally, a short bibliometric analysis visualized co-authorship and keyword co-occurrences, highlighting the key contributors and emerging themes. We also mapped the geographical distribution of research contributions, revealing significant academic output from countries such as China, India, Germany, and the United Kingdom. Our findings reveal a growing body of research focused on conceptual solutions, implemented systems, reviews, and technology analysis. Although theoretical advances in SSI are promising, challenges remain in practical implementation. Issues such as identity wallet management, regulatory compliance, and user experience need to be addressed to foster widespread adoption. Furthermore, we provide a comprehensive map of the literature, elucidating areas of substantial scholarly attention and those necessitating further exploration.

## 1 Introduction

Progress in digital identity has ignited significant interest in utilizing blockchain technology to manage its data. This enthusiasm originates from the robust security features inherent in these distributed ledger systems, such as their decentralization and tamper-proofness. A decentralized identity model, popularly called "self-sovereign identity" (SSI) [7] is emerging as a paradigm shift in digital identification

R. da Silva Costa · P. R. Da Cunha (✉)
University of Coimbra, CISUC, DEI, Coimbra, Portugal
e-mail: rodolfocosta@dei.uc.pt; rupino@dei.uc.pt

 
B. Marcinkowski et al. (eds.), *Advances in Information Systems Development*,
Lecture Notes in Information Systems and Organisation 77,
https://doi.org/10.1007/978-3-031-87880-0_3

models. It empowers individuals with complete autonomy to manage their personal data. Embracing SSI liberates individuals from the constraints of centralized authorities or third-party ID providers.

The management of digital identities is becoming increasingly important today as people conduct more of their lives online, and organizations such as banks, government agencies, and healthcare providers need to verify the identities of citizens, customers, users, and employees. On the other hand, according to the World Bank [16], an estimated 850 million people in the world do not have official proof of identity, which can make it difficult for them to access services, exercise their rights and participate in society. This lack of identity documentation disproportionately affects marginalized and vulnerable populations, such as refugees, stateless people, and people living in poverty [9, 59]. In this context, SSI can help bridge these gaps by offering a secure, decentralized, and verifiable way to manage and share digital identities, while also improving privacy and control for individuals.

This paper extends our original contribution for the 32nd International Conference on Information Systems Development (ISD 2024) [18]. It aligns with the conference theme of "Harnessing Opportunities: Reshaping ISD in the post-COVID-19 and Generative AI Era" by addressing the critical need for secure, decentralized digital identity solutions in a rapidly evolving landscape. The COVID-19 pandemic has accelerated digital transformation, making the demand for privacy-preserving identity management systems like self-sovereign identity more urgent. Blockchain-based SSI systems offer a cutting-edge approach to reshaping information systems development by empowering individuals to control their data, a necessity in the post-pandemic digital era.

Despite its promise, the field of SSI is still in its early stages, with fragmented research and a lack of consolidated knowledge. Conducting a systematic literature review (SLR) is essential to map the current research landscape, identify trends, and pinpoint gaps that need further investigation. Our study contributes by categorizing existing works, analyzing key themes, and highlighting emerging areas in the intersection of blockchain and SSI.

This extension builds on a comprehensive overview of the current state of the art in this area. We present a systematic literature review of current research on blockchain-based SSI, analyzing 94 articles from eight different academic databases, classifying them into six major groups and categorizing them into 18 distinct areas of interest. Although we found a growing number of studies in the area, we also observed that works that do not directly address the topic sometimes misuse the term SSI. Meanwhile, this extended version includes a section with a brief history and an explanation of the concept of SSI. We also added a short bibliographic analysis section. Moreover, the number of figures, tables, and methodology information was increased.

The remainder of this paper is organized as follows. In Sect. 2, we present a brief history and an explanation of self-sovereign identities. Section 3 describes the protocol used to perform the SLR. Section 4 presents our overview of the identified papers. Section 5 gives some bibliometric data. Section 6 provides a discussion and possibilities for future research. Finally, Sect. 7 closes with conclusions.

## 2 Self-Sovereign Identities

Also known as Decentralized Identity, the SSI is a transformative approach that allows individuals and organizations to take control of their identity-related information, moving away from traditional centralized model that relies on third-party management. One of the first and most well-known texts on the subject was written in 2016 by Christopher Allen [5], where the author outlines the concept. He created a group of ten principles specific to self-sovereign identity as a departure point for discussion. They are:

1. Existence: Users must have an independent existence;
2. Control: Users must control their identities;
3. Access: Users must have access to their data;
4. Transparency: Systems and algorithms must be transparent;
5. Persistence: Identities must be long-lived;
6. Portability: Information and services about identity must be transportable;
7. Interoperability: Identities should be as widely usable as possible;
8. Consent: Users must agree to the use of their identity;
9. "Minimalization": Disclosure of claims must be minimized;
10. Protection: The rights of users must be protected.

In the decentralized identity model, the integration of public/private-key cryptography plays an essential role in securing data through cryptographic keys held by each party. Instead of utilizing blockchain technology for cryptocurrencies, identity management employs it for decentralized public key infrastructure (DPKI). This innovative approach enables the direct exchange of public keys, facilitating secure and private connections between peers. This model can be compared to how we confirm our identity in the physical world by presenting credentials from trusted sources. However, in the digital world, this verification occurs via digital wallets, digital credentials, and digital connections [77].

In self-sovereign identity systems, the following roles exist: the Issuer issues the credentials to a Holder, who keeps them in a digital wallet and presents them to a Verifier. All entities involved use a Verifiable Data Registry, which is typically a blockchain, to register and verify the identifiers.

In recent years, the World Wide Web Consortium (W3C) has established standard recommendations for the implementation of a couple of components of SSI systems, namely Verifiable Credentials (VCs) [95] and Decentralized Identifiers (DIDs) [96]. The VCs are digital representations of physical credentials, such as driver's licenses or university degrees, that are cryptographically secure, privacy-respecting, and machine-verifiable. They are issued by an entity and stored in the holder's wallet. Verifiable credentials do not depend on Decentralized Identifiers, and vice versa, but are often used together. However, DIDs serve as unique identifiers for entities (people, organizations, devices) and are used to establish a verifiable digital identity. They allow entities to control their identifiers and associated data, while VCs provide a way to share verified information selectively and securely.

## 3 Methodology

To execute the Systematic Literature Review, we followed the recommendations of [103] and [46]. First, we defined the Research Question, namely: *What is the state of the art for Self-Sovereign ID using Blockchains?* We intended to discover what status of academic research in the field, which technologies the researchers are using and developing, and in which scenarios the blockchain based SSIs have been tested and implemented.

Second, we initiated the process of formulating search expressions to gather the relevant literature. Initially, we conducted a search on Google Scholar using the term "Blockchain Self-Sovereign Identity" and examined the obtained results to identify additional keywords to refine our search. This iterative process was repeated a few times until we finalized the following search expressions:

*(Blockchain OR "Distributed Ledger Technology") AND ("Digital ID" OR "Digital IDs" OR "Digital Identity" OR "Digital Identities" OR KYC OR "Know Your Customer" OR "Self-Sovereign Identity" OR SSI OR "Decentralised identity" OR "Decentralised id")*

Third, we executed the search, which was held in November 2023. Since different databases have different user interfaces, we tried to perform the searches in a way closest to the defined search expression.

Table 1 lists the databases and the number of results obtained in each. We searched, utilizing titles, abstracts, and keywords to identify the papers, filtered by conferences and journals when possible. Initially, we identified 1046 articles, subsequently exported to Rayyan, a collaborative systematic literature review web tool. After the removal of duplicate papers, the remaining unique studies totaled 808.

In the fourth step of our review process, the authors conducted independent blind reviews to determine the inclusion of each article. Each author examined the titles, abstracts, and keywords of the identified papers independently, applying the predefined criteria, without discussing their assessments with each other. Disagreements were discussed and resolved at the end of the process.

The predefined inclusion criteria were: (i) the study must focus on SSI for individuals, (ii) it must be published in conferences or journals, and (iii) it must be written in English. The exclusion criteria were: (i) works that do not address SSI systems, (ii) works that focus on SSI for IoT devices, and (iii) works published in workshops, book chapters, or lectures.

**Table 1** Numbers of search results by database

| Database | Results | Database | Results |
|---|---|---|---|
| ACM | 55 | Scopus | 474 |
| EBSCO | 62 | SpringerLink | 94 |
| IEEExplore | 317 | Taylor & Francis | 5 |
| ScienceDirect | 29 | Wiley Online Library | 10 |
| Total: | 1046 | Unique: | 808 |

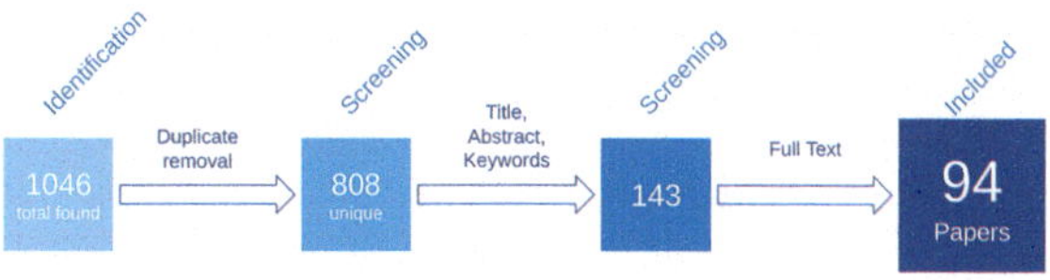


**Fig. 1** Numbers of papers from identification in databases to included

A total of 665 articles were excluded during the initial screening based on titles and abstracts. Subsequently, 49 additional articles were removed after full text review because they did not meet the predefined inclusion criteria. As a result, 94 articles were selected for further analysis. An overview of the screening process is presented in Fig. 1.

## 4 Overview of Blockchain-Based SSI Papers

We have observed a growing interest in research at the intersection of digital identities and blockchain over the years, as evidenced by the increasing number of publications. The trend began in 2017 with the first study we found. Subsequently, there was an increase to seven papers in 2018, followed by six papers in 2019. Since then, there has been a steady rise, with 13 publications in 2020, 16 in 2021, and a peak of 51 publications in 2022. Figure 2 illustrates this evolution of the number of publications.

To categorize the included papers, we progressively classified them into six major groups as we read through and analyzed each one. These groups emerged organically based on recurring themes and focus areas, allowing us to organize the papers into distinct categories, as follows:

**Conceptual Solutions (29 papers):** propose innovative approaches to address problems or challenges related to blockchain and digital identities. Often, new frameworks, theories, or models based on general or theoretical ideas are introduced.

**Implemented Solutions (20 papers):** present the development of new processes, systems, or the application of existing theories or frameworks to solve specific problems within the realm of blockchain and digital identity.

**Reviews or Case Studies (14 papers):** offer critical analyses of technologies, specific situations, or examples related to blockchain and digital identity. Provide valuable insights into real-world applications and examine their effectiveness.

**Technology Analysis (21 papers):** focus on the study and evaluation of projects, protocols, and the utilization of various technologies within digital identity ecosystems. Delve into the technical aspects and assess their implications.

**Systematic Mappings (6 papers):** literature reviews that systematically research, select, and evaluate existing research from different perspectives. Provide a comprehensive overview of the existing body of knowledge in the field.

**Views and Opinions (4 papers):** express personal perspectives or discuss blockchain and self-sovereign identity. Some of these papers present new ideas and challenges associated with the emerging identity paradigm.

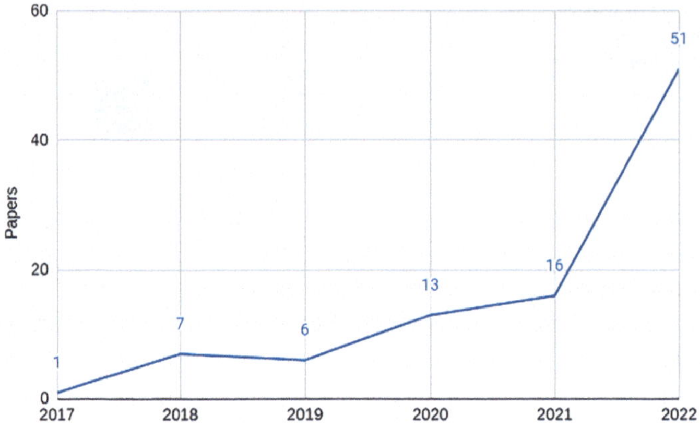


**Fig. 2** The evolution of the number of papers published by year

Among the **Systematic Mappings** addressing the intersection of blockchain and self-sovereign identity, six studies were identified. Two of these focused on specific topics: [84] explicitly reviewed the current state of SSI in healthcare applications, while [104] discussed how blockchain technology could process sensitive and large identity datasets across different domains.

The other four studies adopted a broader and more general perspective on blockchain-based SSI. In [20], the authors analyzed 120 papers published between January 2013 and January 2021, in IEEE Xplore and the Science Direct databases. In [79], Rathee and Singh selected 30 primary studies about blockchain and identity management, published from 2009 to 2020 in five electronic databases: IEEE Xplore, ACM Digital Library, Science Direct, Springer Link, and Wiley. In [6], the authors present a bibliometric analysis of 1395 peer-reviewed articles and their 44,412 references, where the primary studies were collected from the Web of Science database in April 2020. Another paper we found, [3], discusses 63 articles published between October 2015 and January 2022 in academic databases (e.g., IEEE Xplore, ScienceDirect, ACM Digital Library, Wiley, Springer Link, Taylor & Francis, and MDPI), patents, and Google Scholar.

Additionally, [84] focused explicitly on reviewing the current state of healthcare applications. Furthermore, [104] discusses how blockchain could process sensitive and large identity datasets among different domains.

Our review complements existing ones by including the most up-to-date dataset focused on academic articles dealing with blockchain-based SSI, presenting a comprehensive map of the literature and elucidating areas that garner substantial academic attention and those needing further exploration.

In addition to the systematic mapping studies, we encountered four papers presenting authors' **Views and Opinions** on blockchain-based self-sovereign identity. Kubach et al. [48] discuss the challenges faced in the realm of digital identity. In [26], the authors emphasize the socio-technical nature of self-sovereign identity, offering insights on social and technological aspects and suggesting directions for future research. In [88], Seifert explores the prospects of SSI, specifically in the context of national identification implementation, addressing considerations, benefits, and challenges. Lastly, [12] investigates information sharing and governance in the digital society using blockchain-based SSI.

As suggested by Webster and Watson [103], after completing the reading, we grouped the papers by identified concepts. We did it by categorizing them into 18 distinct areas of interest that emerged from our analysis: Architecture and Design Patterns, Authentication and Authorization, Banks and Financial, Blockchain Redaction, Education, Formal Definitions, Government and National IDs, Healthcare, Interoperability, Laws and Regulations, Metaverse, Morals and ethics, Organizational Management, Other Applications, Privacy and Security, SaaS, Trustworthiness, Vulnerable Individuals.

Figure 3 presents a distribution of the papers considering their contributions to Blockchain-based Digital Identities literature. Larger circles represent a higher number of papers on the topic, with the exact quantity written inside. The lines and rows presented in Fig. 3 are detailed in Table 2, below.

In the **Conceptual Solutions** category, we encountered a diverse range of articles proposing innovative ideas and frameworks for blockchain-based self-sovereign

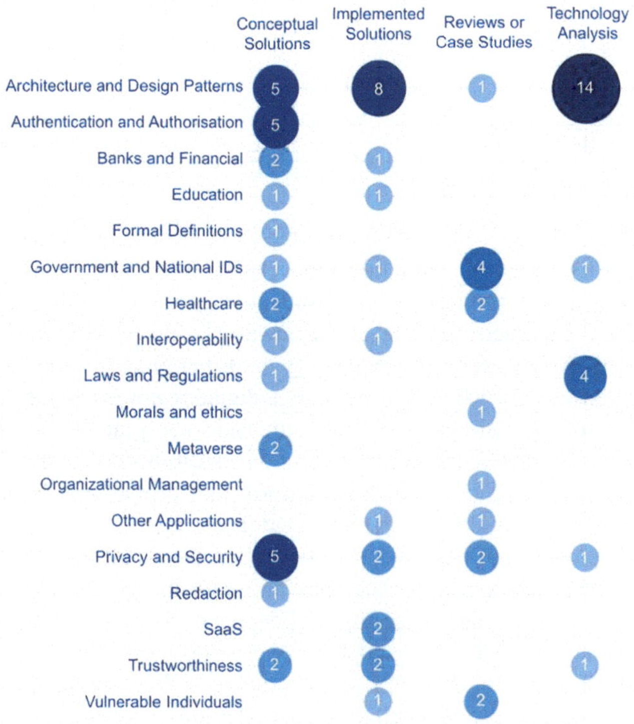


**Fig. 3** Current landscape—number of papers in the intersection of the groups

**Table 2** Current landscape of SSI contributions

| | Conceptual solutions | Implemented solutions | Reviews or case studies | Technology analysis |
|---|---|---|---|---|
| Architecture and design patterns | [49, 54, 62, 76, 82] | [15, 55, 101, 106]<br>[22, 34, 78, 99] | [64] | [4, 8, 19, 26, 28, 29, 35, 40, 43, 50, 68, 69, 75, 102] |
| Authentication and authorization | [25, 36, 38, 57, 80] | | | |
| Banks and financial | [2, 87] | [94] | | |
| Education | [60] | [100] | | |
| Formal definitions | [30] | | | |
| Government and national IDs | [53] | [97] | [10, 39, 58, 98] | [23] |
| Healthcare | [44, 83] | | [89, 90] | |
| Interoperability | [21] | [93] | | |
| Laws and regulations | [73] | | | [47, 61, 70, 71] |
| Morals and ethics | | | [41] | |
| Metaverse | [13, 33] | | | |
| Organizational management | | | [66] | |
| Other applications | | [31] | [91] | |
| Privacy and security | [45, 51, 56, 63, 74] | [1] [86] | [42, 105] | [67] |
| Redaction | [11] | | | |
| SaaS | | [24, 92] | | |
| Trustworthiness | [37] [65] | [52, 85] | | [32] |
| Vulnerable individuals | | [72] | [14, 17] | |

identity systems. These contributions include [54], which introduced 17 distinct design patterns specifically tailored for blockchain-based SSI systems. In [57], the authors present a decentralized SSI authentication protocol, while [36] proposed the OrgID, a comprehensive data management platform incorporating identity registration and authorization procedures. A multi-tiered architecture for scalable SSI is presented in [62], while [76] presents a digital agent (ssDA) as an essential building block for a grassroots digital economy and society, and in [49] the authors prototype a system with document attestation credibility checking and record sharing. Finally, [82] proposes an SSI platform that provides a ZeroKnowledge Proof (ZKP) mechanism to verify the information.

The Conceptual Solutions category also featured articles on authentication architectures, SSI frameworks for the banking sector in [2] and [87], and an SSI framework specifically tailored for Higher Education Institutions [60]. In [80] the authors proposed the EASEID model for a Session-based Single sign-on SSI, and [25] describes a hybrid of SSI, cryptographic authentication, and biometric authentication. We also encountered a formal and rigorous treatment of the concept of self-sovereign identity, employing a mathematical model [30]. Two papers bring

Conceptual Solutions to SSI and Healthcare [44, 83], and another two propose solutions to SSI and metaverse [13], including interoperability [33]. The papers in this category further explored evaluation models for international engagement in decentralized identity systems in [53]. Besides, [21] introduced an identity relationship model that spans multiple Identity Management systems, facilitating interoperability and integration. Moreover, [73] presented a compliance SSI system property set. In addition, we encountered a paper focusing on access control and data security in permissionless blockchains, as well as architecture and system protocols for Sybil-Resistant SSI [63]. Frameworks and models emphasizing the importance of trust and reputation mechanisms were found in [37] and [65]. In [51] the authors propose a decentralized attribute-based SSI, in [74] a method for detecting common weaknesses, and [56] a scheme to strike a balance between privacy and accountability. Finally, we found one paper that analyses the possible use cases for blockchain redaction (to modify or delete some data) in SSI [11].

Most articles in the **Implemented Solutions** category deal with system architecture and design patterns, such as in [106], where authors constructed a blockchain-based framework for verification, authorization and recovery of self-sovereign identity using smart contracts. Moreover, [55] presented a platform architecture that supports the idea of the design pattern as a service (DPaaS). In [99], the authors propose a decentralized access control system for inter-enterprise data sharing, and in [22], a selective disclosure method based on keying hash functions.

Many authors proposed different Digital Identity platforms based on blockchain, such as [78, 101], and [15] using Hyperledger and Ethereum technologies. Moreover, [34] presents the design and implementation of the Elesto protocol as an identity infrastructure, and [100] proposes the AlgoCert as a solution to educational certificates with Non-transferable NFT and DIDs. Furthermore, [93] implemented a trusted and robust authentication mechanism for users who share data between distinct blockchain platforms, [31] provided an SSI-based event ticketing framework, and [86] introduced a novel tool to perform metadata matching on Sovrin. Regarding processes banks and other financial institutions use to confirm the identity of the organizations and individuals (Know Your Customer), [94] created a framework to take a step toward tackling weaknesses in old KYC models. Furthermore, [97] presents a digital identity with passport-level attributes. A group of papers is focused on SSI as a Service [24] and Credentials as a Service [92], while [52] addresses audit and accountability issues in self-sovereign identity Blockchain Systems using Archival Science Principles. Abraham et al. [1] proposed "deriving identity data from an existing identity system into an SSI in a fully privacy-preserving way by additionally supporting offline verification." Additionally, [85] presents a framework for online document verification using SSI. Lastly, [72] proposes a novel solution to address identity issues faced by Indian migrant workers.

As **Reviews or Case Studies**, we encountered a survey focusing on the essential components of an SSI [64], opportunities for the public sector [58], and discussion about national digital identities in India [39], Finland, Sweden, Taiwan [10], and the Estonian E-Residency [98]. Other authors review the applicability of SSI solutions in the healthcare domain [89] and the aspects of these applications during pandemic situations like COVID-19 [90]. In more analyses of SSI technologies, we found [42] that illustrated three distinct paths in the evolution of digital identity and some key technical elements in decentralized identity. In [66], Mulaji and Roodt explain how technological, organizational and environmental (TOE) factors affect organizations' adoption behavior toward SSI. The authors in [105] conducted a comprehensive study comparing 31 blockchain-based Identity management (IdM) solutions against various functional and non-functional requirements and emerging SSI standards. The article [91] highlights the limitations of existing identity solutions, the advantages of SSI, and its application in the blockchain-based land registry system. Additionally, [47] examined issues related to the European Union General Data Protection Regulation (GDPR) associated with three specific systems (uPort, Sovrin, and Jolocom). Furthermore, [41] outlined the moral foundation for claims on the desirability of SSI solutions. In the context of human rights, [17] conducted a thorough survey on the utilization of blockchain technology to support the rights of migrants and refugees. The study examined two cases: the Building Blocks initiative by the World Food Programme in Jordan and the Rohingya Project. Finally, [14] examines the implications of self-sovereign identity for border politics and migration management, identifying a series of competing logics in the debates around SSI's emancipatory potential.

Lastly, within the **Technology Analysis** category, most papers focused on evaluating architecture and design patterns. In [69], the authors conducted an assessment specifically on uPort, while [28] and [68] provided comparisons of uPort with other systems like Sovrin and Civic. Furthermore, [40] and [27] analyzed uPort, Sovrin, and Shocard systems. On the other hand, some authors expanded their analyses to include additional technologies. For instance, [35] examined Blockstack and Selfkey, while [43] added EverID, Life ID, Sora, and Selfkey technologies to their analysis. In [8], the authors analyzed and compared ShoCard, WeIdentity, Microsoft DID, Cambridge Blockchain, uPort, and Sovrin. Nevertheless, [75] presents a detailed latency analysis of a permissioned blockchain system built with Indy and Aries, and [19] provides an overview and analysis of SSI properties from the literature. Related to government use, [23] analyzed SSI and Blockchain to access services of a Public Administration (Italy). While [61] collected and presented the major technological and regulatory information related to Identity and Access Management and blockchain technology, [71] examined the real sovereignty of digital identity in the SSI model. In [4], Alizadeh et al. explored six different Decentralized Identifier methods encompassing various architectural designs, such as public permissioned, public permissionless, and pairwise DIDs. Furthermore, [50] conducted a systematic criteria-driven survey of blockchain-based IdM solutions, covering features, prerequisites, market availability, readiness for enterprise integration, costs, and estimated maturity. In [29], the authors focused on evaluating a selection of distributed identity methods and analyzing their properties based on the categorization specified in the W3C recommendation rubric. Moreover, [81] evaluated six decentralized identifiers (DID) methods based on the guidelines provided by the W3C DID method rubric. Regarding security breaches, [67] proposed an approach for evaluating potential attacks on the SSI system, and in [32], the authors aimed to uncover the benefits that blockchain can bring to SSI systems. Finally, [47] not only analyzed Sovrin, uPort, and Jolocom but also engaged in a discussion on the GDPR compliance of the blockchain-based identity concept. Similarly, [70] evaluated this aspect of SSI, analyzing compliance and alignment with the principles of GDPR. Their findings suggest SSI systems based on a public permissioned blockchain can comply with the most key GDPR principles.

## 5 Bibliometric Data

This section presents a brief bibliometric analysis of the selected papers in this review. By applying bibliometric methods, with aid of VOSviewer 1.6.20, a software tool to build and visualize bibliometric networks, we aim to quantify academic output, identify key trends, and highlight influential contributions within this growing field. By analyzing research volume, identifying leading authors and collaborations, and highlighting the most cited works, we aim to map the intellectual structure of SSI research and identify emerging themes and future avenues for investigation.

The VOSviewer was set up as follows: bibliographic data was extracted from the papers' Digital Object Identifiers (DOIs) using the OpenAlex API, and maps were created based on this information.

Table 3 shows the top 13 authors who have published three or more papers, ranked by their total citations and the number of articles included in this study.

Figure 4 represents a co-authorship network. The links between circles indicate co-authorship relation. The visualization reveals distinct and isolated groups of authors that are publishing without connection to others, highlighting clusters of independent research efforts.

The co-occurrence network in Fig. 5 reveals a complex and interconnected landscape of concepts within self-sovereign identity. As expected, terms like "blockchain," "digital identity," "computer security," and "decentralization" occupy central positions, reflecting their fundamental role in SSI. However, the analysis also uncovers a broader range of interconnected fields, including economics, law,

**Table 3** Top 13 most cited authors and number of publications

| Citations | Papers | Author | Citations | Papers | Author |
|---|---|---|---|---|---|
| 348 | 2 | Mühle, Alexander | 184 | 5 | Naik, Nitin |
| 348 | 2 | Grüner, Andreas | 184 | 5 | Jenkins, Paul |
| 348 | 2 | Meinel, Christoph | 73 | 3 | Paik Hye-Young |
| 348 | 2 | Gayvoronskaya, Tatiana | 73 | 3 | Turkanovic, Muhamed |
| 345 | 2 | Petitcolas, Fabien A. P. | 73 | 3 | Lu, Qinghua |
| 345 | 2 | Dunphy, Paul | 73 | 3 | Cucko, Špela |
| 186 | 2 | Ferdous, Md Sadek | | | |

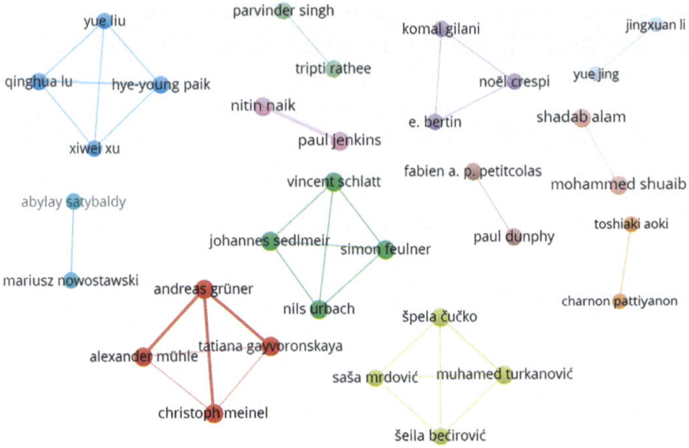


**Fig. 4** Co-authorship map

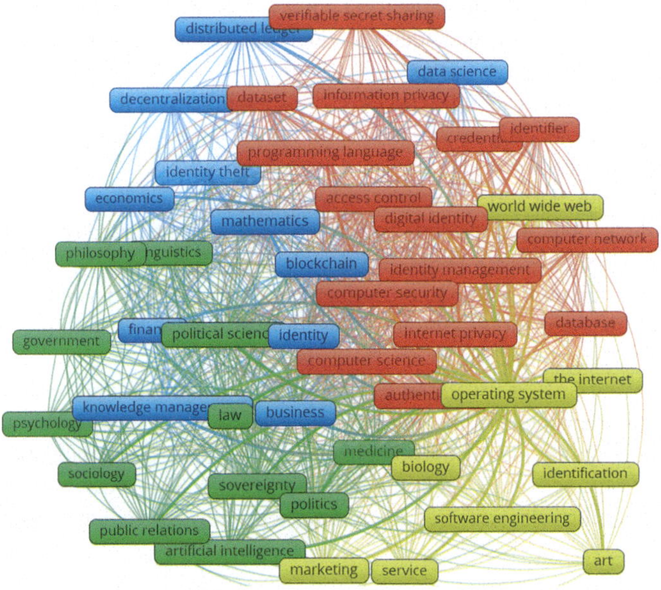


**Fig. 5** Keyword co-occurrences network

sociology, philosophy, and marketing. Notably, the prominence of government, politics, and law in the network underscores the significant societal implications of SSI and the need for robust regulatory frameworks.

Furthermore, we analyzed the articles according to the country of affiliation of the first author. This offers valuable insights into the geographical distribution of research contributions, highlighting the countries with leading academic output.

China is at the forefront with 11 papers, followed by India with 10, and Germany and the United Kingdom with 9 papers, reflecting their strong research capabilities and investment in digital identity technologies. Other notable contributors include Japan, Italy, Norway, and the USA, each with four or more papers during the analyzed period.

## 6 Further Analysis and Research Implications

After analyzing the studies identified in this literature review, it becomes evident that Self-Sovereign Identities are a central focus of much research. While a growing number of studies directly address the SSI topic, there are also instances where the term was used without proper alignment with the concept. Some studies misapply the term, describing systems that do not truly adhere to the principles of self-sovereign identity, such as storage control, portability, or interoperability.

Many selected works present architectures and design patterns for SSI systems, but few have been tested in production. Additionally, we observed that, despite being relatively new standards, Verifiable Credentials (VC) and Decentralized Identifiers (DID) were already present in some analyzed papers, suggesting a potential trend toward their adoption. However, we did not find any comparison between these W3C standards and other approaches.

Additionally, bibliometric data from our review shows that a few countries, such as China, India, Germany, and the UK, lead in research output on SSI and related digital identity technologies. The high output of these countries reflects a growing investment and interest in identity solutions that prioritize privacy, security, and user sovereignty. However, cooperation between groups is low, indicating a potential need for greater global collaboration and support to extend research and development in SSI.

Another recurring theme is the technical complexity associated with SSI, particularly concerning identity wallet management and secure recovery of cryptographic keys. These aspects remain critical barriers to user adoption and call for simplified, user-friendly designs that can make SSIs accessible to non-technical users.

Other points we highlight in the evolution of these systems include concerns about wallet key recovery and compliance with data protection regulations such as GDPR, especially regarding the right to be forgotten, given the immutable nature of blockchains. In this sense, we also note opportunities for debate and research on how SSIs can be used or integrated by official national identity systems, such as the European electronic identity system eIDAS.

In summary, our review underscores the importance of continued research in standardizing SSI principles, expanding global participation, addressing usability challenges, and exploring legal integration. As SSI matures, these areas will be instrumental in realizing the potential of decentralized identity systems in diverse contexts.

## 7 Conclusions

This systematic literature review on blockchain-based Self-Sovereign Identities (SSIs) sheds light on this field's growing interest and significance in digital identity research. By analyzing ninety-four articles from various academic databases, this review underscores the dynamic landscape of SSIs and their far-reaching implications for privacy, security, and regulatory compliance. We also present bibliometric data to highlight key trends and contributions in SSI research. This includes insights into the most published and highly cited authors, a co-authorship network revealing unconnected clusters, leading countries in academic output, and a keyword co-occurrence network. Among the key findings, it becomes evident that SSIs have the potential to revolutionize digital identity management by empowering individuals with unprecedented control over their personal data. The review highlights proposed approaches and architectural designs for SSI systems, along with practical implementations in various sectors such as finance, healthcare, and education. However, the review also exposes specific gaps and challenges in the current state of research. Some studies misuse the term "SSI," failing to adhere to its core principles. Furthermore, while theoretical models and design patterns abound, empirical validation and real-world testing of these solutions remain scarce. Key recovery, data privacy, and regulatory compliance concerns present significant hurdles to widespread SSI adoption. Future research should address these issues and explore pathways for integrating SSIs into existing identity systems, including official national identity frameworks. In conclusion, this systematic literature review provides valuable insights into the current state of blockchain-based Self-Sovereign Identities. Identifying trends, gaps, and future research directions contributes to the ongoing discourse on digital identity management and lays the groundwork for further advancements in the field. A limitation of this study is that our review only encompasses papers published up to the end of 2022. Therefore, broadening our analysis to include more recent publications is essential.

**Acknowledgments** This work is financed through national funds by FCT—Fundação para a Ciência e a Tecnologia, I.P., in the framework of the Project UIDB/00326/2020 and UIDP/00326/2020.

## References

1. Abraham, A., Koch, K., More, S., Ramacher, S., & Stopar, M. (2021). *Privacy-preserving eID derivation to self-sovereign identity systems with offline revocation*. Institute of Electrical and Electronics Engineers (pp. 506–513).
2. Ahmed, K. A., Saraya, S. F., Wanis, J. F., & Ali-Eldin, A. M. (2020). *A self-sovereign identity architecture based on blockchain and the utilization of customer's banking cards: The case of bank scam calls prevention*. Institute of Electrical and Electronics Engineers.
3. Ahmed, M. R., Islam, A. K. M. M., Shatabda, S., & Islam, S. (2022). Blockchain-based identity management system and self-sovereign identity ecosystem: A comprehensive survey.

*IEEE Access, 10*, 113436–113481. Retrieved February 01, 2024, from https://ieeexplore.ieee.org/document/9927415/
4. Alizadeh, M., Andersson, K., & Schelen, O. (2022). Comparative analysis of decentralized identity approaches. *IEEE Access, 10*, 92273–92283.
5. Allen, C. (2016). The path to self-sovereign identity. *Life with alacrity*. Retrieved September 21, 2024, from http://www.lifewithalacrity.com/2016/04/the-path-to-selfsoverereign-identity.html
6. Ante, L., Fischer, C., & Strehle, E. (2022). A bibliometric review of research on digital identity: Research streams, influential works and future research paths. *Journal of Manufacturing Systems, 62*, 523–538.
7. Avellaneda, O., Bachmann, A., Barbir, A., Brenan, J., Dingle, P., Duffy, K. H., Maler, E., Reed, D., & Sporny, M. (2019). Decentralized identity: Where did it come from and where is it going? *IEEE Communications Standards Magazine, 3*(4), 10–13.
8. Bai, Y., Lei, H., Li, S., Gao, H., Li, J., & Li, L. (2022). *Decentralized and self-sovereign identity in the era of blockchain: A survey* (pp. 500–507). Institute of Electrical and Electronics Engineers.
9. Bank, W. (2014). Global ID coverage, barriers, and use by the numbers: Insights from The ID4D-findex survey. http://documents.worldbank.org/curated/en/953621531854471275/Global-ID-Coverage-Barriers-and-Use-by-the-Numbers-Insights-from-the-ID4D-Findex-Survey
10. Bazarhanova, A., Magnusson, J., Lindman, J., Chou, E., & Nilsson, A. (2019). Blockchain-based electronic identification: Cross-country comparison of six design choices. https://aisel.aisnet.org/ecis2019_rp/79
11. Becirovic, S., Cucko, S., Turkanovic, M., Supic, H., & Mrdovic, S. (2022). Blockchain redaction in self-sovereign identity. In *2022 International Conference on Software, Telecommunications and Computer Networks (SoftCOM)* (pp. 1–6). IEEE. Retrieved February 01, 2024, from https://ieeexplore.ieee.org/document/9911445/.
12. Benchaya Gans, R., Ubacht, J., & Janssen, M. (2022). Governance and societal impact of blockchain-based self-sovereign identities. *Policy and Society, 41*(3), 402–413.
13. Cali, U., Ferdous, M. S., Karaarslan, E., Gourisetti, S. N. G., & Mylrea, M. (2022). SSI meets metaverse for industry 4.0 and beyond. In *2022 IEEE 1st global emerging technology blockchain forum: Blockchain & beyond* (iGETblockchain) (pp. 1–6). IEEE. Retrieved February 01, 2024, from https://ieeexplore.ieee.org/document/10087134/
14. Cheesman, M. (2022). Self-sovereignty for refugees? The contested horizons of digital identity. *Geopolitics, 27*(1). Retrieved February 01, 2024, from https://www.tandfonline.com/doi/full/10.1080/14650045.2020.1823836
15. Chen, Y., Liu, C., Wang, Y., & Wang, Y. (2021). A self-sovereign decentralized identity platform based on blockchain (vol. 2021). Institute of Electrical and Electronics Engineers.
16. Clark, J., Metz, A., & Casher, C. (2023). 850 million people globally don't have ID—Why this matters and what we can do about it. Retrieved September 21, 2024, from https://blogs.worldbank.org/en/digital-development/850-million-people-globallydont-have-id-why-matters-and-what-we-can-do-about
17. Connolly, D., Nam, S., & Goodman, K. (2022). Solving old problems or making new ones? Blockchain technology for the protection of refugees and migrants. *Journal of Human Rights, 22*, 109–134.
18. Costa, R., & Rupino Da Cunha, P. (2024). Blockchain-based self-sovereign identities: Current landscape and research opportunities. In *Harnessing Opportunities: Reshaping ISD in the post-COVID-19 and Generative AI Era (ISD2024 Proceedings)*.
19. Cucko, S., Becirovic, S., Kamisalic, A., Mrdovic, S., & Turkanovic, M. (2022). Towards the classification of self-sovereign identity properties. *IEEE Access, 10*, 88306–88329. Retrieved February 01, 2024, from https://ieeexplore.ieee.org/document/9858139/.
20. Čučko, Š., & Turkanović, M. (2021). Decentralized and self-sovereign identity: Systematic mapping study. *IEEE Access, 9*, 139009–139027.

21. Dabrowski, M., & Pacyna, P. (2022). Blockchain-based identity dicovery between heterogenous identity management systems (pp. 131–137). Institute of Electrical and Electronics Engineers.
22. De Salve, A., Lisi, A., Mori, P., & Ricci, L. (2022). Selective disclosure in self-sovereign identity based on hashed values. In: *2022 IEEE Symposium on Computers and Communications (ISCC)* (pp. 1–8). IEEE. Retrieved February 02, 2024, from https://ieeexplore.ieee.org/document/9913052/.
23. Dell'Era, M. (2022). Blockchain and Self-Sovereign Identity for Public Administration. *Neural Networks, 7–8*, 10.
24. Ding, Y., & Sato, H. (2022). *Self-sovereign identity as a service: Architecture in practice* (pp. 1536–1543). Institute of Electrical and Electronics Engineers.
25. Drusinsky, D. (2022). Cryptographic. Biometric self-sovereign personal identities. *Computer, 55*(6), 96–102. Retrieved February 01, 2024, from https://ieeexplore.ieee.org/document/9789304/
26. Dunphy, P., Garratt, L., & Petitcolas, F. (2018). *Decentralizing digital identity: Open challenges for distributed ledgers* (pp. 75–78). Institute of Electrical and Electronics Engineers.
27. Dunphy, P., & Petitcolas, F. A. P. (2018). A first look at identity management schemes on the blockchain. *IEEE Security & Privacy, 16*, 20–29.
28. Eddine, B. N., Ouaddah, A., & Mezrioui, A. (2021). *Exploring blockchain-based self sovereign identity systems: Challenges and comparative analysis* (pp. 21–22). Institute of Electrical and Electronics Engineers.
29. Fdhila, W., Stifter, N., Kostal, K., Saglam, C., & Sabadello, M. (2021). Methods for decentralized identities: Evaluation and insights. In *Business process management: Blockchain and robotic process automation forum* (pp. 119–135). Springer.
30. Ferdous, M. S., Chowdhury, F., & Alassafi, M. O. (2019). In search of self-sovereign identity leveraging blockchain technology. *IEEE Access, 7*, 103059–103079.
31. Feulner, S., Sedlmeir, J., Schlatt, V., & Urbach, N. (2022). Exploring the use of self-sovereign identity for event ticketing systems. *Electronic Markets, 32*(3), 1759–1777. Retrieved February 01, 2024, from https://link.springer.com/10.1007/s12525-022-00573-9
32. Fraser, A., & Schneider, S. (2022). On the role of blockchain for self-sovereign identity. In *Competitive Advantage in the Digital Economy (CADE 2022)*. Hybrid Conference (pp. 17–21). Institution of Engineering and Technology. Retrieved February 01, 2024, from https://digital-library.theiet.org/content/conferences/10.1049/icp.2022.2032
33. Ghirmai, S., Mebrahtom, D., Aloqaily, M., Guizani, M., & Debbah, M. (2022). Self-sovereign identity for trust and interoperability in the metaverse. In *2022 IEEE Smartworld, Ubiquitous Intelligence & Computing, Scalable Computing & Communications, Digital Twin, Privacy Computing, Metaverse, Autonomous & Trusted Vehicles* (pp. 2468–2475). IEEE. Retrieved February 01, 2024, from https://ieeexplore.ieee.org/document/10189537/
34. Giacobino, A., Grierson, D., Sorà, G., Singh, H. P., Schäffner, M., McHale, P., & Maggs, S. (2022). Elesto protocol: Self-sovereign identity system. In *2022 IEEE 1st Global Emerging Technology Blockchain Forum: Blockchain&Beyond (iGETblockchain)* (pp. 1–6). IEEE. Retrieved February 01, 2024, from https://ieeexplore.ieee.org/document/10087121/
35. Gilani, K., Bertin, E., Hatin, J., & Crespi, N. (2020). A survey on blockchain-based identity management and decentralized privacy for personal data. In *2nd Conference on Blockchain Research & Applications for Innovative Networks and Services (BRAINS)* (pp. 97–101).
36. Gilani, K., Ghaffari, F., Bertin, E., & Crespi, N. (2022). *Self-sovereign identity management framework using smart contracts*. Institute of Electrical and Electronics Engineers.
37. Gruner, A., Muhle, A., Gayvoronskaya, T., & Meinel, C. (2018). A quantifiable trust model for blockchain-based identity management. In *2018 IEEE International Conference on Internet of Things (iThings) and IEEE Green Computing and Communications (GreenCom) and IEEE Cyber, Physical and Social Computing (CPSCom) and IEEE Smart Data (SmartData)* (pp. 1475–1482).
38. Gulati, H., & Huang, C.-T. (2019). Self-sovereign dynamic digital identities based on blockchain technology. In *2019 SoutheastCon* (pp. 1–6). IEEE.

39. Gururaj, P. (2020). Identity management using permissioned blockchain. In *2020 International Conference on Mainstreaming Block Chain Implementation (ICOMBI)* (pp. 1–3).
40. Haddouti, S. E., & Kettani, M. D. E.-C. E. (2019). Analysis of identity management systems using blockchain technology. In *2019 International Conference on Advanced Communication Technologies and Networking (CommNet)* (pp. 1–7).
41. Ishmaev, G. (2021). Sovereignty, privacy, and ethics in blockchain-based identity management systems. *Ethics and Information Technology, 23*, 239–252.
42. Jing, Y., Li, J., Wang, Y., & Li, H. (2021). *The introduction of digital identity evolution and the industry of decentralized identity* (pp. 504–508). Institute of Electrical and Electronics Engineers.
43. Kaneriya, J., & Patel, H. (2020). *A comparative survey on blockchain based self sovereign identity system* (pp. 1150–1155). Institute of Electrical and Electronics Engineers.
44. Kang, Y., & Park, Y. B. (2022). Secure access control realization based on self-sovereign identity for cloud CDM. *Applied Sciences, 12*(19), 9833. Retrieved February 01, 2024, from https://www.mdpi.com/2076-3417/12/19/9833
45. Kirupanithi, D. N., & Antonidoss, A. (2021). Self-sovereign identity creation on blockchain using identity based encryption. In *2021 5th International Conference on Intelligent Computing and Control Systems (ICICCS)* (pp. 299–304).
46. Kitchenham, B. (2004). Procedures for performing systematic reviews. https://www.researchgate.net/publication/228756057
47. Kondova, G., & Erbguth, J. (2020). *Self-sovereign identity on public blockchains and the GDPR* (pp. 342–345). Association for Computing Machinery.
48. Kubach, M., Schunck, C. H., Sellung, R., & Rosnagel, H. (2020). Self-sovereign and decentralized identity as the future of identity management? In *Open Identity Summit 2020*.
49. Kumar, S. R., & Goyal, M. (2022). Administration of digital identities using blockchain. In *2022 5th International Conference on Contemporary Computing and Informatics (IC3I)* (pp. 2179–2183). IEEE. Retrieved February 01, 2024, from https://ieeexplore.ieee.org/document/10072845/
50. Kuperberg, M. (2020). Blockchain-based identity management: A survey from the enterprise and ecosystem perspective. *IEEE Transactions on Engineering Management, 67*, 1008–1027.
51. Lee, Y.-H., Liu, Z.-Y., Tso, R., & Tseng, Y.-F. (2022). Blockchain-based self-sovereign identity system with attribute-based issuance. In *International Conference on Information Security Practice and Experience* (pp. 21–38). Springer.
52. Lemieux, V., Voskobojnikov, A., & Kang, M. (2021). *Addressing audit and accountability issues in self-sovereign identity blockchain systems using archival science principles* (pp. 1210–1216). Institute of Electrical and Electronics Engineers.
53. Li, J., & Jing, Y. (2022). Establishing an international engagement model of digital identity based on blockchain. *Mobile Information Systems, 2022*, 6988211.
54. Liu, Y., Lu, Q., Paik, H. Y., & Xu, X. (2020). Design patterns for blockchain-based self-sovereign identity. *Association for Computing Machinery*. In *Proceedings of the European Conference on Pattern Languages of Programs, 2020*, (pp. 1–14).
55. Liu, Y., Lu, Q., Paik, H. Y., Xu, X., Chen, S., & Zhu, L. (2020). Design pattern as a service for blockchain-based self-sovereign identity. *IEEE Software, 37*, 30–36.
56. Lyu, Q., Cheng, S., Li, H., Liu, J., Shen, Y., & Wang, Z. (2022). NSSIA: A new self-sovereign identity scheme with accountability. In D. Zhao (Ed.) *Security and Communication Networks* (pp. 1–17).
57. Ma, B., Zheng, X., Zhao, C.,Wang, Y.,Wang, D., & Meng, B. (2022). A secure and decentralized SSI authentication protocol with privacy protection and finegrained access control based on federated blockchain. *PLoS ONE, 17*, e0274748.
58. Mahula, S., Tan, E., & Crompvoets, J. (2021). *With blockchain or not? Opportunities and challenges of self-sovereign identity implementation in public administration: Lessons from the Belgian case*. Association for Computing Machinery (pp. 495–504).

59. Manby, B. (2016). Identification in the context of forced displacement: Identification for development (ID4D). *World Bank*. Retrieved February 02, 2024, from https://documents.worldbank.org/en/publication/documents-reports/documentdetail/375811469772770030/
60. Mansoori, S. A., & Maheshwari, P. (2022). *HEI-BCT: A framework to implement blockchain-based self-sovereign identity solution in higher education institutions*. Institute of Electrical and Electronics Engineers (pp. 6–10).
61. Mecozzi, R., Perrone, G., Anelli, D., Saitto, N., Paggi, E., & Mancini, D. (2022). Blockchain-related identity and access management challenges: (de)centralized digital identities regulation. In *2022 IEEE International Conference on Blockchain (Blockchain)* (pp. 443–448). IEEE. Retrieved February 01, 2024, from https://ieeexplore.ieee.org/document/9881832/
62. Misic, J., Misic, V. B., & Chang, X. (2022). Scalable self-sovereign identity architecture. *IEEE Network, 36*(3), 114–121. Retrieved February 01, 2024, from https://ieeexplore.ieee.org/document/9829377/
63. Moriyama, K., & Otsuka, A. (2022). *Permissionless blockchain-based sybil-resistant self-sovereign identity utilizing attested execution secure processors*. Institute of Electrical and Electronics Engineers (pp. 1–10).
64. Mühle, A., Grüner, A., Gayvoronskaya, T., & Meinel, C. (2018). A survey on essential components of a self-sovereign identity. Comput. Sci. Rev. **30**, 80–86 (2018).
65. Mukta, R., Paik, H. Y., Lu, Q., & Kanhere, S. S. (2022). *CredTrust: Credential based issuer management for trust in self-sovereign identity*. Institute of Electrical and Electronics Engineers (pp. 334–339).
66. Mulaji, S. M., & Roodt, S. (2022). Factors affecting organisations' adoption behaviour toward blockchain-based distributed identity management: The sustainability of self-sovereign identity in organisations. *Sustainability, 14*(18), 11534. Retrieved February 01, 2024, from https://www.mdpi.com/2071-1050/14/18/11534
67. Naik, N., Grace, P., Jenkins, P., Naik, K., & Song, J. (2022). An evaluation of potential attack surfaces based on attack tree modelling and risk matrix applied to self-sovereign identity. *Computers & Security, 120*, 102808. Retrieved February 01, 2024, from https://linkinghub.elsevier.com/retrieve/pii/S0167404822002024
68. Naik, N., & Jenkins, P. (2020). *Self-sovereign identity specifications: Govern your identity through your digitalwallet using blockchain technology*. Institute of Electrical and Electronics Engineers (pp. 90–95).
69. Naik, N., & Jenkins, P. (2020). *UPort open-source identity management system: An assessment of self-sovereign identity and user-centric data platform built on blockchain*. Institute of Electrical and Electronics Engineers.
70. Naik, N., & Jenkins, P. (2020). *Your identity is yours: Take back control of your identity using GDPR compatible self-sovereign identity*. Institute of Electrical and Electronics Engineers.
71. Naik, N., & Jenkins, P. (2022). Is self-sovereign identity really sovereign? *2022 IEEE International Symposium on Systems Engineering (ISSE)* (pp. 1–7). IEEE. Retrieved February 01, 2024, from https://ieeexplore.ieee.org/document/10005404/
72. Otta, S. P., Panda, S., & Hota, C. (2022). Identity management with blockchain: Indian migrant workers prospective. In *2022 IEEE Conference on Interdisciplinary Approaches in Technology and Management for Social Innovation (IATMSI)* (pp. 1–6). IEEE. Retrieved February 01, 2024, from https://ieeexplore.ieee.org/document/10119388/
73. Pattiyanon, C., & Aoki, T. (2022). Compliance SSI system property set to laws, regulations, and technical standards. *IEEE Access, 10*, 99370–99393.
74. Pattiyanon, C., Aoki, T., & Ishii, D. (2022). A method for detecting commonweaknesses in self-sovereign identity systems using domain-specific models and knowledge graph. In *MODELSWARD* (pp. 219–226).
75. Pflanzner, T., Baniata, H., & Kertesz, A. (2022). Latency analysis of blockchain-based SSI applications. *Future Internet, 14*(10), 282. Retrieved February 01, 2024, from https://www.mdpi.com/1999-5903/14/10/282

76. Poupko, O., Shapiro, E., & Talmon, N. (2022). Self-sovereign digital agents for a grassroots digital society. In *2022 IEEE 42nd International Conference on Distributed Computing Systems (ICDCS)* (pp. 202–212). IEEE.
77. Preukschat, A., & Drummond, R. (2021). *Self-sovereign identity*. Manning Publications.
78. Rathee, T., & Singh, P. (2021). A self-sovereign identity management system using blockchain. In: Cyber Security and Digital Forensics (pp. 371–379).
79. Rathee, T., & Singh, P. (2022). A systematic literature mapping on secure identity management using blockchain technology. *Journal of King Saud University - Computer and Information Sciences, 34*, 5782–5796.
80. Reddy, G. S., & Konala, D. R. (2022). Easeid- a session-based single sign-on self-sovereign identity and access management system using block-chain. *Indian Journal of Computer Science and Engineering, 13*(4), pp. 1197–1209. Retrieved February 01, 2024, from http://www.ijcse.com/abstract.html?file=22-13-04-176
81. Reed, D., Sporny, M., Longley, D., Allen, C., Grant, R., Sabadello, M., & Holt, J. (2020). Decentralized identifiers (dids) v1. 0. Draft Community Group Report.
82. Sampath, S., Sanjay, M., Ahmed, N., Bhagavath, A., & Nanjesh, B. R. (2022). Decentralized digital identity wallet using principles of self- sovereign identity applied to blockchain. In *2022 IEEE 7th International Conference on Recent Advances and Innovations in Engineering (ICRAIE)* (pp. 337–341). IEEE. Retrieved February 01, 2024, from https://ieeexplore.ieee.org/document/10054286/
83. Saidi, H., Labraoui, N., Ari, A. A. A., Maglaras, L. A., & Emati, J. H. M. (2022). DSMAC: Privacy-aware decentralized self-management of data access control based on blockchain for health data. In *IEEE Access, 10*, 101011–101028.
84. Satybaldy, A., Hasselgren, A., & Nowostawski, M. (2022). Decentralized identity management for e-Health applications: State-of-the-art and guidance for future work. In *Blockchain in Healthcare Today, 5*, 10–30953. https://doi.org/10.30953/bhty.v5.195
85. Satybaldy, A., Subedi, A., & Nowostawski, M. (2022). A framework for online document verification using self-sovereign identity technology. *Sensors, 22*(21), 8408. Retrieved February 01, 2024, from https://www.mdpi.com/1424-8220/22/21/8408
86. Schardong, F., Custódio, R., Pioli, L., & Meyer, J. (2022). Matching metadata on blockchain for self-sovereign identity. In *International Conference on Business Process Management* (pp. 421–433). Springer.
87. Schlatt, V., Sedlmeir, J., Feulner, S., & Urbach, N. (2022). Designing a framework for digital KYC processes built on blockchain-based self-sovereign identity. *Information and Management, 59*(7), 103553. https://doi.org/10.1016/j.im.2021.103553
88. Seifert, R. (2020). Digital identities-self-sovereignty and blockchain are the keys to success. *Network Security, 2020*, 17–19.
89. Shuaib, M., Alam, S., Alam, M. S., & Nasir, M. S. (2021). Self-sovereign identity for healthcare using blockchain. In *Materials Today: Proceedings*.
90. Shuaib, M., Alam, S., Nasir, M. S., & Alam, M. S. (2021). Immunity credentials using selfsovereign identity for combating COVID-19 pandemic. In *Materials Today: Proceedings*.
91. Shuaib, M., Hassan, N. H., Usman, S., Alam, S., Bhatia, S., Mashat, A., Kumar, A., & Kumar, M. (2022). *Self-sovereign identity solution for blockchain-based land registry system: A comparison*. Wiley
92. Siddiqui, H., Idrees, M., Gudymenko, I., Quoc, D. L., & Fetzer, C. (2021). *Credentials as a service providing self sovereign identity as a cloud service using trusted execution environments* (pp. 210–216). Institute of Electrical and Electronics Engineers.
93. Singh Sidhu, S., Nguyen, M. N. H., Ngene, C., & Rouhani, S. (2022). Trust development for blockchain interoperability using self-sovereign identity integration. In *2022 IEEE 13th Annual Information Technology, Electronics and Mobile Communication Conference (IEMCON)* (pp. 0033–0040). IEEE. Retrieved February 01, 2024, from https://ieeexplore.ieee.org/document/9946562/
94. Soltani, R., Nguyen, U. T., & An, A. (2018). A new approach to client onboarding using self-sovereign identity and distributed ledger. In *IEEE International Conference on Internet of*

*Things (iThings) and IEEE Green Computing and Communications (GreenCom) and IEEE Cyber, Physical and Social Computing (CPSCom) and IEEE Smart Data (SmartData)* (pp. 1129–1136).

95. Sporny, M., Longley, D., & Chadwick, D. (2022). Verifiable credentials data model v 1.1. Retrieved June 04, 2024, from https://www.w3.org/TR/vc-data-model/
96. Sporny, M., Longley, D., Sabadello, M., Reed, D., Steele, O., & Allen, C. (2022). Decentralized identifiers (DIDs) v1.0. Retrieved June 04, 2024, from https://www.w3.org/TR/did-core/
97. Stokkink, Q., & Pouwelse, J. (2018). Deployment of a blockchain-based self-sovereign identity. In *IEEE International Conference on Internet of Things (iThings) and IEEE Green Computing and Communications (GreenCom) and IEEE Cyber, Physical and Social Computing (CPSCom) and IEEE Smart Data (SmartData)* (pp. 1336–1342).
98. Sullivan, C., & Burger, E. (2017). E-residency and blockchain. *Computer Law and Security Review, 33*, 470–481.
99. Tadjik, H., Geng, J., Jaatun, M. G., & Rong, C. (2022). Blockchain empowered and selfsovereign access control system. In *2022 IEEE International Conference on Cloud Computing Technology and Science (CloudCom)*. IEEE. Retrieved February 01, 2024, from https://ieeexplore.ieee.org/document/10005375/
100. Tahlil, T., Gomasta, S. S., & Ali, A. B. M. S. (2022). AlgoCert: Adopt non-transferable NFT for the issuance and verification of educational certificates using algorand blockchain. *2022 IEEE Asia-Pacific Conference on Computer Science and Data Engineering (CSDE)*. IEEE. Retrieved February 01, 2024, from https://ieeexplore.ieee.org/document/10089274/
101. Takemiya, M., & Vanieiev, B. (2018). *Sora identity: Secure, digital identity on the blockchain* (vol. 2, pp. 582–587). IEEE Computer Society.
102. Thomas, A. M., Ramaguru, R., & Sethumadhavan, M. (2022). *Distributed identity and verifiable claims using Ethereum standards* (pp. 621–636). Springer.
103. Webster, J., & Watson, R. T. (2002). Analyzing the past to prepare for the future: Writing a literature review. *MIS Quarterly, 26*, xiii–xxiii.
104. Yang, X., & Chan, J. (2021). Blockchain and identity management. In *Context-Aware Systems and Applications: 10th EAI International Conference, ICCASA 2021, Virtual Event, October 28–29. Proceedings* (vol. 10, pp. 192–204).
105. Zaeem, R. N., Chang, K. C., Huang, T. C., Liau, D., Song, W., Tyagi, A., Khalil, M., Lamison, M., Pandey, S., & Barber, K. S. (2021). Blockchain-based self-sovereign identity: Survey, requirements, use-cases, and comparative study. In *ACM International Conference Proceeding Series* (pp. 128–135).
106. Zhou, T., Li, X., & Zhao, H. (2019). EverSSDI: Blockchain-based framework for verification, authorisation and recovery of self-sovereign identity using smart contracts. *International Journal of Computer Applications in Technology, 60*, 281–295.

# A Framework for Rigorous Execution and Presentation of Expert Interviews in IS and Digital Transformation Research

**Tobias Hassmann and Markus Westner**

**Abstract** This article addresses the inconsistent conceptualization of expert interviews in information systems (IS) research by providing a structured framework for their rigorous execution and presentation. Through a thematic analysis of 28 method-relevant papers, key characteristics and good practices for executing expert interviews are identified. Additionally, 39 highly cited IS studies were reviewed to examine expert interview utilization in IS research and to identify good practices for presenting expert interview outcomes, which are further validated on nine digital transformation (DT) studies. Our findings highlight the adaptability and varied applications of expert interviews in IS research and offer recommendations to strengthen rigor in their preparation, execution, and presentation of outcomes. Theoretical and practical implications are provided to guide a more systematic and rigorous use of expert interviews in IS research.

## 1 Introduction

Conducting rigorous research hinges on employing a sound research design, making well-founded methodological choices, and selecting appropriate data collection procedures [1–5]. Further developing the utilization and comprehension of research methods and associated data collection procedures within the research community, which serves as both consumers and producers of research, is a relevant topic [3, 4]. This article seeks to deepen information systems (IS) scholars' understanding of expert interviews—a qualitative data collection procedure—by exploring its applicability and challenges within the context of digital transformation (DT)

T. Hassmann
Munich Business School, Munich, Germany
e-mail: tobias.hassmann@munich-business-school.de

M. Westner (✉)
OTH Regensburg, Regensburg, Germany
e-mail: markus.westner@oth-regensburg.de

 
B. Marcinkowski et al. (eds.), *Advances in Information Systems Development*, Lecture Notes in Information Systems and Organisation 77,
https://doi.org/10.1007/978-3-031-87880-0_4

research [6–12]. Expanding on a conference paper presented at the 32nd International Conference on Information Systems Development (ISD 2024) [9], this work provides a practical framework to guide IS researchers in the rigorous execution of expert interviews and the presentation of their outcomes.

To ensure rigor and produce valid, reliable, and generalizable outcomes, a data collection procedure must align with a sound research approach and a defined research methodology. In the context of expert interviews, this entails employing them as sole data collection procedure within a mono-method (MOM) research design, combining them with supplementary qualitative methods in a multi-method qualitative approach (MMQ), or mixing them with quantitative methods in a mixed-methods approach (MM) [1–3, 5]. Also, epistemological and theoretical underpinnings need to clearly map and inform the data collection procedure [2, 5]. While expert interviews allow to efficiently collect data [12–14], they still lack a consistent conceptualization and their methodological as well as epistemological status remains debated [15–19]. There is scepticism about considering expert interviews as a standalone research methodology because of their complex nature and their reliance on the expert as the primary source of information [7, 16]. And yet, despite these challenges, expert interviews enjoy widespread popularity in IS research—in-line with a growing adoption of qualitative research methodologies in top IS research [20].

Emerged in the 1990s in social sciences [6, 7, 12–15], expert interviews are employed in a wide range of studies investigating diverse IS-related phenomena. Highly cited IS studies employ expert interviews to, for example, investigate the effect of DT for business model management in small- and medium-sized enterprises [21], to manage organizations' presence on social media [22], or to explore how new technologies shape the value chain in the online music industry [23]. These examples already suggest that expert interviews are utilized in IS research to explore both emerging and established IS phenomena and can provide input for initial exploration of topics and contribute to theory development [23–26].

Considering that expert interviews originated in other disciplines [6, 7, 10, 15], questions arise about their effective transfer and application to IS research that focuses on technology and organizational dynamics [3]. Hence, this article's research questions fall into two buckets: first, we provide conceptual foundations and practical guidelines for executing expert interviews rigorously, focusing on the generation of valid and reliable outcomes irrespective of the discipline (RQ1, RQ2). Second, we augment these insights by analyzing the utilization of expert interviews in frequently cited studies published in leading IS outlets (RQ3) and by identifying good practices for presenting the outcomes of expert interviews (RQ4). We then validate the good practices for outcome-presentation rigor on nine studies published in relevant IS journals that address the research field of DT [23–31] (RQ5). Our five corresponding research questions are:

RQ1: *What are the distinct characteristics of an expert interview?*

RQ2: *What good practices ensure methodological rigor in conducting expert interviews?*

RQ3: *How are expert interviews employed in highly cited articles within relevant IS outlets?*
RQ4: *What good practices are demonstrated in top-cited IS articles for presenting outcomes derived from expert interviews?*
RQ5: *Do studies on DT published in relevant IS journals follow good practices in presenting interview outcomes?*

The article is organized as follows: Sect. 1 introduces the research questions and objectives. Section 2.1 describes the methodology to address RQ1 and RQ2, while Section 2.2 explains the literature selection for RQ3–RQ5. Section 3.1 tackles RQ1 by identifying characteristics of expert interviews, and Sect. 3.2 presents good practices for conducting them. Both chapters treat expert interviews in a discipline-agnostic manner. Section 4.1 answers RQ3 by detailing the use of expert interviews in IS research, with Sect. 4.2 offering good practices for presenting expert interview outcomes (RQ4). These good practices are validated in Sect. 4.3 through an analysis of nine DT-focused articles (RQ5). Section 5 concludes the paper by summarizing its contributions and discussing its limitations.

## 2 Methodology

### *2.1 Literature Retrieval to Address RQ1 and RQ2*

We conducted systematic reviews of recent literature following the PRISMA guidelines [32] to address RQ1 through RQ5, while applying different search strategies to tackle RQ1–2 and RQ3–5. To tackle RQ1–2 and to ensure an interdisciplinary and comprehensive approach, we conducted a two-fold literature research process (Fig. 1): first, we identified method-related literature on expert interviews across all academic disciplines. Second, we conducted a systematic search leveraging studies that employ expert interviews and that are published in leading IS-specific journals to find additional method-relevant literature.

In the first step (s1), we searched Scopus and Web of Science (WoS) using four inclusion criteria: articles, textbooks, book chapters, or conference papers (IC/s1/1), written in English or German (IC/s1/2), peer-reviewed (IC/s1/3), and published after 2002 (IC/s1/4). In April 2024, we searched for '*expert* interview* method**' in titles, keywords, and abstracts, initially yielding 27,549 results in Scopus and 24,100 in WoS. Accordingly, we refined the search to identify documents with '*expert* AND interview**' in the title and '*expert* interview**', '*interview* expert**', '*method**', or '*qualitative*' within the author-provided keywords and abstracts. This reduced the results to 287 in Scopus and 191 in WoS, totaling 478. After deduplication, 198 results remained. We excluded 181 studies using expert interviews only for data collection, leaving eighteen. A backward and forward search [33] added three more, finalizing the list at 21.

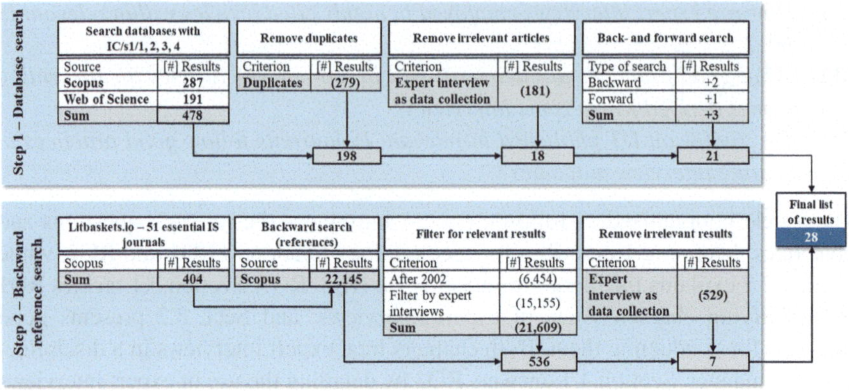


**Fig. 1** Two-step process to find expert interview method-related literature

For comprehensiveness and to ensure the inclusion of relevant results for the IS discipline, we executed a second step (s2): we utilized *litbaskets.io* [34] and its predefined filter *M*, covering *51 essential IS journals*, to search for '*expert* AND interview**'. We intentionally used this broad search term applying no inclusion or exclusion criteria to obtain a comprehensive set of 404 results. We then applied backward search on these results by looking up all cited references from the retrieved 404 articles. This step yielded 22,145 references. To restrict the results to relevant references on expert interviews, we filtered the results with the expression '*expert* AND interview**', or '*expert* interview**', or '*interview* expert**', or '*expert*interview*' and considered results published after 2002. After this filtering step, 536 results remained, which we then carefully screened by applying EC/s1 before selecting seven results. The retrieved results from step 1 and step 2 were then merged and deduplicated, so that 19 articles, seven book chapters, and two textbooks—in total, 28 sources—remained for thematic analysis.

Lastly, a sanity check on the AIS eLibrary using the search terms '*expert* interview* method**' for titles and '*"expert* interview*" OR "interview* expert*" OR "method*" OR "qualitative"*' applied to titles and abstracts yielded no additional results.

To answer RQ1 and RQ2, we applied a six-phased inductive thematic analysis [35]: first, we got acquainted with the 28 sources and then applied descriptive codes to groups of information. Third, we combined the codes into overarching schemes, representing key stages and characteristics of expert interviews. Fourth, we reviewed those to ensure their coherency and consistency. Next, we refined the names for the identified stages and characteristics, which allowed us, in the final sixth step, to summarize the findings in a succinct manner for reporting [35].

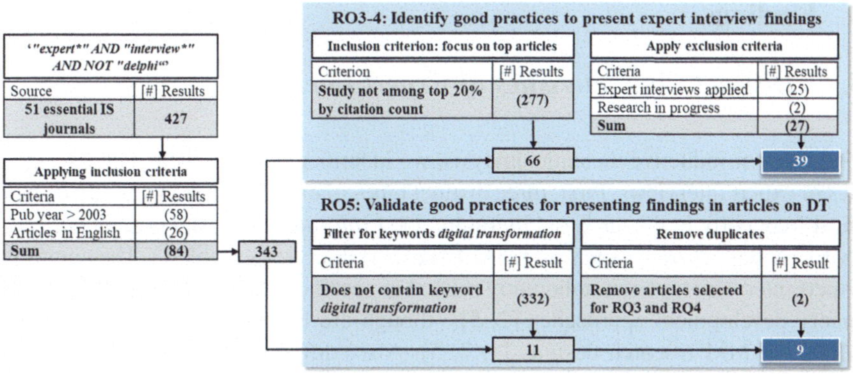


**Fig. 2** Search strategy to identify IS studies employing expert interviews published in important IS outlets

## 2.2 *Literature Retrieval to Address RQ3, RQ4, and RQ5*

To comprehensively address RQ3–5, we searched *litbaskets.io* [34] in September 2024 with its predefined filter *M*, encompassing *51 essential IS outlets* (IC/s3/1), yielding 427 hits. We used the search string '*"expert*" AND "interview*" AND NOT "delphi"*' to exclude the distinct Delphi method [36]. We then removed 58 articles published before 2003 (IC/s3/2) and twenty-six non-English articles (IC/s3/3), leaving 343 articles.

For RQ3–4, we limited the analysis to the top 20% of articles by citation count as in Scopus (IC/RQ3/1), ensuring the identification of good practices for presenting expert interviews' outcomes. Consequently, we excluded articles with less than 40 citations in Scopus, yielding 66 articles. After reviewing titles and abstracts, we applied two exclusion criteria: removing 25 articles not using expert interviews (EC/s3/1) and two describing research in progress (EC/s3/2), resulting in a final sample of 39.

To address RQ5, we filtered the initial 343 results by using the keywords "*digital transformation*", yielding eleven articles. These were assessed against criteria EC/s3/1 and EC/s3/2, both found inapplicable (Fig. 2). After excluding two articles from s3, nine remained to validate best practices for presenting expert interview outcomes.

# 3 Findings

## 3.1 Distinct Characteristics of Expert Interviews

Through our inductive thematic analysis, we identified a set of distinct characteristics of expert interviews. First, three distinct types of expert interviews are described most frequently in the analyzed literature: (1) *exploratory* (E-EI), (2) *systematizing* (S-EI), and (3) *theory-generating* (TG-EI) expert interviews (Table 1). The common expert interview types are inherently related to specific epistemological stances and theory development approaches [2, 5]—though are flexible to be used in MOM, MMQ, or MM research designs [1, 2, 5]. Also, different variations of the same expert interview type are conducted in the same study [26, 40].

E-EI aim to explore a new, poorly defined field to gain first access or to generate basic hypotheses [11, 38]. They show an affinity towards interpretivist epistemology, particularly when used within MOM or MMQ research approaches [1, 2, 5, 8, 37]. However, E-EIs are also used in MM studies with a pragmatist stance, for example, when being leveraged to generate input for subsequent quantitative analyses [41]. Conducted in an unstructured fashion with open-ended questions [10], E-EI help researchers gain insights into the potential ramifications of a new domain, also reflected by a convenience or snowball sampling approach [6, 37–39]. S-EI focus on extracting exclusive knowledge on a specific topic with the goal to systematically obtain and structure expert knowledge, which is not accessible for the researcher [37–39]. S-EI serve different purposes: documenting knowledge or understanding broader social and environmental contexts in which experts operate with the expert as guide [6, 17, 39]. S-EI aim to make the interviews comparable among each other and hence require a structured approach, including the purposeful sampling of experts [11, 15, 39]. TG-EI involve analyzing and reconstructing the subjective, implicit knowledge of experts to generate new theoretical frameworks [37]. By synthesizing perspectives from purposefully sampled experts, novel theories and conceptual frameworks are created with the goal to advance scholarly understanding [6, 37, 39]. Another distinct characteristic of an expert interview is defining who qualifies as expert and what knowledge is sought, which determines the sampling approach [6, 7, 10, 15]. The expert status is solely ascribed by the researcher and hence a subjective assessment [10, 39, 42].

Moreover, expert interviews can address either practical or theoretical expert knowledge. The former denotes the ability to excel in a representative task in a specific context, for instance, in surgery [43]. The main expert interview types presented in our article focus on theoretical expert knowledge, which can be further differentiated into *what* it is that is known and *how* the knowledge is coded [6, 10]. The "what it is that is known" is multifaceted and intertwined, with clear delineations missing. *Technical* knowledge encompasses systematic and factual knowledge, providing experts with distinct advantages within their respective fields [7]. *Experience* knowledge describes individual expertise, whereas *interpretative* knowledge is impacted by the personal biography and networks

**Table 1** Three common expert interview types (EI) and variants

| Type ~ related / Dimension | Epistemology and theory development | Expert knowledge | Knowledge coding | Sampling | Source |
|---|---|---|---|---|---|
| **Common types** | | | | | |
| **Exploratory (E)** | Access new field for exploration to generate basic hypotheses | Technical | Explicit | Snowball, convenience | [6, 10, 11, 15, 18, 37–39] |
| **Systematizing (S)** | Extract exclusive knowledge on a broad topic for theory development | Technical, process, context | Implicit, explicit | Purposeful | [6, 11, 15, 17, 37, 39] |
| **Theory-generating (TG)** | Generate new theoretical frameworks via subjective expert knowledge | Interpretative, explanatory | Implicit | Purposeful | [6, 11, 15, 37, 39] |
| **Other types** (*i.e., variants or mixture of common types, marked with "~"*) | | | | | |
| **Guided** ~S-EI | Systematically generate empirical facts on a phenomenon by using multiple sources | Context, organizational | Implicit, explicit | *Not advised* | [10] |
| **Reconstructive** ~E-EI | Reconstruct individual, subjective perspective of an expert on actions or decisions | Interpretative, experience | Implicit | *Not advised* | [38] |
| **Transformative** ~S-EI, TG-EI | Transfer organizational knowledge beyond an organization | Context, *transgressive*' | Explicit | Purposeful | [38] |
| **Problem-centric** ~TG-EI | Use de- and inductive reasoning to refine a problem | Interpretative, explanatory, process, technical | Implicit, explicit | Probabilistic | [15] |
| **Intersubjective** ~S-EI, TG-EI | Identify common realities within a selected organization, triangulation | Functional | Explicit | Very selective | [38] |
| **Validating conversation** ~ n/a | Hold a conversation after research to validate plausibility of outcomes | Mainly interpretative | Implicit | *Not applicable* | [10] |

[38], allowing experts to interpret situations [10]. *Organizational* knowledge is about knowing institutional or general organizational rules [10, 38]—abstracted and applied to broader contexts, it is also referred to as *process* knowledge [6]. Contrarily, *functional* knowledge describes intra-organizational knowledge [10]. *Context* knowledge denotes expert knowledge about greater societal ramifications [10, 38]. Furthermore, *explanatory* knowledge is considered the expert's ability to provide explanations, meanings, and interpretations on a specific matter [6, 7].

Regarding "how the knowledge is coded", two distinct coding formats can be differentiated: it is either implicit or tacit so that only experts know it, or it is explicit and hence codified, for instance, as an organizational routine, a strategy paper, or a situation assessment [10]. *Context, functional*, and *technical* knowledge have an affinity towards codification, while *interpretative*, *experience*, *organizational*, *explanatory*, and *process* knowledge tend to be implicit [6, 10].

Table 1 also lists additional variants of the three common types: *guided*, *reconstructive*, *transformative*, *problem-centric*, *intersubjective* expert interviews, and *validating conversations*, each of which were mentioned in the analyzed literature once and show parallels to the three common types or are a mixture of the common types.

## 3.2 Good Practices for a Rigorous Expert Interview Procedure

Through our thematic analysis, we identified four distinct stages of a rigorous expert interview procedure. Each stage covers different steps that pose unique challenges. The first stage is defining the research design and objective, which informs the selection of the appropriate expert interview type. The second stage is to prepare and execute the interview, followed by data analysis and summarization of the findings in stage three. Stage four focuses on presenting the outcomes, which is detailed further in Sect. 4.2. Ethical conduct matters throughout the entire expert interview process (Fig. 3).

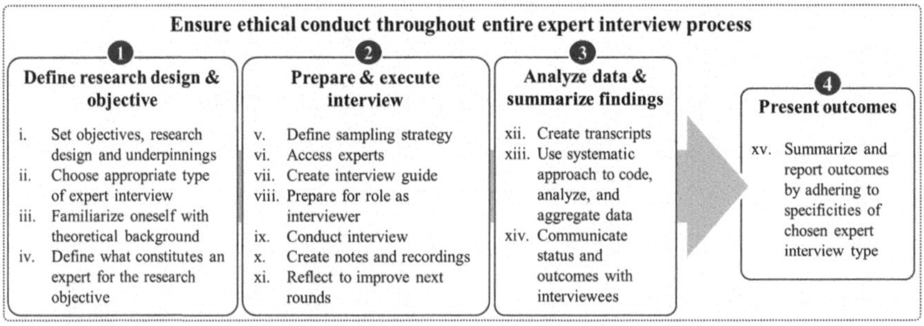


**Fig. 3** The four key stages identified for a rigorous expert interview procedure

***Define research design and objective.*** Researchers should first assess the suitability of expert interviews for their research objectives and design—whether using MOM, MMQ, MM, or other appropriate research designs—and justify their methodological choices and theoretical foundations (step i) [1, 2, 10, 38, 44, 45]. Researchers must also clarify which type of expert interview aligns (step ii) with the research aim [7, 37] to ensure and enhance the validity and relevance of the findings [6, 10, 15, 38, 39]. Choosing an appropriate expert interview type allows for structuring the expert interview procedure [6, 38, 42, 43, 46]: researchers need to be aware that each expert interview type seeks distinct types of expert knowledge. For instance, E-EI focus on extracting technical, explicit knowledge and putting it in context [6]. This means, researchers should pay attention to acquire specific knowledge related to technical applications, information, or data within a particular field to collect insights for practical applications and problem-solving [6, 15]. S-EI aims for technical, process, and context knowledge [6], while TG-EI focus on purposefully delving into the interpretative and explanatory—hence: implicit—knowledge [25].

Prior knowledge on the topic of inquiry—which can be gained, for example, by familiarizing oneself with relevant academic literature [42], publicly available documents [47], or via personal contacts [48]—is key (step iii) to build an intuition what expert knowledge is targeted and identify potential expert interviewees [6, 10, 19, 47]. This helps for step iv, which is to clarify who qualifies as expert by determining what the sought expert knowledge is [6, 10, 37, 38, 42]. Appropriate experts are individuals who possess specialized knowledge that goes beyond common-sense understanding not readily accessible to others [10, 15, 39, 42]. Social representativeness, too, is an expert trait [6, 48]—though it is not intrinsically linked to a professional role or organizational hierarchy [11]. For organizational research, researchers should select individuals who possess institutionalized authority that allows them to construct organizational reality and influence actions in broad contexts [10, 18, 49]. Additional expert attributes are competence, experience, and education in trans-disciplinary and heterogeneous areas requiring cross-discipline collaboration [15, 18, 38, 43].

***Prepare and execute interview.*** After determining who qualifies as an expert, the sampling approach is defined (step v). A diverse set of experts facilitates the generalizability of findings [38, 47, 50]. This can be accomplished by drawing experts from different echelons to avoid positional-biased knowledge and gain different perspectives [14, 19]. The validity of the outcomes is ensured by paying attention to the quality of the experts [51]. Also, the sampling approach must be aligned with the chosen expert interview type. As per Table 1, each expert interview type has an affinity towards different sampling approaches. After having identified the experts, researchers encounter the challenge of accessing (step vi) and persuading them to participate in the research project [42, 46–48, 52]. Good practices are to leverage affiliations with institutions or professional associations, conferences, personal networks, or expert directories [6, 42, 48]. Searching experts via online platforms, such as LinkedIn, allows for quick expert identification [6, 48]. Researchers should also be aware that political organizations or industry sectors such as financial institutions are reluctant to share expert information [45, 48]. Upon completion of the sampling process, researchers are advised to examine the characteristics of experts who declined to participate, as they may possess unique insights compared to those who accepted. A high non-response rate is a matter of concern, as it can impact the findings' generalizability [47].

The next step (vii) is to prepare the interview guide with the questions, which is facilitated by prior knowledge about the domain of inquiry [10, 47]. The guide should avoid ambiguous terms and academic language and thoughtfully order the questions to guide the conversation flow [6, 47]. Typical interview mechanisms are structured interviews with a predetermined script, unstructured and semi-structured interviews with no or partially prepared scripts [44]. Researchers should use the appropriate mechanism based on the chosen interview type: E-EI have an affinity to unstructured interviews with open-ended questions, while S-EI opt for semi-structured formats featuring straightforward questions [11, 37]. TG-EI usually utilize unstructured or semi-structured methods, employing indirect questioning to interpret implicit knowledge and extract experts' perspectives and conceptions on a specific topic [6, 18, 37, 38]. Despite the clear mapping, some flexibility should be allowed, particularly, when novel, unintended topics or themes emerge during the interview [38]. Lastly, the interview guide also needs to consider the interview format—personal, via phone, or video [10, 14, 45]. Online expert meetings have become popular, providing additional benefits such as unintrusive recording capabilities or auto-transcriptions [10] but are suboptimal for observing expert behavior or non-verbal hints [14, 46].

Prior to the interviews (step viii), researchers should prepare by practicing their role as interviewer by conducting a dry run [6, 47]. Having prior knowledge on the topic and the *how* of the inquiry will allow researchers to master demanding situations [37]. The interview process commences with scheduling a time and selecting an appropriate location or medium for the interview. Time scarcity of experts poses scheduling challenges [38, 52]. Researchers should also clarify upfront in which language the conversation is held as additional intricacies arise if participants are not fluent in the used language or translators are required [11]. Upon commencement, the interviewer introduces the study's purpose, confirms informed consent, and builds rapport with the expert [6]. One challenge of expert interviews is managing power imbalances. Experts can exhibit paternalism due to their position or knowledge [39, 42, 47, 53] or are reluctant to share implicit knowledge if they perceive the interviewer as less competent [10]. Additional challenges are when experts start expressing feelings (catharsis effect), are unwilling to share knowledge (iceberg effect), take on the interviewer's role (feedback effect), or use the interview to demonstrate their knowledge (profile effect) [39]. Accurate documentation of the discussion (step x) is critical and contributes to better management of critical situations in subsequent interview rounds (step xi) [6, 14].

***Analyse data and summarize findings***. After completing the interview, data analysis should be applied timely [47], starting with reading, organizing, and coding the recorded and transcribed data (step xii) [6]. IS studies employing expert interviews (see Sect. 4) prefer the works published by Saldaña [54], Miles et al. [55],

Glaser and Strauss [56], and Gioia et al. [57] for systematic coding and iterative inductive analysis (step xiii). During data analysis, researchers should be wary of bias, particularly, expansiveness—where the expert inflates or downplays their status—and attractiveness bias—where the researcher overrates the input of experts due to their status or influence [46, 47]. Ensuring high inter-expert consensus serves as mitigation strategy for these situations [51].

***Ethical conduct.*** Ethical requirements arise during all stages [1, 10, 45, 46, 58]. For sampling [14, 18] and during interviewing researchers must ensure that informed consent is collected, and participants are reminded of their right to withdraw from the project at any time without providing reasons [10, 42]. Further ethical requirements are ensuring anonymity [10] and confidentiality during and after the interview [6, 10, 15, 45]. Upon interview completion, standard ethical procedures are sharing the final transcripts for review (step xiv) and accurately reporting the participants' contributions in the final report (step xv) [1, 42, 58].

# 4 Utilization and Outcome Presentation of Expert Interviews in IS Research

## *4.1 Utilization of Expert Interviews in Highly Cited IS Studies*

In the 39 studies selected from relevant IS journals, we observed a range of research themes, reflecting the broad landscape of contemporary IS research with its multifaceted challenges. In total, we identified and aggregated the research areas into five distinct themes (Appendix 1), with *IT and Business Management* (11 articles) being the most frequent topic and *data-driven services, IT security, and analytics* (10) following. Further research areas are *emerging technology and innovation* (7), *digital transformation, online communities, and e-commerce* (6), and *intellectual capital and knowledge management* (5) (Appendix 1). There were significant variations in the number of experts interviewed—ranging from five to thirty, with an average of fifteen per study, and six articles not advising how many experts were interviewed (Appendix 1). Our analysis also shows a prevalence of S-EI, followed by E-EI, and TG-EI, with four studies exhibiting multiple types (Table 2). The frequent use of E-EI reflects the IS-specific trend of integrating expert interviews within Design Science Research (DSR) protocols and

**Table 2** Distribution of expert interview types across 39 highly cited IS studies

| Expert interview type | [#] Count of studies |
|---|---|
| S-EI | 17 |
| E-EI | 12 |
| TG | 6 |
| E-EI, S-EI | 3 |
| E-EI, TG-EI | 1 |

incorporating expert interviews' outcomes as input for computational modelling, as discussed further below.

Additional differences were observed in the methodological approaches and the role of expert interviews in the research design (Appendix 1). Nine studies use expert interviews as the primary data collection procedure [40, 59–66], with seven supplementing their research by a literature review (LRs) either for initial understanding or to validate outcomes from the LR [40, 59–62, 64, 65]. These nine studies also show significant variations regarding which type of expert interview is employed, how they methodologically fit into the research design, and how they are practically implemented. For example, expert interviews are leveraged to provide input for Analytical Hierarchy Modeling (AHM) [61] or in explorative approaches [59, 60, 63, 66]. Further, we identified 16 studies utilizing expert interviews in MM approaches [22, 25, 41, 67–79]. MM research designs show considerable variations, with a prevalence of sequential approaches. Expert interviews follow quantitative data collection to complement findings in five studies [22, 67, 68, 72, 77], while in eleven studies the outcomes of expert interviews serve as input for subsequent quantitative analysis [41, 69–71, 73–76, 78–80]. MMQ research designs were observed in seven studies [81–87].

A notable phenomenon specific to IS research is the integration of expert interviews within DSR research studies and the utilization of expert interview outcomes for subsequent computational and conceptual modeling. We identified six studies following DSR research protocols [67, 72, 84, 88–90], with expert interviews being instrumental for artifact development [67, 84, 88] and the evaluation of their effectiveness [72, 88–90]. Another seven articles utilized expert interviews to excerpt technical expert knowledge that serves as input for computational models such as Interpretative Standard Modeling (ISM), AHM, or Fuzzy Analytical Hierarchy Models (FAHM) [61, 71, 76, 79, 80, 91, 92] (Table 3). The utilization of DSR principles requires standardized and structured processes for expert interviews, hence there is a tendency towards S-EI. When used for computational modeling, the expert types vary between E-EI, and S-EI. For example, one study applying Fuzzy Petri Nets used expert interviews for both the identification and systematization of factors that can be used for railway control, which were then leveraged to model a risk decision control matrix [71].

## 4.2 Good Practices for Presenting Expert Interview Outcomes

We applied Gioia's two-step inductive coding method [57] on the selected 39 articles for RQ4 to identify good practices for rigorously presenting expert interview outcomes (stage 4, step xv). This process involved first annotating examples of effective and rigorous presentation (first-order concepts), then grouping these into twelve good practices (second-order concepts), and further consolidating them into four primary purposes for presenting expert interview outcomes. We offer

**Table 3** IS research specific use of expert interviews in context of DSR and computational modelling

| Approach | Purpose of expert interview | Sources |
|---|---|---|
| **DSR** | Artifact evaluation | [72, 88–90] |
| | Artifact development | [67, 84, 88] |
| **Modeling** | Analytical Hierarchy Modeling (AHM) | [81] [61] |
| | Fuzzy Petri Nets | [71] |
| | DEMATEL | [80] |
| | Bayesian Belief Network | [76] |
| | Interpretative standard modeling, Fuzzy Analytical Network Process (FANP) | [92] |
| | Fuzzy Analytical Hierarchy Models (FAHP), VIKOR | [79] |

recommendations on where to include each best practice within a research article (Table 4).

***Position expert interview within research design.*** A research report's introduction should outline the interview approach (#1) and connect it to the methodology-section, where the expert interview procedure is detailed. Clearly defined research objectives facilitate the justification of the chosen data analysis method (#2). For example, in [62], the study aims to refine a conceptual model on how features of small- and medium sized enterprises influence IT security investments, with expert interviews used to gain insights from practitioners' perspectives. The methodology section anchors these research goals, guiding the interview preparation, the sampling strategy, and the data analysis approach. Rigor is demonstrated through a well-documented interview protocol, sample questions, and their iterative refinement [62]. Another study offers a strong rationale for an exploratory expert interview approach, particularly suited for uncovering new insights within the evolving context of enterprise cybersecurity [63]. This alignment is maintained as outcomes are presented as propositions, consistent with an exploratory design, with data analysis and annotation methods reflecting the study's inductive, discovery-oriented nature [63].

Adding an *illustrative graphic* to the methodology section effectively positions the expert interview within the overall research design (#3), especially for MM or MMQ research designs [22, 73, 83]. For example, in [22], the research phases addressing impact factors of social media strategies are clearly divided into qualitative and quantitative stages, with the expert interview highlighted as a sixth, complementary step to validate quantitative findings.

***Concise documentation of interview execution.*** Rigor during the expert interview execution stage is demonstrated by a clear presentation of the *sampling strategy, supported by listing the interviewees, and indicating why they qualify as experts* (#4). A description of the sampling approach should be provided within the methodological section, ideally as dedicated subchapter. It should elaborate on who qualifies as expert for the study and why, and how representativeness, and prevention of bias are addressed [62]. The sampling approach can be effectively

**Table 4** Good practices for rigorous presentation of expert interview outcomes

| Purpose | [#] | Good Practice | Section | Sources |
|---|---|---|---|---|
| **Position expert interview within research design** | #1 | Outline interview approach, protocol, and alignment with research goals | Introduction | [62–64, 85, 88] |
| | #2 | Justify the applied data analysis approach | Introduction, methodology | [62, 63, 88] |
| | #3 | Illustrate research design in graphical form to position expert interview within research approach | Introduction, methodology | [22, 40, 73, 75, 83] |
| **Concise documentation of interview execution** | #4 | Articulate sampling approach and support it by listing interviewees with indication of their expertise | Methodology | [40, 41, 59, 60, 62, 63, 65, 66, 72, 84, 86, 89, 93] |
| | #5 | Share interview questions and protocol | Appendix, methodology | [41, 60, 62, 64, 67, 85, 90] |
| | #6 | Use staged interview approach to corroborate findings | Methodology | [78, 84, 86] |
| | #7 | State how anonymity and confidentiality are ensured | Methodology | [40, 64, 89] |
| **Support evidence of findings** | #8 | Collect additional evidence to support explorations | Discussion, appendix | [84] |
| | #9 | Utilize supporting quotes in the final report | Findings, discussion, conclusion | [59, 60, 63, 68, 82–84, 89] |
| | #10 | Add tabular summary of key annotations and outcomes | Findings, discussion, appendix | [40, 64, 65, 68, 70, 77, 78, 85, 86, 89] |
| | #11 | Outline how intercoder agreement was achieved | Methodology, findings, discussion | [59, 66, 88] |
| | #12 | Utilize quantitative techniques to increase validity of outcomes | Findings, discussion | [66, 74, 78, 85, 93] |

summarized by a complete and comprehensive table listing the interviewees with demographics and clear indication of their expertise [40, 41, 59, 60, 62, 63, 65, 66, 84, 86, 89, 93]; for example, providing information about the function of an interviewee within an organization [41, 60, 63, 65, 66, 84, 93] or indicating specific traits and expertise relevant for the research topic [40, 41, 63, 66]. Adding legible and clear identifiers for each interview and interviewee demonstrates that anonymity and confidentiality of the interviewees are respected and can also be referred to when connecting specific findings to a concrete interview or expert, which further increases the transparency and validity of the outcomes [86, 89].

We further propose documenting *the interview protocol and the interview questions* (#5). Authors should decide whether to add the protocol into the methodological section or to the appendix to avoid breaking the flow of the narration [62, 64, 67, 85, 90]. Good practices are to indicate how or which questions were refined throughout the interview process [60] and to structure the protocol by mapping the questions to the respective research questions [41].

A recommendable solution to increase the validity and generalizability of the final outcomes is *staging the interviews to corroborate findings* (#6): the interview process is thereby split into several iterations, whereby specific findings of the first iteration are summarized, and then probed and validated in the subsequent iterations. The concrete procedure should be clearly described in the methodological section. For example, in [86], a group of experts is first interviewed during a case study and the findings are later validated by two different groups of experts, each with a specific expertise. A further example of a staged approach is when the experts are interviewed again and presented with the overall study's outcome for commenting, which adds a further level of validity [78].

It is further recommended to explicitly state in the methodological section that key ethical requirements, specifically those ensuring anonymity and confidentiality (#7), are considered. We suggest including a brief statement explaining how anonymity is maintained, such as by using generic identifiers for interviewees [40, 64, 89].

***Support evidence of findings***. Utilizing *additional means for data collection* (#8) during expert interviews aiming to conceptualize and explore novel ideas is a good example of adding additional layer of data and visualize cohesions, which can be presented in the findings section or in the appendix [84]. One study first explored and collected evidence from expert interviews to create a basic conceptual model for vehicle data-driven services using graphical sketches, which was then used by a second round of expert interviews to further enhance the initial model [84].

The use of *supporting quotes in the final report* (#9) is another good practice widely adopted in the reviewed literature. This approach ensures that individual findings are not only grounded in the data but also clearly linked to the views of the participants and the final outcomes. Quotations interwoven into the text offer a nuanced understanding of the data [63, 93]. Explorative and theory generating expert interviews specifically benefit from a rich use of quotes to illustrate novel cohesions or conceptual claims by adding context and explanation [59, 68, 77,

82–84, 93]. Narrative summaries in particular can substantiate expert interview outcomes and demonstrate their validity [60, 63].

Additionally, *tabular views* (#10) facilitate a concise and readable summarization of the interview outcomes. For example, they can *map findings to individual interviews and interviewees* by providing transparency in how conclusions were drawn [40, 64], allowing for a systematic comparison of findings across interviews [86]. A tabular summary can also support *contrasting findings from different data collection procedures*. For instance, MM and MMQ studies can leverage tables to juxtapose outcomes from the different data collection procedures to draw more comprehensive conclusions and highlight differences [64, 65, 85]. Similarly, insights from preceding literature reviews can be contrasted to show differences and overlaps [65, 85] or underscore key patterns across various sources [89]. A further good practice is to upgrade tabular views with *quotes from the interviews*, which underline the conclusions that were drawn and add thickness to the collected insights [68, 70, 86, 93].

Transparently *outlining how intercoder agreement was achieved* (#11) in either the methodological or discussion sections is a good practice that demonstrates coding rigor and increases the reliability and accuracy of the outcomes. One common approach is the use of independent intercoder reviews [66, 88].

Finally, we found different approaches to leverage *quantitative techniques to support the validity of the outcomes* (#12). An example is counting how often a specific term occurs in the interview transcripts to determine the importance of the concept it denotes [74]. One study tested the statistical significance of term counts in interview transcriptions and further differentiated the final outcomes by providing weights based on different expert levels [85]. These measures help categorize individual findings by importance and provide more objective evidence for drawing final conclusions.

## 4.3 Validation of Presentation Rigor in DT Studies

The selected nine studies for RQ5 show the flexible application of expert interviews in DT research. First, the phenomenon of DT is examined in the context of various different sectors, such as industrial contexts [27], entertainment [23], software services [29], or finance [28], and from multiple perspectives, for example, from organizational viewpoints [26], or from its impact on industry-specific value chains, for example, the music industry [23]. Second, expert interviews' implementation and function within a research design serve different purposes: theory generation, topical exploration, systematizing and structuring information, and validating findings from quantitative data collection. It is remarkable though that six of the selected nine studies have an affinity towards S-EI [24, 27–31]. One explanation is the research design: while five studies used expert interviews in an MOM research design [23, 25–27, 29], the remaining four studies employ research designs that have an affinity towards S-EIs: two studies apply MM [30, 31], one utilizes DSR principles [24], and one study uses expert interviews to evaluate insights gained from applying ISM/AHM [28]. A unique application of expert interviews is their use in an *interview case study* [21], resembling a multiple mini case study [94]. The data is collected solely through interviews across five organizations to systematize and compare insights. Third, a common observation involves conducting interviews in multiple stages and variations; for instance, findings from one round inform subsequent interviews [24] or experts are interviewed in pairs [26].

We validated the nine DT-focused studies against our good practices for presenting expert interview outcomes by assessing their coverage on the three key purposes, marking each as *partially* (↓), *moderately* (↑), or *extensively* (↑↑) covered, or *not advised* (■), based on the detail and comprehensiveness of their descriptions. Additionally, we coded each of the twelve good practices as either applied (*Y*) or not (*empty cell*) (Table 5).

In summary, all studies have taken measures to ensure presentation rigor, but there are areas for improvement: although there was consistency in outlining the research design, research objectives (#1), and in justifying the applied data analysis methods (#2), the methodological sections could provide more detail and better distinguish between exploratory, theory-generating, and systematizing approaches. There was a general trend of justifying sampling strategies (#4), while sharing interview questions and providing a list of interviewees with demographics and expertise were applied more selectively (#5). Staged interview approaches (#6) are commonly adopted [24–26, 28, 30, 31].

Only one study explicitly stated how anonymity requirements (#7) were fulfilled [31]. Also, researchers could leverage experts more to provide additional, non-verbal insights (#8) such as sketches or supporting graphics for their statements, particularly, for E-EI and TG-EI [84]. The studies demonstrated a strong use of supporting quotes (#8) [23, 25–29, 31] and tabular summaries of key findings (#9) [23, 25–27, 29]. However, an opportunity exists to enhance reporting outcomes by incorporating quantitative techniques, such as counting the frequency of occurrence in the transcripts of key terms or applying different weightings to insights identified, to provide additional support for the findings, as done in [66, 74, 85, 93]. Further, only few studies incorporated explicit statements on how intercoder agreement (#10) was achieved [26, 27], indicating another area for improvement.

## 5 Conclusion

This article aims to enhance the understanding and application of expert interviews as a qualitative method in IS research [1, 2, 5, 95] through several key contributions. It presents a structured framework of four stages and fifteen steps to guide the rigorous execution of expert interviews, offering a practical reference for other studies (RQ1–2). Our article also analyses the use of expert interviews in influential IS research, particularly by showing their use within DSR and computational modelling research approaches (RQ3). Additionally, it synthesizes and provides

**Table 5** Assessment of nine expert interviews from relevant IS outlets covering topics of DT

| Study | [1] | [14] | [19] | [30] | [41] | [49] | [54] | [57] | [88] |
|---|---|---|---|---|---|---|---|---|---|
| **Expert interview type (EI)** | S | S (TG) | E (TG) | TG | S | S | TG (S) | S | S |
| **# interviewees** | 16 | 13 | 13 | 22 | 5 | 18 | 22 | 18 | 6 |
| **Research design** | MOM | DSR | MOM | MOM | MM (ISM) | MOM | MOM | MM | MM |
| **Position expert interview within research design** | ↑ | ↑ | ↓ | ↑ | ↓ | ↑ | ↑ | ↑ | ↑ |
| **(#1)** | Y | Y | Y | Y | Y | Y | Y | Y | Y |
| **(#2)** | Y | Y | Y | Y | Y | Y | Y | Y | Y |
| **(#3)** | | Y | | Y | Y | | Y | | |
| **Concise documentation of interview execution** | ↑ | ↓ | ↑ | ↑ | ↓ | ↑↑ | ↑↑ | ↑ | ↑ |
| **(#4)** | Y | | Y | Y | Y | Y | Y | Y | |
| **(#5)** | Y | | | | | Y | Y | | Y |
| **(#6)** | | Y | | Y | Y | | Y | Y | Y |
| **(#7)** | | | | | | | | | Y |
| **Support evidence of findings** | ↑↑ | ■ | ↑↑ | ↑↑ | ↑ | ↑↑ | ↑↑ | ↓ | ↓ |
| **(#8)** | | | | | Y | Y | | | |
| **(#9)** | Y | | Y | Y | Y | Y | Y | | Y |
| **(#10)** | Y | | Y | Y | | Y | Y | | |
| **(#11)** | Y | | | | | | Y | | |
| **(#12)** | | | | | | | | | |

twelve good practices that serve IS researchers as a framework and guide to ensure rigor in presenting interview outcomes (RQ4). Validating these good practices on nine studies on digital transformation (DT), the article reveals opportunities for increasing the rigor of presenting expert interviews' outcomes (RQ5).

The study has three main limitations. First, our recommended good practices focus on the presentation of expert interview outcomes, providing less detail on other stages, including research design and objective definition, preparation and interview execution, as well as data analysis and summary of findings. Second, the sample of 39 IS studies, including nine on DT topics, may not fully represent the entire field. Future research could expand the scope to include more studies for critical review to bolster the reliability of the findings as they relate to IS, and DT specifically. Third, the article does not expand in greater detail on the challenges of expert interviews in rapidly evolving domains, where expert insights can quickly become outdated. Future research could explore the nature of expertise in such novel fields.

In conclusion, this work underscores the versatility of expert interviews in prominent IS publications, illustrating their effectiveness in addressing practical IS and DT challenges. It also aims to equip IS researchers with essential and practical guidance for the rigorous preparation, execution, and reporting of expert interview outcomes to fully leverage expert interviews' potential.

## Appendix 1

Coding and annotation outcomes are available online at https://doi.org/10.6084/m9.figshare.27332217

## References

1. Creswell, J. W., & Creswell, J. D. (2023). *Research design*. SAGE.
2. Davidavičienė, V., Gómez, J. M., & Mouselli, S. (2018). *Research methodology: An introduction*. Springer International Publishing.
3. Farshchian, B. A., Parmiggiani, E., Dahl-Jørgensen, T. C., & Quayyum, F. (2021). How to teach empirical research methods in information systems? Report from a SCIS/IRIS 2019 workshop. *Scandinavian Journal of Information Systems., 33*(1), 65–94.
4. Gunn, A. (2017). Critical debates in teaching research methods in the social sciences. *Teaching Public Administration., 35*(3), 241–259.
5. Saunders, M. N. K., Lewis, P., & Thornhill, A. (2019). *Research methods for business students*. Pearson.
6. van Audenhove, L., & Donders, K. (2019). Talking to people III: Expert interviews and elite interviews. In H. van den Bulck, M. Puppis, K. Donders, & L. van Audenhove (Eds.), *The Palgrave handbook of methods for media policy research* (pp. 179–197). Springer International Publishing.
7. Bogner, A., Littig, B., & Menz, W. (2014). *Interviews mit Experten*. Springer Fachmedien Wiesbaden.

8. Bogner, A., Littig, B., & Menz, W. (2009). Introduction: Expert interviews—An introduction to a new methodological debate. In A. Bogner, B. Littig, & W. Menz (Eds.), *Interviewing experts* (pp. 1–13). Palgrave Macmillan UK.
9. Hassmann, T., & Westner, M. (2024). Enhancing expert interviews: Insights from IS and digital transformation research. In B. Marcinkowski, A. Przybylek, A. Jarzębowicz, N. Iivari, E. Insfran, M. Lang, H. Linger, & C. Schneider (Eds.), *Harnessing opportunities: Reshaping ISD in the post-COVID-19 and generative AI era (ISD2024 Proceedings)*. Gdańsk.
10. Kaiser, R. (2021). *Qualitative Experteninterviews*. Springer Fachmedien Wiesbaden.
11. Littig, B., & Pöchhacker, F. (2014). Socio-translational collaboration in qualitative inquiry. *Qualitative Inquiry., 20*(9), 1085–1095.
12. Meuser, M., & Nagel, U. (2009). The expert interview and changes in knowledge production. In A. Bogner, B. Littig, & W. Menz (Eds.), *Interviewing experts* (pp. 17–42). Palgrave Macmillan UK.
13. Gläser, J., & Laudel, G. (2009). On interviewing "good" and "bad" experts. In A. Bogner, B. Littig, & W. Menz (Eds.), *Interviewing experts* (pp. 117–137). Palgrave Macmillan UK.
14. Soest, C. (2023). Why do we speak to experts? Reviving the strength of the expert interview method. *Perspectives on Politics, 21*(1), 277–287.
15. Döringer, S. (2021). The problem-centred expert interview. *International Journal of Social Research Methodology., 24*(3), 265–278.
16. Liebold, R., & Trinczek, R. (2009). Experteninterview. In S. Kühl, P. Strodtholz, & A. Taffertshofer (Eds.), *Handbuch Methoden der Organisationsforschung* (pp. 32–56). VS Verlag für Sozialwissenschaften.
17. Linderman, A., Baker, J., & Bosacker, S. C. (2011). Surfacing and transferring expert knowledge: The sense-making interview. *Human Resource Development International., 14*(3), 353–362.
18. Meuser, M., & Nagel, U. (2008). ExpertInneninterview: Zur Rekonstruktion spezialisierten Sonderwissens. In R. Becker & B. Kortendiek (Eds.), *Handbuch Frauen- und Geschlechterforschung* (pp. 368–371). VS Verlag für Sozialwissenschaften.
19. Reinhold, A. (2015). Das Experteninterview als zentrale Methode der Wissensmodellierung in den Digital Humanities. *Information–Wissenschaft & Praxis., 66*(5–6), 327–333.
20. Mazaheri, E., Lagzian, M., & Hemmat, Z. (2020). Research directions in information systems field, current status and future trends. *Academic Journal of Interdisciplinary Studies, 24*, 1–25.
21. Fischer, M., Imgrund, F., Janiesch, C., & Winkelmann, A. (2020). Strategy archetypes for digital transformation: Defining meta objectives using business process management. *Information & Management., 57*(5), 103262.
22. Benthaus, J., Risius, M., & Beck, R. (2016). Social media management strategies for organizational impression management and their effect on public perception. *Journal of Strategic Information Systems., 25*(2), 127–139.
23. Darvish, M., & Bick, M. (2024). The role of digital technologies in the music industry—A qualitative trend analysis. *Information Systems Management., 41*(2), 181–200.
24. Breiter, K., Crome, C., Oberländer, A. M., & Schnaak, F. (2024). Dynamic capabilities for the twin transformation climb: A capability maturity model. *Information Systems Frontiers., 26*, 2205–2226.
25. Faro, B., Abedin, B., & Cetindamar, D. (2022). Hybrid organizational forms in public sector's digital transformation: A technology enactment approach. *Journal of Enterprise Information Management., 35*(6), 1742–1763.
26. Lorenz, F., & Buchwald, A. (2023). A perfect match or an arranged marriage? How chief digital officers and chief information officers perceive their relationship: A dyadic research design. *European Journal of Information Systems., 32*(3), 372–389.
27. Abiodun, T., Rampersad, G., & Brinkworth, R. (2023). Driving industrial digital transformation. *Journal of Computer Information Systems., 63*(6), 1345–1361.
28. Hughes, L., Seddon, J. J. M., & Dwivedi, Y. K. (2023). Disruptive change within financial technology: A methodological analysis of digital transformation challenges. *Journal of Information Technology., 1–28*, 756–783.

29. Laato, S., Mäntymäki, M., Islam, A. K. M. N., Hyrynsalmi, S., & Birkstedt, T. (2023). Trends and trajectories in the software industry: Implications for the future of work. *Information Systems Frontiers., 25*(2), 929–944.
30. Mazumder, S., & Garg, S. (2021). Decoding digital transformational outsourcing: The role of service providers' capabilities. *International Journal of Information Management., 58*, 102295.
31. Tsai, J. C.-A., Jiang, J. J., Klein, G., & Hung, S.-Y. (2023). Task conflict resolution in designing legacy replacement systems. *Journal of Management Information Systems., 40*(3), 1009–1034.
32. Shamseer, L., Moher, D., Clarke, M., Ghersi, D., Liberati, A., Petticrew, M., Shekelle, P., & Stewart, L. A. (2016). Preferred reporting items for systematic review and meta-analysis protocols (PRISMA-P) 2015: elaboration and explanation. *eBMJ, 354.*
33. Watson, R. T., & Webster, J. (2020). Analysing the past to prepare for the future: Writing a literature review a roadmap for release 2.0. *Journal of Decision Systems., 29*(3), 129–147.
34. Boell, S., & Wang, B. (2019). www.litbaskets.io, *an IT artifact supporting exploratory literature searches for information systems research.* Presented at the ACIS 2019 Proceedings.
35. Braun, V., & Clarke, V. (2006). Using thematic analysis in psychology. *Qualitative Research in Psychology., 3*(2), 77–101.
36. Okoli, C., & Pawlowski, S. D. (2004). The Delphi method as a research tool: An example, design considerations and applications. *Information & Management., 42*(1), 15–29.
37. Bogner, A., & Menz, W. (2009). The theory-generating expert interview: Epistemological interest, forms of knowledge, interaction. In A. Bogner, B. Littig, & W. Menz (Eds.), *Interviewing experts* (pp. 43–80). Palgrave Macmillan UK.
38. Dreiack, S., & Niederberger, M. (2018). Qualitative Experteninterviews in Internationalen Organisationen. *Polit Vierteljahresschr., 59*(2), 293–318.
39. Korkea-Aho, E., & Päivi, L. (2019). Interviewing lawyers: A critical self-reflection on expert interviews as a method of EU legal research. *European Journal of Legal Studies., 12*, 17–47.
40. Schöbel, S. M., Janson, A., & Söllner, M. (2020). Capturing the complexity of gamification elements: A holistic approach for analysing existing and deriving novel gamification designs. *European Journal of Information Systems., 29*(6), 641–668.
41. Spiegel, O., Abbassi, P., Zylka, M. P., Schlagwein, D., Fischbach, K., & Schoder, D. (2016). Business model development, founders' social capital and the success of early stage internet start-ups: A mixed-method study. *Information Systems Journal., 26*(5), 421–449.
42. Trinidad, J. E. (2024). Interviewing K-12 education experts and elites. *Frontiers in Education., 9.*
43. van de Wiel, M. (2017). Examining expertise using interviews and verbal protocols. Frontline learning. *Research, 5*(3 (special issue)), 94–122.
44. Myers, M. D., & Newman, M. (2007). The qualitative interview in IS research: Examining the craft. *Information and Organization., 17*(1), 2–26.
45. Steiman, D., & Suhay, E. (2023). Conducting interview projects in the US congress: Analyzing the methods of experts in the field. *Legislative Studies Quarterly., 48*(4), 699–730.
46. Nasar, W. (2023). *Impact of expert interviews in software engineering: Challenges and benefits.* Presented at the Proceedings of the International MultiConference of Engineers and Computer Scientists 2023.
47. Beyers, J., Braun, C., Marshall, D., & Bruycker, I. (2014). Let's talk! On the practice and method of interviewing policy experts. *Interest Groups & Advocacy, 3*(2), 174–187.
48. Robinson, G. (2021). Capturing a moving target: Interviewing fintech experts via LinkedIn. *Area, 53*(4), 671–678.
49. Morris, A., Onwuegbuzie, A. J., & Gerber, H. R. (2018). Using expert interviews within MODES in online and offline spaces to extend comprehensive literature review processes. *The Qualitative Report., 23*(8), 1777–1798.
50. Muskat, M., Blackman, D., & Muskat, B. (2012). Mixed methods: Combining expert interviews, cross-impact analysis and scenario development. *The Electronic Journal of Business Research Methods., 10*(1), 9–21.

51. Dorussen, H., Lenz, H., & Blavoukos, S. (2005). Assessing the reliability and validity of expert interviews. *European Union Politics., 6*(3), 315–337.
52. Ma, S., Seidl, D., & McNulty, T. (2021). Challenges and practices of interviewing business elites. *Strategic Organization., 19*(1), 81–96.
53. Sharma, D. R. (2023). Expert as interviewer—Methodological challenges in use of qualitative interviews in maritime research. *The International Journal on Marine Navigation and Safety of Sea Transportation., 17*(3), 637–642.
54. Saldaña, J. (2021). *The coding manual for qualitative researchers*. SAGE.
55. Miles, M. B., Huberman, A. M., & Saldana, J. (2020). *Qualitative data analysis*. SAGE.
56. Glaser, B. G., & Strauss, A. L. (2017). *The discovery of grounded theory*. Routledge.
57. Gioia, D. A., Corley, K. G., & Hamilton, A. L. (2013). Seeking qualitative rigor in inductive research. *Organizational Research Methods., 16*(1), 15–31.
58. Sieber, J., & Tolich, M. (2013). *Planning ethically responsible research*. SAGE Publications, Inc.
59. Bedué, P., & Fritzsche, A. (2022). Can we trust AI? An empirical investigation of trust requirements and guide to successful AI adoption. *JEIM., 35*(2), 530–549.
60. Drummer, D., & Neumann, D. (2020). Is code law? Current legal and technical adoption issues and remedies for blockchain-enabled smart contracts. *Journal of Information Technology., 35*(4), 337–360.
61. Haghighi, M., Divandari, A., & Keimasi, M. (2010). The impact of 3D e-readiness on e-banking development in Iran: A fuzzy AHP analysis. *Expert Systems with Applications., 37*(6), 4084–4093.
62. Heidt, M., Gerlach, J. P., & Buxmann, P. (2019). Investigating the security divide between SME and large companies: How SME characteristics influence organizational IT security investments. *Information Systems Frontiers., 21*(6), 1285–1305.
63. Naseer, A., Naseer, H., Naseer, H., Ahmad, A., Maynard, S. B., & Siddiqui, A. M. (2021). Real-time analytics, incident response process agility and enterprise cybersecurity performance: A contingent resource-based analysis. *International Journal of Information Management., 59*, 102334.
64. Nidhra, S., Yanamadala, M., Afzal, W., & Torkar, R. (2013). Knowledge transfer challenges and mitigation strategies in global software development—A systematic literature review and industrial validation. *International Journal of Information Management., 33*(2), 333–355.
65. Paagman, A., Tate, M., Furtmueller, E., & Bloom, J. (2015). An integrative literature review and empirical validation of motives for introducing shared services in government organizations. *International Journal of Information Management., 35*(1), 110–123.
66. Vigo, M., Bail, S., Jay, C., & Stevens, R. (2014). Overcoming the pitfalls of ontology authoring: Strategies and implications for tool design. *International Journal of Human Computer Studies., 72*(12), 835–845.
67. Adomavicius, G., Bockstedt, J. C., Gupta, A., & Kauffman, R. J. (2008). Making sense of technology trends in the information technology landscape: A design science approach. *MIS Quarterly., 32*(4), 779–809.
68. Ariyachandra, T., & Watson, H. (2010). Key organizational factors in data warehouse architecture selection. *Decision Support Systems., 49*(2), 200–212.
69. Birkmeyer, S., Wirtz, B. W., & Langer, P. F. (2021). Determinants of mHealth success: An empirical investigation of the user perspective. *International Journal of Information Management., 59*, 102351.
70. Chang, S. E., Liu, A. Y., & Shen, W. C. (2017). User trust in social networking services: A comparison of Facebook and LinkedIn. *Computers in Human Behavior, 69*, 207–217.
71. Cheng, Y.-H., & Yang, L.-A. (2009). A fuzzy petri nets approach for railway traffic control in case of abnormality: Evidence from Taiwan railway system. *Expert Systems with Applications., 36*(4), 8040–8048.
72. Denner, M.-S., Püschel, L. C., & Röglinger, M. (2018). How to exploit the digitalization potential of business processes. *Business & Information Systems Engineering., 60*(4), 331–349.

73. Dickinger, A., Arami, M., & Meyer, D. (2008). The role of perceived enjoyment and social norm in the adoption of technology with network externalities. *European Journal of Information Systems., 17*(1), 4–11.
74. Dong, X., Chang, Y., Wang, Y., & Yan, J. (2017). Understanding usage of internet of things (IOT) systems in China: Cognitive experience and affect experience as moderator. *Information Technology and People., 30*(1), 117–138.
75. Kim, J. K., Sharman, R., Rao, H. R., & Upadhyaya, S. (2007). Efficiency of critical incident management systems: Instrument development and validation. *Decision Support Systems., 44*(1), 235–250.
76. Lee, E., Park, Y., & Shin, J. G. (2009). Large engineering project risk management using a Bayesian belief network. *Expert Systems with Applications., 36*(3), 5880–5887.
77. Sai, A. R., Buckley, J., Fitzgerald, B., & Gear, L. (2021). A.: Taxonomy of centralization in public blockchain systems: A systematic literature review. *Information Processing and Management., 58*(4), 102584.
78. van der Valk, H., Haße, H., Möller, F., & Otto, B. (2022). Archetypes of digital twins. *Business & Information Systems Engineering., 64*(3), 375–391.
79. Wu, H.-Y., Chen, J.-K., & Chen, I.-S. (2010). Innovation capital indicator assessment of Taiwanese universities: A hybrid fuzzy model application. *Expert Systems with Applications., 37*(2), 1635–1642.
80. Fan, Z.-P., Suo, W.-L., & Feng, B. (2012). Identifying risk factors of IT outsourcing using interdependent information: An extended DEMATEL method. *Expert Systems with Applications., 39*(3), 3832–3840.
81. Chen, M. K., & Wang, S.-C. (2010). The critical factors of success for information service industry in developing international market: Using analytic hierarchy process (AHP) approach. *Expert Systems with Applications., 37*(1), 694–704.
82. Harison, E., & Boonstra, A. (2009). Essential competencies for technochange management: Towards an assessment model. *International Journal of Information Management., 29*(4), 283–294.
83. Jöhnk, J., Weißert, M., & Wyrtki, K. (2021). Ready or not, AI comes—An interview study of organizational AI readiness factors. *Business & Information Systems Engineering., 63*(1), 5–20.
84. Kaiser, C., Stocker, A., Viscusi, G., Fellmann, M., & Richter, A. (2021). Conceptualising value creation in data-driven services: The case of vehicle data. *International Journal of Information Management., 59*, 102335.
85. Palas, M. J. U., & Bunduchi, R. (2021). Exploring interpretations of blockchain's value in healthcare: A multi-stakeholder approach. *Information Technology and People., 34*(2), 453–495.
86. Subsermsri, P., Jairak, K., & Praneetpolgrang, P. (2015). Information technology governance practices based on sufficiency economy philosophy in the Thai university sector. *Information Technology and People., 28*(1), 195–223.
87. Tseng, S.-M. (2008). The effects of information technology on knowledge management systems. *Expert Systems with Applications., 35*(1–2), 150–160.
88. Ebel, P., Bretschneider, U., & Leimeister, J. M. (2016). Leveraging virtual business model innovation: A framework for designing business model development tools. *Information Systems Journal., 26*(5), 519–550.
89. van Pelt, R., Jansen, S., Baars, D., & Overbeek, S. (2021). Defining Blockchain governance: A framework for analysis and comparison. *Information Systems Management., 38*(1), 21–41.
90. Putz, B., Dietz, M., Empl, P., & Pernul, G. (2021). EtherTwin: Blockchain-based secure digital twin information management. *Information Processing and Management., 58*(1), 102425.
91. Kazancoglu, Y., Ozbiltekin Pala, M., Sezer, M. D., Luthra, S., & Kumar, A. (2021). Drivers of implementing big data analytics in food supply chains for transition to a circular economy and sustainable operations management. *Journal of Enterprise Information Management., 44*, 235–250.

92. Valmohammadi, C., & Dashti, S. (2016). Using interpretive structural modeling and fuzzy analytical process to identify and prioritize the interactive barriers of e-commerce implementation. *Information and Management., 53*(2), 157–168.
93. Spruit, M., Vroon, R., & Batenburg, R. (2014). Towards healthcare business intelligence in long-term care. *Computers in Human Behavior, 30*, 698–707.
94. Käss, S., Brosig, C., Westner, M., & Strahringer, S. (2024). Short and sweet: Multiple mini case studies as a form of rigorous case study research. *Information Systems and e-Business Management., 22*, 351–384.
95. Skinner, R. J., Nelson, R. R., & Chin, W. (2022). Synthesizing qualitative evidence: A roadmap for information systems research. *Journal of the Association for Information Systems., 23*(3), 639–677.

# Growing Pains of Digital Transformation: Navigating the Challenges in Non-profits

**Alexandra Radu, Gideon Mekonnen Jonathan , and Erik Perjons**

**Abstract** Digital transformation promises strategic and operational benefits for organisations regardless of size, sector, or industry. However, its antecedents and value realisation mechanisms are highly context-dependent, influenced by factors within and beyond an organisation. While the focus of prior digital transformation studies seems to be on for-profit and relatively well in public organisations, the challenges for non-profit organisations (NPOs) remain under-investigated. Based on a systematic literature review and a case study in one Swedish NPO, this study reveals digital transformation barriers within NPOs. The barriers identified through thematic analysis encompass internal and external environmental factors grounded in recent digital transformation frameworks. The study contributes to the literature on digital transformation specific to NPOs. Practitioners can also use these insights to inform the development of robust strategies and the effective implementation of their digital transformation initiatives.

## 1 Introduction

Scholars recognise that the emergence of new technologies, innovative business models, shorter product life cycles, highly customised or differentiated products, value-added services, synchronised product-service combinations, and the dynamic environment calls for a paradigmatic shift and new appropriate strategic responses [1]. Indeed, today's organisations and leaders have also realised that technology-enabled organisational change is necessary to drive new business models. To this end, digital transformation—"*a fundamental change to a process utilising digital technologies that results in an improvement to all stakeholders so dramatic that demand for a new way of working or thinking, such as new digital platforms, new methods, new cultures, new strategies, and new structures*" [2, p. 10]—is expected

A. Radu · G. M. Jonathan (✉) · E. Perjons
Department of Computer and Systems Sciences (DSV), Stockholm University, Kista, Sweden
e-mail: alra0560@su.se; gideon@dsv.su.se; perjons@dsv.su.se

 
B. Marcinkowski et al. (eds.), *Advances in Information Systems Development*,
Lecture Notes in Information Systems and Organisation 77,
https://doi.org/10.1007/978-3-031-87880-0_5

to bring about strategic and operational benefits for organisations [3] across sectors and industries. In the private sector, new digital technologies have facilitated the execution of innovative business models, improving the offering of value propositions. In the public organisations context, digital transformation results in synchronised product-service combinations [4, 5]. On the other hand, the primary motivation for embarking on the digital transformation journey for non-profit organisations (NPOs) is that it shapes the communication between various stakeholders to improve fundraising and delivery of services. The rationale is that digital transformation can enhance transparency, accountability, and stakeholder relationships by facilitating more inclusive, high-quality, and impactful provision of services to beneficiaries [6]. However, despite the availability of advanced technologies and attempts to embrace digital transformation, NPOs, even in leading countries like Sweden [7], face challenges in integrating and implementing emerging technologies in their existing processes [8]. While the Swedish government actively supports the works towards modernising the digital infrastructures, drafting favourable legislations, and improving citizens' digital skills [9], a report by Sweden's Open Government Partnership [10] highlights the ongoing difficulties NPOs face as they attempt to embrace digital transformation.

Even though there is little disagreement about the benefits of digital transformation among researchers and practitioners, the diversity of expected outcomes across organisational contexts highlights the intricate interplay of technological, organisational, and environmental factors that shape its success. According to Vial [3], digital transformation antecedents and the way it creates value for different organisations are contingent upon the internal organisational settings as well as the external (i.e., market, industry, and political) dynamics. Thus, Verhoef et al. [11] underscores the significance of aligning digital capabilities, strategic orientation, and environmental contingencies for the successful realisation of the benefits of digital transformation. Among others, these include industry-specific variations in the relationship between digital transformation initiatives and organisational performance, moderated by factors like regulatory frameworks, competitive pressures, and technological readiness. The findings of prior studies also suggest that it is in organisations' best interest to tailor their digital transformation strategies and approaches to their specific context with appreciation for particular antecedents and expected benefits. However, a closer look into the extant research within the Information Systems (IS) indicates that digital transformation is predominantly studied within commercial and private organisations, referred to as for-profit organisations (FPOs), as well as agencies and administrations in the public sector. Thus, there is a dearth of scholarly attention towards investigating digital transformation within the context of NPOs. This is unfortunate, given the pronounced differences between NPOs and organisations in the private and public sectors.

NPOs are organisations that are legally prohibited from distributing profits to shareholders or managers, often relying on donations and operational revenue to fulfil their mission of addressing societal needs that the private and public sectors cannot adequately meet, such as public health, education, charity, and social justice [12, 13]. Thus, NPOs operate in different contextual settings pursuing missions that deviate from the ultimate objectives of the private (i.e., financial) and public organisations (i.e., politically viable) goals. We argue that digital transformation needs to be studied considering the NPO's context, particularly in light of the rapid proliferation of digital technologies within the industry in the aftermath of the COVID-19 pandemic. It is also worth noting that suppliers of services and products within the Information Technology (IT) industry recognise the burgeoning demand for diverse emerging digital technologies, including those operating in non-profit domains [12]. Using Swedish NPOs as a case, this study attempts to reveal the various barriers to digital transformation in the sector. A prior publication of this study [14] attempted to draw the relationship between various barriers affecting the success of digital transformation efforts in NPOS. We argue that the results of our research will contribute to answering the calls for further studies, offering insights for NPOs to develop strategies to overcome digital transformation barriers [15].

The following research question guides the study:

*What specific barriers hinder the digital transformation efforts of non-profit organisations?*

The remainder of the paper is structured as follows. The next section presents the multiple barriers to digital transformation based on the literature review we conducted, which covered studies in the IS and cognate fields. Subsequently, the methodology section outlines the research strategy, data collection, and analysis methods. The results section presents the key findings and discussions. Finally, the implications of the findings for both research and practice are discussed.

## 2 Related Studies

### *2.1 Digital Transformation in Non-profit Organisations*

The abundance of emerging technologies and their adoption across organisations, as well as the potential of these technologies to shape how organisations create value, is cited as the reason for the evolution of digital transformation as a phenomenon. While closely linked to digitalisation [16], digital transformation encompasses a broader scope, focusing on the strategic and operational changes that emerge from the integration of digital technologies into an organisation [3]. IS scholars emphasise that the two concepts differ in scope and complexity [16]. Digitalisation, even though regarded as a critical component of digital transformation, is limited to improving processes or products with mainly economic-driven outcomes (i.e., improved efficiency and effectiveness). Digital transformation goes beyond the technological dimension as it is aimed at not only improving but also changing the organisational processes, models, and activities, focusing on the human dimension and having capability-driven outcomes [2, 7]. Thus, the conceptual boundaries of the phenomenon have expanded from mere technological implementation to encompass fundamental changes in value-creation processes, organisational structures, and business models.

The extant literature indicates that digital transformation is known to have implications for almost every aspect of an organisation. Thus, it is considered a means that supports organisation-wide changes towards enhancing new capabilities. On the other hand, scholars have also found that several factors can influence the digital transformation process enabled by emerging digital technologies, which are also referred to as barriers. According to the findings of a series of empirical studies (e.g., [17]), organisational or sectoral differences determine the various factors considered barriers or success factors to digital transformation. Prior studies suggest that digital transformation barriers are particular organisational elements due to a lack of alignment between people, processes, and technology [15].

On the other hand, Vial [3] argues that digital transformation barriers emerge due to disruptions associated with customer behaviour and expectations, competitive landscape and data availability. The combinations of these barriers are also related to the NPO's organisational characteristics, which is relevant to our work. Due to their size, profile, market coverage, and purpose diversity, NPOs present various characteristics that can affect their digital transformation journey [13, 18]. For instance, customer behaviour and expectations in NPOs closely relate to the long list of stakeholders, determining their expectations and propensity to adopt digital solutions. Thus, stakeholder theory [19–21] is relevant to reveal one of the challenges facing non-profit organisations attempting to succeed in their digital transformation journey. Specifically, the multi-stakeholder nature of NPOs complicates the understanding of consumer behaviour and expectations, making it more challenging to meet diverse needs and application of digital technologies [22]. Sanderse et al. [23] present a non-traditional business model for NPOs to address value creation misalignments, emphasising the accurate expression of the organisation's reality in terms of multi-stakeholder needs and requirements. With limited research on NPO's challenges in digital transformation, insights from previous studies on digital transformation in both FPOs and public organisations presented by Jonathan [17] are recalled for adjusting the structure based on [2] and [6] as well as the already revealed barriers to NPOs digital transformation in the literature.

## 2.2 Barriers to Digital Transformation

Researchers agree that digital transformation is a complex process that challenges entities to align different organisational elements with the technology to gain value from the implemented disruptive technologies. Vogelsang et al. [15] define barriers as obstacles or things that can prevent organisations from successful implementation of digital transformation. Identifying and recognising the challenges and striving to overcome them allows organisations to achieve capabilities that can support the alignment, enable the transformation, and realise the anticipated benefits. According to the author, there is a gap in the research regarding a general framework that captures most barriers and draws a relationship between them. Moreover, both

Brink et al. [24] and Vogelsang et al. [15] underline that prior research identifying various barriers focuses on specific profit-oriented sectors. Even though numerous taxonomies have been developed on barriers to digital transformation in FPOs, only a few have been identified in NPOs. The following are some digital transformation barriers in NPOs identified in the literature.

1. Vogelsang et al. [15] revealed some of the most pressing challenges in NPOs by comparing FPOs and German NPOs. These include lack of managerial skills, lack of acceptance, lack of adapted IT solutions, lack of new roles, lack of agile environment, rigorous legal requirements, and lack of customers.
2. Balacescu [25] excludes limited resources as a barrier per se, instead identifying a lack of planning, goals and vision; lack of strategy, lack of qualitative data, and lack of collaboration are highlighted.
3. Cavicchi and Vagnoni [26] also point out that funding challenges can be resolved in different ways. The barriers identified are lack of awareness, managerial skills, collaboration, data quality, and resistance.
4. Nahrkhalaji et al. [22] analyse digital transformation in NPOs on different maturity levels where barriers might differ. According to the author, the main barriers that hinder digital transformation in NPOs are inertia, lack of resources, lack of tech expertise, fear of change, damage to corporate image, and lack of leadership and management.
5. Brink et al. [24] find a list of barriers to digital transformation based on empirical studies in German NPOs consisting of a lack of adapted technology-based communication structures, a lack of customer pull, a lack of acceptance, and legal barriers.
6. O'Grady and Robert's [27] findings from studies in Irish NPOs are a lack of funding, a lack of public trust, inefficient management, a lack of Information and Communications Technology function, a lack of awareness of digital transformation benefits, resistance, a lack of leadership, a lack of data, a lack of collaboration, a lack of planning, a lack of innovation.
7. Schiffhauer and Seelmeyer [28] found digital transformation barriers in NPOs. These include a lack of adapted guidelines, systematic concepts for evaluating technologies that fit welfare organisations, ethical aspects, and a lack of collaboration.

# 3 Research Methodology

## *3.1 Research Strategy*

Qualitative research was deemed appropriate for this study as it is best suited to reveal the factors related to a phenomenon, aligning with the exploratory reason of the research. Thus, a qualitative case study was adopted as it allows researchers to gain a detailed understanding of a phenomenon in a natural setting

[29]. Additionally, the strategy accommodates the application of multiple data types collected from different sources. Case studies have been long recognised among IS researchers exploring the barriers to digital transformation in FPOs, public organisations and NPOs [12, 15, 17]. Scholars argue that a case study is an appropriate research strategy to gather insights into the interconnection and relationships between organisations' structure, processes, and implemented technology under the digital transformation journey [29]. Moreover, we argue that NPOs present a unique organisational setting and list of stakeholders with varying interests compared to both public organisations and FPOs, providing the opportunity to further our understanding of the digital transformation process and its challenges. A single case study rather than multiple case studies was deemed appropriate to achieve the aim of our study—an in-depth investigation and rich description of digital transformation in NPOs. While multiple case studies are popular among researchers interested in comparing cases and testing and replicability of empirical findings and theoretical applications, single cases provide richer insights [29].

### *3.2 The Case Organisaton*

In line with the aim of this study, we selected a case organisation that is relatively representative of NPOs and is also known to be undertaking digital transformation. To choose the case organisation, we followed the typical characteristics of NPOs as presented in the literature (e.g., [6])—organisations that operate for purposes other than generating profit but engaged in furthering social causes and shared goals contributing to, for instance, sustainable socio-economic growth of local communities. The motivation for choosing the case organisation was to gain a natural setting (i.e., with various unique characteristics of NPOs' missions, resources, and operational models) that could have implications for digital transformation. Thus, we selected a large, well-established Swedish NPO (also referred to as "*ideell förening*" in Swedish). The case organisation, which remains anonymous, is based in Stockholm, with approximately 600 employees and 400 volunteers. It is part of an umbrella of national NPOs operating in different districts in the country with similar features (but different territorial coverage). The NPO based in Stockholm organises its offerings in three areas, i.e., social services, social enterprises, and education. The organisations' beneficiaries are people with different backgrounds, both nationals and migrants from all ages. The organisation's goal is to advocate for equity and support the beneficiaries in overcoming a vulnerable life situation by offering an extensive range of services: job training, juridic support, social assistance, housing, education, economic support, and well-being conversations. It is worth noting that both private entities and governmental organisations finance the organisation. The second criterion for selecting the NPO for the study is the digital transformation it is currently undertaking. According to the documents obtained, the NPO is introducing various emerging technologies to support its processes, including Cloud Services, Data Warehouse, and Power BI. The organisation says that digital transformation is a means to improve the relationship with its stakeholders, value propositions to the beneficiaries, and operational efficiencies.

### *3.3 Data Collection Methods*

Yin [29] argues that the results from case studies can provide deeper insight and a better understanding of a phenomenon when mixed data collection methods (also referred to as multiple sources of evidence) are applied. In the initial stage of the study, we conducted a systematic literature review to establish the state-of-the-art of digital transformation research within NPOs. Using a combination of keywords (i.e.,"*digital transformation*", "*digitalisation*", and "*non-profit organisations*", "*not-for-profit organisations*", "*challenges*", and "*barriers*"), the search for relevant articles was conducted in databases indexing basket of 11 journals and premier information systems conferences. The appraisal of the final papers selected for the review was based on the inclusion and exclusion criteria set at the beginning of the search. Articles in languages other than English, studies that had not been peer-reviewed, incomplete articles, book chapters, research-in-progress articles, and duplicate articles were excluded. Complete and peer-reviewed articles published between 2016 and 2024 on digital transformation in NPOs were included in the review.

The empirical part of the study adopts interviews and documents as data collection methods. However, one-to-one semi-structured interviews were the primary data sources for the study. Our objective is to gather data, as provided by participants, to capture the holistic view and unique situation in a natural environment. The interview questions were formulated to reveal the various challenges facing the case organisation as it introduces and manages emerging digital technologies. Probability sampling was deemed inappropriate for our study because we aimed to provide in-depth insight, not a generalisation, of a phenomenon on the broader population. Thus, we adopted a purposive sampling strategy according to selection criteria in line with the study aim. We were interested in recruiting those with the knowledge and responsibility for the ongoing digital transformation at the organisation. To ensure we have selected respondents who could provide us with the richest information, we consulted the organisational structure of the case organisation. The final list of participants (referred to in the paper only by randomly generated codes) includes product owners, project leaders, team leaders, and a digitalisation manager. The interview data was complemented with internal organisational documents (i.e., 2023–2025 Digital Strategy, financial policy, organisational chart, IT strategy and project roadmaps).

### 3.4 Data Analysis Method

The study adopted a thematic data analysis approach, which is widely recognised among qualitative researchers since it provides flexibility while enabling a rich and detailed account of data [30]. Researchers argue that thematic analysis can be used in studies where complex phenomena are explored. Prior digital transformation studies have applied thematic analysis (e.g., [17]. The thematic analysis method was deemed appropriate for our study as our aim was exploratory, focusing on digital transformation in a complex organisational setting.

We followed the six phases of the thematic analysis procedure by Braun and Clarke [30]—familiarising with data, generating initial code, searching for themes, reviewing themes, defining and naming themes, and producing the report. The aim of the procedure is to search and identify common threads. The themes emerge as researchers carefully read and familiarise themselves with the raw data. To help us describe the phenomenon under investigation, we considered one of the two forms of coding: inductive or deductive. Even though inductive coding is common among exploratory studies, we chose a hybrid approach incorporating both inductive and deductive theme generation to improve the rigour of our study. First, we developed the initial codes and sub-themes from our transcribed data following the inductive approach. Later, we mapped and grouped these themes deductively using a priori template.

## 4 Results

The aim of this study was to establish the various barriers to digital transformation within the context of NPOs. However, the starting point for the empirical study was the findings of the literature review, which has already provided with the list of both internal and external factors preventing NPOs from realising the benefits of digital transformation. As shown in Fig. 1, the analysis of our interviews and documents revealed fifteen additional barriers (shown in light green sharp rectangle boxes). The thematic map also shows the seventeen barriers (in white boxes) identified in this study. The complete list of barriers presented in eight categories was organised based on the priori template we developed from our literature review and the common attributes of NPOs. A brief discussion of the category of barriers is presented in the following sub-sections.

### 4.1 Organisational Structure

The case organisation under investigation presents a hierarchical and siloed organisational structure, resulting in fragmented processes across different units. To

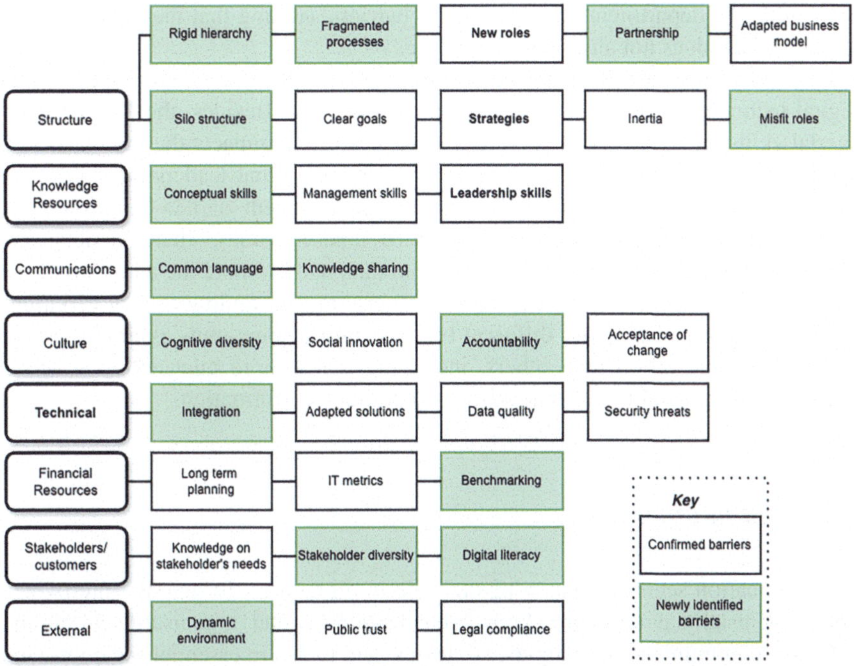


**Fig. 1** Thematic map with the barriers to DT in the Swedish NPO

address these inefficiencies, the organization initiated a restructuring effort in 2022, aiming to flatten the hierarchy and streamline processes. Despite these efforts, the organization's business model lacks a robust foundation to effectively leverage its knowledge resources and develop adaptive capabilities. While respondents acknowledged the potential benefits of adaptive business models, maintaining a balance between process-oriented approaches and the organization's unique identity remains a critical challenge. As one respondent stated, "You cannot go into this kind of organisation being totally process-oriented because then we would probably lose our soul and all the people working within this. But I still think it can be combined" (MP15).

## *4.2 Knowledge Resources*

To determine the extent to which a lack of a participatory environment hinders the digital transformation process, we focus on the organisation's capabilities and how it manages its knowledge resources. Our analysis suggests a shortage of diverse conceptual skills (e.g., systems thinking, service thinking, abstract thinking, and process thinking) has implication on the implementation of emerging technologies.

Staff in the IT department anticipate these barriers, arguing that the organisation's digital skillset does not align with its profile.

Concerns have also been raised regarding the experience of employees using digital technologies integrated with existing processes. Besides, the lack of managerial skills and a forward-thinking approach directly impacts the organisation's agility and innovation potential. Our analysis indicates that leaders must do more to encourage employee input and foster the development of new solutions. For instance, since the implementation of Power BI, it has become evident that managers require additional skills to extract value from data and promote the adoption of the technology throughout the organisation. Furthermore, our findings reveal variations in management styles across different business units. Some units exhibit a greater openness to innovation than others, indicating that a more nuanced approach is needed to foster a culture of innovation and digital transformation.

### *4.3 Communications*

Communication seems to play a pivotal role in digital transformation, intertwined with organisational structure, knowledge resources, and organisational culture. Effective communication methods, strategies, and tools are essential for improving understanding and synergy across different levels of the organisation. The barriers identified within this category include a lack of common language and a lack of knowledge sharing and organisational learning. The organization's profile and self-presentation influence its use of language. Our respondents agree that a shared language facilitating mutual understanding between IT and the rest of the organisation is crucial for enhancing its capabilities and the utilisation of digital technologies. As one respondent stated, "One thing that is hard while working with data is that you have to make sure you really use the same kind of definitions" (MP15). Instead of formal arrangements, the NPO relies on diverse, informal knowledge-sharing and organisational learning approaches. Consequently, a centralised knowledge-sharing strategy encompassing various organisational units is lacking.

### *4.4 Organisational Culture*

Our research identified several cultural barriers hindering NPO digital transformation. For instance, the lack of cognitive diversity and fear of accountability emerged as significant challenges. Organisational resistance to innovation and change further impeded progress. Particularly, varying technological understanding among employees affected motivation and belonging. Furthermore, a homogeneous culture fostered self-censorship and hindered talent acquisition. Top management's fear of failure and decision avoidance suppressed agile practices and innovation.

We argue that overcoming these challenges requires fostering an open, innovative culture that encourages risk-taking and experimentation, as NPOs tend towards conservative norms that hinder digital adoption.

## 4.5 Technical Barriers

The technical barriers identified in this study relate to applications, systems, and data-related challenges. As the case organisation is in the early stages of its digital transformation journey, a common challenge is the lack of integration between various systems, often described as an "archipelago" or "spaghetti" application landscape. While digital technologies offer flexible and out-of-the-box solutions, adapting these solutions to the specific needs of NPOs, which often have complex requirements, can be resource-intensive. Assigning responsibility for ensuring the alignment of digital technologies with organisational needs presents a challenge. IT ownership can sometimes lead to the development of solutions that do not adequately address business requirements. This risk is particularly pronounced in NPOs that lack a deep understanding of business development. Data quality issues, particularly related to data standardisation, are another significant technical barrier. Additionally, information security threats pose a potential risk to digital transformation efforts. Respondents argue that while shared IT resources may mitigate some supplier risks in the short term, long-term ethical and societal implications are challenging to anticipate and address.

## 4.6 Financial Resources

NPOs often face financial constraints, with a significant portion of their budget allocated to operational costs and projects. This limited financial flexibility hinders long-term IT planning, leading to challenges in developing existing projects and implementing new ones. While the IT team recognises the benefits of long-term resource planning, external factors like economic uncertainty and compliance requirements, as well as the difficulty of measuring IT benefits, pose significant obstacles. The participants recognise that measuring IT benefits is crucial for influencing leadership decisions and securing long-term budget allocations. However, quantifying the benefits of IT investments can be complex, as costs and benefits are often distributed across various areas of the organisation. On the other hand, the implementation of IT metrics in NPOs is further complicated by a lack of standardised models and benchmarks. While benchmarking practices can help organisations identify best practices and tailor solutions to their specific needs, the absence of established benchmarks within the NPO sector presents an additional challenge.

## *4.7 Customers/Stakeholders*

One characteristic of NPOs, in contrast with organisations in different sectors, is a diverse range of stakeholders, including donors, suppliers, partner institutions, volunteers, employees, and beneficiaries. The NPO's digital transformation initiatives aim to improve efficiency and communication with these stakeholders. However, the diversity of stakeholders poses challenges in tailoring digital solutions to meet their specific needs. As one respondent noted, "We have customers and beneficiaries, and then we have some mix with those two. But one thing we have a challenge with is to think about the user, and users can come in many different shapes" (MP15). The organisation aspires to become data-driven and provide more digital services to its stakeholders. However, the analysis suggests that the needs of beneficiaries are not sufficiently prioritised during the digital strategy formulation. Additionally, there is a lack of recognition of the need to address beneficiaries' digital literacy. As one respondent emphasised, "Even more important is that we can provide work training places for people that need to train and update their skills in an environment that is demanded in the future. We need to provide work training places within the digital area" (MP15).

## *4.8 External Barriers*

The success of NPOs, as demonstrated in the case organisation's digital transformation, is contingent upon external environmental factors, including the dynamic social landscape, diverse stakeholder needs, and rapid technological and market developments. Thus, NPOs are expected to navigate these complexities while simultaneously creating public value through the adoption of new digital technologies and adhering to regulatory and compliance requirements. This delicate balancing act can both hinder and facilitate digital transformation. As one respondent noted, "it's in our DNA to just do a lot of stuff. I think that we need to be able to adapt quickly to change because that is the nature of our business in general!" (KD87). Besides, public trust is a critical factor for NPOs' sustainability, as it influences their ability to secure financial resources. Consequently, NPO leadership may be cautious about adopting innovative solutions due to concerns about potential failure and negative public perception. While the organisation has taken steps to comply with GDPR, the regulatory landscape can also pose additional challenges and resource constraints.

Overall, the external environment plays a significant role in shaping the trajectory of NPOs' digital transformation efforts. By understanding and responding to these external factors, NPOs can mitigate risks and maximize the benefits of digital innovation.

## 5 Discussions and Concluding Remarks

The heterogeneous nature of organisations' goals in pursuing digital transformation, along with the varied antecedents and contextual settings affecting its successful implementation, justifies empirical studies conducted in various sectors and industries. We argue that NPOs present unique organisational settings that can influence the adoption of emerging technologies to improve the value they need to create for their beneficiaries. Based on two frameworks from the extant literature [2, 3], we present the various challenges NPOs face as they undertake digital transformation. The starting point for us was the findings of our literature review [15, 22, 24, 26–28] which were invaluable to not only developing a taxonomy but also in explaining how they are correlated with each other, and which barriers were recognised by the organisation (See [14] for the correlation of the identified barriers).

The developed taxonomy in our study substantiated the previously identified barriers in extant literature. The findings corroborated existing barriers across seven thematic areas whilst contributing a novel theme, "Communications". The study also revealed fifteen previously unidentified barriers: rigid hierarchy, fragmented processes, lack of partnership misfit roles, siloed business structure, lack of diverse conceptual skills, lack of common language, lack of systematic knowledge sharing and organisational learning, fear of accountability, lack of integration, lack of benchmarking, mixed stakeholder's journey, digital literacy, and environmental complexity. These findings augment our understanding of the challenges organisations face in their digital transformation endeavours, particularly within the NPOs context. We argue that the emergence of these additional barriers underscores the evolving nature of digital transformation and highlights the necessity for a more nuanced approach to addressing these barriers.

The new barriers we identified provide a broader perspective on NPOs' challenges in adopting emergent technologies that have not been approached in other studies. The organisational core—structure, culture, knowledge, and communications—brings the barriers together within one main organisational challenge: lack of systematic knowledge management and organisational learning. Under communications barriers, we find a lack of conceptual skills, a lack of new roles [15] and a lack of a culture of change [22, 23, 27]. New specialised roles have the capacity to accelerate the development of needed capabilities and to increase cognitive diversity. Lack of cognitive diversity, in turn, is related to both lack of acceptance and lack of awareness previously presented in the literature [22, 26, 27]. These barriers are assumed to be rooted in both the organisation's historical development, influenced by the constraints of the public sector, and a lack of effective communication management.

The barriers that are closely related to Vial's [3] disruptions are found to be embedded in technical, financial, stakeholder, and external themes. Data availability relates to a lack of data quality [25, 26], legal barriers and compliance [22] and lack of benchmarking. Lack of benchmarking is a specific challenge for digital transformation in NPOs, unrevealed in the consulted literature. NPOs encounter challenges in measuring IT benefits [15] because they rely on benchmarking. The NPO's competitive landscape is shaped by both external challenges—public trust and environmental complexity -and the ability to innovate [27]. Lack of adapted IT solutions [28] and lack of knowledge of stakeholders' needs [22] are elements of consumer behaviour and expectations disruptions.

## 6 Contributions and Future Research

Through a literature review and a single case study, we uncovered digital transformation barriers specific to NPOs, which can serve as a foundation for future research. By applying existing frameworks and considering the unique characteristics of NPOs, we developed a taxonomy of barriers that encompasses both internal organisational and external environmental factors. This research contributes to further understanding the challenges and opportunities facing NPOs in their digital transformation journeys.

While our study provides rich insights into the barriers to digital transformation within a specific NPO, the findings may not be generalisable, particularly to organisations operating in different contexts and settings. However, as Yin [17] suggests, case studies can facilitate analytical generalisation, allowing for the exploration of links between specific findings and broader theoretical constructs. Thus, our findings can be a foundation for further comparative qualitative or quantitative studies within the NPO sector and other public or private organisations. Practitioners can also leverage these insights to gain a deeper understanding of the various factors hindering their digital transformation efforts. By identifying and addressing these barriers, organisations can improve their planning and execution of digital transformation initiatives.

## References

1. Bellantuono, N., Nuzzi, A., Pontrandolfo, P., & Scozzi, B. (2021). Digital transformation models for the I4. 0 transition: Lessons from the change management literature. *Sustainability, 13*(23), 12941.
2. Gong, C., & Ribiere, V. (2021). Developing a unified definition of digital transformation. *Technovation, 102*, 102217.
3. Vial, G. (2019). Understanding digital transformation: A review and a research agenda. *The Journal of Strategic Information Systems, 28*(2), 118–144.
4. Luna-Reyes, L. F., & Gil-Garcia, J. R. (2014). Digital government transformation and internet portals: The co-evolution of technology, organizations, and institutions. *Government Information Quarterly, 31*(4), 545–555.
5. Mergel, I., Edelmann, N., & Haug, N. (2019). Defining digital transformation: Results from expert interviews. *Government Information Quarterly, 36*(4), 101385.
6. Ibrahim, S. S., Muhamat, A. A., Ahmad, M., Hassan, W. A. W., & Bakar, A. J. A. (2021). Empowering NGOs and social entrepreneur through digitalization for sustainable

socioeconomic growth of the society: Post Covid-19. *The Empirical Economics Letters, 20*(2) 215–225.
7. OECD. (2018). *OECD reviews of digital transformation: Going digital in Sweden*. OECD Publishing.
8. Bidrag med anledning av Covid-19 till organisationer som arbetar med människor i socialt särskilt utsatta situationer. Retrieved October 25, 2024, from https://tinyurl.com/3xsye2zy
9. Digitala Sverige. (2022). En samlad analys av samhällets digitalisering. Retrieved October 23, 2023, from https://tinyurl.com/2auyyn6w
10. Sweden's Open Government Partnership Action Plan 2023–2025. Retrieved October 23, 2024, from https://tinyurl.com/43cxeu7m
11. Verhoef, P. C., Broekhuizen, T., Bart, Y., Bhattacharya, A., Dong, J. Q., Fabian, N., & Haenlein, M. (2021). Digital transformation: A multidisciplinary reflection and research agenda. *Journal of Business Research, 122*, 889–901.
12. Hansmann, H. B. (1980). The role of nonprofit enterprise. *The Yale Law Journal, 89*(5), 835–901.
13. McDonald, R. E., Weerawardena, J., Madhavaram, S., & Sullivan Mort, G. (2015). From "virtuous" to "pragmatic" pursuit of social mission: A sustainability-based typology of nonprofit organizations and corresponding strategies. *Management Research Review, 38*(9), 970–991.
14. Radu, A., Jonathan, G. M., & Perjons, E. (2024). Barriers to digital transformation in non-profit organisations. In *Proceedings of the 32nd International Conference on Information Systems Development (ISD)* (p. 19). Association for Information Systems (AIS), Gdańsk.
15. Vogelsang, K., Packmohr, S., & Brink, H. (2021). Challenges of the digital transformation – comparing nonprofit and industry organizations. In *Proceedings of the International Conference on Wirtschaftsinformatik* (pp. 297–312). Essen.
16. Verina, N., & Titko, J. (2019). Digital transformation: Conceptual framework. In *Proceedings of the International Scientific Conference "Contemporary Issues in Business, Management and Economics Engineering* (pp. 9–10). Vilnius Tech, Vilnius.
17. Jonathan, G. M. (2023). *Information Technology Alignment in Public Organisations: Towards Successful Digital Transformation*. Doctoral Dissertation. Department of Computer and Systems Sciences, Stockholm University.
18. Lundström, T., & Wijkström, F. (1995). Defining the nonprofit sector: Sweden. Johns Hopkins Institute for Policy Studies, Maryland.
19. Van Veenstra, A. F., Klievink, B., & Janssen, M. (2011). Barriers and impediments to transformational government: Insights from literature and practice. *Electronic Government, An International Journal, 8*(2–3), 226–241.
20. Lewis, D. (2014). *The management of non-governmental development organizations: An introduction*. Routledge.
21. Arvidson, M., Johansson, H., Meeuwisse, A., & Scaramuzzino, R. (2018). A Swedish culture of advocacy? Civil society organisations' strategies for political influence. *Sociologisk Forskning, 55*(2–3), 341–364.
22. Nahrkhalaji, S. S., Shafiee, S., Shafiee, M., & Hvam, L. (2018). Challenges of digital transformation: The case of the non-profit sector. In *Proceedings of the IEEE International Conference on Industrial Engineering and Engineering Management (IEEM)* (pp. 1245–1249). IEEE.
23. Heikkinen, A., Kujala, J., & Inha, M. (2019). Stakeholder engagement in a non-profit organisation: An issue-based perspective. *International Journal of Human Resources Development and Management, 19*(1), 5–20.
24. Brink, H., Packmohr, S., & Vogelsang, K. (2020). Fields of action to advance the digital transformation of NPOs–development of a framework. In *Proceedings of the International Conference on Business Informatics Research* (pp. 82–97). Springer.
25. Mato-Santiso, V., Rey-García, M., & Sanzo-Pérez, M. J. (2021). Managing multi-stakeholder relationships in nonprofit organizations through multiple channels: A systematic review and

research agenda for enhancing stakeholder relationship marketing. *Public Relations Review, 47*(4), 102074.
26. Sanderse, J., de Langen, F., & Salgado, F. P. (2020). Proposing a business model framework for nonprofit organizations. *Journal of Applied Economics and Business Research, 10*(1), 40–53.
27. O'Grady, J., & Roberts, P. (2019). The digital transformation of Irish non-profit organisations. In *Proceedings of the 27th AIAI Irish Conference on Artificial Intelligence and Cognitive Science* (pp. 388–399). CEURL.
28. Balacescu, A. (2021). Visibility and communication of small NGOs in the context of digital transformation. *Journal of Research and Innovation for Sustainable Society, 3*(2), 201–208.
29. Yin, R. K. (2018). *Case study research and applications: Design and methods*. SAGE.
30. Braun, V., & Clarke, V. (2006). Using thematic analysis in psychology. *Qualitative Research in Psychology, 3*(2), 77–101.

# Digital Innovation, Strategic and Lean Management as Success Factors in IT

**Elżbieta Wojnicka-Sycz, Jacek Rybicki, and Piotr Sycz**

**Abstract** The article presents the specificity of innovativeness in software development companies in Europe from the perspective of its connection with Industry 4.0/5.0 technologies and closed versus open innovation methods, as well as its role in innovation systems. Empirical research in 142 European computer programming companies shows that they are involved in the development of software supporting the digital transition. The findings also show that high innovation in collaboration with external partners as well as closed innovation are success factors for the software industry. Consistent strategic management and wastage reduction are also important. Further promotion of the software industry as an intermediary in innovation systems is recommended. The methods used were literature review, web survey and statistical and econometric analysis.

## 1 Introduction

The aim of this paper is to analyse the impact of innovativeness on the success of computer programming companies in Europe and the role of software supporting digital transformation in the innovative efforts of IT companies. Therefore, we also examine whether digital innovations developed by IT firms increase their competitiveness as measured by the assessment of growth prospects. We also examine whether strategic management in its various forms and lean management are determinants of IT success. We present the results of a survey of 142 European software development companies.

E. Wojnicka-Sycz (✉)
University of Gdańsk & Gdańsk University of Technology, Gdańsk, Poland
e-mail: elzbieta.wojnicka-sycz@ug.edu.pl

J. Rybicki · P. Sycz
University of Gdańsk, Gdańsk, Poland
e-mail: jacek.rybicki@ug.edu.pl; piotr.sycz@ug.edu.pl



B. Marcinkowski et al. (eds.), *Advances in Information Systems Development*, Lecture Notes in Information Systems and Organisation 77,
https://doi.org/10.1007/978-3-031-87880-0_6

Computer programming (CP) is a high-tech industry that is crucial for today's innovativeness. It is innovative itself and supports the innovativeness of other industries. As such, it belongs to the sector of knowledge-intensive business services (KIBS), which are an important component of innovation systems, but are not included in the existing concepts of triple, quadruple and quintuple helix innovation models. These models show the helixes of science, business, administration, as well as users and the natural environment, represented by environmental activists and other actors [1, 2]. We show an additional helix in the innovation system model that includes intermediary institutions such as KIBS, clusters, pro-innovation infrastructure (technology parks, incubators, technology transfer centres) (Fig. 1). CP companies are an example of advanced KIBS that support the innovative capacity of all other types of companies and the entire economy undergoing digital transformation. The digital transformation of industry is visible in the use of digital innovations associated with Industry 4.0/5.0 technologies. Digital technologies supporting digital transformation are technological process innovations according to the OSLO Manual [4]. Progress in the implementation of digital technologies

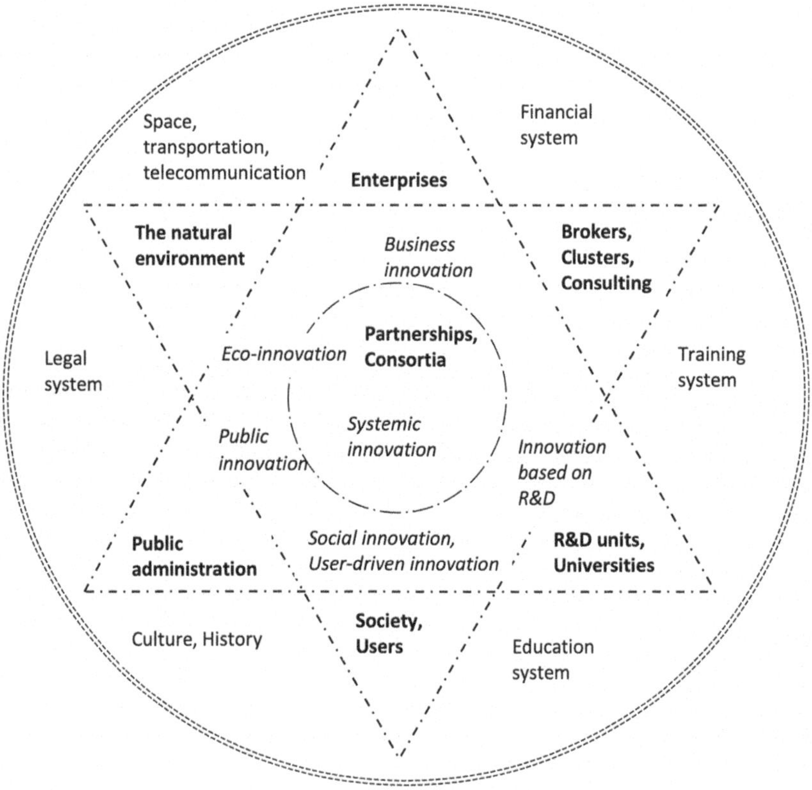


**Fig. 1** Innovative system according to the sextuple helix model. Source: [3]

drastically changes products, processes and business models, i.e. innovations [5]. Digital technologies related to Industry 4.0 and 5.0 include the Internet of Things, big data analytics and cloud computing, artificial intelligence, robotic process automation, augmented and virtual reality, blockchain, digital twins of factories and people, autonomous vehicles, sensors and cybersecurity or green IT [6].

Strategic management consists of the development of long-term strategic plans that define strategic goals with specific measures that enable strategic control. It can be a formalized plan or a more behavioral and emergent strategy. Emergent strategy results from the exploitation of emerging opportunities and the adjustment of the strategic plan and objectives. As a result, the realized strategy is a mixture of intended and emergent strategy. Behavioral strategy means that a company takes actions that become its pattern of behavior. Intended formal strategy establishes the meaningful direction of an organization. Emergent strategy means that an organization is able to learn and adapt to the changing environment [7]. It reflects the dynamic capabilities of organizations that is the ability to sustain competitive advantage by sensing opportunities and threats in the environment. Behavioral strategy is based on the adaptability of individuals and teams, which further depends on their cognitive, emotional and social behavior [8].

Lean management is a concept derived from the Toyota Production System (TPS), which consists in using such ways of the company's activities to achieve the best possible results with the least possible effort under the given conditions. This is achieved by eliminating wastage, such as activities that do not add value to the external or internal customer and take time [9, 10]. The Lean concept adapted to the specific work of IT companies was first demonstrated in Mary and Tom Poppendieck's (2003) "Lean Software Development: An Agile Toolkit for Software Development Managers. Lean IT is a set of practices that slims down structures and streamlines processes. Lean philosophy describes the "what" to do to reduce waste, while Agile is a way to eliminate low value-added activities [11, 12].

The following research questions are examined in this article:

RQ1. What is the innovation intensity of CP companies in Europe; RQ2. Whether computer programming firms in Europe are involved in the development of software that is the basis of digital innovations related to Industry 4.0/5.0; RQ3. Whether this type of software is an important part of IT companies' innovation efforts; RQ4. What type of innovation, closed or open, based on collaboration with external partners, is characteristic of CP enterprises; RQ5. Can CP firms be considered as intermediaries in the innovation system; RQ6. What strategic options are chosen by IT firms; RQ7. What is the intensity of wastage in IT firms as measured by the incidence of different sources of wastage; RQ 8. Which strategic options lead to better development prospects for firms. We also test the hypothesis H1. that innovation is a crucial factor that increases the probability of good and very good development prospects of firms, accompanied by specific strategic and lean management. Strategic objectives are often associated with firms' innovative efforts. In an era of hypercompetition, cost efficiency is as important as creating new value for customers. Strategies aimed at swimming in a "blue ocean" without competitors, i.e. aimed at radical innovation, are based not only on adding some new features to products/services, but also on reducing some of the standard features, thus allowing cost optimisation [13]. In IT, lean management is becoming a dominant management concept [3].

In Web of Science from October 2024 we found 4 publications with topic containing words digital innovation or digital transition and lean management and strategic management and software or computer programming. In [14], the authors analyse the changes in the business models of software vendors in the light of the digital transition and the use of cloud computing technology for digital innovation, which changes the business processes of software vendors. Cloud computing has changed the business processes of user companies, but it has also changed the activities of the software industry. In [15], the strategic behaviour and collaboration in digital innovation ecosystems involving digital innovation firms is considered [16]. Lermen et al. [17] analyzed the use of lean management methods by 6 digital startups to deliver value to customers and improve performance. Wolfert et al. [18] showed that the ecosystem perspective is important in digital innovations related to IT solutions for the agri-food industry, as many different stakeholders with different roles are involved in these innovations. Therefore, they designed and tested the concept of a "lean multi-actor approach to testing and case development". Every digital innovation should be designed with the business and technology environment in mind.

We also searched WoS for publications containing the words "success factors" and "software development companies" or "computer programming industry". We found 144 publications in which we also found 46 articles containing the words innovation or digital innovation. Finally, we searched for publications that also contained the words "strategic management" and found 11. We did not find any articles that also included lean management in the topic. Thus, our article fills the gap in analyzing the success factors in software development from the holistic perspective of digital innovation and strategic and lean management.

The conclusions of the most relevant publications on success factors in IT show that the innovative ability of software companies is enhanced by an analytical, future-oriented and proactive innovation strategy. Another critical success factor is customer orientation [19]. In the software industry, new ventures with a formal technology strategy succeed by aligning their technology choices with their business environment [20]. The success of high-tech companies should be measured not only in financial terms, but also in terms of market position and preparation of assets for future development [21]. The success factor for software process improvement is the dynamic learning capacity of the organization [22]. According to Akgün et al. [23], the success factors of software development projects are team efficiency increased by trust among project team members, their experience and team empowerment. Pereira et al. [24] found that the success factors of Brazilian ICT start-ups in terms of revenue and customer base were the use of product development and market interaction methods, the selection of employees based on a model, and the experience of the founders. Gobeli et al. [25] analyzed the specificity of conflict management for the success of software development projects. Negative impact on product success and customer satisfaction had unresolved conflict, while its high intensity decreases organizational and project satisfaction. Positive impact on organizational success had problem-solving confrontation and give-and-take style of conflict management. Negative effects had forcing, smoothing, and withdrawing in case of conflict.

In the article we present the theoretical background for the article based on the literature review, followed by the presentation of data sources and methods, the results section and the conclusions with discussion.

## 2 Literature Review and Theoretical Background

Innovation is a new or significantly improved product or business process, but also social innovation, eco-innovation, systems innovation and public innovation. Innovation is new value that satisfies human needs and, in the case of business, generates revenue. The recent OSLO Handbook on Innovation [4] provides new recommendations for measuring innovation, changing and adapting the definitions to include a broader vision of innovation-generating entities, now including social and public organisations, and emphasising the systemic nature of innovation. However, business innovation remains the basis of innovation systems and the main source of growth of economies.

The reductionist approach to innovation implies closed innovation. In the closed model, innovation is based on human resources, in-house R&D and self-financing by firms aiming to be first to market with new products for which they secure intellectual property rights [26]. In this model, producers view R&D as covering the value chain from design to technology. Thus, in-house R&D substitutes for any potential contribution from users as innovators [27]. The concept of open innovation (OI) relies on extensive collaboration between external entities and the firm, integrating external and internal knowledge [28]. The OI concept implies that both knowledge and skills can be created or used outside the boundaries of the firm. For example, internal research may be complemented by external research. It is not necessary to be the first in R&D in a particular field to achieve positive results. For a company to benefit from open innovation, it must have a business model that integrates external and internal knowledge and thus values collaboration with external partners [28]. The OI concept is based on absorptive capacity, that is, the ability of organisations to recognise the value of external knowledge, assimilate it and use it to create new value [26]. In this article, we examine how closed and open innovation models are related to the innovation intensity and development prospects of CP firms.

The sextuple helix model of the innovation system [29] takes into account the role of intermediary institutions, which has been omitted from previous models of the innovation system (triple [1], quadruple and quintuple helix models [2]). Brokers facilitate the diffusion of knowledge as well as independently generate innovations. Intermediaries and pro-innovation infrastructure facilitate contacts between science and business. These are such organisations as technology transfer centres, technology parks and clusters, as well as knowledge-intensive business services (KIBS)—such as computer programming companies.

The development of the Internet has made it possible to involve users more closely in the innovation process and to create social networks and initiatives. Public administration has started to support and manage the development of innovative systems and is now becoming an active entity inventing new solutions in the field of social and public innovation (participatory budgeting, new solutions in the field of road systems in terms of autonomous vehicles, smart cities, etc.). Environmental organisations and movements are now also agents of innovation systems representing the natural environment [29]. In the most advanced innovation systems, co-creation and interdisciplinary efforts are crucial. The aim is to connect different units of innovation systems so that they develop new solutions to societal challenges. Moreover, current technologies and knowledge are too complex and extensive to be known by individual entities, so networking is often required in innovation processes. The sextuple helix requires appropriate conditions, such as a pool of skills provided by an education and training system, so that society can generate and/or use new solutions. It also relies on funding at the idea stage. In addition, transport and telecommunications infrastructures are important for the exchange of knowledge. Regulations facilitate the implementation of innovative activities. Finally, innovation systems are rooted in a specific culture and history, which influence their development path (Fig. 1). We used this concept of innovation system to indicate varied potential partners of CP firms in innovation processes as well to check their intermediary role in the innovation system.

KIBS are commercial enterprises that operate at the interface between science and industry and can therefore be regarded as knowledge brokers. They are also innovators themselves. Interaction with KIBS is particularly important for companies that develop radical innovations, such as the bundling of services with products [30]. KIBS are often high-tech service providers. They have stronger links to science than traditional sectors, while interaction with KIBS promotes innovation in traditional companies. KIBS are companies that provide services with high intellectual added value, mainly to other companies [31]. The first type of KIBS are traditional professional services that are intensive users of new technologies (marketing, advertising, etc.). The second type is KIBS based on new technologies, such as software and other computer-related activities. KIBS are knowledge-intensive services with a consulting—problem-solving function that is highly interactive and individualised for the client.

The relevance of KIBS for the innovation system is twofold: directly, through the innovativeness of KIBS as a provider of new knowledge, and indirectly, through the impact on the innovativeness of customer companies [31–33]. For example, CP firms become more innovative through the implementation of digital technologies, such as cloud computing, and their innovation also includes the development of software for these digital solutions, which are later implemented as digital innovations by their customers.

The latest changes in industry and the economy as a whole are linked to digital transformation. The terms used are Industry 4.0 or 5.0. However, these changes are driven by computer programming companies that respond to their customers' needs by developing software that supports digital transformation. This software and the innovations resulting from its use can be called digital innovations. In the era of Industry 4.0, digitalisation encompasses a wide range of data operations, digital interfaces, automation and connectivity [34, 35]. Firms' growth and innovation increasingly depend on their ability to analyse large amounts of data from systems, business processes and products in real time. Methods for analysing big data sets turn the collected data into information for decision making.

Cloud computing is the use of shared IT resources made available over the Internet. In virtual reality (VR), users are transported into a virtual world, usually with a set of headsets and goggles, while in augmented reality (AR) applications show the illusion of layers of graphical information superimposed on a particular part of the user's field of view. The combination of both technologies is mixed reality. In smart factories, cyber-physical systems monitor physical processes, create a virtual copy of the physical world and make decisions. Based on the Internet of Things, cyber-physical systems communicate and cooperate with each other and with humans in real time [36]. The Internet of Things is the direct communication between machines and things. Industry 4.0 is also about the extensive use of artificial intelligence, and therefore robots. Examples include autonomous vehicles and drones. The data and information shared as part of Industry 4.0 solutions must be protected by cybersecurity solutions. Blockchain technology is a new business-to-business settlement system and proof of identity. New digital solutions are based on wireless connectivity and sensors [3]. Quantum computers currently exist as experimental models, but business applications are being developed. They are based on the principles of quantum physics for information processing, enabling much faster performance than conventional computers [30].

Businesses must digitise to remain competitive. Sustainability requirements to reduce waste and pollution are also driving the development of new digital technologies. The fourth revolution is related to mobile technology, machine learning and artificial intelligence. It is characterised by widespread access to the internet, a decrease in the cost of digital storage, portable devices, smart sensors, the use of renewable energy sources and artificial intelligence [37, 38]. The Fifth Industrial Revolution is about the combination of humans and machines. It also emphasises clean industrial technologies that promote sustainability and conserve natural resources [39, 40].

Innovation is not only technological development driven by competition, but also a range of strategic options that enable a firm to maintain and develop a particular form of production [41]. Entrepreneurial strategies are those that enable people to be innovative, creative and accountable for their decisions. Therefore, the diffusion of strategic capabilities throughout the firm and the empowerment of individuals to actively participate in the strategic management process are critical to the development and implementation of strategies [42]. Innovating actors engage in discursive strategies to create and manipulate the meaning of modern technologies, products and services. In doing so, they seek to change formal and informal institutional environments such as norms, practices, knowledge and relationships [43].

Strategic intelligence [44] relates to top management, teams and the organisation. Organisations with different levels of strategic intelligence can be identified by the impact of their strategic behaviour in a particular business ecosystem. Strategic behaviour is the result of strategic decisions made by members. Strategic thinking is a dynamic process that continuously influences mission, strategy and operations in relation to customer and market needs [45]. Strategic thinking needs to be integrated with the context of action [46]. In the research, we asked the computer programming companies whether their strategy takes different forms, from more formalised to more informal and emergent. We examined which forms of strategic behaviour, in addition to innovativeness, are associated with better development prospects for firms.

Johnson & Mulder [47] show that Flow-like micro-projects based on Lean IT principles have the highest success rate - 71%. Flow modernization reduces decision latency because it is based on self-directed teams that can make their own decisions. Infinite Flow" software development increases customer satisfaction. Flow-like projects generate higher net value because improved software functionality is delivered quickly in small chunks. Infinite Flow reduces overhead costs to 20%, compared to 80% in waterfall projects and 52% in agile projects [47]. There are no budgets or project plans in Infinite Flow. There is a budget for direct software development costs. There are also costs for managing the pipeline of activities, but with greatly reduced project overhead. This is achieved by reducing and eliminating most of the current project management activities. Changes to the project occur continuously, but in small steps that are useful and more acceptable to the users. It means a very "lean" implementation of software development projects with the elimination of non-value adding activities [3, 47].

The Toyota Production System (TPS) originally defined the following types of wastage: overproduction, waiting, transport and movement, extra processing, inventory, defects, wasted talent [48, 49]. In the context of software development projects, losses include extra features, delays and waiting, hand-offs and partially done work, defects and failures, context and task switching, unnecessary movement, extra processes, and unused employee creativity [50, 51]. Lean principles relevant to software development are such as wastage elimination, built-in quality, knowledge creation, addressing bottlenecks, proper reward system, continuous improvement in the form of kaizen, pull instead of push system, use of kanban boards, work in progress control, value stream mapping, using fast feedback loops, understanding the behavior of queues, decentralized control, exploiting variability, reducing batch size, making process rules explicit, using models to identify improvement opportunities [51, 52].

## 3 Data and Methods

In December 2023–January 2024 we sent an online questionnaire to about 20 thousand computer programming firms in Europe and received 142 responses. We sent the survey to all computer programming companies registered in the Orbis database[1] that have an e-mail address. The questionnaires were sent by the IT Centre of the University of Gdansk. Questionnaires were sent to companies in both English and the native language. Questionnaires were sent to Polish companies in Polish only. We received responses from Poland, Estonia, Hungary, Lithuania, Bulgaria, Slovenia, Slovakia, Romania and the Czech Republic, which we define as Central and Eastern European (CEE) countries. From the Western European (WE) countries, we received responses from Portugal, Finland, Germany, the United Kingdom and Norway. The highest number of responses came from Poland - 40, followed by Portugal - 20, Finland - 20 and Germany - 17. Of the respondents, 115 were CEOs or directors or owners, while the rest were IT project managers or IT specialists. Low response rate causes that the results may be treated only as opinnions of the respondents about their organisations and we cannot generalize them to the whole CP industry in Europe. Moreover Polish companies are overrepresented.

In the survey we asked respondents about the perceived innovation level: the percentage of software development projects that are innovative in nature (development of software that is significantly different from existing software on the market or significant changes to your own software).

We also asked whether the software developed by the firms is related to the following areas: virtual/augmented reality, blockchain and/or cybersecurity, autonomous vehicles and drones, smart factories, reduction of environmental impact, wireless communication, quantum computers and big data or cloud computing. In this article, we analyse whether the CP companies surveyed are developing software related to the digital transformation of industry and the economy. We took into account both relatively widely used technologies as Wireless communications as well as emerging such as Quantum computers. We believe the latter could be the source of a new industrial revolution. We wanted to check which of the digital technologies are the subjects of CP firms' software development projects.

We then aksed with which partners from the six helixes of the innovation system the respondents cooperate. We asked precisely about cooperation with (1) Firms: a. customers multinational corporations, other customers, b. technology suppliers, c. competitors: other IT companies, d. companies from other industries other than customers; (2) Administration, (3) Academia: a. universities, b. individual experts from science or outside science, (4) Society: non-governmental organizations, (5) Intermediaries: a. KIBS—consulting firms, b.organizations such as technology transfer centers, clusters, technology parks; (6) Other... We also asked about closed innovation. The responets could choose the option "We do not cooperate, we implement them internally".

The respondents answered also how the company's strategy is created and implemented. We analysed the following options: strategy as a formalised action plan, strategic goals and measures of success are formulated only by the CEO of the company, strategic plans are strictly implemented in business practice, the path of

[1] https://login.bvdinfo.com/R0/Orbis

implementation of the strategy is defined only piecemeal, the strategy is a market improvisation, the strategy is formed in the course of operations in the market, the strategy is oriented towards the exploitation of emerging opportunities.

In the questionnaire we also asked about the causes of wastage in companies such as poor communication within the project team, poorly diagnosed customer requirements, overly ambitious schedule, execution of several projects simultaneously, poor distribution of tasks among project team members, lack of effective monitoring and control, overly ambitious customer requirements, excessive tasks of the project manager, too small project budget, insufficient staff qualifications and use of outdated technology. We also asked about development prospects of the companies.

We conducted a statistical analysis of the significance of the differences in the proportions. We used the two-sample test for large samples, depending on the proportion and size of the population in question. In addition, the two-sample z-test for significance of differences in means was performed based on population size and standard deviation [53]. We also estimated logistic regressions to assess whether the development of digital innovation software by enterprises increases the probability of high innovation activity of companies. We also tested whether collaboration in the innovation process increased the odds of high innovation. We also estimated whether innovation and its specific type and form of strategic management, as well as waste, affect the development prospects of firms. Logistic regressions are used to determine which factors increase the likelihood that an explained variable has a certain character. They determine the probability that the explained variable will be 1 or 0, given the parameters and values of the explanatory variables. An odds ratio was calculated to indicate how much more likely it is that a company with a given characteristic will excel in innovation and stand out in terms of development prospects [54].

We also used a path model, which can capture direct and indirect relationships. In a path model, variables are placed in the model once as explained variables by other variables and a second time as explanatory variables, depending on the concept of the relationships. The result is a set of paths that illustrate the relationships between variables [31].

## 4 Results

Most of the CP companies surveyed reported that more than 50% of their software development projects are innovative, that is, the software developed is significantly different from existing software on the market or significantly different from the company's own software (42.3%). One in four companies had a share of innovative projects of 31–50% and around 22% of companies had a share of 11–30%. Only about 11% of the enterprises had less than 10% innovative projects. The only significant difference was found between enterprises from CEE and WE, namely a higher share of enterprises with a share of innovative projects in the 11–30% range

**Table 1** Percentage of innovative software development projects versus type of innovation, good development prospects, company's location and size

| | Share of innovative software | | | | |
|---|---|---|---|---|---|
| Dimension | More than 50% | 31–50% | 11–30% | Less than 10% | n |
| **The whole sample** | 42.3% | 24.6% | 21.8% | 11.3% | 142 |
| **Intensity versus type of innovation and development prospects** | | | | | |
| **Closed innovation** | *3%* | 12%** | 13%** | 6% | (11) |
| **The average number of different types of innovation partners—Open innovation** | *2.5* | 2.4 | 2* | 1.5* | 2.3 |
| **Good & vg prospects** | *65%* | 56% | 42%** | 38%** | (78) |
| **Differences between firms in CEE and WE countries in innovation intensity** | | | | | |
| **CEE** | 38.9% | 25% | 27.8%** | 9.7% | 72 |
| **WE** | 45.7% | 24.3% | *15.7%* | 12.9% | 70 |
| **Differences between size classes in innovation intensity** | | | | | |
| **Micro** | 46.7%* | 24.4% | 17.8% | 11.1% | 45 |
| **Small** | 46.6%* | *17.2%* | 20.7% | 15.5%* | 58 |
| **Medium and large** | *31.6%* | 34.2%** | 28.9% | *5.3%* | 38 |
| **n** | 60 | 34 | 31 | 16 | |

Note: n in brackets given for information issues, not used for calculations; ** statistically significant on 0.05 level, * statistically significant on 0.1 level, the statistically significant difference of values in the subgroups of a given variable to the value/s of the subgroup in italics. Source: authors calculations in Stata based on the research

in CEE. Among the size classes, micro (up to 9 employees) and small enterprises (10–49 employees) had a higher share of companies with more than 50% innovative projects than enterprises with more than 49 persons employed (medium and large). However, the latter had more enterprises with innovative projects in the 31–50% range. Small enterprises were more likely to have less than 10% innovative projects than the largest enterprises (Table 1).

Comparing the types of innovation: closed versus open and the share of innovative projects, only 1 enterprise among the most innovative enterprises did not cooperate with external partners but carried out innovative projects internally. Among the medium innovators, significantly more companies relied on closed innovation. We calculated the average number of the types of partners that the enterprises involved in their innovative projects. Firms with a share of innovative projects above 30% had a significantly higher average number of the types partners than those with a lower level of innovativeness. This means that high innovativeness requires open innovation.

Collaboration with other companies was the strongest: with customers (especially multinationals) and other IT companies as well as technology suppliers and other companies. Another important partner for CP companies is academia: universities and individual experts from academia. This confirms the intermediary role of IT between business and science in the innovation system. Other intermediaries, that is consulting firms and innovation infrastructure, were the third according to intensity of cooperation type of innovation partner for the enterprises surveyed. The fourth-ranked type of partner was administration and non-governmental organisations.

Good and very good development prospects were reported significantly more often by enterprises with more than 50% of innovative software development projects than by those with less than 30% of innovative projects in their project portfolio.

Although management support software is still the main type of software developed by enterprises, software supporting digital transformation, that is, digital innovation, is also the area of activity of CP enterprises in Europe (Table 2). CP companies are mainly concerned with big data or cloud computing and software to reduce environmental impact. Several percent of firms develop software related to smart factories, virtual/augmented reality, and blockchain and/or cybersecurity, as well as software for wireless communications. Few companies are working on autonomous vehicles and drones, as well as quantum computing. Among the enterprises that reported the highest share of innovative projects, the share of enterprises dealing with virtual/augmented reality and management support software was higher than in the whole sample. A higher proportion of enterprises in CEE than in WE were involved in the development of management support software and big data or cloud computing. Only in the WE were there enterprises developing software related to quantum computing, and these were only micro-enterprises. More enterprises in WE than in CEE were involved in projects related to smart factories and autonomous vehicles and drones. A significantly smaller proportion of small than micro enterprises were involved in virtual/augmented reality and smart factories.

Specific types of software developed by the enterprises surveyed are, according to the respondents, related to areas such as artificial intelligence, FinTech, EdTech, Internet applications, green energy, paperless, process automation, WAN network acceleration, medical laboratories and psychological and innovation IT systems.

Table 3 shows the strategic options used by the companies surveyed. Intended strategy is represented by the options: strategy as a formalized plan of action and strict implementation of strategic plans in business practice. The emergent strategy is represented by the option "strategy is oriented to the use of emerging opportunities". Centralization of strategy means that "strategic goals and measures of success are formulated only by the CEO of the company". The low intensity of any strategic planning and the dominance of behavioral strategy are reflected in the options: "the path of implementation of the strategy is only partially defined" and "the strategy is a market improvisation". Strategic behavior without strategic planning and mostly reactive, not proactive market behavior means that "the strategy is formed in the course of operations on the market". Overall, emergent and behavioral strategy dominates in IT. However, the real strategy is often a mixture of emergent and intended strategy, as quite often respondents indicated having a formalized plan. But market improvisation is also popular among IT companies, as is centralizing goal setting at the CEO level. In the CEE countries, IT companies were more likely to report an emergent strategy rather than an

**Table 2** Type of software versus innovation, prospects, location and size

| Dimansion | Software, innovation, prospects | | | Location | | Size | | |
|---|---|---|---|---|---|---|---|---|
| Type of software | Europe | Over 50% innov | Good & vg prospects | CEE | WE | Micro | Small | Medium and Large |
| **Virtual/augmented reality** | *13.8%* | 21.7%* | 14.1% | 15.5% | 11.9% | 19.1%* | *8.8%* | 15.8% |
| **Blockchain and/or cybersecurity** | *13.8%* | 16.7% | 11.5% | 15.5% | 11.9% | 11.9% | 17.5% | 7.9% |
| **Autonomous vehicles and drones** | *5.8%* | 8.3% | 9% | *2.8%* | 9%* | 7.14% | 5.3% | 5.3% |
| **Smart factories** | *14.5%* | 18.3% | 15.4% | *8.5%* | 20.9%** | 19.1%* | *8.8%* | 18.4% |
| **Reducing environmental impact** | *18.1%* | 21.7% | 19.2% | 14.1% | 22.4% | 16.7% | 19.3% | 18.4% |
| **Wireless communications** | *12.3%* | 15% | 14.1% | 11.3% | 13.4% | 9.52% | 17.5% | 7.9% |
| **Quantum computers** | *2.2%* | 1.7% | 2.6% | *0%* | 4.5%** | 7.1%** | *0%* | *0%* |
| **Big data or cloud computing** | *34.1%* | 33.3% | 38.5% | 42.3%** | *25.4%* | 28.6% | 33.3% | 42.1% |
| **Management support software** | *60.1%* | 53.3%** | 60.3% | 73.2%*** | *46.3%* | 52.4% | 63.2% | 65.8% |
| **n** | 138 | 60 | 78 | 71 | 67 | 42 | 57 | 38 |

Note: *** statistically significant on 0.01 level, ** statistically significant on 0.05 level, * statistically significant on 0.1 level, difference to the value in italics.
Source: authors calculations in Stata based on the research

**Table 3** Strategy options used by IT companies

| Category | Europe | CEE | WE | Micro | Small | Medium and Large |
|---|---|---|---|---|---|---|
| **As a formalized plan of action** | 21,2% | *23,6%* | 18,5% | 14,3%*** | 15,5%*** | *37,8%* |
| **Strategic plans are strictly implemented in business practice** | 16,1% | *18,1%* | 13,8% | 9,5%** | 12,1%** | *29,7%* |
| **The path of implementation of the strategy is defined only partially** | 14,6% | *12,5%* | 16,9% | 14,3% | 17,2% | *10,8%* |
| **The strategy is a market improvisation** | 21,9% | *26,4%* | 16,9%* | 21,4% | 24,1% | *18,9%* |
| **The strategy is formed in the course of operation on the market** | 37,2% | *50,0%* | 23,1%*** | 31,0%* | *44,8%* | 32,4% |
| **Strategy is oriented to the use of emerging opportunities** | 29,9% | *43,1%* | 15,4%*** | 14,3%** | *41,4%* | 29,7% |
| **Strategic goals and measures of success are formulated only by the CEO of the company** | 20,4% | *26,4%* | 13,8%** | 21,4% | 15,5%* | *27,0%* |
| n | 137 | 72 | 65 | 42 | 58 | 37 |

Note: *** statistically significant on 0.01 level, ** statistically significant on 0.05 level, * statistically significant on 0.1 level, difference to the value in italics.
Source: authors based on the research results

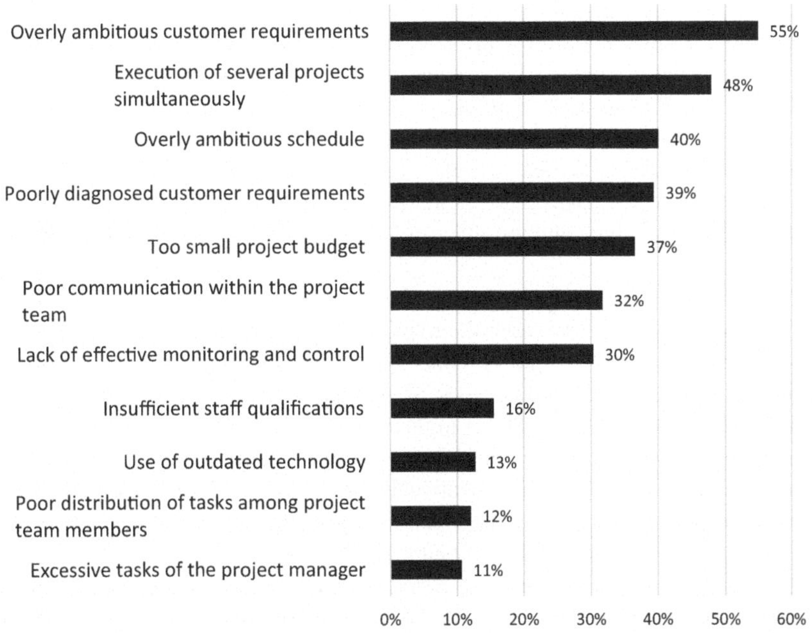


**Fig. 2** The main causes of wastege in the implementation of software development projects in the company

intended strategy, strategic behavior rather than strategic planning, and centralized strategic goal setting. Medium and large companies more often have an intended strategy accompanied by emergent strategy and strictly implement the plans. Micro companies are the least likely to have any kind of strategic management, either intended or emergent, and the strategic goals are mainly set by the CEO. In the case of small companies, strategic goals are less often set by the CEO than in the case of medium and large companies. Especially in the case of small companies, only emergent strategy and strategic behavior dominate (strategy formed during market operation and oriented towards emerging opportunities).

The main causes of wastage in software development projects are overly ambitious customer requirements and running multiple projects at the same time (Fig. 2). Other important causes are an overly ambitious schedule, poorly diagnosed customer requirements, too small a project budget, poor communication within the project team, and a lack of effective monitoring and control. The least important causes are excessive responsibilities of the project manager, poor distribution of tasks among project team members, inadequate staff skills, and the use of outdated technology.

Other problems identified by companies were mainly related to customer issues, such as "problems caused by missing or changed customer data, insufficient customer involvement despite requests, immaturity and over-ambitiousness of customer representatives, inability of customer representatives to make decisions, excessive time spent on customer-side approvals, inability of customer representatives to formulate project objectives, lack of customer-side knowledge of their own processes". Imprecise business requirements and too many changes to specifications were also mentioned. Sub-optimal team size is also a cause. As one respondent noted, "Sometimes a larger team is organized to get the project done faster, which is not effective because it takes much more time to organize the work than in a smaller team. Micromanagement and too little automation were also identified as causes of waste [12].

Logistic regression analysis showed that only the development of virtual/augmented reality software increased the likelihood of companies reporting more than 50% innovative projects (Table 4). Other types of technology were not significant. In another model, we included types of partners that in other estimations have been found to increase the odds of high innovativeness, that is, cooperation with universities and customers, as well as the size variable. The results show that there is an increased likelihood of high innovativeness in the case of firms engaged in V/AR, cooperation with universities and cooperation with customers. Being a medium or large firm reduces the probability of being highly innovative.

In another set of estimations, we tested for factors that increase the likelihood of very good and good prospects of the firms reported by the respondents. We created an interaction variable to show firms with the highest innovativeness and the number of innovation partners to reflect the open innovation method used by firms. We also introduced a variable reflecting the number of sources of wastege in the firm. We also looked at which types of strategic thinking and management correlate with good prospects for companies. Only the option that reflected consistent implementation of strategic plans increased the chances of an optimistic outlook. The more formal or emergent type of strategy was not important. However, the completely unplanned behavior, in which the strategy is formed in the course of operating on the market, as a reaction to market forces, had a negative impact on the chances of prosperous development in the future. Finally, we estimated a model that showed that both closed and open innovation increase the likelihood of an optimistic outlook. Consistency in implementing strategic plans in business practice was also a success factor for the IT companies surveyed (Fig. 3).

The likelihood of declaring good and very good prospects decreased in the case of strategy formed during market operations and a higher number of causes of waste identified in the organisation (Table 4). Innovation is therefore a success factor for CP companies, as is appropriate strategic management in the form of real implementation of the strategic plan. Furthermore, the elimination of wastage should also lead to better prospects, as more sources of wastage in companies reduce the chances of good development. The numerous regressions carried out in the analysis of the survey data, in addition to the four presented in Table 4, showed an indirect relationship between the type of digital innovation developed and cooperation with external partners and the development prospects of the companies (Fig. 2).

**Table 4** Estimations of logistic regressions

| Explained variables | Over 50% innovative projects | | Very good and good prospects | |
|---|---|---|---|---|
| **Explaining variables** | Odds ratio(z-statistic) | | | |
| **Virtual/augmented reality** | 3.2 (2.10**) | 3.2 (2.02**) | . | . |
| **Blockchain and/or cybersecurity** | . | 1.5 (0.79) | . | . |
| **Autonomous vehicles and drones** | . | 1.2 (0.24) | . | . |
| **Smart factories** | . | 1.5 (0.82) | . | . |
| **Reducing environmental impact** | . | 1.4 (0.75) | . | . |
| **Quantum computers** | . | 0.28 (−0.88) | . | . |
| **Big data or cloud computing** | . | 0.9 (−0.26) | . | . |
| **Management support software** | . | 0.66 (−1.11) | . | . |
| **Cooperation with universities** | 2.4 (2.06**) | . | . | . |
| **Cooperation with customers** | 2.2 (2.17**) | . | . | . |
| **Over 49 employees** | 0.38 (−2.15**) | . | . | . |
| **Number of waste causes** | . | . | 0.77(−2.24**) | . |
| **Number of innovation partners and over 50% innovative software (interaction)** | . | . | 1.3(2.14**) | . |
| **Closed innovation—No partners** | . | . | 15.05 (2.42**) | . |
| **Strategy as a formalized action plan** | . | . | | 1.28 (0.53) |
| **Strategic plans are strictly implemented in business practice** | . | . | 3.82 (2.31**) | 3.35 (2.1**) |
| **The path of implementation of the strategy is defined only partially** | . | . | . | 1.34 (0.56) |
| **The strategy is a market improvisation** | . | . | . | 1.09 (0.19) |
| **The strategy is formed in the course of operation in the market** | . | . | 0.35(−2.54**) | 0.44 (−2.01**) |
| **The strategy is oriented to the use of emerging opportunities** | . | . | . | 1.09 (0.22) |
| **Strategic goals and measures of success are formulated only by the company's CEO** | . | . | . | 1.12(0.26) |
| **Constant** | 0.4 (−2.92***) | 0.68 (−1.17) | 2.4(1.8*) | 1.24(0.77) |
| **Pseudo $R^2$** | 0.09 | 0.06 | 0.14 | 0.06 |
| **n** | 138 | 138 | 137 | 137 |

Note: in brackets value of z statistic Chi-square Pearson test, ***—statistically significant on 0.01 level, ** statistically significant on 0.05 level, * statistically significant on 0.1 level. Source: authors calculations based on the research

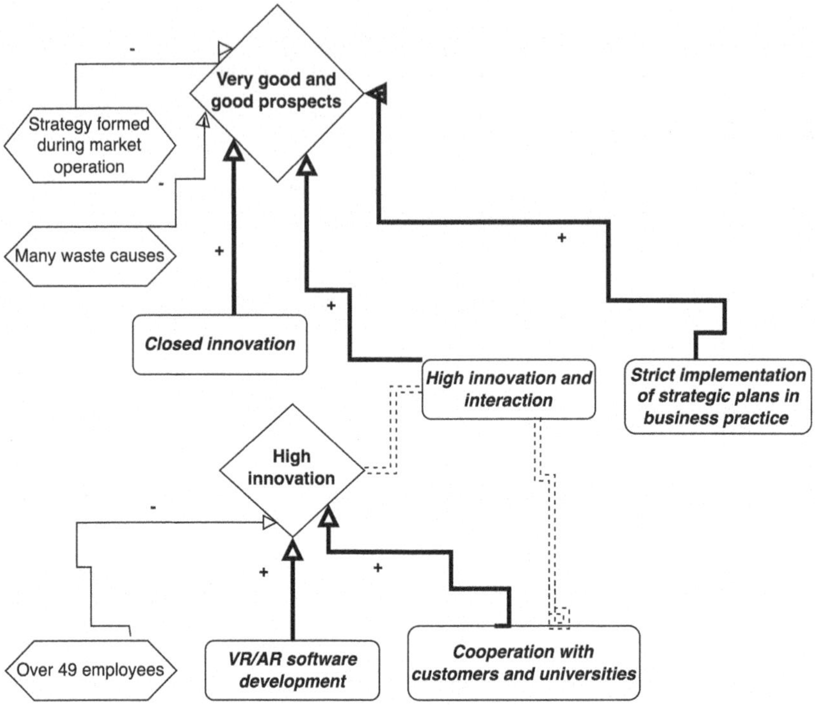


**Fig. 3** The path of the success factors for the companies surveyed. Note: (+)—positive impact, (−)—negative impact

The development of V/AR software and cooperation with universities and customers were significant for high innovation intensity in CP enterprises, but insignificant as explanatory variables for good development prospects. However, high innovation intensity, especially when accompanied by a higher number of the types of innovation partners (out of customers, suppliers, universities, experts, consultancies, administration, innovation infrastructure such as technology parks) was crucial for good development prospects of the firms. We can conclude that the involvement of CP firms in the development of digital technologies indirectly, through high innovativeness, increases the chances of a prosperous development of the firms. However, high innovativeness requires innovation partners, especially customers and academia.

## 5 Conlusions and Discussion

Computer programming companies are high-tech business services that play a crucial intermediary role in innovation systems. This role of software development companies has been confirmed in our research on European enterprises (RQ5). CP companies are highly innovative. None of the respondents reported that their projects were not innovative (RQ1). The software developed by the surveyed firms is often connected with digital innovation, especially big data and cloud computing, software that reduces environmental impact, virtual and augmented reality, and blockchain and cybersecurity (RQ2). However, only software related to VR/AR increased the likelihood of high innovativeness for CP firms (RQ3). The main innovation partners of the surveyed enterprises are customers, mainly multinational organisations, as well as universities and individual researchers. Both closed and open innovation models have been successful for CP companies. However, external partners are crucial for the highest levels of innovation (RQ4).

High innovativeness combined with consistent strategic management and proper lean management further increased the likelihood of firms having an optimistic outlook (H1). Many sources of wastage in firms, such as poor communication in a project team, multi-tasking, insufficient monitoring in an organization, reduced the chances of success for the CP firms surveyed. The strategic management options positively correlated with the very good and good prospects of companies were strict implementation of strategic goals, which means that some formal or more emergent strategic planning must be present in IT organizations. On the contrary, a reactive strategy formed during operation in the market was unsuccessful in terms of the companies' prospects for further development (RQ8). However, IT companies often form strategy in the course of market operations. In addition, their strategy is often oriented towards the exploitation of emerging opportunities (RQ6). Intended strategy in the form of a formalized plan is less popular than emergent strategy or just strategic behavior. The most important causes of wastage in software development projects, according to about every second IT respondent, are overly ambitious customer requirements and the execution of several projects at the same time (RQ7).

The intermediary role of CP firms in the innovation system means that when they develop innovative software, they do so mostly for their customers who want to increase their innovativeness. In order to be successful in this, CP companies often establish links with academia. Currently, digital innovation is a critical type of innovation leading to the digital transformation of organisations and the economy.

The types of digital innovations developed and, in particular, the growth prospects of the companies surveyed are largely similar in CEE and WE. Some differences were observed in the shares of enterprises with innovative projects of 11–30%, which were higher in CEE. In CEE, relatively more CP companies are involved in big data or cloud computing and developing management support software. Firms in WE develop more advanced software related to smart factories, autonomous vehicles and drones, and quantum computers. Smaller companies in CP are more likely to report more than 50% of their projects as being related to the development of innovative software. Microenterprises stand out mainly in terms of software development related to VR/AR, smart factories and quantum computers.

Our respondents were primarily chief executives, directors and owners of the companies. Therefore, their opinions can be seen as related to the perspective of the whole organisation. However the limitation of the research is the low response rate. The results may be attributed only to the respondents' companies.

Further research on success factors and innovation in IT could include types of innovation other than the digital innovations identified in the research as increasing the efficiency of the intermediary role of CP firms in innovation systems. Perhaps a stronger promotion of innovation networks and innovation infrastructure among CP firms would increase their intermediary role in the innovation process. To some extent this role is visible in the strong involvement of the IT sector in regional innovation strategies in Europe, mostly as a horizontal smart specialisation providing key enabling technologies for other sectors of the economy. As intermediaries in the innovation system, CP companies also need methods to diagnose the digital transition needs of their customers. Such methods would also help to reduce waste in IT projects. In addition, some sort of strategic planning should be present in CP firms, especially in the form of formulating strategic plans that would later be rigorously implemented.

## References


1. Leydesdorff, L., & Zawdie, G. (2010). The triple helix perspective of innovation systems. *Technology Analysis & Strategic Management., 22*(7).
2. Carayannis, E. G., Barth, T. D., & Campbell, D. F. (2012). The quintuple helix innovation model: global warming as a challenge and driver for innovation. *Innovation Entrepreneur, 1*(2).
3. Sycz, P. (2023). *Methodology for reducing waste in IT projects (in Polish)*. Doctoral dissertation. University of Gdansk.
4. OSLO Manual. (2018). *OECD & Eurostat*.
5. Lamperti, S., Cavallo, A., & Sassanelli, C. (2024). Digital servitization and business model innovation in smes: A model to escape from market disruption. *IEEE Transactions on Engineering Management., 71*.
6. Seeger, S., Hurley, B., & Bhat, R. (2020). *Innovation in Europe. A deloitte survey on european companies and how digital technologies can strategically enhance innovation*. Deloitte. Insights.
7. Mintzberg, H. (1983). *Power in and around organizations*. Prentice-Hall.
8. Piórkowska, K. (2016). Behavioural strategy: Adaptability context. *Management, 20*(1), 256–276. https://doi.org/10.1515/manment-2015-0038
9. Womack, J. P., Jones, D. T., & Roos, D. (2008). *Maszyna, która zmieniła świat*. ProdPress.
10. Liker, J. K. (2004). *The heart of the Toyota Production System: Eliminating waste, [w:] The Toyota Way: 14 Management Principles from the World's Greatest Manufacturer*. McGraw-Hill.
11. Jorge, G. F. (2017). Continuous improvement and waste reduction for leaner it organizations—an introduction to lean IT project management development–practice and perspectives. In *Sixth International Scientific Conference on Project Management in the Baltic Countries*.
12. Sycz, P., & Wojnicka-Sycz, E. (2024). Wastage and its elimination in software development projects in Europe in the context of lean IT. In B. Marcinkowski, A. Przybylek, A. Jarzębowicz, N. Iivari, E. Insfran, M. Lang, H. Linger, & C. Schneider (Eds.), *Harnessing opportunities: Reshaping ISD in the post-COVID-19 and generative AI Era (ISD2024 proceedings)*. University of Gdańsk. https://doi.org/10.62036/ISD.2024.123
13. Chan, K. W., & Mauborgne, R. A. (2005). *Blue Ocean Strategy*. Harvard Business Review Press.
14. Schneckenberg, D., Benitez, J., Klos, C., Velamuri, V. K., & Spieth, P. (2021). Value creation and appropriation of software vendors: A digital innovation model for cloud computing. *Information & Management., 58*(4).

15. Chen, D., Fu, M., & Wang, L. (2024). Study on the symbiosis evolution mechanism of the digital innovation ecosystem: Considering government regulation. *Kybernetes*.
16. Wojnicka-Sycz, E., Rybicki, J., & Sycz, P. (2024). Innovation as a success factor in IT–The role of software supporting digital transition. In B. Marcinkowski, A. Przybylek, A. Jarzębowicz, N. Iivari, E. Insfran, M. Lang, H. Linger, & C. Schneider (Eds.), *Harnessing opportunities: Reshaping ISD in the post-COVID-19 and generative AI Era (ISD2024 proceedings)*. University of Gdańsk. https://doi.org/10.62036/ISD.2024.68
17. Lermen, F. H., de Moura, P. K., Bertoni, V. B., Graciano, P., & Tortorella, G. L. (2023). Does maturity level influence the use of agile UX methods by digital startups? evaluating design thinking, Lean Startup, and Lean User experience. *Information and Software Technology., 154*, 107107.
18. Wolfert, S., Verdouw, C., van Wassenaer, L., Dolfsma, W., & Klerkx, L. (2023). Digital innovation ecosystems in agri-food: Design principles and organizational framework. *Agricultural Systems., 204*, 103558.
19. Sarja, J. (2018). Success factors of Radical Breakthgrough ICT projects—comparison of hardware and software cases. *International Journal of Innovation., 6*, 40–53.
20. Zahra, S. A., & Bogner, W. C. (2000). Technology strategy and software new ventures' performance. *Journal of Business Venturing., 15*, 135–173.
21. Dvir, D. (1990). Success factors of high-tech sbus: Towards a conceptual model based on the Israeli electronics and computers industry. *Journal of Product Innovation Management., 7*, 288–296.
22. Lee, J.-C., & Chen, C.-Y. (2019). The moderator of innovation culture and the mediator of realized absorptive capacity in enhancing organizations' absorptive capacity for SPI Success. *Journal of Global Information Management., 27*, 70–90.
23. Akgün, A. E., Keskin, H., Byrne, J., & Imamoglu, S. Z. (2007). Antecedents and consequences of team potency in software development projects. *Information & Management., 44*, 646–656.
24. de Souza Pereira, J. H., Lopes, J. E., & Porto, G. S. (2018). *Success factors to improve the life cycle of information and communication technology start-ups in Brazil*. 2018 Portland International Conference on Management of Engineering and Technology (PICMET). 1–9.
25. Gobeli, D. H., Koenig, H. F., & Bechinger, I. (1998). Managing conflict in software development teams: A multilevel analysis. *Journal of Product Innovation Management., 15*, 423–435.
26. Lopes, A. P. V. B. V., & de Carvalho, M. M. (2018). Evolution of the open innovation paradigm: Towards a contingent conceptual model. *Technological Forecasting and Social Change., 132*.
27. Gambardella, A., Raasch, C., & von Hippel, E. (2016). The user innovation paradigm: Impacts on markets and welfare. *Management Science., 63*(5).
28. Chesbrough, H. W. (2003). The era of open innovation. *MIT Sloan Management Review., 44*(3).
29. Wojnicka-Sycz, E., & Sycz, P. (2023). Innovative Ecosystem Based on a Sextuple Helix on the Example of the Podkarpackie Voivodeship (in Polish). *Journal of Modern Science, 52*(3), 172–189. after Wojnicka-Sycz, E., Piróg, K., Sycz, P. & Mularz K. (2023). Good practices in strengthening stakeholder engagement in regional innovation systems (in Polish). Marshall Office of Podkarpackie Voivodeship. Rzeszów.
30. Bustinza, O. F., Gomes, E., Vendrell-Herrero, F., & Baines, T. (2019). Product-service innovation and performance: The role of partnerships and R&D intensity, R&D. *Management., 49*(1).
31. Muller, E., & Zenker, A. (2000). Knowledge-intensive business services (KIBS) and regional innovation capacities. In E. Muller, A. Zenker, & F. Meyer-Krahmer (Eds.), *Technology and infrastructures policy in the knowledge-based economy. The impact of the tendency towards codification of knowledge*.
32. Miles, I., Kastrinos, N., Bilderbreek, R., & den Hertog, P. (1994). Knowledge-intensive business services. Users, carriers and sources of innovation. In *EIMS No 15*. European Commission.
33. Wojnicka, E. (2004). Poland's innovation system from the perspective of enterprises (in Polish),

34. Abdelkader, A., Camille, S., & Gianluigi, V. (2016). Innovation capacity and the role of information systems: A qualitative study. *Journal of Management Analytics., 3*, 4.
35. Sehlin, D., Truedsson, M., & Cronemyr, P. (2019). A conceptual cooperative model designed for processes, digitalization and innovation. *International Journal of Quality and Service Sciences, 11*.
36. Bongomin, O., Gilibrays, G., Oyondi, N. E., Musinguzi, A., & Omara, T. (2020). Exponential disruptive technologies and the required skills of industry 4.0. *Journal of Engineering, 1*.
37. Walentynowicz, P. (2020). Industry 4.0 and innovation in organizations. Do industry 4.0 solutions foster organizational innovation? (in Polish). In Z. Malara & M. Rutkowska (Eds.), *Innovation in the Era of IT: Areas, concept, tools* (pp. 265–274). Publishing House of Wroclaw University of Technology.
38. Sycz, P., & Wojnicka-Sycz, E. (2023). *Significance of digital innovations of industry 4.0. for Polish enterprises on the example of podkarpackie and lubuskie voivodeships* (Vol. 182). Scientific Papers of Silesian University of Technology. Organization and Management Series.
39. Wang, B., Zhou, H., Li, X., Yang, G., Zheng, P., Song, C., Yuan, Y., Wuest, T., Yang, H., & Wang, L. (2024). Human digital twin in the context of industry 5.0. *Robotics and Computer-Integrated Manufacturing., 85. February*.
40. Ruiz-de-la-Torre, A., Rio-Belver, R. M., Guevara-Ramirez, W., & Merlo, C. (2023). Industry 5.0 and human-centered approach. A bibliometric review. In F. P. García Márquez, I. Segovia Ramírez, P. J. Bernalte Sánchez, & A. Muñoz del Río (Eds.), *IoT and data science in engineering management. CIO 2022 lecture notes on data engineering and communications technologies. 160*. Springer.
41. Walsh, S. (2021). Subsumption and the critique of innovation. *Organization., 1*(16).
42. Nambisan, S., & Baron, R. A. (2013). Entrepreneurship in innovation ecosystems: Entrepreneurs' self-regulatory processes and their implications for new venture success. *Entrepreneurship Theory and Practice., 37*(5).
43. Purtik, H., & Arenas, D. (2019). Embedding social innovation: Shaping societal norms and behaviors hroughout the innovation process. *Business & Society., 58*(5).
44. Wells, J. R. (2012). *Strategic IQ: Creating smarter corporations*. Wiley.
45. Moon, B.-J. (2012). Antecedents and outcomes of strategic thinking. *Journal of Business Research., 3*.
46. Terra, L. A., & Passador, J. L. (2018). Strategic thinking in the context of complexity, system research and behavioral. *Science., 35*(6).
47. Johnson, J., & Mulder, H. (2020). *Endless modernization: How infinite flow keeps software fresh*. The Standish Group International, Inc..
48. Sedano, T., & Cécile, P. R. (2017). *Software development waste*. International Conference on Software Engineering.
49. Guedes, J. F. (2018). A lean mind-set on the information technologies sector: Targeting and addressing waste for an increased performance. In J. Mejia, M. Muñoz, Á. Rocha, Y. Quiñonez, & J. Calvo-Manzano (Eds.), *Trends and applications in software engineering. CIMPS 2017. Advances in Intelligent Systems and Computing. 688*. Springer.
50. Power, K., & Conboy, K. (2014). Impediments to Flow: Rethinking the Lean Concept of 'Waste' in Modern Software Development. *Lecture Notes in Business Information Processing, 179*. LNBIP, 203–217.
51. Cvetkovic, N., Morača, S., Jovanović, M., Medojević, M., Lalić, B. (2017). *Enhancing the agility and performances of a project with lean manufacturing practices*. Annals of DAAAM and Proceedings of the International DAAAM Symposium, pp. 661–670.
52. O'connor, M., Conboy, K., Dennehy, D., & Carroll, N. (2024). Temporal complexity in information systems development flow: Challenges and recommendations. *Communications of the Association for Information Systems., 54*.
53. Szymczak, W. (2010). Fundamentals of statistics for psychologists (in Polish). *Difin*.
54. Greene, W. H. (2003). *Econometric analysis*. Prentice Hall.

# A Solution for Developing Corpora for Polish Speech Enhancement in Complex Acoustic Environments

**Mariusz Kleć, Krzysztof Szklanny, and Alicja Wieczorkowska**

**Abstract** This paper presents a solution for generating corpora of simulated Polish speech recordings in complex acoustic environments. The proposed method introduces a layer of unpredictable sound events, in addition to the acoustic scene noise and reverberation, making the solution unique. Each sound layer is stored in separate files, allowing users to mute specific layers selectively via phase cancellation. We applied this technique for data augmentation and trained two speech enhancement models. Experimental results show that the models trained with our data augmentation strategy effectively generalize across various background noise complexities. Moreover, we highlight the crucial role of integrating speech enhancement methods within the speech separation pipeline in conditions characterized by diverse background noises. Our publicly available code allows researchers to create their corpora tailored to the Polish language and train speech enhancement or separation models.

## 1 Introduction

Speech recordings are invaluable in many scientific fields, including linguistics, history, psychology, sociology, and medicine. Many information systems use voice communication and automatic speech recognition. Generative artificial intelligence tools are also becoming more and more common. A lot of data are needed to train these systems. Some of the data are recorded in studios, whereas some recordings are made outside recording studios. In particular, the real-life speech recordings are often made during spontaneous situations, in various locations, both indoors and outdoors, in uncontrolled acoustic environments. Non-professional microphones and casual settings can significantly impact the speech intelligibility of these

M. Kleć (✉) · K. Szklanny · A. Wieczorkowska
Polish-Japanese Academy of Information Technology, Warsaw, Poland
e-mail: mklec@pjwstk.edu.pl; kszklanny@pjwstk.edu.pl; alicja@poljap.edu.pl

 
B. Marcinkowski et al. (eds.), *Advances in Information Systems Development*,
Lecture Notes in Information Systems and Organisation 77,
https://doi.org/10.1007/978-3-031-87880-0_7

recordings. Therefore, the acquired audio files often contain noise, reverberation, and random sounds, like car horns or dog barking.

The role of speech enhancement (SE) systems is to increase speech intelligibility. It can be accomplished by speech denoising [36], increasing the resolution of the audio signal [23], or by conditional speech synthesis [1]. This process is essential before applying further signal processing techniques, such as Automatic Speech Recognition (ASR) or Speech Separation (SS). Noise present in the recordings significantly affects the performance of these systems. Therefore, developing SE and SS methods is crucial for ASR, speech corpus analysis, and real-time communication. The work presented in this paper aims to improve speech intelligibility by isolating it from complex and non-stationary background noise, including reverberation and unexpected sound events. This is an extended version of the paper [18], where the presented ideas were introduced.

Standard techniques like spectral subtraction [42], non-negative matrix factorization [15] or Wiener filtering [6, 39] rely on the numerical differentiation between speech and noise characteristics, and they can effectively denoise the speech when the noise is stationary. However, background noise is often non-stationary, consisting of multiple sound sources in the speaker's environment that cannot be controlled.

Recent studies have shown that Deep Learning (DL) techniques are more effective for speech denoising compared to traditional methods [36]. The DL-based techniques encompass such models as Wave-U-Net [8, 47], Convolutional Neural Networks (CNN), Long Short-Term Memory (LSTM) networks [6, 9, 13], Generative Adversarial Networks (GAN) [31, 38], Transformers [19], and, more recently, models that can be trained without the need for clean data [16].

SE techniques to remove noise from speech signals can be found in various studies [10, 17, 22]. Researchers predominantly use time-domain models to achieve this, which offer greater accuracy than time-frequency representation-based models. The latter necessitates phase information estimation, potentially causing distortions and inaccuracies during signal reconstruction [41].

Among the effective time-domain models, the Conv-TasNet neural network [25] has demonstrated high efficacy in single-channel SS, surpassing other time-frequency methods. Another notable model is the Hybrid Tasnet network [44], which combines time and frequency domains to enhance the separation performance. A model leveraging Recurrent Neural Networks [24] for utterance-level sequence modelling has also been explored. Wavesplit [45] is another end-to-end speaker separation model that excels in various tasks, including clean mixtures of two speakers from the WSJ0-2Mix dataset [11] and noisy, reverberated settings from the WHAMR dataset [26]. In [45], the authors reported achieving 22.2 dB on WSJ0-2Mix and 13.2 dB of SI-SDR on WHAMR. Furthermore, a recent study investigated the SepFormer transformer architecture for speech separation [41], yielding promising results of 22.3 dB of SI-SDR on WSJ0-2Mix. Additionally, the MossFormer2 model [46] currently achieves top results for the Libri2Mix [4] and

WSJ0-2Mix [11] datasets, with 24.1 dB and 21.7 dB of SI-SDR, respectively. The newest benchmarks are presented on www.paperswithcode.com, primarily as arXiv papers. The best-achieved results are 25.2 dB for WSJ0-2Mix and 18.7 dB of SDRi for the WHAM dataset [40].

## *1.1 Contribution*

Our approach is unique because we specifically designed the solution for generating speech corpora that include reverberation and unpredictable sound events as an additional layer of noise alongside acoustic scene signals. We also performed experiments on SS and SE with these data. We used the Polish speech data in our work, but this approach is universal, and other languages can also be used instead of Polish.

The script for Polish Speech Enhancement and Speech Separation (Pol-SESS) is publicly available[1] and allows users to generate an unlimited number of recordings. The recordings consist of audio components downloaded from publicly available data sources. These components include clean speech, sound events (E), acoustic scenes (S), and reverberation (R). In addition to the final mixed recordings, the script saves each component in separate files. Users can mute specific components from the mix by adding their phase-inverted versions. This technique will be called Mix Modification by Inverted Phase Cancellation (MM-IPC).

This organized structure prepares the created corpora for training deep learning models and enables users to select components from the mix without generating the corpus again. It also allows addressing other problems, such as event recognition or dereverberation in complex and non-stationary background noise. Moreover, this technique can also be used as a data augmentation for training deep models, which we did in this paper.

Using the script, we created two data corpora for further experiments. The first corpus simulates indoor recordings with reverberation, while the second consists of outdoor recordings; thus, these recordings simulate environments without reverberation. Each corpus contains 4000 training examples, each lasting 4 seconds, totalling over 133 minutes of continuous speech in complex, noisy environments.

We trained two models for speech enhancement. The first model enhances single speech (ES) by separating it from complex noise, while the second model enhances both concurrent speakers (EB) by separating their speech from the complex noise. To train these models, we employed the MM-IPC technique, utilizing both the originally generated examples—which encompass all possible background components (S, E, and optionally R)—and their modified versions. These modifications introduce various noise complexities, such as simple scenes or scenes with reverberation, without including the events themselves. Thus, modifying the data during training

[1] https://github.com/mklec/PolSESS.

using MM-IPC is used here as a data augmentation technique. Our two datasets contain ~8.88 hours of continuous speech, which can be further augmented by an additional ~22.22 hours of recordings with diverse background complexities using the MM-IPC method.

We hypothesize that the models trained in this manner will generalize better across various background types and complexity, resulting in a more universal solution better suited for various real-life cases.

The second hypothesis is that speech enhancement used as preprocessing helps achieve higher speech separation performance. The role of the EB model was to separate both speakers from the background noise. Once the two speakers were enhanced, they were further separated using a pre-trained SepFormer model [41]. We evaluated the SepFormer performance on noisy data and examined how the preprocessing step, performed with the EB model, helps in speaker separation in the presence of various background noises.

## 2 Corpus for Polish Speech Enhancement and Speech Separation (Pol-SESS)

Deep learning models for speech enhancement require many noisy recordings and their corresponding clean speech signals for training. However, obtaining clean speech signals can be difficult and expensive, often requiring access to professional recording studios. To address this problem, we have developed a Pol-SESS script that generates noisy speech corpora from the corresponding clean speech signals, which makes it ready to be used for training deep models. We use publicly available high-quality data sources in the script to create the corpora. The speech data sources are in Polish, and each generated audio file comprises a mix of seven distinct layers, as shown in Fig. 1.

### *2.1 Mix Modification by Inverted Phase Cancellation (MM-IPC)*

Each layer of the mix is saved as a separate audio file in its designated folder. This allows for easy cancellation of a component from the mix by adding the component's phase-inverted version to the mix. This technique is called Mix Modification by Inverted Phase Cancellation (MM-IPC). The MM-IPC technique allows adjusting the created corpora to a specific task. For instance, one speaker can be removed from the mix. The same should be done with the reverberation for this speaker in such a case, to remove this speaker completely. Therefore, obtaining the corpus with one speaker instead of two is easy without generating the corpus again. Other possibilities are feasible; exemplary ideas are presented in Table 1.

**Fig. 1** The structure of a simulated speech recording generated by the Pol-SESS script. The first four layers consist of two speech signals and the corresponding reverberation signals based on room impulse responses. The speech signals are sourced from the Polish Read Speech corpus (PRS) [20] and the Polish section of The Multilingual LibriSpeech (MLS) [34]. Layers five and six contain additional sound events and their corresponding reverberation. The recordings of sound events are sourced from the ESC50 [33] and FSD50K [5] datasets. The final layer of the mix comprises the sound of the environmental scene taken from TUT Acoustic Scenes 2017 [28], TAU Urban Acoustic Scenes 2019 [27], and the WHAM [43] datasets

**Table 1** Possible corpus adjustments using the MM-IPC method to make the corpus suitable for training various speech enhancement or speaker separation problems. This can be achieved by cancelling a given component from the mix without generating the new corpus from scratch. Each column shows the layers left in a mix to solve a particular problem. For instance, one can remove one speaker while leaving another or cancel out all reverberation. Other examples include cancelling the background scene while retaining only the sound events, with or without reverberation, etc

| Layers of the mix | | Speaker separation | | | | | | | Speech enhancement | | | | |
|---|---|---|---|---|---|---|---|---|---|---|---|---|---|
| Speaker 1 | ($Sp_1$) | ✓ | ✓ | ✓ | ✓ | ✓ | ✓ | ✓ | ✓ | ✓ | ✓ | ✓ | ✓ |
| Speaker 2 | ($Sp_2$) | ✓ | ✓ | ✓ | ✓ | ✓ | ✓ | ✓ | | | | | |
| Scene sound | ($S$) | ✓ | | | ✓ | | ✓ | | ✓ | ✓ | ✓ | | |
| Event sound | ($E$) | ✓ | ✓ | | ✓ | ✓ | | | ✓ | ✓ | | ✓ | |
| Reverb for speaker 1 | ($R_1$) | ✓ | ✓ | ✓ | | | | | ✓ | | | | ✓ |
| Reverb for speaker 2 | ($R_2$) | ✓ | ✓ | ✓ | | | | | | | | | |
| Reverb for event | ($R_e$) | ✓ | ✓ | | | | | | ✓ | | | | |

## 2.2 *Review of Existing Data Sources*

We aim to develop a solution accessible to everyone and stimulate research in this field. To achieve this, we assumed that each mix layer should contain publicly available, high-quality data sources. An overview of the most popular data sources is presented below in our quest for data sources to be used in particular layers of the mixes.

Many data sources are released when scientific challenges and workshops are organized. Still, most are in English, and noisy and corresponding clean data sources are provided only occasionally. For example, the CHiME[2] challenge frequently releases new datasets. The CHiME-5 [3] provides conversational speech recordings in everyday home environments, but it is intended to advance ASR performance rather than improve speech enhancement. On the other hand, the Deep Noise Suppression challenge (DNS) [36] focuses on improving overall speech quality when recorded in a challenging background. The dataset from this challenge contains over 10000 hours of noise and over 1000 hours of clean speech signals for training the noise suppression models and a representative test set of real-world scenarios consisting of both synthetic and real recordings.

The Wall Street Journal (WSJ0) corpus provides a speech source for creating other corpora. WSJ0-2Mix [11] takes two speakers and mixes them at speech-to-speech ratios (SSR) between 0 and 5 dB. It provides 30 hours of training examples. However, WSJ0 is not open-sourced. An alternative to WSJ0 is the Libri2Mix [4] dataset, based on LibriSpeech [30]. It consists of mixes of two speakers combined with ambient noise sampled from the WHAM [43] dataset and provides 212 hours of training examples. The WHAMR dataset [26] extends the WSJ0-2Mix by noise from the WHAM, reverberation, and mixes with the loudest speaker at SNR between $-6$ and 3 dB. It provides 58 hours of noisy and corresponding clean speech examples for training.

Other corpora can also provide valuable speech sources. However, their recordings often contain distortions and reverberation and are made with poor-quality microphones. The use of speech data for speech enhancement should include a selection of candidates of the best quality. One example of such a data source is VoxCeleb [14], containing over 100,000 utterances from more than 6000 speakers. Another example is the multi-language Common Voice dataset [2], which also contains the Polish subset of 177 hours of spontaneous speech. The Librivox project[3] is another example of a multi-language source of speech data. It contains recordings of volunteers reading over 10,000 public-domain books in various languages, also in Polish. The Polish clean and high-quality recordings are available from the Polish Read Speech corpus (PRS) [20]. The PRS provides 56 hours of recordings featuring phonetically rich words and sentences spoken by 317 speakers in an acoustically treated recording studio. The Multilingual LibriSpeech (MLS) [34] is a multilingual dataset of read books (audiobooks), and the Polish section contains 137 hours of clean speech from 16 speakers, reading 25 books. Finally, there are over 140 corpora available in the Common Language Resources and Technology Infrastructure (CLARIN) for the Polish language [12, 32].

[2] https://www.chimechallenge.org/.

[3] https://librivox.org/.

As for the environmental scene and noise data sources, Audioset [7] provides a collection of about 2 million human-labeled 10-second sound clips extracted from YouTube videos, which belong to about 600 audio classes. The TUT Acoustic Scenes 2017 dataset [28] includes 52 hours of audio recordings from 15 locations, such as homes, city centres, forest paths, grocery stores, metro stations, and more. The WHAM dataset [43] provides 80 hours of background noise from urban environments, such as restaurants, bars, cafes, and parks. The TAU Urban Acoustic Scenes 2019 dataset, introduced in [27], features 40 hours of audio recordings from various urban acoustic scenes, such as pedestrian streets, trams, and airports.

The sound events can also be downloaded from the ESC50 [33], which comprises 2000 recordings, each five-second long, classified into 50 semantic classes, such as clapping, vacuum cleaners, fireworks, and more. The FSD50K [5] contains over 50,000 audio clips, amounting to more than 100 hours of audio, organized into 200 classes drawn from the AudioSet Ontology. Examples of these classes include various musical instruments, splashes, zippers, telephones, and many others.

## 2.3 *The Data Generation Process*

In generating speech corpora, as reported in this work, we considered such factors as license, accessibility, language, and data quality when selecting the sources for our solution. Considering all these factors, we chose two sources of spoken Polish recordings, PRS and MLS, and obtained the sounds of real-world environments from the TUT, WHAM, and TAU datasets. Sound events were sourced from the ESC50 and FSD50K datasets. Finally, we created simulated recordings of noisy speech by combining signals from the sources above and applying reverberation using the following formula:

$$y(t) = \sum_{i=1}^{C=2} (s_i(t) + r_i(t)) + b(t) + e(t) + r_e(t) \tag{1}$$

where $y(t)$ represents the simulated noisy speech recording in the time domain with a maximum of $C$ speakers, $C = 2$ in our case. The signal $s_i(t)$ represents the $i$th speaker in the mix, which is mixed with their corresponding room response $r_i(t)$, generated earlier as reverberation. The signal $b(t)$ denotes the scene's ambient sound, and $e(t)$ represents a non-speech sound event, along with its corresponding reverberation $r_e(t)$. In this context, the background noise refers to the sum of four components: $r_i(t)$, $b(t)$, $e(t)$, and $r_e(t)$. The signals $s_i(t)$, $b(t)$, and $e(t)$ are randomly selected from the sources mentioned above. Since most of the signals are of low sound level, these signals are added without scaling. The obtained mix is then checked for overdrive, and overdriven mixes are discarded.

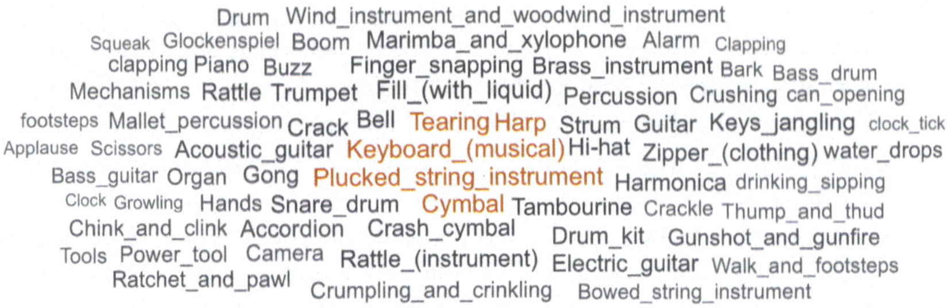


**Fig. 2** The word cloud shows the classes of events that occur in corpora created using the PolSESS script. This word cloud was created based on the pilot corpus containing 2,500,000 files. For the sake of clarity, the least common events have been excluded. Four of the most frequent event classes have been highlighted in red. The most common event classes are related to musical instruments

First, we divided all files from different sources into three subsets for training, validation, and testing, according to the instructions provided by each data source. This ensures no mixed component in the training subset is used for testing or validation. Next, we excluded files with speech-related events, such as whispering or singing, from the event sources to avoid conflicts with speech layers. Figure 2 shows the distribution of event classes when the script generates a new corpus. The two randomly selected speakers are mixed at a speech-to-speech ratio randomly selected from a range of −5 to 5 decibels, rounded to the nearest whole decibel. The resulting mix includes a randomly selected 4-second fragment from the given source files, yielding always different final mixes.

To render the actual recording conditions as much as possible, we considered several recordings' characteristics. To ensure that the selected sound events suit a particular scene, we created a matrix that maps scene classes to possible event classes. This step helps prevent the random selection of mismatched events, such as the sound of a cow at an airport, which would be absurd. The matrix provides guidelines for the event and specific scene classes when preparing mixes using our script. Additionally, reverberation was generated using Matlab, but only when the scene class represented an indoor category. We manually defined a list of possible reverb parameter ranges for the indoor classes to ensure that the characteristics of the generated room reflections match the specific scene class. Random selection of the reverb parameters was limited to the predefined ranges to avoid generating unsuitable reverbs, such as long reverbs for the library class that typically has a short decay time. We controlled the following parameters: decay time reflection, the strength of diffusion, high-frequency damping, and the time of early reflections in this manner. The same values of these parameters were applied to the speech and event sources, except for different early reflection times for events and the second speaker. These sound sources usually have different placements in the recording room, which affects the time of their first reflections captured by the microphone.

# 3 Experiments

We performed experiments on training SE models using data generated by Pol-SESS and augmented by MM-IPC. The experiments aimed to investigate the influence of various background complexities on speech enhancement performance. Our second goal was to incorporate the SE models into the preprocessing step for speech separation and evaluate the influence of that preprocessing on the speech separation performance.

Background noise in speech recordings can include various acoustic environments, unexpected sound events, and reverberation. Depending on the recording conditions and location, these elements can occur individually or in different combinations. For example, a recording made while walking in a park may feature only ambient sounds without reverberation. In contrast, a recording made at home while cooking might include reverberation, an acoustic scene, and unexpected events. Therefore, to effectively enhance speech, the model must be robust against unexpected sound events and adaptable to changing and complex background environments. However, capturing speech recordings in such diverse and complex acoustic backgrounds is challenging. The proposed Pol-SESS solution addresses this problem, and the MM-IPC method enables the creation of various background noise variants from the created corpus. Our experiments aimed to show the following:

- Demonstrate the feasibility of the Pol-SESS script.
- Investigate how background noise complexity affects speech enhancement performance for various background noise versions.
- Showcase using MM-IPC as a data augmentation method for training deep learning models.
- Validate the impact of speech enhancement on the performance of speech separation algorithms.

## *3.1 Data Generation for the Experiments*

To start with, we created a training subset of 250,000 files according to Eq. 1 (i.e. representing $y(t)$), using the Pol-SESS script. The testing and validation subsets contain 5000 files each. All created audio recordings consist of all possible sound layers (see Fig. 1 and Table 1). However, this amount of data was too significant for the available computational resources. Therefore, we randomly selected only a portion of the data, from which we created the two smaller corpora.

The first corpus simulates indoor recordings, featuring reverberation ($C_{in}$). The second corpus consists of recordings made outdoors, i.e., in an environment without reverberation ($C_{out}$). Consequently, each corpus contains a unique set of sound scene classes and sound event classes. For instance, the $C_{in}$ corpus includes sound scene classes such as "home", "library", "metro", and others, as well as sound event classes including sounds of machines, musical instruments, applause, and others. In contrast, the $C_{out}$ corpus features sound scene classes like "park", "forest", "street", and others, along with sound event classes such as "car horn", "chainsaw", and "rain", among others. Besides the distinct scene and event classes in each corpus, another difference is that the mixes belonging to the $C_{out}$ corpus do not contain the layers with reverb, as they simulate speech recorded outside.

Each corpus consists of 4-second recordings. Specifically, each corpus contains 4000 training examples (approximately 4.4 hours), 400 test examples (around 0.44 hours), and 20 validation examples (80 seconds total). Both corpora have balanced event classes in each subset. The validation set is relatively small to speed up computations. Still, it represents the event class distribution in the testing set well, as each example in the validation set represents one (and different) event.

## 3.2 The Models Used in the Experiments

We trained the two models to separate speech from complex background noise. More specifically, our goal was to estimate $s_i(t)$ from $y(t)$ (see Eq. 1). The first model was designed to enhance a single speaker by isolating their speech from the background noise (ES). The second model was designed to enhance two speakers by separating their concurrent speech from the background noise (EB).

The purpose of the EB model is to preprocess the noisy signal with the data representing two speakers to prepare it for speech separation. To evaluate the influence of this preprocessing step on the speech separation process, we used an already pre-trained SepFormer [41] model. Figure 3 illustrates the objective of training the models based on the provided input data and desired output.

For all the ES and EB models, we used the Convolutional Time-domain Audio Separation Network (CTN) architecture [25], designed initially for speaker separation. We adapted this architecture to speech enhancement by separating the speech from the background noise instead of separating the two speakers.

### Convolutional Time-Domain Audio Separation Network

CTN uses a linear encoder to generate a representation optimized for learning masks for the target speakers. Next, the mask is applied to the encoder output, which is then inverted back to the waveforms, representing the speech of separated speakers (see

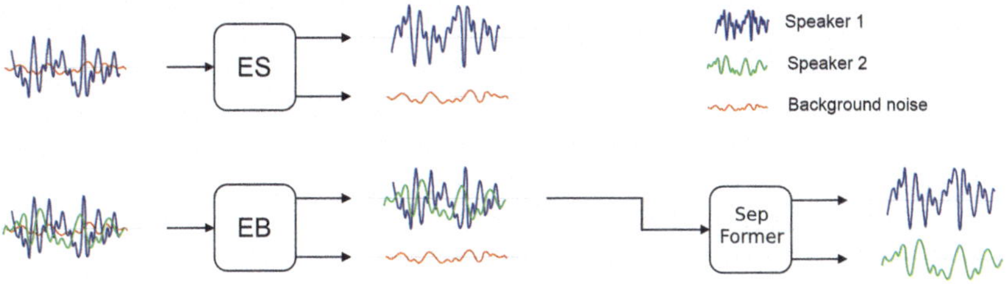


**Fig. 3** The inputs and target outputs applied in our experimental models. The two models, ES and EB, were trained to enhance a single speaker (ES) and both speakers (EB). In our experiments, the output from EB was further processed using the pre-trained SepFormer model [41] to achieve final clean speech separation. The SepFormer was pre-trained using the Libri2Mix-Clean dataset from SpeechBrain [35]

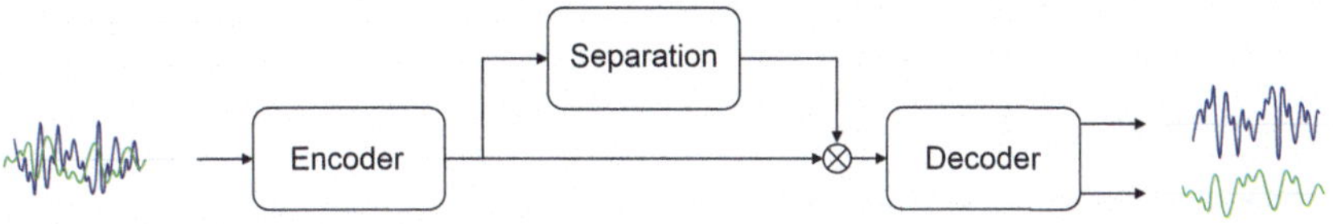


**Fig. 4** The general architecture of the Conv-Tas-Net network [25]

Fig. 4). The network finds the masks using a temporal convolutional network (TCN) consisting of stacked 1-D dilated convolutional blocks.

The hyperparameters of our networks are the length of the input filters, equal to 20 samples, and 32 convolutional blocks in the TCN. The loss functions and training procedure followed [25], with the initial learning rate set to 1e-3 and Adam used as the optimizer. If the validation set's accuracy did not improve over two consecutive epochs, the learning rate was multiplied by 0.95. For evaluation purposes, we took the parameters which obtained the lowest validation loss through fifty epochs. The models were implemented in Matlab and trained from scratch for fifty epochs on a single GPU GeForce RTX 3080.

## 3.3 The Training Procedure

The ES and EB models were trained using examples from two corpora simultaneously, i.e. $C_{in}$ and $C_{out}$. The ES model was trained with data containing one speaker, while the EB was trained with data containing two speakers. The training loop for these two models was implemented as described in the following simplified pseudocode:

```
epochs = 50;
CTNmodel = initRandomCTNParameters();

% The training data contains both indoor and outdoor recordings.
trData = [C_in_SER, C_out_SE];

for i=1:epochs
  while hasData(trData)

    % In each training iteration, a pair of training examples is read:
    % one representing an indoor recording
    % and the other representing an outdoor recording.
    trEx = read(trData);

    % Transforming the indoor training example into
    % a randomly selected variant of background complexity: SER, SR, ER, R.
    trExIndoor = MMIPC(trEx(1));

    % Transforming the outdoor training example into
    % a randomly selected variant of background complexity: SE, S or E.
    trExOutdoor = MMIPC(trEx(2));

    trEx(1) = trExampleIndoor;
    trEx(2) = trExampleOutdoor;

    % the model optimization
    CTNmodel.optimize(trEx.mix, trEx.cleanSpeech, trEx.bgNoise);
  end
end
```

Using the MM-IPC technique, the MMIPC function randomly transforms the background noise present in the training examples. For indoor examples, it converts the background into one of four variants: SER, SR, ER or R, while for outdoor examples, it converts each training example to one of three variants: SE, S or E, as detailed in Table 2. The ES and EB model training results are presented in Tables 3 and 5, respectively.

### *3.4 The Influence of Background Noise Complexity on the Speech Enhancement*

To investigate the influence of background noise complexity on speech enhancement, we trained seven CTN models with one specific background complexity for one model. This means the MM-IPC method was applied to the data once before training, which differs from the approach described in Sect. 3.2, where the MM-IPC was used every time in each training iteration. The seven models covered all possible background complexities obtained via MM-IPC (see Table 2). We used the Scale-Invariant Signal-to-Distortion Ratio (SI-SDR) [21] to evaluate the models' performance. Higher SI-SDR values indicate better separation quality. The results in Table 4 provide insights into the models' performance when evaluated against all the possible background complexities in the testing set.

**Table 2** The background complexity variants for both corpora, ($C_{in}$ and $C_{out}$). $X$ in the acronyms represents the number of speakers in the dataset, which can be either 1 or 2. The originally generated corpus $C_{in}$ include all possible background components in the recordings: scene (S), event (E), and reverb (R)—(SER). The originally generated corpus $C_{out}$ include scene (S) and event (E)—(SE). The range of background components in the background can be modified using the MM-IPC method, which can remove one or more components from the original recording. The last part of the subscript in the acronym indicates the components in the mix. For instance, $SER$ represents all background components present in the recording, $SR$ indicates that only the scene and reverberation components are retained (with the event component $E$ having been removed by the MM-IPC method), and so on

| | | |
|---|---|---|
| Indoor recordings | | |
| 1 | $C_{in-X-SER}$ | Recordings with scene, events and reverberation. With this background complexity the corpus is originally generated by means of Pol-SESS. Additional variants can be obtained using the MM-IPC method. |
| 2 | $C_{in-X-SR}$ | Recordings with scene and reverberation. |
| 3 | $C_{in-X-ER}$ | Recordings with events and reverberation. |
| 4 | $C_{in-X-ER}$ | Recordings with reverberation. |
| Outdoor recordings | | |
| 1 | $C_{out-X-SE}$ | Recordings with scene and events. With this background complexity the corpus is originally generated by means of Pol-SESS. Additional variants can be obtained using the MM-IPC method. |
| 2 | $C_{out-X-S}$ | Recordings with scene. |
| 3 | $C_{out-X-E}$ | Recordings with event. |

**Table 3** SI-SNR, expressed in dB, is used to evaluate a single speech enhancement (ES) model. The ES model was trained using the data from both training datasets, $C_{tr-in-1}$ and $C_{tr-out-1}$. The transformation process was applied using the MM-IPC method in every training iteration for each training batch data. The "MMIPC" at the end of the subscript denotes this transformation. The model was evaluated using varying levels of background complexities in the testing sets $C_{test-in-1}$ and $C_{test-out-1}$. Additionally, the model was evaluated using the external Libri1Mix-Noisy dataset ($L.1Mix$). Finally, the average results were calculated across all testing sets, covering all background complexities and the Libri1Mix dataset

| | | $C_{test-in-1}$ | | | | $C_{test-1-out}$ | | | | |
|---|---|---|---|---|---|---|---|---|---|---|
| | Model | $SER$ | $SR$ | $ER$ | $R$ | $SE$ | $S$ | $E$ | L.1Mix | Mean |
| $C_{tr-in-1-MMIPC}$ $C_{tr-out-1-MMIPC}$ | ES | 8.3 | 12.27 | 9.4 | 13.96 | 12.61 | 23.32 | 13.44 | 9.47 | 12.85 |

Finally, we compare the average results from all the trained CTN models with the performance of the single ES model described in Sect. 3.2. The results from this comparison are presented in Fig. 6.

**Table 4** SI-SNR, expressed in dB, applied to evaluate our seven CTN models for single speech enhancement. Each model was trained with one specific background complexity. These models were also evaluated using the external Libri1Mix-Noisy ($L.1Mix$) dataset, containing English speech and scenes without events and reverberation. Finally, for each model, average results were calculated across all testing sets, encompassing all background complexities and Libri1Mix-Noisy. The results were also averaged across all trained models for each testing set

| | | | $C_{test-in-1}$ | | | | $C_{test-out-1}$ | | | | |
|---|---|---|---|---|---|---|---|---|---|---|---|
| | | Model | $SER$ | $SR$ | $ER$ | $R$ | $SE$ | $S$ | $E$ | L.1Mix | Mean |
| $C_{tr-in-1}$ | $SER$ | $CTN_{SER}$ | 8.33 | 12.2 | 9.36 | **13.72** | 7.06 | 9.42 | 7.85 | 9.47 | 9.68 |
| | $SR$ | $CTN_{SR}$ | 5.63 | 12.93 | 6.50 | **14.74** | 4.51 | 9.15 | 5.15 | 9.66 | 8.53 |
| | $ER$ | $CTN_{ER}$ | 8.15 | 12.06 | 9.54 | **14.35** | 6.9 | 9.25 | 7.93 | 9.02 | 9.65 |
| | $R$ | $CTN_{R}$ | 2.31 | 9.62 | 5.14 | **15.67** | 1.35 | 5.5 | 3.54 | 5.07 | 6.03 |
| $C_{tr-out-1}$ | $SE$ | $CTN_{SE}$ | 6.21 | 9.62 | 7.04 | 10.75 | 11.94 | **22.58** | 12.62 | 7.74 | 11.06 |
| | $S$ | $CTN_{S}$ | 1.78 | 7.64 | 2.51 | 8.80 | 6.24 | **25.64** | 6.94 | 7.29 | 8.36 |
| | $E$ | $CTN_{E}$ | 6.26 | 9.62 | 7.15 | 10.96 | 11.87 | **23.28** | 13.21 | 8.16 | **11.31** |
| | | $CTN_{Mean}$ | 5.52 | 10.53 | 6.75 | 12.71 | 7.12 | **14.97** | 8.18 | 8.02 | 9.23 |

The bold values indicate the maximum SI-SNR for each model. In addition, the highest mean value across all testing subsets is also highlighted.

**Table 5** SI-SNR, measured in dB, for the evaluated speech enhancement model for both speakers (EB). The training procedure for the EB model was identical to that of the ES model (refer to Table 3), except that the EB model was trained using data containing two speakers, referred to as $C_{tr-in-2}$ and $C_{tr-out-2}$. Instead of evaluating it with Libri1Mix-Noisy, the model was evaluated with the Libri2Mix-Noisy dataset containing two speakers ($L2.Mix$)

| | | $C_{test-in-2}$ | | | | $C_{test-out-2}$ | | | | |
|---|---|---|---|---|---|---|---|---|---|---|
| | Model | $SER$ | $SR$ | $ER$ | $R$ | $SE$ | $S$ | $E$ | L.2Mix | Mean |
| $C_{tr-in-2-MMIFC}$ $C_{tr-out-2-MMIFC}$ | EB | 7.79 | 11.01 | 8.65 | 12.31 | 12.53 | 24.16 | 13.24 | 9.78 | 12.43 |

## 3.5 *The Influence of Speech Enhancement on Speech Separation*

To check the influence of speech enhancement on speech separation, we trained the single EB model, which denoises the two speakers, and once the two speakers were enhanced, they were further separated using a pre-trained SepFormer model [41]. We evaluated the model's performance on noisy data and examined how this preprocessing step with EB helps in speaker separation in the presence of various background noises. The results are presented in Fig. 5 and Table 6.

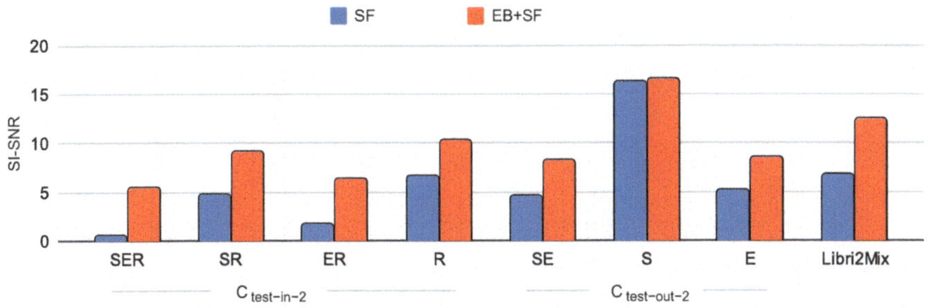


**Fig. 5** The performance of SepFormer for the testing datasets ($C_{test-2-in}$ and $C_{test-2-out}$) of various background complexities, and for the Libri2Mix-Noisy test set. The figure illustrates the performance of the two scenarios for speech separation. In the first scenario, the SepFormer model is tested without any preprocessing applied to the testing set. In the second scenario, the testing examples undergo preprocessing to remove noise using our EB model

**Table 6** SI-SNR, measured in dB, obtained from the tests of the speech separation approaches. The EB+SF approach involves first denoising the testing signals using the EB model (as shown in Table 5) before processing the denoised signal with a pre-trained external SepFormer model (SF) to separate two speakers into two channels, one channel per speaker. The SF model was also tested across all background complexities in our test sets. Additionally, these two approaches were evaluated using the external Libri2Mix-Noisy dataset. Finally, the results were averaged across all testing sets, encompassing all background complexities and the Libri2Mix dataset

| Model | $C_{test-in-2}$ | | | | $C_{test-out-2}$ | | | | |
|---|---|---|---|---|---|---|---|---|---|
| | $SER$ | $SR$ | $ER$ | $R$ | $SE$ | $S$ | $E$ | L.2Mix | Mean |
| EB+SF | 5.54 | 9.11 | 6.37 | 10.31 | 8.27 | 16.49 | 8.53 | 12.4 | 9.63 |
| SF | 0.61 | 4.81 | 1.67 | 6.6 | 4.57 | 16.23 | 5.14 | 6.84 | 5.81 |

## 4 Results

When analyzing the results presented in Table 4, we can conclude that the recordings primarily containing reverberation are most effectively enhanced by all models trained on indoor examples (no matter for which background complexity), yielding the highest SI-SNR (Scale-Invariant Signal-to-Noise Ratio). On the other hand, recordings that primarily feature outdoor scenes (S) are best enhanced by models trained on outdoor examples (no matter with which background complexity). This can be caused by the fact that the scene and reverb represent the stationary types of noise, compared to other possibilities, and all the models learned their characteristics very well. However, models trained on indoor examples tend to perform poorly when tested on outdoor recordings and vice versa. When analyzing the results averaged across all possible testing background complexities from the same Table, the $CTN_E$ model achieves the highest average value of SI-SNR. This indicates that the events present in the training set generalize well to various other background complexities found in the testing examples.

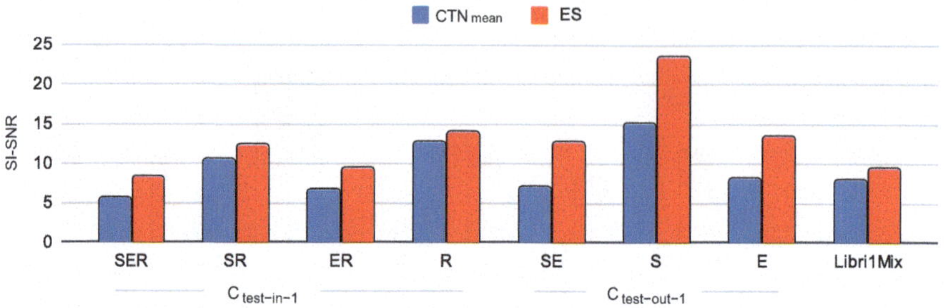


**Fig. 6** The performance of two different speech enhancement approaches. The first approach involves training seven models, each trained to handle different background complexities, and then averaging their results (see Table 4). This approach is labelled in the figure as $CTN_{mean}$. The second approach integrates the MM-IPC technique into the training process and trains a single enhanced speech (ES) model using all possible background complexities

In our comparison of the average results from all trained CTN models ($CTN_{mean}$) with those from the ES model (see Fig. 6), we find that the ES model produces a higher SI-SNR across all testing sets, compared to the $CTN_{mean}$. These results underscore the importance of the MM-IPC method in training speech enhancement models that effectively generalize across different types of background complexity.

When analyzing the impact of the EB model on speech separation performance (see Table 6), we observe a significant improvement, with an average SI-SNR of 9.63 dB compared to 5.81 dB across all tested sets. The most substantial gain occurs for the most complex background (SER) cases, where speech separation without the EB model results in only 0.61 dB. In contrast, using the EB preprocessing boosts the SI-SNR to 5.52 dB.

## 5 Discussion and Conclusion

This paper addresses the challenges of enhancing and separating speech from noisy, reverberant, and disrupted environments. The proposed publicly available Pol-SESS solution for developing corpora has enabled us to generate simulated speech recordings and train speech enhancement models, thereby improving speech intelligibility and separation across various levels of background complexity present in the recordings. Achieving this would not have been possible without sufficient training data, which is difficult to obtain, and without the introduction of the MM-IPC technique. This technique leverages the phenomenon of phase cancellation to suppress specific layers of background noise from the recordings. The Pol-SESS solution and the MM-IPC technique are valuable resources for training deep learning models and advancing further research. Although the work presented in this paper focuses on the Polish language, the methodology can also be adapted for use with other languages.

The research detailed in [17] demonstrated that a single-channel time-domain denoising technique could reduce the word error rate (WER) by 30%. These findings motivate us to enhance our models in the future by integrating more data sources, generating additional training examples, increasing the model's capacity, and extending the model training time. Furthermore, the speech data sources should include transcriptions to help other researchers evaluate their models with ASR in terms of WER. Currently, only the MLS data source contains the transcription. Another potential source is the newly released Polish speech corpus discussed in [32], which offers transcriptions and conversational Polish speech, complementing the supervised speech recordings used in the current study.

The created corpora using Pol-SESS can also be applied to train voice activity detection, which is crucial for effectively operating in unpredictable and noisy environments; for example, to recognize speech in cars or voice-controlled machines [29, 37]. Accurately distinguishing between noise and speech is essential in such scenarios.

We hope the proposed solution will contribute to developing new models and be a valuable resource for further research.

## References


1. AlBadawy, E. A., Gibiansky, A., He, Q., Wu, J., Chang, M.-C., & Lyu, S. (2022). Vocbench: A neural vocoder benchmark for speech synthesis. In *2022 IEEE International Conference on Acoustics, Speech and Signal Processing (ICASSP)* (pp. 881–885). IEEE.
2. Ardila, R., Branson, M., Davis, K., Kohler, M., Meyer, J., Henretty, M., Morais, R., Saunders, L., Tyers, F., & Weber, G. (2020). Common voice: A massively-multilingual speech corpus. In *Proceedings of the Twelfth Language Resources and Evaluation Conference* (pp. 4218–4222).
3. Barker, J., Watanabe, S., Vincent, E., & Trmal, J. (2018). The fifth'chime'speech separation and recognition challenge: Dataset, task and baselines. In *Interspeech 2018-19th Annual Conference of the International Speech Communication Association*.
4. Cosentino, J., Pariente, M., Cornell, S., Deleforge, A., & Vincent, E. (2020). Librimix: An open-source dataset for generalizable speech separation. arXiv preprint arXiv:2005.11262
5. Fonseca, E., Favory, X., Pons, J., Font, F., & Serra, X. (2021). Fsd50k: An open dataset of human-labeled sound events. *IEEE/ACM Transactions on Audio, Speech, and Language Processing, 30*, 829–852.
6. Garg, A. (2022). Speech enhancement using long short term memory with trained speech features and adaptive wiener filter. *Multimedia Tools and Applications, 82*(3), 3647–3675.
7. Gemmeke, J. F., Ellis, D. P., Freedman, D., Jansen, A., Lawrence, W., Moore, R. C., Plakal, M., & Ritter, M. (2017). Audio set: An ontology and human-labeled dataset for audio events. In *2017 IEEE International Conference on Acoustics, Speech and Signal Processing (ICASSP)* (pp. 776–780). IEEE.
8. Guimarães, H. R., Nagano, H., & Silva, D. W. (2020). Monaural speech enhancement through deep wave-u-net. *Expert Systems with Applications, 158*, 113582.
9. Hao, X., Su, X., Horaud, R., & Li, X. (2021). Fullsubnet: A full-band and sub-band fusion model for real-time single-channel speech enhancement. In *2021 IEEE International Conference on Acoustics, Speech and Signal Processing (ICASSP)* (pp. 6633–6637). IEEE.
10. Hasumi, T., Kobayashi, T., & Ogawa, T. (2021). Investigation of network architecture for single-channel end-to-end denoising. In *2020 28th European Signal Processing Conference (EUSIPCO)* (pp. 441–445). IEEE.

11. Hershey, J. R., Chen, Z., Le Roux, J., & Watanabe, S. (2016). Deep clustering: Discriminative embeddings for segmentation and separation. In *2016 IEEE International Conference on Acoustics, Speech and Signal Processing (ICASSP)* (pp. 31–35). IEEE.
12. Hinrichs, E., & Krauwer, S. (2014). The CLARIN research infrastructure: Resources and tools for e-humanities scholars. In *Proceedings of the Ninth International Conference on Language Resources and Evaluation (LREC-2014)* (pp. 1525–1531).
13. Hu, Y., Liu, Y., Lv, S., Xing, M., Zhang, S., Fu, Y., Wu, J., Zhang, B., & Xie, L. (2020). DCCRN: Deep complex convolution recurrent network for phase-aware speech enhancement. arXiv:2008.00264.
14. Huh, J., Brown, A., Jung, J.-W., Son Chung, J., Nagrani, A., Garcia-Romero, D., & Zisserman, A. (2023). Voxsrc 2022: The fourth voxceleb speaker recognition challenge. arXiv e-prints, arXiv–2302.
15. Kagami, H., Kameoka, H., & Yukawa, M. (2018). Joint separation and dereverberation of reverberant mixtures with determined multichannel non-negative matrix factorization. In *2018 IEEE International Conference on Acoustics, Speech and Signal Processing (ICASSP)* (pp. 31–35). IEEE.
16. Kashyap, M. M., Tambwekar, A., Manohara, K., & Natarajan, S. (2021). Speech denoising without clean training data: A noise2noise approach. arXiv:2104.03838.
17. Kinoshita, K., Ochiai, T., Delcroix, M., & Nakatani, T. (2020). Improving noise robust automatic speech recognition with single-channel time-domain enhancement network. In *2020 IEEE International Conference on Acoustics, Speech and Signal Processing (ICASSP)* (pp. 7009–7013). IEEE.
18. Kleć, M., Szklanny, K., & Wieczokowska, A. (2024). Developing a corpus for polish speech enhancement by reducing noise, reverberation, and disruptions. In *Harnessing Opportunities: Reshaping ISD in the Post-COVID-19 and Generative AI Era (ISD2024 Proceedings)*.
19. Koizumi, Y., Yatabe, K., Delcroix, M., Masuyama, Y., & Takeuchi, D. (2020). Speech enhancement using self-adaptation and multi-head self-attention. In *ICASSP 2020-2020 IEEE International Conference on Acoustics, Speech and Signal Processing (ICASSP)* (pp. 181–185). IEEE.
20. Koržinek, D., Marasek, K., & Brocki, Ł. (2016). Polish read speech corpus for speech tools and services. In *CLARIN Annual Conference 2016 in Aix-en-Provence*.
21. Le Roux, J., Wisdom, S., Erdogan, H., & Hershey, J. R. (2019). SDR–half-baked or well done? In *ICASSP 2019-2019 IEEE International Conference on Acoustics, Speech and Signal Processing (ICASSP)* (pp. 626–630). IEEE.
22. Lee, D., Kim, S., & Choi, J.-W. (2021). Inter-channel conv-tasnet for multichannel speech enhancement. arXiv:2111.04312.
23. Lim, T. Y., Yeh, R. A., Xu, Y., Do, M. N., & Hasegawa-Johnson, M. (2018). Time-frequency networks for audio super-resolution. In *2018 IEEE International Conference on Acoustics, Speech and Signal Processing (ICASSP)* (pp. 646–650). IEEE.
24. Luo, Y., Chen, Z., & Yoshioka, T. (2020). Dual-path RNN: Efficient long sequence modeling for time-domain single-channel speech separation. In *ICASSP 2020-2020 IEEE International Conference on Acoustics, Speech and Signal Processing (ICASSP)* (pp. 46–50). IEEE.
25. Luo, Y., & Mesgarani, N. (2019). Conv-tasnet: Surpassing ideal time–frequency magnitude masking for speech separation. *IEEE/ACM Transactions on Audio, Speech, and Language Processing, 27*(8), 1256–1266.
26. Maciejewski, M., Wichern, G., McQuinn, E., & Le Roux, J. (2020). Whamr! Noisy and reverberant single-channel speech separation. In *ICASSP 2020-2020 IEEE International Conference on Acoustics, Speech and Signal Processing (ICASSP)* (pp. 696–700). IEEE.
27. Mesaros, A., Heittola, T., & Virtanen, T. (2018). A multi-device dataset for urban acoustic scene classification. In *Scenes and Events 2018 Workshop (DCASE2018)* (p. 9).
28. Mesaros, A., Heittola, T., & Virtanen, T. (2018). Acoustic scene classification: An overview of dcase 2017 challenge entries. In *2018 16th International Workshop on Acoustic Signal Enhancement (IWAENC)* (pp. 411–415). IEEE.

29. Mihalache, S., & Burileanu, D. (2022). Using voice activity detection and deep neural networks with hybrid speech feature extraction for deceptive speech detection. *Sensors, 22*(3), 1228.
30. Panayotov, V., Chen, G., Povey, D., & Khudanpur, S. (2015). Librispeech: An ASR corpus based on public domain audio books. In *2015 IEEE International Conference on Acoustics, Speech and Signal Processing (ICASSP)* (pp. 5206–5210). IEEE.
31. Pascual, S., Bonafonte, A., & Serrà, J. (2017). Segan: Speech enhancement generative adversarial network. In *Proceedings of Interspeech* (pp. 3642–3646).
32. Pęzik, P., Karasińska, S., Cichosz, Ł. Jałowiecki, A., Kaczyński, K., Krawentek, M., Walkusz, K., Wilk, P., Kleć, M., Szklanny, K., & Marszałkowski, S. (2023). Spokesbiz–an open corpus of conversational polish. arXiv–2312.
33. Piczak, K. J. (2015). ESC: Dataset for environmental sound classification. In *Proceedings of the 23rd ACM International Conference on Multimedia* (pp. 1015–1018).
34. Pratap, V., Xu, Q., Sriram, A., Synnaeve, G., & Collobert, R. (2020). MLS: A large-scale multilingual dataset for speech research. arXiv preprint arXiv:2012.03411.
35. Ravanelli, M., Parcollet, T., Plantinga, P., Rouhe, A., Cornell, S., Lugosch, L., Subakan, C., Dawalatabad, N., Heba, A., Zhong, J., Chou, J.-C., Yeh, S.-L., Fu, S. W., Liao, C.-F., Rastorgueva, E., Grondin, F., Aris, W., Na, H., Gao, Y., De Mori, R., et al. (2021). Speechbrain: A general-purpose speech toolkit. arXiv:2106.04624.
36. Reddy, C. K., Gopal, V., Cutler, R., Beyrami, E., Cheng, R., Dubey, H., Matusevych, S., Aichner, R., Aazami, A., Braun, S., Rana, P., Srinivasan, S., Gehrke, J. (2020). The interspeech 2020 deep noise suppression challenge: Datasets, subjective testing framework, and challenge results. arXiv preprint arXiv:2005.13981.
37. Rho, D., Park, J., & Ko, J. (2022). Nas-vad: Neural architecture search for voice activity detection. In *Proceedings of the Annual Conference of the International Speech Communication Association, INTERSPEECH* (vol. 2022, pp. 3754–3758). International Speech Communication Association.
38. Satheesh, A., & Muthu-Manivannan, K. (2022). Denoising speech signals with hifi-coulombgans. *Journal of Student Research, 11*(3). https://www.jsr.org/hs/index.php/path/article/view/3501.
39. Scalart, P., & Filho, J. V. (1996). Speech enhancement based on a priori signal to noise estimation. In *1996 IEEE International Conference on Acoustics, Speech, and Signal Processing Conference Proceedings* (vol. 2, pp. 629–632). IEEE.
40. Shin, U.-H., Lee, S., Kim, T., & Park, H.-M. (2024). Separate and reconstruct: Asymmetric encoder-decoder for speech separation. arXiv:2406.05983.
41. Subakan, C., Ravanelli, M., Cornell, S., Bronzi, M., & Zhong, J. (2021). Attention is all you need in speech separation. In *ICASSP 2021-2021 IEEE International Conference on Acoustics, Speech and Signal Processing (ICASSP)* (pp. 21–25). IEEE.
42. Upadhyay, N., & Karmakar, A. (2015). Speech enhancement using spectral subtraction-type algorithms: A comparison and simulation study. *Procedia Computer Science, 54*, 574–584.
43. Wichern, G., Antognini, J., Flynn, M., Zhu, L. R., McQuinn, E., Crow, D., Manilow, E., & Roux, J. L. (2019). Wham! Extending speech separation to noisy environments. arXiv:1907.01160.
44. Yang, G.-P., Tuan, C.-I., Lee, H.-Y., & Lee, L.-S. (2019). Improved speech separation with time-and-frequency cross-domain joint embedding and clustering. arXiv:1904.07845.
45. Zeghidour, N., & Grangier, D. (2021). Wavesplit: End-to-end speech separation by speaker clustering. *IEEE/ACM Transactions on Audio, Speech, and Language Processing, 29*, 2840–2849.
46. Zhao, S., Ma, Y., Ni, C., Zhang, C., Wang, H., Nguyen, T. H., Zhou, K., Yip, J. Q., Ng, D., & Ma, B. (2024). Mossformer2: Combining transformer and RNN-free recurrent network for enhanced time-domain monaural speech separation. In *ICASSP 2024-2024 IEEE International Conference on Acoustics, Speech and Signal Processing (ICASSP)* (pp. 10356–10360). IEEE.
47. Zhao, S., Nguyen, T. H., & Ma, B. (2021). Monaural speech enhancement with complex convolutional block attention module and joint time frequency losses. In *2021 IEEE International Conference on Acoustics, Speech and Signal Processing (ICASSP)* (pp. 6648–6652). IEEE.

# Data-Driven Assessment of Practical Skills in Cybersecurity Challenges

**Austėja Bauraitė, Agnė Brilingaitė, and Linas Bukauskas**

**Abstract** Practical problem-solving provides information technologies and information systems professionals with various learning and assessment opportunities to build, operate, and test cloud infrastructures. When carried out under simulated conditions, the challenge-oriented exercises offer a hands-on approach to highlight the importance of skills related to structured decision-making and detailed configuration in a command line. Therefore, this paper proposes a novel information system design solution for skill evaluation. It contains a data analysis component as an integral part, incorporates a secure sandbox, and analyses user-supplied command line data from cybersecurity training sessions. The proposed solution focuses on command-line input parsing, tokenization, and structured analysis, providing a viewpoint on the knowledge level in simulated scenarios. The paper aligns the needs of trainees and instructors with the learning process. The work provides insight into structured command-line data analysis and the complexities of command execution. The prototype is based on modular Bourne-Again Shell and Python modules and asynchronous data collection. The paper contributes to the educational processes by offering an information system solution to satisfy the assessment needs in the exemplified field of penetration testing of information systems.

## 1 Introduction

A rapidly evolving cybersecurity domain impacts a vast sector of information technologies (IT) and information systems (IS). IT specialists take measures to keep systems resilient against cyber incidents and various threats. IS specialists require skills to design, develop, and support systems and processes involving the cybersecurity dimension. Thus, comprehensive training of IT and IS specialists is crucial. As cyber threats become more sophisticated, robust training, which

A. Bauraitė (✉) · A. Brilingaitė · L. Bukauskas
Institute of Computer Science, Vilnius University, Vilnius, Lithuania
e-mail: austeja.bauraite@mif.vu.lt; agne.brilingaite@mif.vu.lt; linas.bukauskas@mif.vu.lt



B. Marcinkowski et al. (eds.), *Advances in Information Systems Development*,
Lecture Notes in Information Systems and Organisation 77,
https://doi.org/10.1007/978-3-031-87880-0_8

encompasses self-learning, instructing others, and continuous skill development, becomes vital. Cybersecurity is a critical topic by its nature, and the component of practical security in education is vital [21]. Hands-on cybersecurity exercises bridge the gap between theoretical concepts and their application in real-world scenarios, offering a dynamic and interactive method of education. The application of practical skills in cybersecurity tasks is routinely based on the quality of domain-specific commands and the parametrisation of command execution.

Training activities range from academic education to training programs to enhance cybersecurity awareness, influence user behaviour, and develop a culture of cybersecurity [3]. Efficient training must be relevant, current, and tailored to the needs of participants, creating simulations for these situations to provide an environment where they can improve their skills. This learning is indispensable for grasping cybersecurity's intricate and changing nature, putting theoretical knowledge to the test in diverse circumstances.

Training exercises focusing on command-line (CLI; command-line interface) proficiency are crucial in developing a more advanced skill set [14]. They allow learners to apply academic knowledge in various simulated scenarios that closely resemble actual cyber-threat landscapes [16]. Such hands-on experiences are invaluable in comprehending the complexities of cybersecurity, where learners are challenged to adapt and apply their expertise. IT and IS specialists must employ command-line skills to perform system penetration testing, mitigate vulnerabilities, or tune-up system configuration. The role of assessment modules in training and educational programmes is critical [5]. Additionally, employing IT and AI-ready tools provides a structured approach to understanding learning outcomes, identifying areas for improvement, and tailoring future training to tackle existing and evolving challenges [9]. The data from cybersecurity exercises offers rich insights for learners and educators, enabling feedback that enhances the learning experience [10]. However, the richness of collected data obscures the aiding process for data-driven qualitative evaluation. The community expects to gain a toolset for knowledge and data mapping for training performance evaluation.

This paper contributes by establishing novel methods to analyse command-line-based user activity to identify user experience levels and assess competences during training without prior knowledge and pre-testing. Specifically, the novelty is focused on formalisation, evaluation criteria, and metrics to derive trainee expertise. This work outlines the method from understanding the command line structure to developing the solution and its operational methods, aiming to create a prototype for analysis and transform data into insights. The paper discusses hands-on cybersecurity exercises, CLI complexities, the design of the data analysis tool, its technical implementation, and the results gathered from testing with the openly available data set.

The emphasis on hands-on exercises and IS development for the education of IT and IS specialists in cybersecurity targets several critical aspects of the interaction processes among systems, technology, and people in modern and hybrid work environments. These exercises enhance the ability to sustain performance and promote high levels of interactivity and collaboration, even in remote settings, as the environments are cloud-based but still resemble real-world challenges. The data-driven approach of assessing CLI input provides a structured method to evaluate productivity and engagement while supporting skill development. Furthermore, the solution's design, which emphasises modularity and asynchronous data collection, facilitates social cohesion by enabling transparent performance evaluation processes.

This paper extends our previous research work [1]. Firstly, it aligns the needs of actors in the learning process that is part of the cybersecurity training challenge execution. Secondly, it gives a more precise picture of the potential of the proposed solution by providing illustrative complementary examples of results from the prototype experimentation.

The rest of the paper is structured as follows. Section 2 covers the analysis of related work as the research background. Section 3 reviews cybersecurity challenges through the lens of the learning process. Section 4 defines the process and methodology of CLI command evaluation. Section 5 covers the design of the information system as a proposed solution. Section 6 presents the experimental setup of the proof of concept implementation. Section 7 provides experimentation results and discusses assessment viewpoints. Section 8 concludes the paper, outlines limitations, and reviews future work.

## 2 Background

Penetration testing [25], as a part of the cybersecurity area, assists organisations in security compliance and includes finding vulnerabilities and their mitigation. Typically, professionals advance their skills to tackle cyber threats, mirroring real-world challenges, during intensive hands-on training sessions called cyber defence exercises (CDX). CDXs offer technical, hands-on experience in active defence against simulated incidents, testing participants' technical expertise and response agility [11]. Participants engage in CDX roles across different teams in a cyber range environment, simulating real-world IT infrastructures to prepare for a spectrum of cybersecurity challenges, such as crisis situations during cyber incident handling [13].

The command-line interface (CLI) plays a pivotal role in cybersecurity training tasks [12] and the professional environment [19], demanding specific command inputs and a deep understanding of systems for tasks like network configuration and penetration testing. CLI's efficiency, especially for experienced users, is explored by Voronkov, Martucci, and Lindskog [22], highlighting its preference among system administrators for certain tasks over graphical user interfaces (GUIs). CLI allows for scripting and command piping, enhancing task performance efficiency and requiring fewer system resources, making it ideal for high-performance computing environments. Moreover, CLI-based training in cybersecurity is instrumental in improving problem-solving skills and adaptability. CLI command learning can also be specialised in using one or more commands, e.g. for learning the git tool or networking scenarios [4, 23]. Previous research exists on assessing tasks and challenges encoded and labelled by instructors [12, 15]. However, in the case of problem-solving tasks, when different approaches can be taken to achieve the results, they are unsuitable because of a high degree of freedom regarding several possible solutions.

Švábenský et al. [17] demonstrate how hands-on exercises that require quick and innovative thinking enhance professionals' analytical capabilities. Although the CLI may present a steep learning curve for beginners, its precision, flexibility, and efficiency are unmatched for IT professionals, developers, and system administrators, making it an essential tool for complex tasks or automating repetitive ones in computing environments. This hands-on experience with the CLI significantly enhances the learning process, preparing students for future developments in this technical area and allowing educators to adjust their teaching strategies for improved training effectiveness [8, 16].

Maennel [10] covers the application of learning analytics in cybersecurity training, focusing on cybersecurity exercises to enhance effectiveness in skill development. Learning analytics and metrics provide evidence of the learning process and related improvements. Online cybersecurity exercises are a powerful tool for teaching cybersecurity content, but they have a challenge related to individual assessment [7].

Analysis of CLI artefacts includes string tokenization and context analyses. Trizna [20] introduces the Shell Language Preprocessing (SLP) library, which focuses on the tokenization and encoding of Unix and Linux Shell commands. It outlines the limitations of traditional NLP methods in this context and proposes alternative encoding strategies such as label, one-hot, and TF-IDF encodings, implemented through *bashlex* and additional syntactic logic for complex command syntax handling. Analysis of command similarities [6] enables pattern recognition and its application to attribute actions to the adversary. Structured features of the Shell command can be used to identify malicious commands [2].

Quantitative and qualitative data analyses of CLI can identify the efficacy of command-line tool usage in cybersecurity training simulations. Švábenský et al. [16] focused on the frequency and types of commands employed by trainees, with a particular emphasis on tools like *nmap*, *ls*, and *cd*. The study further explored terminal command usage, identifying common errors and misconceptions among trainees. However, they did not analyse the variability of commands in terms of parameter or option usage.

As users may track their progress over time, see trends in their errors, and modify their learning tactics accordingly, error analysis of this kind encourages self-improvement and independent learning in a self-learning environment. The relationship between user error and cognition is examined by Wu et al. [24]. In order to create more user-friendly user interfaces and instructional materials, it is imperative that user errors be understood from a cognitive point of view, as the study highlights. It also highlights that distinct user groups, such as novice, ordinary, and expert, show differing error rates.

This paper presents a solution for analysing user activities at the command structure level in the CLI environment to ensure individual assessment in online training. Analysis of correct and erroneous commands and result aggregation in the group context enables evaluation of the individual performance for the defined tasks.

## 3 Learning Process in Cybersecurity Challenges

Most cybersecurity training exercises implement a challenge-based learning approach where trainees solve tasks practically. Then, they submit artefacts such as IP addresses, passwords, and breached usernames as evidence in reports or specialized forms. The scoring modules assign points for correctly provided evidence.

Figure 1 interrelates people, processes, and technology in the context of cybersecurity challenges and provides an abstraction of the learning process in training activities. Instructor and trainee are the actors with responsibilities and needs. The instructor designs the scenario considering the trainee audience and simulated cases. This sub-process involves designing a realistic system, i.e., a technological digital twin working in a safe environment. The trainee practices in the system and self-assesses the performance when solving the tasks, i.e., challenges. The trainee has an overview of the performance and can provide contextual feedback, i.e., depending on the trainee group, goals, and scenario. Typically, the feedback involves guidelines and hints about the challenge. However, the assessment of skills is not involved because the path to solving the challenge still needs to be clarified. Some artefacts can even be guessed accidentally. Even if the users leave digital traces, i.e., their actions are logged, the collected data typically stays unused for assessment and feedback at its total capacity.

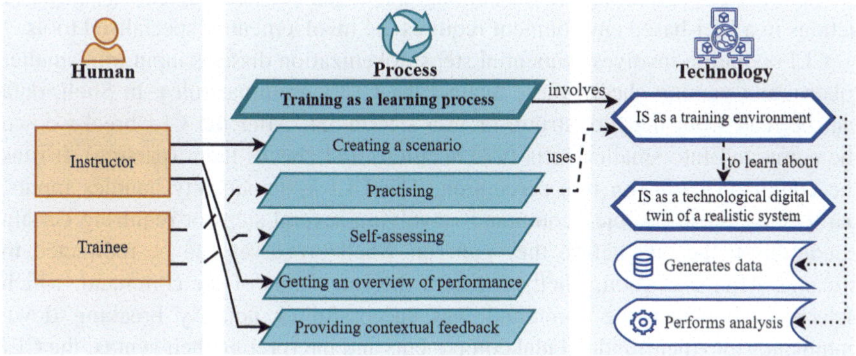


**Fig. 1** People, process, and technology in cybersecurity challenges

Evaluating trainees' progress becomes rigid as the number of participants increases. The more trainees involved in a training program, the more data is generated. Thus, processing and analysing the data to indicate the performance of an individual or group in terms of competences becomes only possible with technological solutions. The instructors need to find a balance between providing individualised feedback and managing the large number of data generated by the trainees' performance.

Similarly, from the trainee's perspective, receiving relevant feedback is critical for learning and development. Without clear and immediate feedback, trainees may struggle to understand where they went wrong or where they can improve their approach. This can lead to frustration, decreased motivation, and even slower progress. Therefore, the need for automated feedback mechanisms increases as bridging the gap between trainees' need for feedback and instructor's capacity to provide support becomes crucial.

Technology plays a central role in the learning process during cybersecurity challenges. Firstly, IS as a training environment is required to ensure and enhance the training experience even with existing complexities, especially regarding evaluation and feedback mechanisms. Secondly, IS, as a digital twin of the realistic system, is a mandatory element as an object of learning and practising. Instructors should have access to tools that could help them manage and interpret the large amount of data generated by the trainees, while the trainees should get timely feedback and make further steps to improve their learning experience.

## 4 CLI Evaluation Metrics

The most common interface for security developers and operators is the feature-rich CLI. Therefore, systematically handling CLI command sequences and analysing the richness and correctness of the command is essential. The assessment of trainee actions in a CLI-based environment requires the involvement of specialised tools.

CLI operation involves sequential steps: tokenization dissects input into smaller tokens, and parsing checks these against the CLI's grammar rules. In Shell, data can be read from the file, string, or user's terminal. After the CLI breaks down the command into smaller parts (tokenization) and checks them (parsing), it runs the command based on this perception. The CLI systematically handles inputs, particularly those complex commands involving several steps or requiring certain conditions to be met before they can run. Shell processes can be redirected to streams. After execution, Shell processes the exit status of the command, which determines whether the command was successful or not. By breaking down commands into their fundamental components and interpreting their syntax, the CLI gains the ability to analyse command structures and usage patterns. This depth of analysis is valuable for both educators and practitioners, offering more profound insights into the nuances of command-line interactions.

The lexical analysis breaks the input into words and phrases, known as tokens. Each token carries a specific meaning, and it surrounds everything from the commands themselves to various options and arguments. The role of the tokenizer is to categorise each segment of the command accordingly. Tokenization can be represented using the formal constructs.

Each command is a string $s \in S$ composed of a sequence of characters $s = \langle c_1 c_2 c_3 \ldots c_n \rangle$, where each $c_i \in CH$ represents a character in the command, and set $S$ denotes a set of strings. The tokenization function $tf$ maps the string $s \in S$ to a sequence of tokens $T = \langle t | \forall t \in S \wedge \exists s' = \sqcup t : s' = s \rangle \subset S$. A token set is a subset of a string set, and concatenation of tokens can make the original string $s$.

Meta-characters play a crucial role in the tokenization and influence command parsing process. A set of meta-characters, $M \subset CH$, includes delimiters such as a pipe, ampersand, semicolon, relational operators, parentheses, spaces, tabs, and newlines. The presence of the meta-characters in the command string $s$ determines the boundaries of each token. Each token $t \in T$ is classified based on its composition. A *word* is a token without any characters from $M$ and not enclosed in quotes. An *operator* contains at least one character from $M$ and is unquoted. Operators are categorised into control and redirection types, denoted as $C$ and $R$, respectively. Set $C$ includes control operators such as a newline, a vertical pipe, and parentheses. Set $R$ includes redirection operators such as '<<'.

Let us consider a complex *Nmap* command represented as a string $s =$ "*nmap -p 80,443 --open -sV example.com*". The tokenizer identifies *nmap* as the foundational command token. Then, it separates the options *-p*, *--open*, and *-sV*, alongside with *80,443* and *example.com* as arguments. The tokenization function $tf$ applied to the command string $s$ returns a token sequence, $T$=⟨"nmap", "-p", "80,443", "--open", "-sV", "domain-example.com"⟩. Figure 2 illustrates the tokenization result and context information. As illustrated in this example, the tokenization successfully breaks down the command into individual components. However, these components, or tokens, lack meaning when isolated. For instance, the token *-p* is ambiguous on its own but, when used with the *nmap* command, specifies the ports to scan. Similarly, the token 80,443 is a basic string of characters until it is understood as the argument for the *-p* option, specifying the selection of ports for the *nmap* command. Tokenization prepares tokens for parsing, but the semantic understanding arises in later stages, where syntax is analysed, and commands are executed.

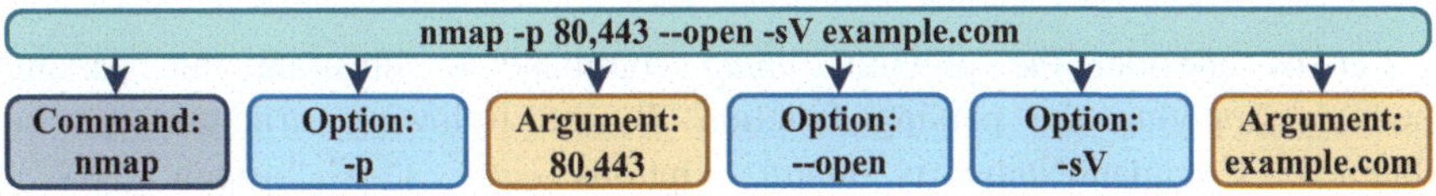


**Fig. 2** Tokenization of the Nmap command

Analysis of the parser involves examining tokens to establish their relationships and determining command components like names, options, and arguments combined into coherent instructions for execution. Understanding CLI conventions, such as delimiters, the role of flags as boolean options to indicate true or false states, and the significance of the *--help* flag in providing detailed command information is essential. In Shell command line processing, the parsing function, denoted as $P$, transforms a sequence of tokens into a structured command representation.

Here, each token $t_i \in T$ represents a distinct element of the original command. The function $P$ meticulously maps these tokens to their corresponding roles in the command structure. The CommandName is the first token $t_1$, while OptionsList and ArgumentsList are formulated from subsequent tokens based on their syntactical and contextual properties. Additionally, special tokens indicating pipes and redirections are categorized into RedirectionOperator and ControlOperator, respectively. Pipes and Redirections, integral to command execution flow, are identified by specific Meta-characters. These elements, besides the first element, can have variable order and presence in the command structure, reflecting the flexible nature of Shell command syntax. This mapping ensures that the sequence and hierarchical relationship of the tokens are preserved, leading to an accurate interpretation of the command as a whole unit. Options in a Shell command, signified by '-' or '--', are often paired with their subsequent Arguments. Arguments are tokens that do not qualify as Options or Meta-characters. The mapping function $F_{\text{oa}}$ is defined to identify these pairs (see Eq. 1.) Applying $F_{\text{oa}}$ to the command tokens, option-argument pairs are constructed, $\text{Pairs} = \{(t_i, F_{\text{oa}}(t_i)) \mid t_i \in \text{Options}\}$.

$$F_{\text{oa}}(t_i) = \begin{cases} t_{i+1} & \text{if } t_{i+1} \notin \text{Options} \\ \emptyset & \text{otherwise} \end{cases} \tag{1}$$

In the case of specific commands like *nmap*, where the last token often represents the target of the scan, a modified option-argument mapping function $F_{\text{oa}}^{nmap}$ is defined as presented in Eq. 2. Applying $F_{\text{oa}}^{nmap}$ to *nmap* command tokens, it identifies both option-argument pairs and standalone arguments: $\text{Pairs}^{nmap} = \{(t_i, F_{\text{oa}}^{nmap}(t_i)) \mid t_i \in \text{Options}\}$ and $\text{StandaloneArgument} = t_m$ if $t_m \notin \text{Pairs}^{nmap}$.

$$F_{\text{oa}}^{nmap}(t_i) = \begin{cases} t_{i+1} & \text{if } t_{i+1} \notin \text{Options} \wedge i+1 < m \\ \emptyset & \text{if } i+1 = m \vee t_{i+1} \in \text{Options} \end{cases} \tag{2}$$

Let us consider the previous *nmap* command to illustrate this parsing method. Applying the parsing function $P$, the following structure can be obtained: CommandName is *nmap*, Options = {"-p", "--open", "-sV"}, $\text{Pairs}^{nmap}$ = {("-p", "80,443"), ("--open", ∅), ("-sV", ∅)} *example.com* is a StandaloneArgument, and Pipes and Redirections are empty sets.

Statistical methods can be used to analyse the frequency and patterns of command usage (Command Structure Analysis; CSA.) For instance, using a counter to count the occurrences, can provide specific patterns like *Command-Option* or *Command-Argument-Option*. A high frequency of *Command-Argument-Option* might indicate a preference for commands with specific configurations, suggesting a user's skill level or the complexity of tasks they are performing. A CSA function *sf* maps each sequence of tokens $T$ to a command structure $cs \in CS$, where $CS$ is the set of all the possible command structures. A command structure can be defined as a sequence of token types representing the syntactic structure of a command. Each command structure $cs$ is a sequence of elements $cs = \langle t_1, t_2, t_3, \ldots, t_m \rangle$ where each $t_i$ corresponds to a type of token (such as Command, Option, Argument, etc.). The frequency of each command structure $cs$ in the dataset is calculated using the function $F(cs)$, defined as the sum of occurrences of $cs$ for each command string $s \in S$: $F(cs) = \sum_{s \in S}[sf(tf(s)) = cs]$. Here, $[sf(tf(s)) = cs]$ this function checks whether the structure identified by $sf(tf(s))$ is equal to a particular command structure $cs$ and if they are the same, the function returns 1, otherwise, it returns a 0. The formula counts how many times each unique command structure appears in the dataset. The unique command structure function *usf* maps each tokenized command to its unique structural pattern. The frequency function $F_{ucs}$ counts the occurrences of each unique command structure within the dataset. This analysis provides insights into the complexity and variety of command usage, highlighting common patterns or unusual combinations in command structures for individual commands. By identifying the most frequently used options and arguments, it can be defined, which features of a command are most valued, and its usage suggests the users' proficiency and sophistication level in command-line operations. Frequent use of complex metacharacters could indicate a high level of user expertise. Additionally, this analysis could aid in uncovering patterns or anomalies in command usage. Unusually high or low usage of certain options or arguments might suggest either a lack of awareness about these features or their irrelevance to the users' needs. In security-sensitive environments, these anomalous patterns could also be an indication of misuse, potentially flagging security concerns.

For any given command $s$, the function $cef(tf(s))$ provides the frequency distribution of elements in $s$, therefore, linking a tokenized command to its element frequencies. To be able to extend this analysis across all commands in the dataset, a frequency function $F_{all}$ is defined: $F_{all}(e) = \sum_{s \in S} n$ where $(e, n) \in cef(tf(s))$. This general function aggregates the frequencies of each element $e$ across the entire dataset, which then provides a comprehensive insights into user interactions with command-line elements. Such an analysis is valuable for understanding user behaviour patterns and preferences, in particular command usage. The average complexity $K$ for a set of commands by the user can be calculated as follows: $\bar{K} = \frac{1}{M} \sum_{i=1}^{n} m_i K(c_i)$, where $c_i$ is a command from the set of all certain command structures, $K(c_i)$ is a command complexity (based on the number of elements in a command), $m_i$ is a count of $c_i$ occurrences, and $M$ is a total number of command usages. The complexity variation $V$, which measures the spread of these complexities, is the standard deviation of complexity: $V = \sqrt{\frac{1}{M} \sum_{i=1}^{n} m_i (K(c_i) - \bar{K})^2}$.

In a command line, error analysis is essential for identifying common mistakes users make. In order to provide insights into user behaviour, this analysis can focus on classifying and evaluating the success or failure of instructions that are executed in the command-line environment. Examination of unsuccessful commands, stemming from syntax errors, improper command usage, or a lack of understanding of the purpose of command functions, might reveal error patterns. This data is essential for creating more focused teaching materials that could address prevalent areas of misunderstanding.

## 5 IS Design and Architecture

We propose the IS design to support cybersecurity-related education and data-driven assessment of the trainee who is an IT or IS specialist. The proposed solution is a heterogeneous environment (see Fig. 3), fulfilling the needs of the instructor and trainee in challenge-based training activities. As an actor, a *Course instructor* designs a *Training task* that requires the execution of CLI commands. The task represents a challenge to overcome, and it includes several subtasks. As a *Training group* participant, the *Trainee* performs the task in an individual training *Sandbox* that is a part of the *Training environment*. Each sandbox is a digital twin of a realistic system designed for the challenge scenario. There, the CLI actions of the trainee are recorded and sent to the *Analytics component*. Once CLI-based data is collected, the instructor proceeds to the next steps. Within the *Analytics component* section, the *Course instructor* begins with anonymisation and performs *Data cleaning* to ensure the private data is not disclosed, for example, private keys and possible plain-text passwords. Then, the instructor launches the *Analysis* process. The *Data analysis tool* applies the predefined metrics on the collected and cleaned CLI data to generate trainee performance results (see *Performance report* in the figure) in a structured format. The trainee and instructor can view the generated results. The instructor can provide additional feedback for an individual trainee in the context of the trainee group and challenge scenario.

The execution architecture of the proposed IS (see Fig. 4) uses a dual virtual machine configuration. The proposed design enables the separation and management of two fundamental processes, CLI usage pattern extraction and Shell command execution, in the *Data analysis tool* of the *Analytics component* presented in Fig. 3. *The Main Virtual Machine*, running as a Linux host, is responsible for data handling tasks, i.e., receiving and organising collected data. The main scripts of the component *Command-line Data Tool* orchestrate the entire process. They control the intake and parsing of data (see *Command-line Data*) and manage workflows to save and retrieve patterns (see database *Commands*), check command correctness, execute analytical tasks, and save the analysis results (see *Generated Results*). The *Sandbox Virtual Machine* is employed to identify errors in the usage pattern during the extraction process. It enables the execution of commands in an isolated environment and returns the execution output to the main machine. Ideally, the sandbox is Kali or Parrot Linux OS distribution equipped with core utils and penetration and security testing tools.

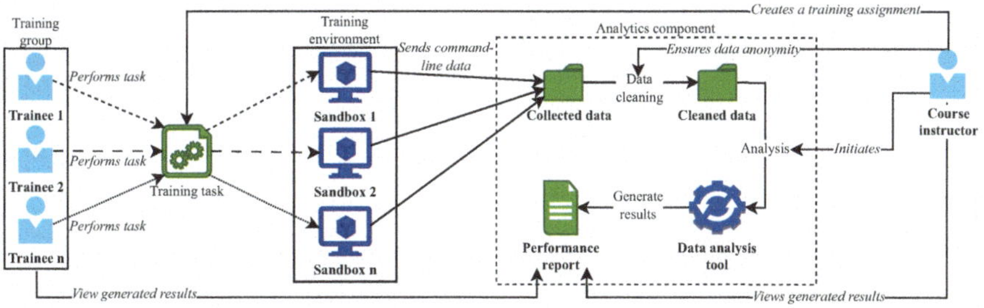


**Fig. 3** Information system solution design

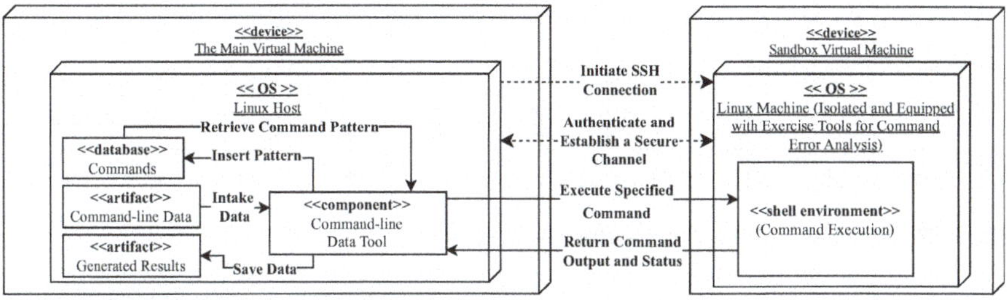


**Fig. 4** Execution architecture of the solution's analytics component

Figure 5 presents the relational model of the database component and illustrates the tokenized CLI command data insertion. Table CommandSequences stores an original CLI command with a unique identifier. A record of CommandExecutionLog represents the output of the command execution in the sandbox. Table CommandElements refers to CommandSequences, as it records the order of options and arguments, i.e., a single record corresponds to a parameter. Each CLI command and its options and arguments are stored in dedicated tables (see tables at the right). Therefore, before inserting new arguments and options, the system checks already saved elements. This design enables analysis of the options and arguments among all commands within the trainee group.

Figure 6 presents the flow of the error-checking logic and command pattern extraction for an individual trainee. Firstly, the command is checked for the base exception. Configuration files define command types to skip, e.g., Python script execution. If such a command is detected, the system raises a base exception. Otherwise, the tool sanitises the commands from the outbound file or network operations, such as switching IP addresses to localhost for scanning tools, and checks if it is already in the database (found in the logs of other trainees or previously detected in the log of this trainee). If the command is not in the database, the error-checking module sends it to the sandbox for execution. Command execution status is recorded, i.e., successful execution or failed (see Fig. 5). The performance report explicitly counts the trainee's errors.

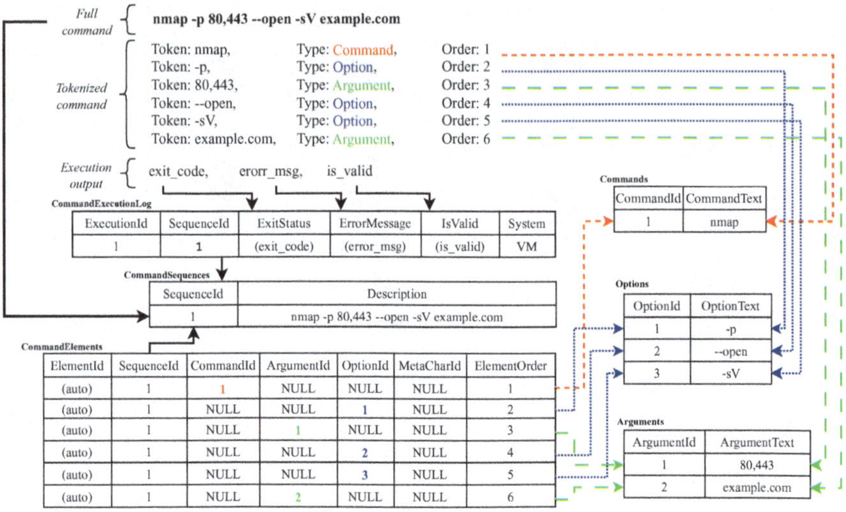


**Fig. 5** Relational model and data insertion example

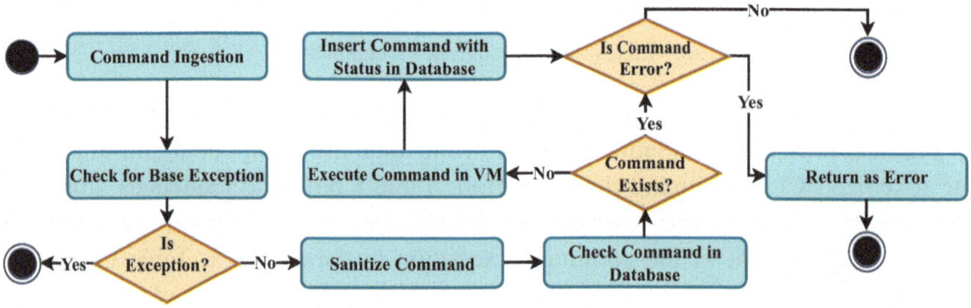


**Fig. 6** The flowchart of the error-checking logic

The sandbox virtual machine serves as a controlled testing ground. It replicates or closely resembles the trainee's operating environment. The sandbox usage ensures isolated execution of Shell commands and integrity of the main machine, working as a central IS hub.

## 6 Experimental Setup

The IS prototype was implemented as a proof of concept for the proposed solution. The prototype reflected the designed execution architecture (see Fig. 4) for the experimental setup. OpenNebula, Infrastructure as a Service (IaaS) open-source platform with KVM hypervisor for virtualization, was used to create two virtual machines. The Main Virtual Machine, built using a Debian OS template, had the developed tool installed with the corresponding SQLite3 database and the dataset for experimentation. The tool comprised Bash and Python scripts. Bash scripts orchestrated the flow of the tool. They performed remote Bash execution, while Python scripts performed data loading, tokenization, parsing, and the analysis part. The Sandbox Virtual Machine was used as a separate environment to execute sanitised CLI commands over SSH connection, i.e., get execution output and perform error analysis. Therefore, the machine was equipped with main exercise tools to test the commands and return the output to the analysis tool on a central machine.

We used the open dataset [18] to execute the simulated experiments, test our analytical components, and demonstrate proof of concept of the proposed design. The dataset consists of 13,446 Shell commands from 175 individuals participating in cybersecurity training. The dataset contains several subsets associated with different tasks. We selected the "Junior Hacker Adaptive" subset for experimentation because it contained the most significant number of participants and commands. It included 58 participants who executed 12–148 commands to familiarise themselves with the environment, scan the network, connect to the server, find and retrieve the required file, and crack its password.

The dataset offers realistic content of user interactions in a cybersecurity training context. The data was gathered during actual training activities using a transparent, open-source logging system, accurately showing command-line operations typical in cybersecurity, such as penetration testing. The dataset includes a variety of commands used in Bash, ZSH, and Metasploit shells, all stored in a JSON format, making it a valuable tool for diverse research activities. Each sandbox file is formatted using newline delimited JSON.

The provided JSON files represent recorded user actions in a cybersecurity training environment. Each entry in each dataset file includes attributes like `cmd_type`, indicating the nature of the command executed (e.g., Bash command), and `pool_id` and `sandbox_id`, which are identifiers for the specific training environment. The `timestamp_str` attribute timestamps each action, allowing for temporal analysis of user activities. The `hostname` and `username` fields provide context on the system and user account from which the trainee executed the commands, and the fields are vital to follow access levels and system interactions. The `cmd` attribute records the exact command executed, offering insights into the user's primary focus and command-line efficiency. Additionally, the `wd` (working directory) and `ip` (IP address) fields provide further context, revealing the user's navigation patterns and network interactions.

Some participants performed tasks with long breaks, sometimes lasting days. The long breaks, more extended than 1800 seconds, were subtracted from the total task duration time to get a more concentrated view of time. Thus, the duration of task solving included only shorter breaks as part of the training process. In the configuration file of the prototypes' error-checking module, the base exception list included the execution of specific console-based commands that open environments or require user input to operate or stop the processes, i.e. interactive commands such as terminal editors (vim), password changing (passwd) or device availability utilities (ping), and Bash or Python scripts, as such data is not logged and cannot be processed or analysed.

## 7 Results and Discussion

The experiments were executed on the open dataset (see Sect. 6) to demonstrate the proof of concept and the potential of the proposed IS design. The developed prototype performed lexical and syntax analysis of the logged CLI commands. It also produced a structured output and generated visual reports as performance indicators of an individual (or several individuals) in the context of the group results and challenge scenario.

The compiled insightful diagrams reveal key patterns and improvement areas based on the commands the trainees executed. This interpretation of the results is based exclusively on the data from a single dataset, without prior knowledge of the trainees and their level of expertise. Consequently, trainee performance during this training session determines the evaluation. In each figure of this section, visual markers are used to distinguish particular trainees to illustrate and track individual performance indicators: diamonds represent User 1, and squares represent User 2. These markers visually *represent how these participants interact with the task and tools compared to the average team performance*. The figures also show the distribution of individual results within a team. Figure 7a plots the number of CLI commands against the number of errors, allowing the accuracy of command usage to be assessed within the average group performance. It highlights that higher command usage does not necessarily lead to more errors, *indicating the participants' learning curve*. For example, User 1 executed almost the same number of commands as User 2 but experienced many more errors. Both users executed fewer commands than the average number of executions within a group (represented as a horizontal dashed line).

Figure 7b aligns the task duration (on the x-axis) with error counts and unique command counts (on the y-axis) to *gain perspective on the performance of the unique tool usage based on task completion time and its correlation with command line inaccuracy*. The lower horizontal line shows an average number of errors, and the upper horizontal dashed line shows the average number of unique commands. For all users, except Users 1 and 2, the duration is aligned with a count of unique commands (the filled circle sign) and a count of errors (the times sign). The figure demonstrates that longer duration does not necessarily correlate with error frequency, as a bigger part of participants with longer task execution time managed to stay below average error count. For example, User 1 spent less time on the task than User 2, using fewer unique commands but experiencing more errors. As shown in Fig. 7, User 2 executed all correctly formed CLI commands, and a count of unique commands is the average of unique commands within a group. Another important observation is the relationship between unique command usage and errors. Sessions with a higher variety of commands only sometimes led to more

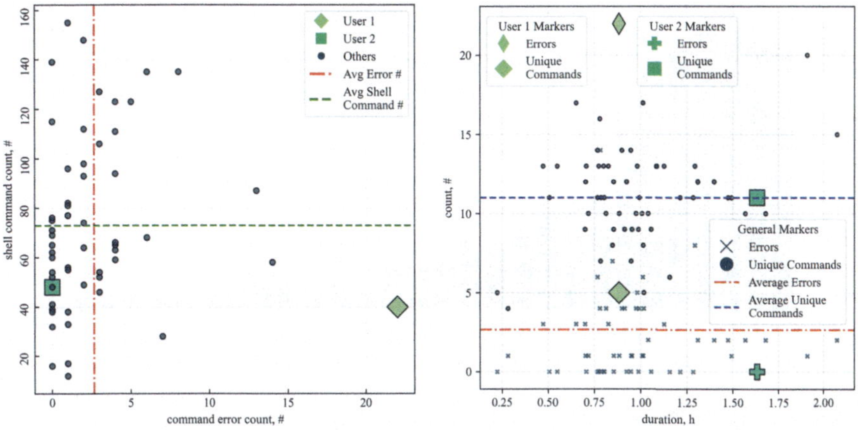


**(a)** CLI command count vs. command error count

**(b)** Task duration vs. error count vs. unique command count

**Fig. 7** Error count alignment with execution duration and CLI command count. (**a**) CLI command count vs. command error count. (**b**) Task duration vs. error count vs. unique command count

errors. This suggests that *proficiency in command usage and familiarity with tools can significantly impact performance outcomes.*

A deeper analysis of the specific command usage can reveal a user's expertise and involvement. Session data along the timeline offers valuable insights into users' behaviour, and a granular look into command usage patterns can suggest their proficiency level. Frequent use of advanced options or niche commands might indicate higher expertise, whereas reliance on basic commands could suggest a novice or task-focused approach. Each of Figs. 9, 10, and 11 includes two diagrams. One diagram illustrates the command usage, and the second highlights the corresponding options applied. The diagrams show the count, complexity, and variation of command structures. This view indicates the trainee's familiarity with the specific tools and describes how well they can use the commands with minimal effort compared to the average indicators within the group. The figures order the users according to the command count, where high command complexity suggests a more advanced level. Moderate complexity variation reflects consistency in command execution (see equations in Sect. 4). *High command complexity variations might indicate experimental approaches*, while beginners with consistently low complexity scores and minimal variations indicate less experience. Low complexity scores and minimal variations reflect a more cautious approach to command usage, potentially avoiding errors.

Figure 8 highlights some of the most frequently executed commands during the task, offering insight into the primary focus and scope of the users' actions. It also provides clues about the depth of their engagement, such as whether they explored additional commands or stuck to basic ones. The diagram contrasts the two users considered exemplary cases in this section. While both users relied heavily on basic

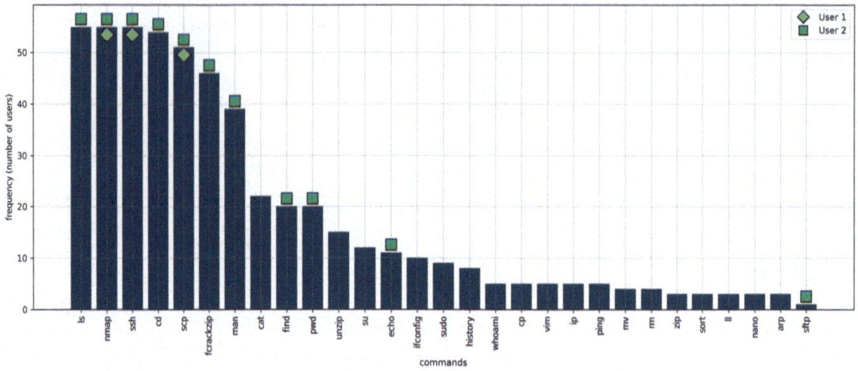


**Fig. 8** Command usage frequency amongst users

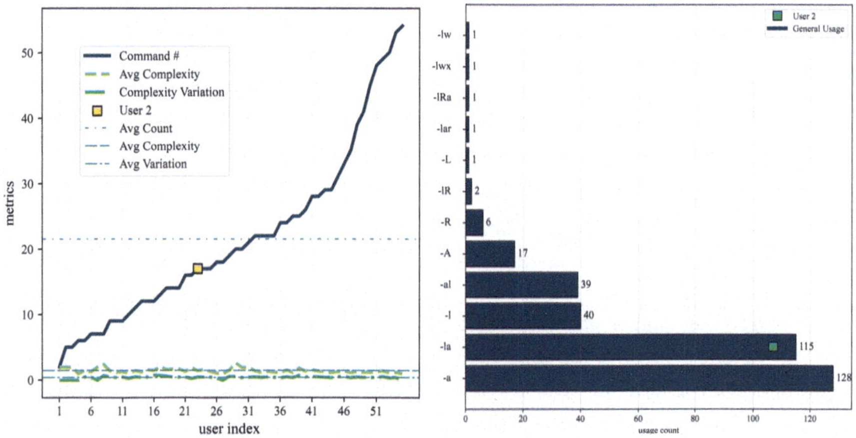


**(a)** `ls` command complexity **(b)** `ls` options

**Fig. 9** Analysis of `ls` command usage. (**a**) `ls` command complexity. (**b**) `ls` options

commands such as `Nmap` and `ssh`, User 2 showcased a higher level of involvement, executing a broader range of commands. In contrast, User 1 used fewer commands and notably did not use the `fcrackzip` (for password cracking) and `ls` (for listing information about the directories and files) commands. The diagram suggests that User 1 may have struggled to complete the task.

Heavy usage of basic commands can be observed in the diagrams. For example, command `ls` is a fundamental command (see Fig. 9 for a more detailed analysis). However, its utility varies significantly among individuals (see Fig. 9a). Some users employ simple, straightforward executions. Others use more advanced flag combinations to tailor the output to their needs (see Fig. 9b). In this case, User 1 did not even employ Fig. 9 to list the file system contents. On the other hand, User 2 leveraged one of the most common and powerful flag combinations `-la`, to display

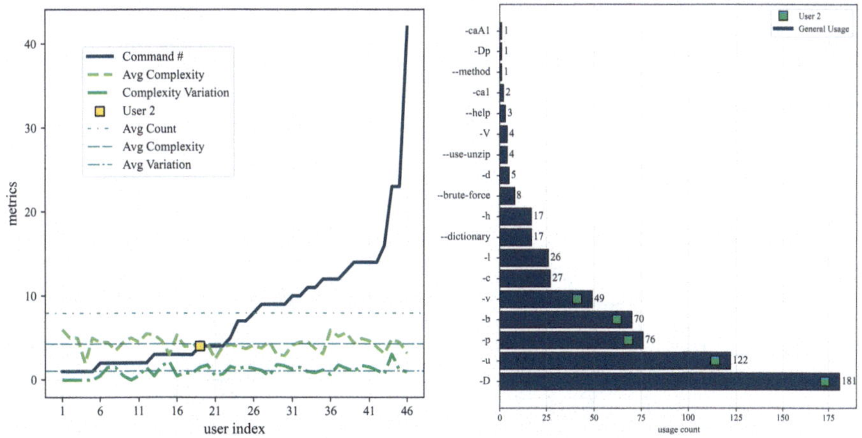


**(a)** `fcrackzip` command complexity **(b)** `fcrackzip` options

**Fig. 10** Analysis of `fcrackzip` command usage. (**a**) `fcrackzip` command complexity. (**b**) `fcrackzip` options

hidden files and provide detailed directory listings, indicating a more strategic and informed approach to the task. *The detailed analysis with a designed metric enables assessment of the command complexity and identifies the level of proficiency.*

Sometimes, challenges require additional, more advanced, and non-standard CLI tools, such as `fcrackzip`. The analysis of this command usage shows varying levels of engagement and expertise among users (see Fig. 10a). Note that not all users executed the command; therefore, the maximum value of the x-axis is smaller than in other diagrams. The diversity in usage is evident, as some users employ specific brute force methods while others take a more generalized approach. For instance, User 2 opted for one of the most commonly used techniques, such as the dictionary attack (see Fig. 10b), which is often favoured for its efficiency when the password is likely to be found in a pre-compiled wordlist. On the other hand, as mentioned before, User 1 did not attempt this part of the challenge and did not use the command. This contrast highlights the different strategies and familiarity levels with the tool, showcasing a spectrum of proficiency from basic to advanced. *The visual analysis gives evidence regarding participant evaluation and suggests directions the instructor should take when providing feedback, considering the challenge scenario.*

Diagrams of Fig. 11a offer insights into the participants' usage of the `Nmap` command, a tool for network scanning and security auditing. The figure highlights the differences in tool usage. User 1 relied on standard parameters used by their peers, and User 2 experimented with less frequently used options (see Fig. 11b), further demonstrating their more profound knowledge. Based on the figures, User 1 struggled with command execution, as seen by a high error rate in the CLI command analysis. The trainee executed 40 commands, but 22 errors indicate a

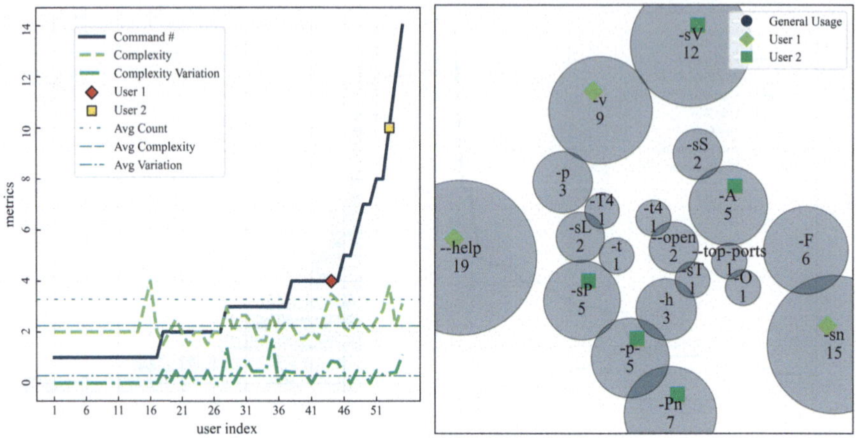


**(a)** `Nmap` command usage **(b)** `Nmap` options

**Fig. 11** Analysis of `Nmap` command usage. (**a**) `Nmap` command usage. (**b**) `Nmap` options

substantial error rate of 55%. This result suggests a lack of familiarity with the commands and the system. The frequent usage of the `--help` option in `Nmap` and the most common option usage further supports the hypothesis that User 1 is in a learning phase, potentially lacking knowledge of some commands. In contrast, User 2 displayed superior command execution skills, executing 48 commands with no errors, indicating high proficiency and confidence in handling hands-on tasks. Using `Nmap` with complex options like `-A` for aggressive scanning and `-sV` for service version detection showcases a strategic and thorough approach. These options are critical for in-depth system analysis, showing the readiness of User 2 for participation in actual penetration testing missions.

Overall, the diagrams from Figs. 8, 9, 10, and 11 complement each other and work as a visual tool for the instructor to indicate the skill level of the particular trainee in the assessment process. This detailed analysis highlights the varying skill levels and areas for improvement among the participants. It also shows the importance of personalised and group training programs, which could tackle arising issues and enhance training efficiency. In addition, *certain users can be identified as taking on more complex tasks to further engage in more challenging activities*. In contrast, others might need more basic training to reach a certain level.

## 8 Conclusions, Limitations, and Future Work

The professional development of IT and IS specialists includes training using hands-on exercises. However, the training process should be part of the educational system that employs tools for semi-automated and AI-ready assessment and evaluation of performance proficiency. The proof of concept, implemented according to the design of the analytics component of the proposed solution and executed with an open dataset, demonstrated individual performance assessment based on command execution patterns, frequency of errors, and task duration. The performance report offered insights into the trainee's confidence and familiarity with tasks. Diverse command structures, from basic Command-Argument to complex sequences, suggested varying technical skill levels among participants. The community of educators benefits from the designed solution for *the formative assessment of the trainee, getting the report of command usage patterns, and aligning individual performance with a group and command usage patterns detected within the group*. Therefore, it could work as a tool to *increase training efficiency, ensure transparency, and shape training plans*.

This study has potential limitations. Firstly, using one specific dataset to gain insights into student performance could cover only part of the diverse possibilities of command usage. Other data sets could reveal the necessity of adding alternative dimensions to provide a multi-perspective view of trainee performance. Then, the interpretation of the results may yield different insights depending on the type of exercise conducted and the competence of the course instructor. Command usage patterns might correlate and allow instructors to distinguish skill levels. Some advanced patterns are out of scope for novices, and the advanced trainees could solve tasks using many alternatives. Furthermore, the data did not include the background information, e.g., what engagement elements the exercise included or if the system provided hints. The data set description lacks details about sampling procedures. Thus, the same performance does not mean the same required training approach. Technical limitations could also pose challenges. For example, different CLI environments may require different parsing of command elements to identify their exact meaning within the command structure correctly. Also, some specific and non-core Unix commands require a non-typical parameter passing. Finally, the proposed method identifies syntax errors but cannot detect logical ones. Thus, the system would indicate a good trainee performance even when the parameter values are illogical in the scenario setting.

Future research directions could include investigating probabilistic methods for user behaviour prediction for dynamic hint and training help invocation. Other improvements could enhance the system's resilience, safety, and flexibility, adapting to training scenarios. More accurate identification and sanitisation of complex data types, advancing error detection, and accommodating different command execution environments would be crucial for a broader application spectrum. Additionally, incorporating AI tools for refined data pattern recognition, anomaly detection, and user behaviour forecasting could significantly enrich the tool's analytical capabilities. These advancements elevate the tool's utility in more complex scenarios and provide deeper, AI-driven insights into cybersecurity training and education.

## References


1. Bauraitė, A., Brilingaitė, A., & Bukauskas, L. (2024). Designing trainee performance assessment system for hands-on exercises. In *Proceedings of Harnessing Opportunities: Reshaping ISD in the Post-COVID-19 and Generative AI Era (ISD2024)* (pp. 1–13). AIS.
2. Chen, S., Yang, R., Zhang, H., Wu, H., Zheng, Y., Fu, X., & Liu, Q. (2023). SIFAST: An efficient unix shell embedding framework for malicious detection. In *Proceedings of Information Security: 26th International Conference (ISC)* (pp. 59–78).
3. Chowdhury, N., Katsikas, S., & Gkioulos, V. (2022). Modeling effective cybersecurity training frameworks: A delphi method-based study. *Computers & Security, 113*, 102551.
4. Conte de Leon, D., Goes, C. E., Haney, M. A., & Krings, A. W. (2018). ADLES: Specifying, deploying, and sharing hands-on cyber-exercises. *Computers & Security, 74*, 12–40.
5. Foster, C., & Francis, P. (2020). A systematic review on the deployment and effectiveness of data analytics in higher education to improve student outcomes. *Assessment & Evaluation in Higher Education, 45*(6), 822–841.
6. Hobert, K., Lim, C., & Budiarto, E. (2023). Semantic similarities for honeypot collected linux shell commands. In *Proceedings of the 11th International Conference on Information and Communication Technology (ICoICT)* (pp. 172–177). IEEE.
7. Karjalainen, M., Kokkonen, T., & Taari, N. (2022). Key elements of on-line cyber security exercise and survey of learning during the on-line cyber security exercise. In M. Lehto & P. Neittaanmäki (Eds.), *Cyber security: Critical infrastructure protection* (pp. 43–57). Springer.
8. Kendon, T., & Stephenson, B. (2016). Unix literacy for first-year computer science students. In *Proceedings of the 21st Western Canadian Conference on Computing Education (WCCCE)* (pp. 1–4). ACM.
9. Ley, T., Tammets, K., Pishtari, G., Chejara, P., Kasepalu, R., Khalil, M., Saar, M., Tuvi, I., Väljataga, T., & Wasson, B. (2023). Towards a partnership of teachers and intelligent learning technology: A systematic literature review of model-based learning analytics. *Journal of Computer Assisted Learning, 39*(5), 1397–1417.
10. Maennel, K. (2020). Learning analytics perspective: Evidencing learning from digital datasets in cybersecurity exercises. In *European Symposium on Security and Privacy Workshops (EuroS&P)* (pp. 27–36). IEEE.
11. Maennel, K., Brilingaitė, A., Bukauskas, L., Juozapavičius, A., Knox, B. J., Lugo, R. G., Maennel, O., Majore, G., & Sütterlin, S. (2023). A multidimensional cyber defense exercise: Emphasis on emotional, social, and cognitive aspects. *SAGE Open, 13*(1), 1–12.
12. Mirkovic, J., Aggarwal, A., Weinman, D., Lepe, P., Mache, J., & Weiss, R. (2020). Using terminal histories to monitor student progress on hands-on exercises. In *Proceedings of the 51st ACM Technical Symposium on Computer Science Education (SIGCSE)* (pp. 866–872).
13. Seker, E., & Ozbenli, H. (2018). The concept of cyber defence exercises (CDX): Planning, execution, evaluation. In *2018 International Conference on Cyber Security and Protection of Digital Services* (pp. 1–9). IEEE.
14. Singh, T. D., Khilji, A. F. U. R., Divyansha, Singh, A. V., Thokchom, S., & Bandyopadhyay, S. (2021). Predictive approaches for the UNIX command line: Curating and exploiting domain knowledge in semantics deficit data. *Multimedia Tools and Applications, 80*(6), 9209–9229.
15. Šuppa, M., Jariabka, O., Matejov, A., & Nagy, M. (2021). Term adventure: Interactively teaching UNIX command line, text adventure style. In *Proceedings of the 26th Conference on Innovation and Technology in Computer Science Education V. 1 (ITiCSE)* (pp. 108–114). ACM.
16. Švábenský, V., Vykopal, J., Tovarňák, D., & Čeleda, P. (2021). Toolset for collecting shell commands and its application in hands-on cybersecurity training. In *Frontiers in Education Conference (FIE)* (pp. 1–9). IEEE.
17. Švábenský, V., Vykopal, J., Čeleda, P., Tkáčik, K., & Popovič, D. (2022). Student assessment in cybersecurity training automated by pattern mining and clustering. *Education and Information Technologies, 27*(7), 9231–9262.

18. Švábenský, V., Vykopal, J., Seda, P., & Čeleda, P. (2021). Dataset of shell commands used by participants of hands-on cybersecurity training. *Data in Brief, 38*, 107398.
19. Tevault, D. A. (2020). *Mastering linux security and hardening: Protect your linux systems from intruders, malware attacks, and other cyber threats* (2nd edn.). Packt Publishing.
20. Trizna, D. (2022). Shell language processing: Unix command parsing for machine learning. arXiv:2107.02438.
21. Vigna, G. (2003). Teaching hands-on network security: Testbeds and live exercises. *Journal of Information Warfare, 2*(3), 8–24.
22. Voronkov, A., Martucci, L. A., & Lindskog, S. (2019). System administrators prefer command line interfaces, don't they? An exploratory study of firewall interfaces. In *Proceedings of the Fifteenth USENIX Symposium on Usable Privacy and Security, SOUPS*.
23. Winder, J., Falor, E., Poulsen, S., & Edwards, J. (2024). The shell tutor: An intelligent tutoring system for the UNIX command shell and git. In *Proceedings of the 2024 on Innovation and Technology in Computer Science Education V. 1 (ITiCSE)* (pp. 548–554). ACM.
24. Wu, X., Huang, X., Xu, R., & Yang, Q. (2013). An experimental method study of user error classification in human-computer interface. *Journal of Software, 8*, 2890–2898.
25. Zabicki, R., & Ellis, S. R. (2017). Chapter 75 – penetration testing. In J. R. Vacca (Ed.), *Computer and Information Security Handbook* (3rd edn., pp. 1031–1038). Morgan Kaufmann.

# A Circular Digital Twin for Climate-Smart Soils through Community Composting

**José Monteiro and João Barata**

**Abstract** This paper presents a Circular Digital Twin (DT) applied to climate-smart soils in a UNESCO Global Geopark, oriented towards the sustainable management of water use and organic matter, with a focus on climate change mitigation through carbon sequestration. Based on the Design Science Research approach, the study follows an iterative design and development cycle, which includes an ex-ante evaluation of technical and human risks. The Circular DT's architecture integrates sensors with real-time data analysis, using the Spiral Knowledge Management and Strong Structuration Theory to propose design principles. The results indicate that the Circular DT can promote efficient resource management in the agricultural context and contributes to closing the loop in the food supply chain, encouraging community composting and the use of organic waste in the soil. It also facilitates adaptive and inclusive management of soils and natural resources, which aligns with the sustainability standards of UNESCO Geoparks and the GEOfood initiative. The main contribution is a replicable DT for smart soils that support sustainable agricultural practices in the circular economy. The design principles strengthen the body of knowledge on DTs applied to natural resources, with the potential to support the transition to regenerative agricultural systems.

A prior version of this paper has been published in the ISD2024 Proceedings: Monteiro, J. & Barata, J. (2024). The Circular Digital Twin: Climate-Smart Soils as a Use Case. In B. Marcinkowski, A. Przybylek, A. Jarzębowicz, N. Iivari, E. Insfran, M. Lang, H. Linger, & C. Schneider (Eds.), *Harnessing Opportunities: Reshaping ISD in the post-COVID-19 and Generative AI Era (ISD2024 Proceedings)*. Gdańsk, Poland: University of Gdańsk. ISBN: 978–83–972,632-0-8. https://doi.org/10.62036/ISD.2024.107

J. Monteiro (✉) · J. Barata
University of Coimbra, CISUC/LASI, DEI, Coimbra, Portugal
e-mail: jafmonteiro@dei.uc.pt; barata@dei.uc.pt



B. Marcinkowski et al. (eds.), *Advances in Information Systems Development*, Lecture Notes in Information Systems and Organisation 77,
https://doi.org/10.1007/978-3-031-87880-0_9

# 1 Introduction

The European Green Deal is clear about the need to promote sustainable soil management practices, emphasizing the importance of protecting this vital natural resource from degradation that threatens biodiversity, carbon sequestration capacity, and ecological resilience [1]. In response to these concerns, the concept of climate-smart soils emerged for mitigating the adverse effects of climate change [2]. Climate-smart soils can be defined as those managed to optimize agricultural productivity and resilience while minimizing carbon emissions and contributing to soil carbon sequestration [2, 3]. In this context, Digital Twins (DTs) play a key role in enabling continuous monitoring of soil conditions [4], providing producers and managers with accurate data to implement sustainable management practices that respond to the objectives of the European Green Deal and corroborated by the 2030 Agenda [5], such as biodiversity conservation and increased climate resilience.

DTs are a strategic tool for regenerative agriculture [6, 7], offering a digital replica of physical systems for real-time monitoring and forecasting [8]. By tracking the state of the soil and its evolution, DTs facilitate the analysis of environmental and agronomic data, enabling informed decisions that support productivity and sustainability. The circularity of the supply chain is reinforced with the introduction of composted organic waste into the soil, promoting the continuous improvement of soil health [9]. The process of returning waste to the soil is central to regenerative agriculture practices, as it encourages an increase in organic matter, improves water retention, and strengthens the soil's structure [10].

A Design Science Research (DSR) [11] project was conducted in cooperation with Estrela UNESCO Global Geopark (Estrela Geopark) [12]. The first design cycle focused on community composting [13], and the present study expands this concept to cover the management of climate-smart soils through Circular DT. This manuscript is an extension of our previous work in Circular DTs [14], strengthening the theoretical analysis using the lenses of Strong Structuration Theory (SST) [15] and Knowledge Spiral Model (KSM) [16], and extending the design principles to support regional sustainability. This research focuses on developing a DT architecture to monitor, evaluate, and optimize C sequestration and resource management in Estrela Geopark, in line with the GEOfood manifesto [17]. The Research Objectives (RO) are:

- ***RO1.*** *Investigate the interdependencies between different segments of the food supply chain (return and source), laying the foundations for a Circular DT.*
- ***RO2.*** *Design and evaluate a Circular DT to continuously monitor the implementation of the GEOfood in Estrela Geopark, closing the loop of food waste and its incorporation into climate-smart soils.*

This study contributes to the digital transformation agenda in the development of Information Systems (IS) in the post-COVID-19 era, integrating the emerging opportunities brought by Artificial Intelligence (AI) to improve the accuracy, adaptability, and regulation of DTs [18]. The use of data analytics is critical for digital resilience and sustainability.

The rest of this paper is structured as follows. Section 2 explores the theoretical foundations of this work. Next, Section 3 describes the research approach and Sect. 4 details the design and development of Circular DT. The demonstration and evaluation of this solution are presented in Sections 5 and 6, respectively. Subsequently, Section 7 presents a critical reflection through the lens of the selected theories and establishes design principles for developing Circular DTs. Finally, Section 8 summarizes the main conclusions and future lines of research.

## 2 Theoretical Background

### *2.1 Digital Twins in Smart Soils*

The concept of DT has its roots in aerospace and military industry [19], but it has expanded into various fields, including manufacturing, healthcare and smart cities [20–22]. According to Raj and Surinayanan [8], *"a digital twin is a computer program that takes real-world data about a physical object or system as input and produces as outputs (predications or simulations of how that physical object or system will be affected by those inputs)"*. This definition underscores the ability of DTs to monitor and predict the behavior of physical systems in real-time, allowing for process optimization and improved operational efficiency. The application of DTs has been growing in agriculture and smart soils, as detailed in the bibliometric analysis shown in Fig. 1.

The bibliometric analysis was performed with VOSviewer software, using data from Scopus and Web of Science. The search was performed with the query "digital twin" AND "soil", yielding 479 articles in Scopus and 274 in Web of Science. The keyword co-occurrence network from the Scopus results (Fig. 1a) shows DT as a central term linked to concepts such as agriculture, AI, the Internet of Things (IoT), precision agriculture, and climate change. This network reveals a strong

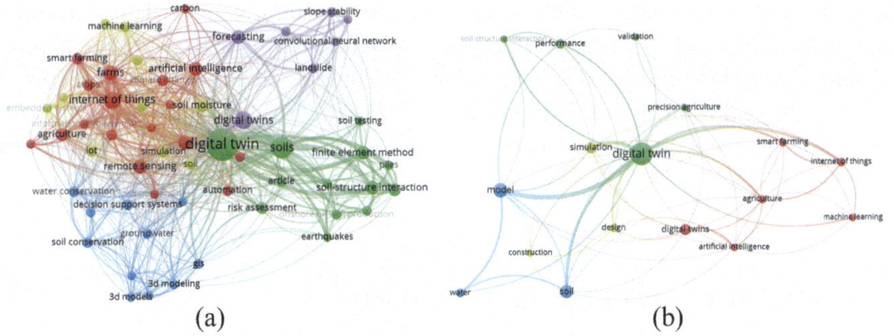


**Fig. 1** DTs and smart soils bibliometric analysis—keyword co-occurrence networks: (**a**) Scopus; and (**b**) Web of Science (Source: Authors own work)

intersection between the application of digital technologies and the need for more sustainable agricultural practices, demonstrating the potential of DTs to optimize agricultural and environmental processes. On the right, Fig. 1b exhibits the network constructed with the data from the Web of Science, which emphasizes technical aspects such as simulation, validation, performance, and soil models, reflecting a focus on the practical implementation of DTs for soil monitoring and analysis. Through these networks, research is evolving in two directions: one focused on agricultural optimization through new technologies and the other on the validation and technical performance of digital models applied to soil.

Silva et al. [23] conducted a systematic literature review on using DTs to assess soil quality. The authors found that although DTs are still in their infancy in agriculture, they have great potential to control and improve soil conditions in real-time. However, the study also emphasizes the need to overcome technical challenges, mainly due to the variability of agricultural data. Another example is provided by An and Chen [24], who propose a DT model with explicable AI for managing soil C emissions. This makes processes more transparent and decisions more understandable, reinforcing the potential of DTs in mitigating climate change.

In geotechnical engineering, Wu et al. [25] explore how DTs can be applied to monitoring underground structures and soil-structure interaction and suggest that the principles adopted in this sector can be transferred to agriculture, particularly for soil management and conservation. Tsakiridis et al. [26] propose a cognitive DT that integrates different data sources to monitor the health of soil ecosystems, using technologies such as IoT and AI to provide holistic information that enables more effective agricultural decisions.

Alves et al. [27] address the efficient management of water resources and describe how DTs can optimize smart irrigation by combining IoT sensors with water management platforms, enabling more rational and sustainable water use in agricultural contexts. Evert et al. extend this concept in their study [28], showing how DTs can be applied to crop and livestock farming, providing real-time solutions to monitor soil and crop conditions.

Finally, An and Chen [29] propose a DT model based on the internet of living things, which uses proximity sensors and UAVs (Unmanned Aerial Vehicles) to measure and manage soil carbon content in large agricultural areas. This innovative approach aims to improve the accuracy of carbon accounting and contribute to more sustainable agricultural practices. In the area of control and automation, the work of Silva et al. [30] reinforces the importance of DTs in the automation of agricultural processes, with a focus on increasing efficiency through the combination of robotics, AI, and DTs.

## 2.2 *Digital Twins in Circular Economy*

The Circular Economy (CE) appeared to address the environmental, economic, and social challenges caused by the traditional linear economic model. As defined by

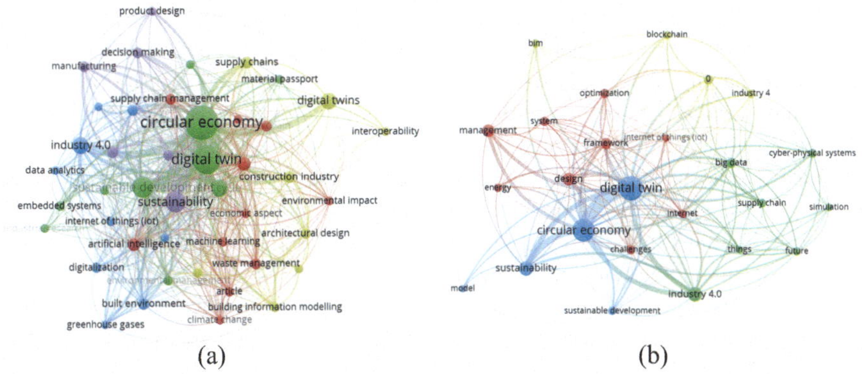


**Fig. 2** DTs and CE—keyword co-occurrence networks: (**a**) Scopus; and (**b**) Web of Science (Source: Authors own work)

Prieto-Sandoval et al. [31], the CE *"aims to prevent the depletion of resources, close energy and material loops, and facilitate sustainable development through its implementation at the micro (enterprises and consumers), meso (economic agents integrated in symbiosis) and macro (city, regions and governments) levels"*. This model requires circular and regenerative environmental innovations, integrating new modes of production and consumption. DTs play a critical role in achieving these goals by enabling real-time monitoring and optimization of products and product lifecycles. Figure 2 provides an overview of the current adoption of DTs in the CE through a brief bibliometric analysis.

The bibliometric analysis performed on Scopus and Web of Science using the keywords "digital twin" AND "circular economy" revealed important patterns in scientific publications. A total of 152 results were identified in Scopus and 98 in Web of Science. In Fig. 2a (Scopus) there is a dense interconnection between the terms "digital twin", "circular economy", and "supply chain management", suggesting a strong relationship between digitalization and sustainable practices. Figure 2b (Web of Science) highlights the concepts of "sustainable development", "IoT", "big data", and "blockchain" confirming the importance of digital technologies in the implementation of a CE in different industries.

There are several examples of DT adoption in CE. For example, Preut et al. [32] identify DTs as an enabler to improve circular supply chain management by providing data throughout the product lifecycle. Chen and Huang [33] explore the use of DTs in remanufacturing construction waste, demonstrating how they can optimize recycling and reuse processes. Meng et al. [34] highlight the importance of these IS in overcoming waste barriers and increasing the value of recovered materials in construction. Keivanpour et al. [35] proposes gamification and DTs as pedagogical tools to improve CE education, while Mügge et al. [36] present a comprehensive DT concept to support decision-making at critical product lifecycle stages. These contributions highlight the main role of DTs in the transition to a more efficient and sustainable economy.

DTs enable monitoring the state of soils in real-time and predict scenarios for the efficient use of materials. This integration is particularly useful in complex systems, such as managing material flows resulting from excavation and demolition, where soils may or may not be contaminated and require specific recycling processes. Recent studies have demonstrated the use of DTs to optimize materials management in construction, promoting soil reuse and waste minimization [37]. On the other hand, projects such as DeepGeo are advancing the application of DTs to create 3D stratigraphic maps that allow the characterization of soils in real-time, facilitating their reuse and integration into new infrastructures [38]. This approach can be extended to the implementation of smart soils, helping to manage soil fertility and health, optimize resource use, and minimize environmental impact, which is in line with the CE principles.

## 2.3 Theoretical Lenses

This research is grounded in Strong Structuration Theory (SST) and Knowledge Spiral Model (KSM) for analyzing the interactions between social structures, agency, and knowledge creation within organizations.

Introduced by Stones [15], SST builds on the original Structuration Theory [39]. Giddens's emphasizes that structures enable and constrain individual actions while those actions simultaneously reproduce or modify the structures themselves [39]. Stones advances this by distinguishing four key elements: (1) *external structures*, the institutional contexts or systems within which agents operate; (2) *internal structures*, representing agents' dispositions, knowledge, and motivations; (3) *active agency*, which captures how individuals act within and upon structures; and (4) *outcomes*, the result of these interactions [15, 40]. SST provides a practical framework for examining how agents in various positions interact with structures, enabling or constraining their actions while reshaping those structures over time.

KSM [16], explains the process of knowledge creation through the continuous interaction between tacit and explicit knowledge. The SECI model (Socialization, Externalization, Combination, Internalization) describes how knowledge evolves and transforms within organizations. *Socialization* captures how tacit knowledge is shared through personal experience, while *Externalization* converts tacit knowledge into explicit forms such as documentation or codified data. *Combination* refers to the synthesis of multiple explicit knowledge sources, and *Internalization* involves absorbing explicit knowledge into tacit understanding [16, 41]. According to KSM, knowledge creation is an iterative, dynamic process crucial for innovation and decision-making.

The integration of SST and KSM provides a comprehensive lens for analyzing socio-technical systems. SST focuses on the structural dimensions of human action (how individuals are shaped by and, in turn, shape their environments), while KSM focuses on the knowledge dimensions, specifically how knowledge is created, shared, and applied within these structures. These theories offer a robust framework for understanding how structures and knowledge interact to influence organizational practices, decision-making processes, and innovation capacity.

## 3 Research Approach

DSR aims to develop and evaluate novel artifacts that address real-world problems [11], generating knowledge through design [42, 43]. The DSR approach adopted in this paper is developed in six phases: (1) problem identification and motivation, (2) setting goals for a solution, (3) design and development, (4) demonstration, (5) evaluation, and (6) communication [44].

According to the structure of the DSR grid [45], we can summarize our research as follows: The *problem* is related to the lack of community-focused IS to optimize the management of climate-smart soils. The *research process* implements a second DSR design cycle (the first one focused on community composting [13]), and for theory building, the theoretical lenses of SST and KSM were used to create design principles. The proposed *solution* consists of the design and development of a Circular DT for smart soil management, including support for a community composting network. The *input knowledge* required for this research was based on various sources, such as Agenda 2030, the European Green Deal, the Farm to Fork strategy, the GEOfood initiative, and the Smart Regions model. The key *concepts* underpinning the development of this artifact include DTs, climate-smart soils, C sequestration, community composting, and the circular economy. Based on these concepts and sources, the *output knowledge* focuses on developing design principles for the development of Circular DTs, which follow the anatomy proposed by Gregor et al. [46].

Estrela Geopark, one of the 177 UNESCO Global Geoparks, is located in the interior region of Portugal. It was the setting chosen for this study. Covering an area of 221,600 ha in nine municipalities around Serra da Estrela [12], only around 1.93% of the territory is occupied by agricultural land, with a total of 9324 farms, of which approximately 24.47% are business-related [47, 48]. Agriculture represents a significant part of the regional economy, with around 1909 agricultural businesses and a total turnover of 60.345 million euros, employing approximately 2550 people, which corresponds to around 5.87% of total employment in the Geopark region [48, 49]. Since 2020, Estrela Geopark has been part of GEOfood network, currently with five certified producers who grow a variety of crops, such as aromatic herbs, teas, pears, cheeses, wine and olive oils, on areas ranging from a few square meters to over 60 ha. The entity responsible for the Geopark showed interest in DT solutions to help monitor compliance with sustainable development policies, promote the regional growth and support local communities.

The evaluation of our DSR design cycle followed the FEDS (Framework for Evaluation Design Science Research), which consists of four steps: *"(1) explicate the goals of the evaluation, (2) choose the evaluation strategy or strategies, (3) determine the properties to evaluate, and (4) design the individual evaluation episode(s)"* [50]. In this work, we used the ISO/IEC 25010:2023 standard [51] to evaluate the technical risk and efficacy of the DT and the Sustainability Evaluation Checklist established by Schroeter [52] to evaluate human risk and effectiveness. Additionally, the theory building focused on the conception of design principles for the development of Circular DTs, which were supported by the theoretical lenses of SST and KSM.

## 4 Design and Development

The Circular DT aims to manage and monitor the sustainability of climate-smart soils in Estrela Geopark, promoting a feedback loop that integrates food waste and soil health data. The architecture is shown in Fig. 3, using the C4 container diagram to describe the main components, data flows, and interactions of different users in the system [53].

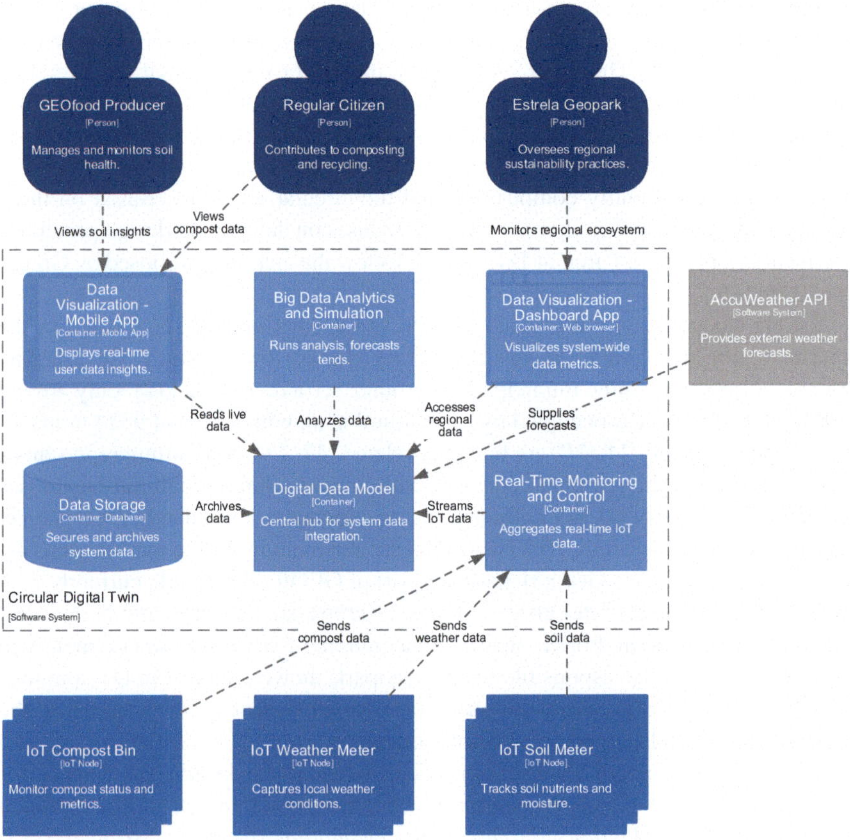


**Fig. 3** C4 container diagram (Source: Authors own work)

Circular DT is made up of five main components: (1) Digital Data Model, (2) Real-Time Monitoring and Control, (3) Data Storage, (4) Big Data Analytics and Simulation, and (5) Data Visualization (mobile app and web dashboard). These components are integrated to collect, process, and provide critical data on soil and compost, enabling efficient and sustainable management of local resources.

The Digital Data Model is the core of Circular DT, responsible for integrating and structuring data from IoT devices, external sources, and user interactions. This model ensures that data is accessible in an integrated way to all the other components of Circular DT, allowing information on soil and composting to be consistently used for analysis and decision-making.

Real-Time Monitoring and Control manages the reception and aggregation of data transmitted in real-time by IoT devices distributed throughout the area. These devices include the IoT Compost Bin, which monitors the status of the community composting network; the IoT Weather Meter, which collects weather data; and the IoT Soil Meter, which measures critical soil health parameters. This data is transmitted via the LoRaWAN network, which enables long-distance communication with low power consumption, which is essential for the rural areas of Estrela Geopark with limited network coverage.

Data Storage is implemented through a non-relational MongoDB database, which retains all historical data from the IoT infrastructure and other external sources. This storage is essential to ensure data persistence and integrity, allowing efficient retrieval for future analysis and visualization. MongoDB was chosen because of its scalability and flexibility, enabling the system to support a significant volume of data generated by the sensors over time without compromising performance.

Big Data Analytics and Simulation process the data collected to generate operational insights and forecasts for soil and crop management. This component carries out detailed soil fertility assessments, calculating, for example, the specific fertilization needs of each crop based on the indicators collected by the IoT Soil Meters. Fertilizer needs are determined using specific calculation formulas [54, 55]: if, for example, a crop requires 150 kg/ha of nitrogen, and the soil only contains 50 kg/ha, with the available fertilizer containing 20% nitrogen, the system will recommend an application of 500 kg/ha of fertilizer to meet the crop's need. Fertilization recommendations also consider the crop's stage of growth, prioritizing the use of natural fertilizers (such as compost generated by the community composting network) during the sowing phase and suggesting mineral fertilizers at later stages. The proposed architecture also allows to estimate carbon sequestration in the soil, using the organic matter data collected by the IoT Soil Meters and applying a conservation factor (usually 0.58), which makes it possible to calculate the amount of carbon sequestered and monitor the soil's contribution to climate change mitigation.

Data Visualization is carried out through two interfaces: the mobile app and the web dashboard. Two main groups use the mobile application: GEOfood producers and regular citizens. GEOfood producers can access real-time soil data and use a decision support module to manage their crops. This module includes features for irrigation and fertilization planning, land management, and monitoring soil conditions in real-time. The application allows producers to register IoT devices via a QR code, associating each sensor with their specific plots for personalized monitoring. Regular citizens can locate the nearest composting point and monitor the amount of organic waste recycled, visualizing their contribution to reducing carbon emissions. The web dashboard is aimed at Estrela Geopark managers, allowing them to monitor regional metrics and guarantee producers' compliance with GEOfood standards, making it easier to control the sustainability of the practices adopted in the territory.

To complement the local data, Circular DT integrates the AccuWeather API, which provides external weather forecasts to the Digital Data Model. This integration allows the system to align local data with forecasts of future weather conditions, which is essential for planning agricultural activities, giving GEOfood producers a robust database for making informed decisions.

The IoT infrastructure is made up of specialized sensors that collect continuous data on soil and environmental conditions. The IoT Compost Bin monitors the capacity and condition of the compost, evaluating the factors that promote composting, such as fill level and temperature. The IoT Weather Meter collects weather data, including wind, precipitation, temperature, and humidity parameters. The IoT Soil Meter collects critical soil health metrics for agronomic decision-making, including nutrient levels (nitrogen, phosphorus, potassium—NPK), pH, electrical conductivity, temperature, and moisture. This data is transmitted to the Real-Time Monitoring and Control component, which processes it and forwards it to the Digital Data Model.

On the one hand, GEOfood producers can benefit from accurate data and recommendations based on predictive analysis, which enables efficient and sustainable management of their agricultural activities. On the other hand, regular citizens can contribute to the composting cycle, promoting the circular economy and reducing environmental impact by recycling organic waste. Finally, Geopark managers can use the web dashboard to monitor and evaluate the implementation of sustainable practices, aligning local activities with Geopark's preservation and sustainability objectives.

## 5 Demonstration

The mobile application is the primary interaction between GEOfood producers and regular citizens in the community composting network and climate-smart soil management. Figure 4 shows the four prototypes of the mobile application, covering essential functionalities for both user groups.

The first interface (Fig. 4a) presents a production list showing monitored crops and plots. Each entry provides contextual information such as crop type, fertilization needs, and alerts about its association with IoT devices. The float action button allows users to add new resources, such as a new production, or associate IoT

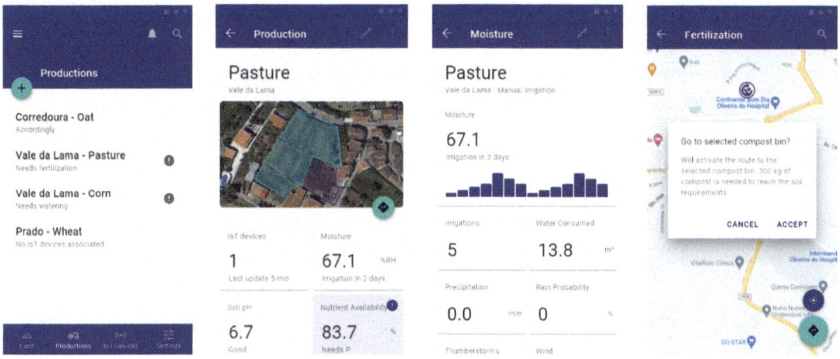


(a) (b) (c) (d)

**Fig. 4** Mobile application: (**a**) list of productions, (**b**) details of a production, (**c**) details of specific condition, and (**d**) location of compost bins (Source: Authors own work)

devices with a specific plot. The interface shown in Fig. 4b displays a specific production, offering a detailed view of the parameters monitored for a plot, including associated IoT devices, soil moisture level, pH, and nutrient availability. This data is updated in real-time, allowing the GEOfood producer to adjust farming practices as necessary, such as planning irrigation based on moisture levels or adjusting fertilization according to nutrient analysis. In Fig. 4c, the third interface zooms in on the details of a specific condition, in this case, soil moisture. This visualization shows recent irrigation history, water consumption in cubic meters, and a forecast of irrigation needs, helping producers efficiently manage water resources. Weather forecasts, such as the likelihood of rain, are also included, which help make irrigation decisions. Finally, the fourth interface (Fig. 4d) is dedicated to locating appropriate compost bins for soil fertilization needs. The user can see a map with the location of the available compost bins and select the most suitable one. When choosing a compost bin, the system estimates the amount of compost required to meet fertilization needs and allows navigation to the selected location. Figures 5 and 6 show the web dashboard.

The web dashboard complements the mobile application. It aims to support Estrela Geopark managers to monitor the composting network and other environmental parameters. The interface in Fig. 5 shows a regional map with the location of the IoT Weather Meters, IoT Compost Bins, and farmland. Colored icons represent the state of compost bins (blue for fully functional and yellow for identified problems), allowing an assessment of conditions and maintenance needs. By selecting a specific compost bin (Fig. 6), the user can view additional details, such as the condition of the compost bin (load, temperature, pH, and composition) and the link between the compost bin and the land using the compost. The thickness of the lines on the map indicates the intensity of the use of the compost bin to fertilize the land, while the color of the land indicates the level of carbon sequestered: red for low, yellow for medium, and green for high sequestration.

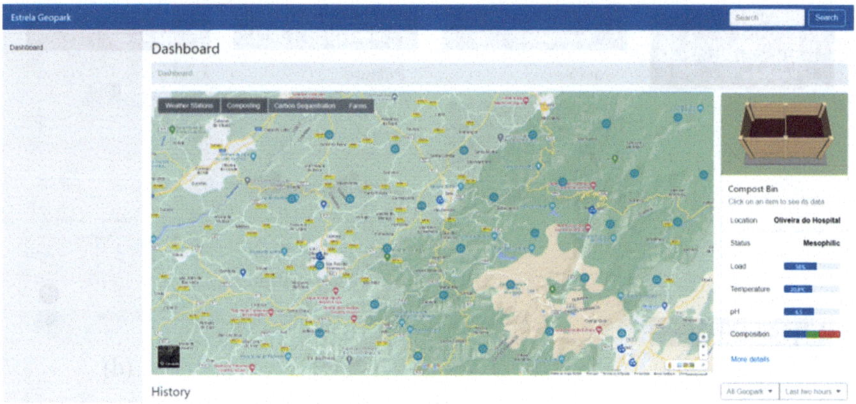


**Fig. 5** Web dashboard: regional map (Source: Authors own work)

**Fig. 6** Web dashboard: compost bin status (Source: Authors own work)

These integrated functionalities between the mobile app and web dashboard provide a comprehensive soil management and composting platform, promoting a circular economy.

# 6 Evaluation

This study's evaluation is formative (ex-ante) and naturalistic, following the two-dimensional characterization proposed by Venable et al. [50]. The evaluation aims to analyze three main aspects: (1) the efficacy and effectiveness of the artifact, (2) the impact of the artifact's prototype, and (3) the resources required to instantiate the artifact. The Technical Risk and Efficacy and Human Risk and Effectiveness strategies [50] were considered critical by the research team, due to the innovative nature of the Circular DT. Our selection is motivated by the novelty of the circular digital twin.

To assess Technical Risk and Efficacy, we used the ISO/IEC 25010:2023 standard [51], which provides an adaptable framework for the quality of DTs, organizing the assessment into nine criteria: (1) *functional sustainability* (functional completeness, functional correctness, and functional appropriateness); (2) *performance efficiency* (time behavior, resource utilization, and capacity); (3) *compatibility* (co-existence, and interoperability); (4) *interaction capability* (appropriateness recognizability, learnability, operability, user error protection, user engagement, inclusivity, user assistance, and self-descriptiveness); (5) *reliability* (faultlessness, availability, fault tolerance, and recoverability); (6) *security* (confidentiality, integrity, non-repudiation, accountability, authenticity, and resistance); (7) *maintainability* (modularity, reusability, analysability, modifiability, and testability); (8) *flexibility* (adaptability, scalability, installability, and replaceability); and (9) *safety* (operational constraint, risk identification, fail safe, hazard warning, and safe integration).

To assess Human Risk and Effectiveness, we used Schroeter's [52] Sustainability Evaluation Checklist, focusing on the following four criteria: (1) *human sustainability* (food security, health, local resources, and resilience); (2) *social sustainability* (social norms, community cohesion, cultural plurality, solidarity, and participation in decision-making); (3) *economic sustainability* (economic benefits for stakeholders, allocation of financial resources, productivity, and cost viability); and (4) *environmental sustainability* (impact on air, water, soil, ecosystem services, ecological balance, resource recycling, and emissions reduction).

Table 1 summarizes the main results of the evaluation process.

The evaluation, carried out in cooperation with experts by the Estrela Geopark management body, did not identify any significant human risks. However, the effectiveness assessment results should be interpreted cautiously, as they are based on estimates derived from a prototype that has not yet been deployed throughout the region.

# 7 Theory Building

## *7.1 Theoretical Reflection*

A Circular DT is a technological artifact and a dynamic socio-technical system that shapes and is shaped by its users while facilitating knowledge creation and dissemination processes. SST emphasizes the mutual shaping between structures (e.g., systems, technologies) and agents (e.g., farmers, policymakers, and community members) [15]. In the context of this research, the DT serves as a technological structure that enables real-time monitoring and decision-making around soil health and carbon sequestration. However, this structure is not static. The design and

**Table 1** Results from the evaluation phase (Source: Authors own work)

| Strategy | Evaluation |
|---|---|
| *Technical risk and efficacy* | – *Functional suitability:* The functionalities of the prototype were evaluated by Geopark experts and local producers, who confirmed that the DT meets the specific needs of the Estrela Geopark. The prototype has functional integrity and accuracy, providing support for soil monitoring and community compost management. However, the prototype has not yet been implemented throughout the region and is in a validation phase.<br>– *Performance efficiency:* The system collects and transmits data from IoT sensors every 15 min, optimizing the frequency of updates without overloading the network. The IoT devices use Arduino microcontrollers and have been configured to meet resource efficiency requirements. Each IoT device generates less than 2 MB of data per year, which reduces the impact on data storage and communication. Battery life varies between 109 and 180 days, depending on the intensity of use, and is extended by energy consumption optimizing strategies, essential for operating in rural areas with limited network coverage.<br>– *Compatibility:* The solution integrates several internal components (real-time monitoring and control, data storage, big data analytics and simulation, data visualization) and external components (AccuWeather API), with the digital data model component being responsible for ensuring compatibility between the different components. This integration allows interoperability between components, ensuring the collected data is processed and visualized cohesively. Although the solution is promising for Estrela Geopark, its application in other regions of the Geopark will require a detailed analysis of regional characteristics due to possible climatic and topographical variations that may influence the application of IoT devices.<br>– *Interaction capability:* The mobile app and web dashboard interfaces were designed following material design and bootstrap guidelines, respectively, ensuring an intuitive and attractive user experience. Initial feedback from users confirms the ease of navigation, error tolerance, and user support, minimizing the learning curve. Physical interaction with the IoT devices is limited to handling the protective cases, which have been designed to ensure the durability of the equipment in adverse conditions, including exposure to the weather and intensive use.<br>– *Reliability:* The DT is at technology readiness level (TRL) 5, which means it has been validated in a relevant environment. Fault tolerance mechanisms have been implemented, including anomaly detection through data triangulation, which increases the accuracy and security of the data collected. The system prevents unauthorized deletion of data and allows recovery in the event of failures. Continuity of operations is maintained despite possible reboots of the IoT devices, guaranteeing the robustness required for continuous monitoring in a rural context.<br>– *Security:* The solution includes various security measures to protect data, such as confidentiality, integrity, authenticity, and accountability, implemented through the flask-security library. Communication between devices and the server is encrypted to guarantee data security in transit. However, the physical security of IoT devices is a challenge, and solutions such as physical locks and location sensors are being explored to reduce the risk of tampering or theft. These measures are particularly important given the geographical dispersion of IoT devices in publicly accessible areas. |

**Table 1** (continued)

| Strategy | Evaluation |
|---|---|
| | – *Maintainability:* The solution's modular design allows it to be adapted to different regional scenarios and facilitates maintenance. The system has self-diagnostic capabilities that identify maintenance needs and optimize operational performance, sending alerts to administrators when necessary. This approach ensures that the system remains operational with minimal interventions, crucial for reducing maintenance costs and extending the life of devices in the field, especially in remote areas with limited access to technical assistance.<br>– *Flexibility:* The DT prototype was explicitly developed for a specific Geopark region but has the potential to be adapted to other areas within the GEOfood initiative, where the integration of food waste into the soil is valued. The flexible and modular architecture makes it easy to adapt the system to different regional requirements while maintaining the essential functionalities. The flexibility allows the system to be adjusted for different types of crops, farming practices, and environmental conditions, meeting the specific needs of various regions and promoting agricultural sustainability.<br>– *Safety:* The physical security of IoT devices is a concern due to their installation in public places and unmonitored access. Options were considered to strengthen physical protection, including the use of locks to prevent theft and unauthorized manipulation, as well as location sensors to track devices in the event of authorized movement. These measures aim to ensure the integrity of the data collected and the continuity of operations and are essential for the system's effectiveness in environments where constant supervision is unfeasible. |
| *Human risk and effectiveness* | – *Human sustainability:* The DT information flows can support the transition to a sustainable food system, providing food security through traceability and minimizing the use of chemical fertilizers, which contributes to soil health and food safety. It also increases regional resilience by encouraging the use of local resources and strengthening control over food production in GEOfood. In addition, the community composting network connects urban food waste producers to rural carbon sequestration areas, promoting a strong regional identity and a circular economy.<br>– *Social sustainability:* The DT application allows Geopark professionals to monitor compliance with GEOfood standards, providing accurate, real-time data to support decision-making. This support increases community cohesion and promotes the sharing of relevant information, strengthening ties between producers and consumers. The system contributes to social sustainability by encouraging responsible agricultural practices and enabling the active participation of stakeholders in local resource management, ensuring that soil management and composting practices are aligned with the Geopark's sustainability objectives.<br>– *Economic sustainability:* The initial implementation cost is estimated at around €84,436.89, with €72,628.89 earmarked for the IoT infrastructure (21 IoT compost bins, 29 IoT weather meters, 61 IoT soil meters, and 29 LoRaWAN gateways) and €11,808 for installation and additional services. This figure does not include development, training, and maintenance costs, estimated at approximately 45% of the total. The expected savings on fertilizer purchases represent a significant economic advantage since reusing locally produced compost partially replaces the need for external inputs. In the long term, this system could reduce dependence on external resources and promote a more sustainable and efficient agricultural economy. |

(continued)

**Table 1** (continued)

| Strategy | Evaluation |
|---|---|
| | – *Environmental sustainability:* IoT devices consume different amounts of energy, and IoT weather meters and LoRaWAN gateways are powered by solar energy, reducing their carbon footprint. It is estimated that a real-scale deployment of the system could sequester up to 419 tons of carbon per year, helping to mitigate climate change. In addition, the community composting system helps divert organic waste from landfills, reducing carbon emissions by between 461 and 922 tons per year. The system contributes to environmental sustainability by promoting the reuse of local organic resources and reducing the need for waste transportation, resulting in a positive environmental impact on both soil conservation and emissions reduction. |

development phase reveals that the DT can evolve based on the actions and feedback of agents interacting with it. For example, farmers using IoT soil sensors influence the data flow and functionality of the system through their actions (decisions about when and where to apply compost, water crops, or monitor environmental conditions). As Giddens [39] posits in Structuration Theory, structures constrain and enable agents, but agents, through their actions, modify and reproduce these structures over time.

This reciprocal relationship became particularly evident during the demonstration and evaluation phases. The initial deployment of the DT revealed areas where the system constrained agent behavior, such as technical limitations in the sensor data or difficulties in interpreting the dashboard. However, users (primarily local farmers and community compost managers) can adapt their practices and provide feedback for system adjustment. This feedback loop is essential for ensuring the technology remains flexible and responsive to local needs. As a structure, the DT is continuously reshaped by the active agency of its users. Thus, SST offers a robust framework for understanding the iterative nature of the DSR processes, where each cycle builds on the previous one through the interaction of structure and agency.

KSM provides a different theoretical perspective on how the DT facilitates knowledge creation. The DT acts as a platform that enables the externalization of tacit knowledge (farmers' and stakeholders' experimental insights into soil management) into explicit knowledge, such as sensor data and analytics. The SECI model of Socialization, Externalization, Combination, and Internalization was evident throughout the design, development, and demonstration stages. Farmers' tacit knowledge about their lands can be transformed into measurable data via IoT sensors (externalization), aggregating data from other sources like weather stations to form a broader understanding of soil health (combination). This explicit knowledge is made available through the DT's dashboard, where stakeholders can analyze and apply it to their specific farming practices, thereby internalizing this knowledge and influencing future actions.

The demonstration phase illustrated how this knowledge spiral operates in practice. Farmers who accessed the DT can see explicit data, such as moisture levels and nutrient content, and make informed decisions about when to water or apply compost. This real-time data integration with local expertise improved decision-making and created new opportunities for shared learning across the community. As knowledge is continuously cycled through the SECI process, the quality of decisions and the sustainability of practices may improve, aligning with KSM's emphasis on dynamic knowledge conversion as a key driver of innovation and performance.

The theoretical lenses of SST and KSM proved essential for understanding how DTs mediate the relationship between human agents and their environments. On the one hand, SST helped clarify the relationship between users and the technological structure, where users' feedback and actions can reshape the system to suit their needs better. On the other hand, KST explained how knowledge is generated, shared, and applied through the DT, ensuring that the system becomes more effective over time as stakeholders refine their practices based on actionable insights.

## *7.2 Design Principles for Circular Digital Twin*

According to Gregor and Hevner [42], *"when the design is complex in terms of the size of the artifact and the number of components (social and technical), then explicit extraction of design principles may be needed"*. Ten design principles were derived from the creation of Circular DTs, following the guidelines of Gregor et al. [46] (*"DP Name: For Implementer I to achieve or allow for Aim A for Use U in Context C, employ Mechanisms M1, M2, ..., Mn involving Enactors E1, E2, ..., En because of Rationale R."*):

- ***DP1. Comprehensive data integration:*** For *developers* to achieve *real-time monitoring and prediction* for *stakeholders* in *areas the geological interest*, employ *real-time data collection tools and advanced analytics* involving *sensors, satellite data, and community-generated data sources* because of *the need to provide a holistic view of the current state of climate-smart soils, community composting, and food supply chain dynamics.*
- ***DP2. Circular supply chain visualization:*** For *interface designers* to achieve *visual mapping of return and source links* for *supply chain managers* in *protected regions with unique brands*, employ *graphical representations, flow diagrams, and intuitive dashboards* involving *GIS tools, interactive charts, and 3D models* because of *the importance of understanding the circular nature of resource flows and material loops.*
- ***DP3. GEOfood implementation monitoring:*** For *brand managers* to allow for *consistent adherence to GEOfood principles* for *consumers and producers* in *areas the geological interest*, employ *brand tracking, audit systems, and feedback loops* involving *QR codes, user reviews, and supply chain metadata* because of *the necessity to ensure brand integrity and authenticity in a protected region.*

- ***DP4. Adaptive learning and simulation:*** For *software engineers* to allow for *predictive insights and scenario planning* for *policymakers and farm managers in protected regions*, employ *simulation tools, and historical data analyzes* involving *climate data, soil health metrics, and community composting outputs* because of *the need anticipate challenges, optimize resource use, and promote sustainable practices.*
- ***DP5. Community and stakeholder engagement:*** For *community managers* to allow for *inclusive decision-making* for *local residents and businesses* in *areas the geological interest*, employ *feedback platforms, interactive workshops, and collaborative tools* involving *mobile apps, web portals, and local community centers* because of *the importance of harnessing local knowledge, ensuring transparency, and fostering community ownership of sustainable initiatives.*
- ***DP6. Stakeholder knowledge integration:*** For *implementers* to allow for *multi-stakeholder knowledge sharing and contextual understanding* for *regional policymakers and agricultural practitioners* in *soil management*, employ *data integration tools and collaborative interfaces* involving *farmers, scientists, and environmental authorities* because of *the need to merge local tacit knowledge with explicit digital insights to enhance soil sustainability.*
- ***DP7. Dynamic adaptation of practices:*** For *developers* to allow for *real-time adaptive management strategies* for *agricultural operators* in *varying climate conditions*, employ *predictive algorithms and real-time feedback systems* involving *IoT sensors and mobile applications* because of *the necessity to respond swiftly to environmental shifts and optimize resource usage.*
- ***DP8. Distributed accountability mechanism:*** For *system designers* to allow for *transparency and shared accountability* for *sustainable practices among community members and policymakers* in *rural and semi-urban composting networks*, employ *transparent data tracking, automated logging, and distributed ledger technology* involving *community compost mangers, producers, and regulatory bodies*, because of *the critical need for traceable and verifiable information in fostering community trust and policy compliance.*
- ***DP9. Resource optimization feedback loop:*** For *implementers* to allow for *continuous improvement and waste reduction practices* for *compost managers and local producers* in *circular food supply chains*, employ *resource feedback loops and waste tracking mechanism* involving *compost metrics, soil health indicators, and yield projections*, because of *the imperative to refine resource application and minimize environmental impact dynamically.*
- ***DP10. Knowledge codification for community empowerment:*** For *community managers* to allow for *the creation of accessible, codified knowledge for educational and operational purposes* for *local farmers and future implementers* in *soil management practices*, employ *instructional dashboards, user-generated insights, and visual data representations* involving *experienced farmers and local experts*, because of *the importance of building a knowledge repository that empowers users and promotes informed decision-making in sustainable agriculture.*

# 8 Conclusions

This study presents a novel approach to the development of Circular DTs, applied to climate-smart soils in a UNESCO Geopark, exploring their potential in circular economy and sustainable land management. Through the theoretical lenses of SST and KSM, it was possible to analyze a model that responds to the demands of monitoring and managing natural resources, as well as adapting and evolving with the intervention of local agents, promoting a cycle of continuous and adaptive improvement. Supported by the results achieved and inspired by Prieto-Sandoval's [31] definition of CE and Raj and Surianarayanan's [8] definition of DT, we proposed the following definition for Circular DT:

> A computational model that incorporates real-world data from physical systems or objects focusing on their relationship with nature and resource dynamics, simulating and predicting how these systems or objects interact within a cyclical and regenerative lifecycle. The main aim is to prevent resource depletion, close energy and material loops, and promote sustainable development at micro, meso, and macro levels.

## *8.1 Study Limitations*

This work was developed based on the specific context of Estrela Geopark, a site with distinct geological and agricultural characteristics, which offers a unique platform for testing and applying Circular DT in community composting and soil management practices. However, this specificity limits the direct generalization of the results to other regions since environmental, social, and economic conditions can differ considerably. In addition, the Circular DT developed has not yet been fully implemented throughout the territory, with the study's results limited to a validated prototyping phase in a controlled environment.

Despite these limitations, the study stands out for its methodological robustness and the development of design principles for Circular DTs. These principles offer a theoretical and practical basis that can be adapted to different contexts. The circularity and scalability of Circular DT allow it to be applied in other scenarios, provided adjustments are made to accommodate regional particularities.

## *8.2 Main Contributions and Next Steps*

This work contributes to the literature on DTs and the circular economy by presenting a replicable DT and specific design principles that respond to the demands of sustainability and resource management in agricultural contexts. Through the integration of IoT data, analytical models, and community feedback, Circular DT allows for the optimization of local practices and establishes a framework for the active engagement of stakeholders and the promotion of regenerative agricultural practices.

Future work opportunities include expanding and longitudinally implementing Circular DT throughout the Estrela Geopark region to assess its long-term impact. Comparative studies with other geographically and climatically distinct regions could also strengthen user engagement and the effectiveness of Circular DT in promoting sustainable practices and regenerative land management.

**Declaration of Competing Interests**
The authors declare that they have no known competing financial interest or personal relationships that could have appeared to influence the work reported in this paper.

**Acknowledgments** This work is partially financed through national funds by FCT - Fundação para a Ciência e a Tecnoloiga, I.P., in the framework of the Project UIDB/00326/2025 and UIDP/00326/2025. The first author is funded by FCT under the Ph.D. grant 2022.09950.BD.

## References

1. European Commission. (2021). EU soil strategy for 2030 reaping the benefits of healthy soils for people, food, nature and climate (COM/2021/699 final).
2. Paustian, K., Lehmann, J., Ogle, S., Reay, D., Robertson, G. P., & Smith, P. (2016). Climate-Smart Soils. *Nature, 532*(7597), 49–57.
3. Hou, D. (2022). Expediting climate-smart soils management. *Soil Use and Management, 38*(1), 1–6.
4. Alves, R. G., Maia, R. F., & Lima, F. (2023). Development of a digital twin for smart Darming: Irrigation management system for water saving. *Journal of Cleaner Production, 388*, 135920.
5. United Nations. (2015). *Transforming our world: The 2030 agenda for sustainable development*
6. Pylianidis, C., Osinga, S., & Athanasiadis, I. N. (2021). Introducing digital twins to agriculture. *Computers and Electronics in Agriculture, 184*, 105942.
7. Verdouw, C., Tekinerdogan, B., Beulens, A., & Wolfert, S. (2021). Digital twins in smart farming. *Agricultural Systems, 189*, 103046.
8. Raj, P., & Surianarayanan, C. (2020). Digital twin: The industry use cases. In P. Raj & P. Evangeline (Eds.), *Advances in computers* (pp. 285–320). Elsevier.
9. Breure, A. M., Lijzen, J. P. A., & Maring, L. (2018). Soil and land Management in a Circular Economy. *Science of The Total Environment., 624*, 1125–1130.
10. Moinet, G. Y. K., Hijbeek, R., van Vuuren, D. P., & Giller, K. E. (2023). Carbon for soils, not soils for carbon. *Global Change Biology, 29*(9), 2384–2398.
11. Hevner, A. R., March, S. T., Park, J., & Ram, S. (2004). Design science in information systems research. *MIS Quarterly., 28*(1), 75–105.
12. Vieira, G., de Castro, E., Gomes, H., Loureiro, F., Fernandes, M., Patrocínio, F., Firmino, G., & Forte, J. (2020). *The Estrela Geopark–from planation surfaces to glacial erosion*. Springer International Publishing.
13. Monteiro, J., Barata, J., Gomes, H., & Castro, E. (2021). Deploying smart community composting in Estrela UNESCO global Geopark: A Mobile app approach. In E. Insfran, F. González, S. Abrahão, M. Fernández, C. Barry, H. Linger, M. Lang, & C. Schneider (Eds.), *Information systems development: Crossing boundaries between development and operations (DevOps) in information systems (ISD2021 proceedings)*. Valencia.

14. Monteiro, J., & Barata, J. (2024). The circular digital twin: Climate-smart soils as a use case. In B. Marcinkowski, A. Przybyłek, A. Jarzębowicz, N. Iivari, E. Insfran, M. Lang, H. Linger, & C. Schneider (Eds.), *Harnessing opportunities: Reshaping ISD in the post-COVID-19 and generative AI era (ISD2024 proceedings)*. University of Gdańsk.
15. Stones, R. (2005). *Structuration theory*. Palgrave Macmillan.
16. Nonaka, I., & Takeuchi, H. (1995). *The knowledge-creating company: How Japanese companies create the dynamics of innovation*. Oxford University Press.
17. Magma Geopark. (2021). *The GEOfood manifesto*.
18. Pfeiffer, J., Lachenmaier, J. F., Hinz, O., & van der Aalst, W. (2024). New Laws and Regulation. Business & Information. *Systems Engineering., 66*, 653–666.
19. Glaessgen, E., & Stargel, D. (2012). The digital twin paradigm for future NASA and U.S. air Force vehicles. In *53rd AIAA/ASME/ASCE/AHS/ASC Structures, Structural Dynamics and Materials Conference, 20th AIAA/ASME/AHS Adaptive Structures Conference, 14th AIAA*. American Institute of Aeronautics and Astronautics.
20. Ferré-Bigorra, J., Casals, M., & Gangolells, M. (2022). The adoption of urban digital twins. *Cities, 131*, 103905.
21. Sarp, S., Kuzlu, M., Zhao, Y., & Gueler, O. (2023). Digital twin in healthcare: A study for chronic wound management. *IEEE Journal of Biomedical and Health Informatics, 27*(11), 5634–5643.
22. Zhou, G., Zhang, C., Li, Z., Ding, K., & Wang, C. (2020). Knowledge-driven digital twin manufacturing cell towards intelligent manufacturing. *International Journal of Production Research, 58*(4), 1034–1051.
23. Silva, L., Rodríguez-Sedano, F., Baptista, P., & Coelho, J. P. (2023). The digital twin paradigm applied to soil quality assessment: A systematic literature review. *Sensors, 23*(2), 1007.
24. An, D., & Chen, Y. (2023). Explainable artificial intelligence (XAI) empowered digital twin on soil carbon emission management using proximal sensing. In *2023 IEEE 3rd International Conference on Digital Twins and Parallel Intelligence (DTPI)* (pp. 1–5). IEEE.
25. Wu, X., Lu, G., & Wu, Z. (2023). Remote sensing Technology in the Construction of digital twin basins: Applications and prospects. *Water (Basel)., 15*(11), 2040.
26. Tsakiridis, N. L., Samarinas, N., Kalopesa, E., & Zalidis, G. C. (2023). Cognitive soil digital twin for monitoring the soil ecosystem: A conceptual framework. *Soil Syst., 7*(4), 88.
27. Alves, R. G., Souza, G., Maia, R. F., Tran, A. L. H., Kamienski, C., Soininen, J.-P., Aquino, P. T., & Lima, F. (2019). A digital twin for smart Darming. In *2019 IEEE Global Humanitarian Technology Conference (GHTC)* (pp. 1–4). IEEE.
28. van Evert, F. K., Berghuijs, H. N. C., Hoving, I. E., de Wit, A. J. W., & Been, T. H. (2021). A digital twin for arable and dairy farming. In *Precision Agriculture'21* (pp. 919–925). Wageningen Academic Publishers.
29. An, D., & Chen, Y. (2022). A digital twin enabled internet of living things (IoLT) framework for soil carbon management. In *2022 18th IEEE/ASME International Conference on Mechatronic and Embedded Systems and Applications (MESA). pp. 1–6*. IEEE.
30. Silva, L., Giugge, R., Rodríguez-Sedano, F. J., Baptista, P. C., & Coelho, J. P. (2022). *Promoting olive Groves's soil quality by a digital Twin's predictive based control: The Sensor's network*. Springer International Publishing.
31. Prieto-Sandoval, V., Jaca, C., & Ormazabal, M. (2018). Towards a consensus on the circular economy. *Journal of Cleaner Production, 179*, 605–615.
32. Preut, A., Kopka, J.-P., & Clausen, U. (2021). Digital twins for the circular economy. *Sustainability., 13*(18), 10467.
33. Chen, Z., & Huang, L. (2020). Digital twin in circular economy: Remanufacturing in construction. *IOP Conference Series: Earth and Environmental Science, 588*(3), 032014.
34. Meng, X., Das, S., & Meng, J. (2023). Integration of digital twin and circular economy in the construction industry. *Sustainability., 15*(17), 13186.
35. Keivanpour, S. (2021). Work-in-Progress digital twin and gamification for designing an educational lab for circular economy. In *2021 7th International Conference of the Immersive Learning Research Network (iLRN)* (pp. 1–3). IEEE.

36. Mügge, J., Seegrün, A., Hoyer, T.-K., Riedelsheimer, T., & Lindow, K. (2024). Digital twins within the circular economy: Literature review and concept presentation. *Sustainability., 16*(7), 2748.
37. Züst, S., Züst, R., Züst, V., West, S., Stoll, O., & Minonne, C. (2021). A graph based Monte Carlo simulation supporting a digital twin for the curatorial management of excavation and demolition material flows. *Journal of Cleaner Production, 310*, 127453.
38. Phoon, K.-K., Ching, J., & Cao, Z. (2022). Unpacking data-centric geotechnics. *Underground Space., 7*(6), 967–989.
39. Giddens, A. (1984). *The constitution of society*. University of California Press.
40. Greenhalgh, T., & Stones, R. (2010). Theorising big IT Programmes in healthcare: Strong structuration theory meets actor-network theory. *Social Science & Medicine, 70*(9), 1285–1294.
41. Nonaka, I., Toyama, R., & Konno, N. (2000). SECI, Ba and leadership: A unified model of dynamic knowledge creation. *Long Range Planning, 33*(1), 5–34.
42. Gregor, S., & Hevner, A. R. (2013). Positioning and presenting design science research for maximum impact. *MIS Quarterly., 37*(2), 337–355.
43. March, S. T., & Smith, G. F. (1995). Design and natural science research on information technology. *Decision Support Systems, 15*(4), 251–266.
44. Peffers, K., Tuunanen, T., Rothenberger, M. A., & Chatterjee, S. (2007). A design science research methodology for information systems research. *Journal of Management Information Systems., 24*(3), 45–77.
45. vom Brocke, J., & Maedche, A. (2019). The DSR grid: Six Core dimensions for effectively planning and communicating design science research projects. *Electronic Markets., 29*(3), 379–385.
46. Gregor, S., Kruse, L., & Seidel, S. (2020). Research perspectives: The anatomy of a design principle. *Journal of the Association for Information Systems, 21*, 1622–1652.
47. PORDATA. (2022). *Agricultural holdings, according to the census: Total and by type of tenure*. https://www.pordata.pt/en/municipalities/agricultural+holdings++according+to+the+census+total+and+by+type+of+tenure-963
48. PORDATA. (2023). *Non-financial enterprises: Total and by sector of economic activity*. https://www.pordata.pt/en/municipalities/non+financial+enterprises+total+and+by+sector+of+economic+activity-346
49. PORDATA. (2023). *Personnel employed in non-financial enterprises: Total and by sector of economic activity*. https://www.pordata.pt/en/municipalities/personnel+employed+in+non+financial+enterprises+total+and+by+sector+of+economic+activity-353
50. Venable, J., Pries-Heje, J., & Baskerville, R. (2016). FEDS: A framework for evaluation in design science research. *European Journal of Information Systems., 25*(1), 77–89.
51. ISO: ISO/IEC 25010:2023. (2023). Systems and software engineering–systems and software quality requirements and evaluation (SQuaRE). *Product Quality Model.*, https://www.iso.org/standard/78176.html
52. Schroeter, D. (2010). Sustainability evaluation checklist.
53. Brown, S. (2023). *The C4 model for Visualising software architecture*. Leanpub.
54. Edwards, T. (2021). *Measuring and reporting soil organic carbon*.
55. Rose, C. (2004). Fertiliser calculations. *Kempsey*.

# Design Principles for Food Heritage Digital Twins

**Ivo Mendes, José Monteiro, and João Barata**

**Abstract** This paper presents the design of a Digital Twin (DT) for the traditional Serra da Estrela cheese production, integrating digital innovation to preserve Intangible Cultural Heritage (ICH) while improving production efficiency and sustainability. The study adopts a Design Science Research approach, combining knowledge from interviews with cheesemakers and theoretical reflections using Strong Structuration Theory, Communities of Practice, and Practice-Based Knowledge Management. The DT prototype replicates the cheesemaking process, ensuring compliance with protected designation of origin standards and preserving tacit knowledge. It provides real-time monitoring, process optimization, and a digital repository of traditional practices. This research pioneers the application of DTs to ICH in food production and introduces the Hybrid Knowledge Structuration Model to integrate traditional and digital knowledge systems. The DT reveals the potential to improve cheesemakers' operational efficiency, compliance, and sustainability, offering a practical tool to optimize production while preserving cultural authenticity. This research contributes to the long-term preservation of cultural heritage, local development, and rural socio-economic sustainability, proposing design principles for the advances of heritage digital twins.

A prior version of this paper has been published in the ISD2024 Proceedings: Mendes, I., Monteiro, J. & Barata, J. (2024). A Heritage Digital Twin for Serra Da Estrela Cheese Production. In B. Marcinkowski, A. Przybylek, A. Jarzębowicz, N. Iivari, E. Insfran, M. Lang, H. Linger, & C. Schneider (Eds.), *Harnessing Opportunities: Reshaping ISD in the post-COVID-19 and Generative AI Era (ISD2024 Proceedings)*. Gdańsk, Poland: University of Gdańsk. ISBN: 978–83–972,632-0-8. https://doi.org/10.62036/ISD.2024.3

I. Mendes · J. Monteiro (✉) · J. Barata
University of Coimbra, CISUC/LASI, DEI, Coimbra, Portugal
e-mail: ivomendes@student.dei.uc.pt; jafmonteiro@dei.uc.pt; barata@dei.uc.pt



B. Marcinkowski et al. (eds.), *Advances in Information Systems Development*, Lecture Notes in Information Systems and Organisation 77,
https://doi.org/10.1007/978-3-031-87880-0_10

# 1 Introduction

Preserving and safeguarding Intangible Cultural Heritage (ICH) is a priority worldwide, especially for traditional practices threatened by industrialization, the decline of rural populations, and global market pressures [1–3]. UNESCO [4] defines ICH as *"the practices, representations, expressions, knowledge, skills—as well as the instruments, objects, artefacts and cultural spaces associated therewith—that communities, groups, and, in some cases, individuals recognize as part of their cultural heritage. This intangible cultural heritage, transmitted from generation to generation, is constantly recreated by communities and groups in response to their environment, their interaction with nature and their history, and provides them with a sense of identity and continuity, thus promoting respect for cultural diversity and human creativity"*. The production of Serra da Estrela cheese [5] is an example of a traditional practice under threat. It plays an important socio-economic role in the central interior region of Portugal. Preserving this artisanal practice while complying with manufacturing standards, hygiene, and food safety rules and adopting sustainable production practices requires innovative solutions.

Digital Twins (DTs) are a promising alternative for solving some of the challenges of ICH protection. A DT is a digital replica of a physical process or entity that allows for real-time monitoring, simulation, and optimization [6]. These Information Systems (IS) have gained prominence in the field of smart manufacturing to enhance operational efficiency and resource management through digital simulations and predictive analytics [7, 8]. Recently, researchers have begun to explore DT potential for ICH, but their application in this field is still in its infancy [9]. The development of a DT for the Serra da Estrela cheesemaking process can enable the digital replication of traditional practices while supporting resource optimization and compliance with production processes and hygiene and food safety standards [10].

Our research contributes to a new era of IS development research characterized by digital transformation of traditional practices and new digital structures that promote collaborative and increasingly distributed work. It follows the Design Science Research (DSR) [11] approach and is being carried out in the Estrela UNESCO Global Geopark (Estrela Geopark) [12], a region with a rich cultural and natural heritage. The research has the dual aim of (1) digitally preserving traditional cheesemaking practices and (2) improving the sustainability and operational efficiency of the production process. This manuscript extends a previous study on the design and development of a DT for regional food products with a protected designation of origin [10], providing new design knowledge and principles for Heritage DTs through three theoretical lenses, namely: (1) Strong Structuration Theory (SST) to explore the dynamic interaction between agents (cheesemakers) and structures (regulations, digital systems) [13]; (2) Communities of Practice (CoP) to understand how knowledge is shared within the cheesemaking community and how the DT can support the transfer of this tacit knowledge [14]; and (3) Practice-Based Knowledge Management (PBKM) to analyze how knowledge embedded in the cheesemaking process can be codified, stored, and transmitted through digital means [15]. The following Research Objectives (ROs) were formulated for this research:

- ***RO1.*** *Design and develop a DT for the traditional Serra da Estrela cheese production.*
- ***RO2.*** *Analyze how the DT interacts with the existing social and structural dynamics.*
- ***RO3.*** *Evaluate how DT can enhance operational efficiency and resource optimization while maintaining cultural authenticity.*

The remainder of this article is structured as follows: Section 2 reviews the literature about DTs in smart manufacturing and ICH and describes the selected theoretical lenses. Section 3 presents the research approach. Next, Section 4 details the design and development stage, and Sect. 5 details the demonstration. Subsequently, Section 6 explains the evaluation, and Sect. 7 focuses on theory building by (1) critically reflecting on the selected theoretical lenses, (2) presenting the theoretical model, and (3) establishing design principles for the development of DTs applied to food heritage DTs. Finally, Section 8 presents the main conclusions, contributions, limitations, and future research directions.

## 2 Theoretical Background

### *2.1 Digital Twins in Smart Manufacturing*

The adoption of DTs in the manufacturing industry has initiated a transformation phase by harnessing the power of digital replication and intelligent automation [6]. The concept of DT emerged in the early 2000s in the aerospace and defense industries as *"an integrated multiphysics, multiscale, probabilistic simulation of an as-built vehicle or system that uses the best available physical models, sensor updates, fleet history, etc., to mirror the life of its corresponding flying twin"* [16]. Over time, this understanding has been consolidated and expanded and is now seen as a complete IS with well-defined characteristics and components such as digital data model, data storage, real-time monitoring and control, big data analytics and simulation, and data visualization [6, 17, 18]. Its broad scope and scalability contribute to its growing adoption in smart manufacturing [19].

Recent studies point to the significant role of DTs in smart manufacturing. For instance, Li et al. [7] discuss their value in facilitating green performance assessment in manufacturing. DTs are transforming manufacturing [8] by dynamically monitoring, analyzing, and improving organizational activities [20], and these abilities are enhanced with the application of emerging digital technologies such as machine learning and 5G networks [21]. Tao et al.'s work [22] is another example of the implementation of DTs in smart manufacturing (DT Shop-Floor), which integrates and optimizes physical and virtual production spaces, promoting data interconnection for more efficient and intelligent production processes.

DT studies are also increasing in food supply chains and Industry 5.0. For example, Gallego-García et al. [23] developed a DT focused on optimizing smallholder farmers' management, control activities, and supply chain operations in response to external crises. Singh et al. [24] use a causal model to identify and classify these factors, highlighting improved coordination as a key indicator. Following a DT approach based on machine learning, the work of Melesse et al. [25] uses thermal images to monitor fruit quality to reduce waste and provide real-time predictions of fruit flavor, achieving a 99% accuracy rate in classifying fruit during storage. Applied to the context of Industry 5.0, Wang et al. [26] present the concept of Human DT as an enabler for human-centred intelligent manufacturing systems, focusing on integrating human characteristics into system design to increase flexibility, resilience, and personal well-being in industrial environments.

DTs can be used to track manufacturing processes and assist in decision-making. This is achieved through simulations and forecasts supported by analysis of large volumes of data, which come from real-time monitoring, historical records, or external sources. Visualization mechanisms usually correspond to the 3D representation of objects and processes, accompanied by contextual information. However, their adoption in traditional sectors of the economy, such as artisanal production, remains limited.

## 2.2 *Digital Twins in Intangible Cultural Heritage*

A search in Scopus and Web of Science revealed six and four results, respectively, when combining DT and ICH. For example, Shi et al. [27] investigated the digital heritage of the traditional Mongolian costumes of the Nayman tribe, using a DT to create their clothes digitally. This study demonstrated the effectiveness of 3D simulation and virtual experimentation for conserving and transmitting cultural traditions at risk of disappearing.

Banfi et al. [1] researched DTs in the archeological and paleontological context, namely preserving finds from the Lamalunga cave, where Neanderthal Man was discovered. Technologies such as photogrammetry and 3D scanning have made monitoring and analyzing the cave's fragile environment possible, providing a digital representation that supports scientific research and the accessibility of heritage without physical intervention on site. This approach highlights the importance of DTs in the conservation of sensitive cultural environments, the promotion of virtual tourism, and knowledge sharing.

Wen and Xu [28] also explore the dissemination of ICH through DTs, focusing on rural settings in China. The proposal includes the creation of DTs of cultural practices to preserve the authenticity and cultural identity of local communities. Using technologies such as BIM (Building Information Modeling), GIS (Geographic Information System), and XR (eXtended Reality), the study proposes the construction of digital scenarios to revitalize rural culture, overcome the physical limitations of ICH transmission, and innovate related business models. Stacchio et al. [29] present DanXe, a platform that combines artificial intelligence and extended reality to analyze and promote dance heritage. Through a case study focused on the legacy of dancer Rudolf Nureyev, the framework offers a new way of organizing, digitizing, and analyzing tangible and intangible dance materials, promoting the accessibility and preservation of choreographic heritage. Both studies contribute to innovation in preserving and disseminating ICH through advanced technological approaches.

Wang and Lau [30] explored the use of NFTs (Non-Fungible Tokens) and DTs to preserve the silver crafts of the Miao ethnic group, a cultural heritage at risk due to urbanization and mass production. The creation of DTs of handcrafted pieces allows (1) the preservation of traditional techniques and (2) the creation of new business models in the context of the metaverse, extending the lifespan and commercial value of the handcrafted heritage. This study highlights the ability of DTs to integrate technological innovation and cultural preservation, adapting traditions to the contemporary context.

Finally, Li et al. [31] applied DTs to the craft of Yangxin Cloth Paste, a Chinese cultural practice. The digital platform developed made it possible to visualize and interact with the craft process, promoting learning and the transmission of cultural heritage. This work exemplifies how DTs can facilitate an experience of cultural immersion, offering a dynamic solution for preserving and disseminating traditions. Thus, DTs are practical tools for strengthening the ICH, providing new ways of engaging with culture and history through technology. However, no studies in our literature review applied DTs to food heritage or its traditional production.

## 2.3 *Theoretical Framework*

This section describes the three focal theories used in our research: (1) SST, (2) CoP, and (3) PBKM. Each theory offers a distinct yet interconnected view of social structures, learning, and knowledge management, forming a comprehensive framework to examine how technology, tradition, and knowledge interact, especially within cultural heritage practices.

SST, developed by Stones [13], builds on Giddens [32]'s original Structuration Theory and aims to refine understanding of the relationship between structure and agency. Whereas Giddens's theory emphasized the *"duality of structure"* (i.e., how structures are both the medium and the outcome of actions), SST introduces a more detailed ontology, distinguishing between external structures (e.g., social norms, systems) and internal structures (e.g., the agent's knowledge and schemas). SST focuses on how agents actively engage with structures, enabling or constraining their actions [13, 33]. One of the SST's key contributions is its emphasis on the *"quadripartite cycle"*, which captures the dynamic interplay between agents' behavior, context, external social structures, and outcomes [13]. This cyclical interaction provides a framework for understanding how social and technological structures evolve through human agency. SST also recognizes the importance of position-practices, which link agents to broader networks and social systems. It is a valuable tool for understanding how individuals interact with both physical and digital systems [34].

Proposed by Lave and Wenger [35], CoP provides a framework for understanding how social participation creates, shares, and maintains knowledge. CoP proposes that learning is not simply an individual activity but occurs within a social context where individuals share a common interest in practice. The community is characterized by mutual engagement, a shared repertoire of practices, and a joint enterprise, which fosters knowledge development and transmission [14, 35]. Within a CoP, knowledge is mainly tacit and situated, meaning that it is embedded in the day-to-day practices of the community members and is often transmitted through direct participation rather than formal instruction [35]. Wenger [14] asserts that learning in a CoP is fundamentally about becoming a practitioner, and thus, the theory focuses on how individuals move from peripheral to full participation within the community. CoP is particularly useful for understanding how collective knowledge is sustained across generations and how new technologies can support or disrupt this process. The theory highlights the role of shared practices and collective meaning-making in maintaining cultural continuity while allowing for the integration of new tools and methods [36].

PBKM articulates knowledge's situated and embodied nature within practices [15]. In contrast to traditional knowledge management approaches that focus on the codification and storage of explicit knowledge, PBKM argues that knowledge is deeply embedded in the activities and routines of practitioners. This approach focuses on the *"knowing-in-practice"* perspective, where knowledge is generated and enacted through ongoing social interactions and engagements within specific contexts [37]. PBKM emphasizes tacit knowledge (knowledge that is difficult to articulate or formalize) and how it is shared and transmitted through practice rather than formal documentation [38]. Orlikowski [15] stated that much of what is valuable in organizations and communities exists in this tacit form and that the challenge is not to reduce it to rigid, codified forms. This perspective recognizes that knowledge constantly evolves as practices change and adapt to new circumstances. It supports the idea that managing knowledge is about facilitating ongoing practice rather than merely storing information [39].

These theoretical frameworks share connection points that allow them to complement and reinforce each other. First, SST and CoP point to the importance of context and social structures in shaping actions and learning. SST focuses on how structures (both external and internal) constrain or enable agency, while CoP highlights how social learning occurs within shared practices and mutual engagement. Together, they offer a holistic understating of how individuals and communities interact with broader systems (such as technology and social norms) and how these interactions shape the development and transmission of knowledge [13, 14]. Second, CoP and PBKM are closely aligned in their emphasis on tacit knowledge and the role of social participation in knowledge sharing. Both theories defend that much of what is valuable within communities and practices is not formally documented but instead exists in the tacit, situated knowledge of practitioners. Both reiterate the importance of participation and engagement in learning and knowledge creation, with CoP focusing more on the social structures of learning and PBKM on the management of knowledge within practices [15, 35]. Third, SST and PBKM intersect in their treatment of agency and the ongoing adaptation of practices. SST provides a dynamic model for understanding how agents interact with and shape structures, while PBKM focuses on how knowledge is enacted and evolves with practices [13, 15]. Both theories highlight the fluid and evolving nature of practices and structures, making them particularly relevant for understanding how new technologies (such as DTs) can be integrated into traditional practices without displacing existing knowledge.

## 3 Research Approach

DSR is a problem-solving paradigm [40] particularly well-suited to fields where knowledge generation is closely tied to innovative artifacts, offering a framework for developing and evaluating new solutions, processes, or models [11, 41]. This approach enables researchers to tackle complex problems through iterative design and development, demonstration, and evaluation cycles, ensuring both rigor and relevance in research outcomes [40, 42]. Table 1 presents an overview of our research using the DSR grid [43].

This research is set in the context of the Estrela Geopark [12], a region of profound geological diversity and rich cultural heritage. The production of Serra da Estrela is a central cultural practice within the Geopark and a key element in the area's social, economic, and environmental sustainability. Estrela Geopark's participation in the GEOfood brand initiative further highlights its commitment to

**Table 1** The heritage DT, according to the DSR grid [43] (Source: Authors own work)

| Problem | Research Process | Solution |
|---|---|---|
| The dwindling knowledge and practice of traditional cheesemaking in the Serra da Estrela region require innovation to ensure sustainability and resilience. | An iterative process of problem identification, artifact design and development, demonstration, evaluation, and refinement based on feedback. | A DT prototype for the artisanal production of Serra da Estrela cheese, acting as a digital repository for preserving memory, a compliance tool, and a resource optimization mechanism |
| **Input knowledge** | **Concepts** | **Output knowledge** |
| Literature on DT in smart manufacturing, preservation of ICH, artisanal cheesemaking practices, SST, CoP, and BPKM. | DTs, ICH, sustainability, smart manufacturing, SST, CoP, PBKM. | Design principles for heritage DTs. Insights into the integration of digital and traditional knowledge. Evaluation of the DT's impact on sustainability and cultural preservation. |

promoting sustainable development by connecting local stakeholders to the region's identity and ensuring the valorization of endogenous products like Serra da Estrela cheese. Through this lens, the DT serves as an innovative tool that addresses the need to preserve the traditional cheesemaking methods that form part of the region's ICH while enhancing productivity and ensuring compliance with modern health standards.

The design and development phase involved gathering detailed insights through interviews with local cheesemakers and visits to cheese dairies to capture the essence and evolution of the cheesemaking process. Venable et al. [44]'s framework guided the evaluation of the prototypes, emphasizing Human Risk and Effectiveness as the evaluation strategy, reflecting the project's focus on cultural sensitivity and practical applicability. Feedback from stakeholders, including cheese dairy representatives and experts in cheese certification and ICH, was instrumental in the evaluation process. We then conducted a reflection using the lenses of SST, CoP, and PBKM. This reflection has resulted in the development of a theoretical model, integrating digital and traditional knowledge systems, which has informed the design principles and guides the practical implementation of the DT to ensure that it preserves the cultural authenticity of traditional cheesemaking practices, as well as increasing operational efficiency and sustainability.

The selected theories align well with the development of a DT for Serra da Estrela cheese production. SST helps examine the evaluation of traditional cheesemaking structures under digital innovation, while CoP emphasizes tacit knowledge sharing within the community. PBKM aids in codifying and preserving artisanal knowledge digitally. Together, these theories ensure the DT supports production optimization, compliance, and cultural preservation, addressing both social and technical dimensions.

## 4 Design and Development

This phase began with the specification and control plan of the Serra da Estrela cheesemaking process, followed by interviews with four cheesemakers. After gathering these insights, we established the system requirements and designed a DT prototype using Microsoft's Azure Digital Twins platform. This platform was selected for its ability to integrate both the digital representation of the cheesemaking process and the underlying data model. However, alternative platforms could be used for similar prototyping needs.

The Serra da Estrela cheesemaking process uses specific raw materials: (1) milk from Bordaleira Serra da Estrela or Churra Mondegueira sheep breeds, (2) salt, and (3) ground thistle flower (*Cynara cardunculus, L.*) as a coagulant. Figure 1 systematizes the main tasks of the Serra da Estrela cheese manufacturing process.

The process begins with manually milking the sheep and filtering the milk through clean cloths. The milk is then heated to 28–32 °C, salted, and mixed with ground thistle (0.2–0.3 g per liter). After resting for 45–60 min, the curd is manually

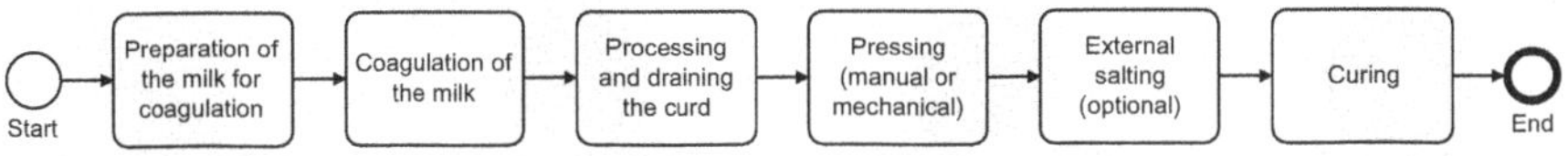


**Fig. 1** Simplified flow of the Serra da Estrela cheese manufacturing process (Source: Authors own work)

cut and filtered to remove any remaining whey. The curd is then placed in molds ("cinchos") for molding, pressed to reduce the mold diameter and extract the whey, and either manually or mechanically pressed with a 4–5 kg weight for about 6 h. Afterward, the cheese is salted externally by rubbing its surface with salt. The maturing process occurs in two stages: (1) drying, which lasts 15–20 days at 6–12 °C with 85–90% relative humidity, requiring daily turning and washing, and (2) curing, which lasts for an additional 25–30 days at 6–14 °C and 90–95% humidity, with periodic turning and washing performed sporadically based on the appearance of the rind. The same temperature and humidity conditions apply for producing Serra da Estrela Velho, but the minimum maturation period is extended to 120 days. The cheese is typically 9–20 cm in diameter and 4–6 cm in height, with a soft, slightly acidic flavor. The older cheese, Serra da Estrela Velho, has a stronger flavor and can be slightly spicy, with dimensions ranging from 11–20 cm in diameter and 3–6 in height.

The interviews were conducted with four participants: two retirees aged 91 and 92 (Q01 and Q02), a 58-year-old educational assistant (Q03), and a 35-year-old food engineer (Q04). Q01 and Q02 were directly involved in agriculture and cheesemaking, selling their cheese at local fairs, while Q03 (Q02's daughter) supplements her income through small-scale production and sells at the municipal market. Q04 operates a small cheese dairy that processes about 100 liters of milk daily despite having no prior cheesemaking experience. All participants confirmed the key steps in the cheesemaking process, though with some variations. For instance, Q01 and Q04 use a cloth to process curd, while Q02 and Q03 use molds directly. Q01-Q03 use manual pressing, but Q04 employs a mechanical system. Other differences include traditional fire heating (Q01 and Q02), stove heating (Q03), and water baths (Q04). The maturation process has also evolved, with Q03 using a refrigerator and Q04 using specialized curing chambers. Tools have been upgraded to comply with HACCP standards, transitioning from wood to stainless steel or plastic.

Figure 2 presents the structure of the Heritage DT system. We applied the C4 Model [45], a framework for visualizing software architecture. The Container Diagram provides a high-level view of the system, illustrating how the various components (containers) interact with each other and the system's users. The four key users of the system are the Cheesemaker, ICH Expert, Certification Body, and the Estrela Geopark. The system itself consists of five core containers: (1) Digital Data Model, (2) Data Storage, (3) Real-Time Monitoring and Control, (4) Big Data Analytics and Simulation, and (5) Data Visualization. Additionally, the system

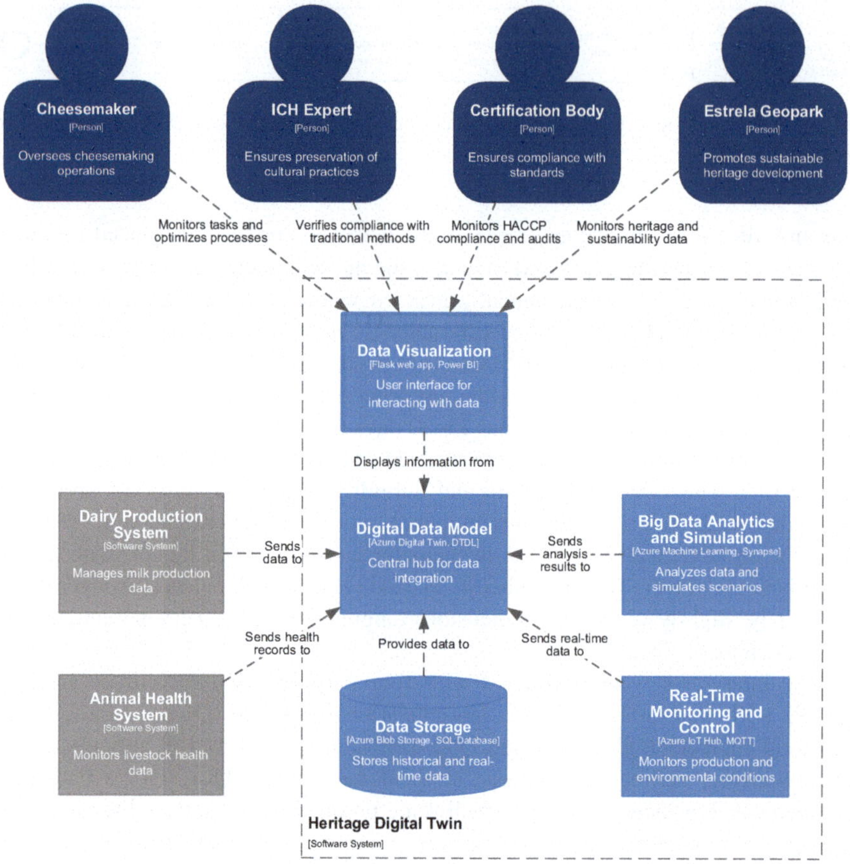


**Fig. 2** Container diagram of the C4 Model representing the Heritage DT for the Serra da Estrela artisanal cheesemaking process (Source: Authors own work)

integrates with two external systems: the Dairy Production System and the Animal Health System.

The Heritage DT provides real-time monitoring and decision support for Cheesemakers, optimizes daily operations, and ensures adherence to traditional methods while complying with modern health and safety standards. The ICH Expert relies on the system to preserve cultural heritage by capturing and validating the authenticity of artisanal cheesemaking practices. Certification Bodies benefit from the system's ability to provide traceability and automated compliance verification, streamlining the auditing process and ensuring that production meets regulatory requirements, such as HACCP (Hazard Analysis and Critical Control Points) standards. Finally, for the Estrela Geopark, the system enables monitoring of sustainability efforts and regional heritage practices, contributing to the Geopark mission's socio-economic development and cultural preservation goals. This targeted functionality ensures that each user group is supported in achieving their respective objectives by integrating traditional knowledge with advanced digital capabilities.

The Digital Data Model is at the heart of the system, the central hub for all data integration. It collects and processes information from both internal system components and external systems, ensuring a cohesive digital representation of the cheesemaking process. This model is implemented using the Azure Digital Twins Definition Language (DTDL), allowing it to map and synchronize real-world processes in real-time. All container and external-system interactions are channeled through the Digital Data Model, ensuring the system remains flexible and adaptable. We choose Azure Digital Twins for the following reasons [46]: (1) the platform provides scalability and flexibility, essential for accommodating the requirements of the cheese-making process; (2) it offers integration capabilities with IoT devices and other Azure services, facilitating the collection and analysis of real-time data, which is crucial for monitoring and optimizing production parameters; (3) the platform's security features ensure the protection of sensitive data related to traditional production methods and standards; and (4) the ease of use and extensive support resources available for Azure make it an accessible choice for local cheese producers who may have different levels of digital literacy.

The Data Storage container supports the Digital Data Model and maintains real-time and historical data. This storage is critical for enabling traceability, auditing, and long-term analysis. The data is stored in a combination of Azure Blob Storage and SQL Databases, which provide the scalability and security required to manage the large volumes of data generated by the IoT (Internet of Things) sensors and user interactions. This container ensures that all relevant data is available for analysis and decision-making.

The Real-Time Monitoring and Control container is responsible for continuously tracking environmental and production conditions within the cheese dairy. Critical factors such as temperature, humidity, and the force applied during pressing are monitored using IoT sensors placed throughout the production environment. These sensors communicate with the system via MQTT (Message Queuing Telemetry Transport) protocol and the Azure IoT Hub, allowing seamless integration with the Digital Data Model. Real-time data is essential for maintaining production quality and ensuring health and safety standards compliance.

The Big Data Analytics and Simulation container performs advanced data analysis and predictive simulations. It leverages the data collected from the monitoring system and historical records to provide insights into the production process. The system can predict outcomes based on different environmental conditions or production variables by running simulations, allowing cheesemakers to optimize their method. This component is built on Azure Machine Learning and Synapse Analytics, enabling large-scale data processing and predictive modeling.

Finally, the Data Visualization container provides an interface through which users interact with the system. Built using a Flask web application and Power BI for graphical dashboards, this container allows users—cheesemakers, certification bodies, ICH experts, and Geopark managers—to access real-time insights, monitor production performance, and review compliance data. The interface is designed to be intuitive and tailored to the needs of each user group, ensuring that the system is accessible to those with varying levels of digital literacy.

Additionally, the system interacts with two external systems: the Dairy Production System and the Animal Health System. The former tracks milk production volumes, quality metrics, and other relevant data fed into the Digital Data Model to monitor the production process comprehensively. The Animal Health System records livestock health data, ensuring that any issues affecting the sheep are reflected in the cheesemaking process. Both systems provide critical input to the Digital Data Model, enabling the Heritage DT to maintain a holistic view of the production ecosystem.

## 5 Demonstration

Figure 3 shows some of the high-fidelity prototypes developed and presented to different stakeholder to validate the alignment of the system's functionalities with their real-world needs.

In Fig. 3a, the left side shows a 3D representation of the cheesemaking facility, offering a real-time view of the status of various rooms and equipment within the DT. This 3D model allows users to visually monitor occupation, environmental conditions, and processes occurring in each space. For instance, the selected "Cure room 2" displays current occupation levels and provides critical metrics such as HVAC (Heating, Ventilation, and Air Conditioning) system status, temperature, and any alerts tied to anomalies in the curing process. This allows the cheesemaker to keep track of essential tasks such as cheese turning or washing, ensuring adherence to the control plan. On the right, users can access contextual information about

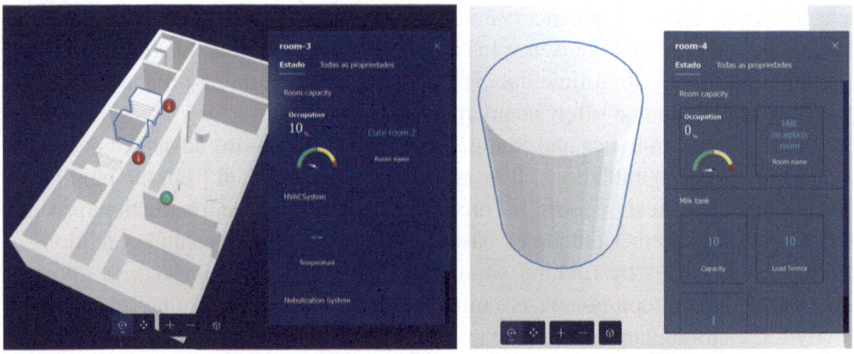


(a) (b)

**Fig. 3** High-fidelity prototypes of the user interaction system: (**a**) curing chamber; and (**b**) milk storage tank (Source: Authors own work) the selected object, such as its status and historical data, providing insights into operational efficiency and warning them of pending tasks or critical issues.

In Fig. 3b, the focus shifts to a specific object within the DT—the milk reception tank. The 3D representation on the left provides a simplified view of the tank, while the contextual information on the right shows key metrics such as current capacity, load sensor data, and other operational parameters. This level of detail allows for precise monitoring of critical points in the cheese production process, ensuring that inputs such as milk volumes are properly tracked and managed. This view simplifies process oversight for the cheesemaker, ensuring optimal resource use and compliance with health standards, such as HACCP.

These prototypes demonstrate the DT's capability to provide a macro- and micro-level view of the cheesemaking process. It supports real-time monitoring and control at the facility level, allowing users to quickly identify and resolve issues. At the object level, it enables detailed tracking of equipment and operational metrics. Together, these functionalities enable a holistic, data-driven approach to managing the cheesemaking process, ensuring that traditional methods are preserved while leveraging modern technology for efficiency and compliance.

## 6 Evaluation

In this DSR design cycle, we conducted an ex-ante evaluation, emphasizing user insights to preemptively address potential human and social barriers in adopting and using the system. Using a human risk and effectiveness strategy [44], we gathered feedback from key stakeholders through open interviews. The goals were (1) to present system requirements and user interface prototypes and (2) to obtain valuable feedback to guide further development. Table 2 summarizes the feedback received from the main stakeholders.

From the feedback gathered in this DSR design cycle, several key insights emerged: (1) the *alignment of stakeholder needs*, i.e., the DT meets the expectations and needs of the various stakeholders, from cheesemakers to certification bodies and cultural heritage experts; (2) *adoption challenges*, i.e., there may be barriers to adoption among cheesemakers, particularly due to system complexity and varying levels of digital literacy; (3) *systematic process control*, i.e., a systematic and methodical approach to controlling artisanal production is necessary, especially for monitoring and compliance; and (4) *cultural heritage preservation*, i.e., it is critical to preserve, protect, and pass on ICH to future generations, leveraging technology as a means of doing so.

**Table 2** Stakeholder feedback on the Heritage DT system (Source: Authors own work)

| Stakeholder | Feedback |
|---|---|
| Cheesemaker | – Benefits: *"A system like this could reduce the amount of paperwork ( . . . ), as well as warning us about important tasks."*<br>– Concerns: *"However, if the system is too complex, it could become a hindrance, and instead of helping, it could get in the way."*<br>– Equipment monitoring: *"Sometimes we have problems monitoring the conditions of the ripening chambers, especially at weekends, and if these problems aren't detected in time, they can lead to spoiled cheese being thrown away."*<br>– Collaboration: *"( . . . ) have access to animal health records, because if there is a problem with a sheep, there will be a problem with the milk it produces and, gradually, with the cheese we make from it."* |
| Certification body | – Relevance: *"There is an urgent need for systems that help us in our mission as certification bodies for regional food products that have a deep link with the territory and heritage of the region."*<br>– Control plan integration: *"An added value of this system is that it is based on the specification and control plan, which gives us a comprehensive view of the whole process and services as a valuable support mechanism to facilitate communication and transparency between the certification body and cheese producers."*<br>– Monitoring assistance: *"We do not have enough inspectors to audit as much as we would like, and we believe that such a system could help us to monitor the work carried out in the various cheese dairies, even at a distance, as well as assisting us in selecting potential inspection targets."*<br>– Concerns: *"Most cheese dairies are small, and the people who run them and work there don't have ( . . . ) a high level of digital literacy, so these factors could be an obstacle; not to mention the fact that they may also think this type of system is only there to control them."* |
| ICH expert | – Importance: *"Recording the traditional ways of making cheese and preserving them for future memory is crucial."*<br>– Step-by-step recording: *"It is necessary to record the step-by-step and check that they comply with the traditional matrix since it is an 'industrialized' cheesemaking process and with the passage of time become forgotten."*<br>– Capturing know-how: *"Capturing video makes it possible to record details related to know-how often omitted from textual or audio records, as well as to understand the occurrence of a deviation that could alter the tradition."*<br>– Cross-referencing: *"By cross-referencing the records of various cheese dairies, we can capture unknown singularities, which may be the results of previous unknown deviations."*<br>– Knowledge transmission: *"Traditionally, the process of passing on a traditional practice is done from generation to generation, but in the absence of an older cheesemaker, this system could do so, complemented by the records of the traditional matrix."*<br>– Applicability to other heritage: *"We can also apply it to other types of manufacture, whether food or handicrafts, for example, the case of Estremoz rattles or Biscainho's black clay crockery."* |

(continued)

**Table 2** (continued)

| Stakeholder | Feedback |
|---|---|
| Estrela Geopark | – Alignment with mission: *"Our main purpose is to contribute to the sustainable development of the Estrela Geopark territory through networking, to enhance the different dimensions of the heritage of this territory and, at the same time, stimulating the socio-economic development of the people who live here, and this project is exactly in line with all of this."*<br>– Endogenous product valorization: *"In recent years, we have been increasingly concerned with the valorization of existing endogenous products, which led us to join the GEOfood brand created by magma Geopark in 2020, and the implementation of the brand in the Geopark territory is one of the challenges we have, and we believe that this system can help us in this monitoring process."*<br>– Cultural heritage protection: *"The conservation and safeguarding of IHC play a fundamental role both for UNESCO, as established in the 2003 convention, and for its Geoparks, which seek to collect traditional practices so that they are not lost and can be passed on to future generations, and this system allows us to both collect and understand how practices evolve and vary from territory to territory."* |

# 7 Theory Building

In this section, we provide a theoretical reflection on the study's findings, employing the lenses of SST, CoP, and PBKM. Integrating these three theoretical frameworks allows us to construct a comprehensive understanding of how the introduction of a DT interacts with traditional artisanal practices. Additionally, we present a model synthesizing key concepts from each theory to guide future implementations of DTs in similar contexts, particularly in preserving ICH.

## *7.1 Theoretical Reflection*

Through the lenses of SST, the findings reveal a dynamic interplay between the agents (cheesemakers) and the structures (DT system and traditional cheesemaking practices). SST points out the duality of structure, where structures both enable and constrain agents' actions [13]. In this case, the DT system serves as an external structure that formalizes and codifies traditional cheesemaking processes, but the cheesemakers' knowledge, values, and practices also shape it. The results suggest that the introduction of the DT can lead to a transformation of the traditional structures. Cheesemakers, as agents, engage with the system to ensure compliance with production standards, resource optimization, and health regulations. However, they also negotiate how much of the traditional methods are preserved versus how much is adapted. SST helps to explain this ongoing negotiation and adaptation process, where the DT becomes a flexible structure that can accommodate both the preservation of heritage and the optimization of production efficiency [33]. The position-practices relations outlined in SST are particularly evident in cheesemakers' role evolving within a broader network of stakeholders, including certification bodies, consumers, and ICH experts.

Applying CoP to our findings highlights the importance of social learning and knowledge sharing within the cheesemaking community. CoP emphasizes that learning is inherently social and occurs through participation in shared practices [14]. In this context, the DT system acts as a tool that supports the transmission of tacit knowledge across generations of cheesemakers while also providing a platform for mutual engagement and collaboration. The findings indicate that the DT fosters a shared repertoire of practices where cheesemakers can contribute their experiential knowledge, enhancing the system's accuracy and relevance. The joint enterprise (the collective goal of preserving traditional cheesemaking methods while optimizing for sustainability) provides coherence to the community's actions. This aligns with Wenger's [14] idea that CoP enables practitioners to move from peripheral to full participation, as younger or less experienced cheesemakers can gradually become more central through their engagement with the DT and interactions with more experienced practitioners.

From a PBKM perspective, the findings reinforce that knowledge is deeply embedded in practice and continuously enacted through everyday activities [15]. The DT captures this knowledge in its tacit and explicit forms, allowing it to be managed, transmitted, and refined over time. PBKM focuses on the situated nature of knowledge, and the DT system successfully integrates with the cheesemaking process to facilitate real-time knowledge sharing and feedback loops that enable iterative improvements [38]. Our results demonstrate that while the DT codifies certain aspects of the cheesemaking process, much of the knowledge remains tacit and context-specific, requiring the expertise and insight of the cheesemakers themselves to interpret the data fully. This affirms the importance of continuous practice and the system's ability to enhance knowledge flow without overly formalizing or rigidifying the processes. PBKM allows us to see how the DT can balance the need for standardization (for certification and optimization purposes) with the fluid evolving nature of artisanal knowledge.

## *7.2 Hybrid Knowledge Structuration Model*

Based on the integration of SST, CoP, and PBKM, we present the Hybrid Knowledge Structuration Model (HKSM) to provide us with a theoretical framework specifically designed to support the study and application of Heritage DTs in the preservation and valorization of ICH. This model synthesizes key elements from each theory, offering a comprehensive framework for understanding how digital tools like DTs interact with traditional practices to preserve cultural heritage while enabling innovation. The HKSM (Fig. 4) consists of the following components:

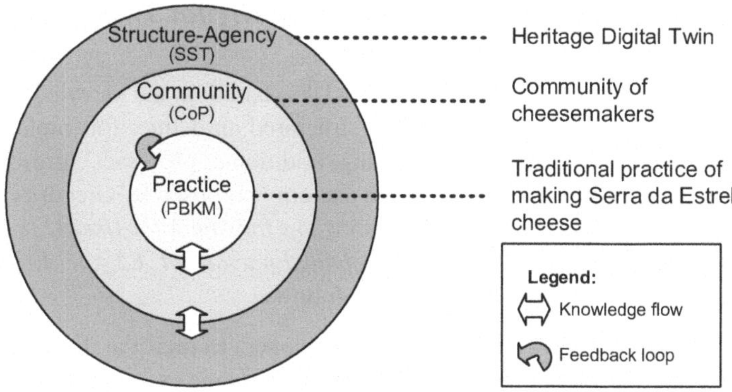


**Fig. 4** Hybrid Knowledge Structural Model (Source: Authors own work)

1. *Dynamic Structure-Agency Interaction (SST)*: At the core of the model is the SST framework, which presupposes those structures (e.g., DTs) and agents (e.g., cheesemakers) are dynamically intertwined. The DT is an evolving structure that constrains and enables agent actions, while agents continuously shape the DT based on their practices and experiences. This interaction is not static; the system adapts as the technology and the users evolve.
2. *Community-Based Knowledge Sharing (CoP)*: The model emphasizes the role of social learning with communities. The DT facilitates mutual engagement, allowing practitioners to contribute to and benefit from a shared knowledge base. Through the DT, community members can observe the best practices, share insights, and engage in collective sense-making, which fosters the transmission of tacit knowledge across generations.
3. *Situated Knowledge Flow (PBKM)* The model incorporates the PBKM perspective, recognizing that knowledge is enacted through practice. The DT enables capturing and enhancing situated knowledge, supporting real-time decision-making and process improvements. This perspective ensures that while explicit knowledge is codified, tacit knowledge remains flexible, adaptive, and contextualized within the cheesemaking process.

The HKSM aligns with the case of Serra da Estrela cheesemaking by addressing the complexities of integrating digital technology with ICH. The model illustrates how the DT can support the preservation of traditional practices while providing tools for process optimization and compliance with modern standards. The dynamic interaction between agents and the DT, as captured by SST, is particularly relevant as it highlights the adaptability of tradition in the face of technological change.

Furthermore, the HKSM is transferable to other domains where traditional practices intersect with digital technologies. This model can benefit contexts that involve craftsmanship, heritage preservation, or artisanal production. For example, the HKSM could be applied to traditional handicrafts, textile production, or agriculture, where both the conservation of tacit knowledge and the adoption of technological innovations are critical.

## 7.3 Design Principles for Food Heritage Digital Twins

This section presents nine Design Principles (DPs) based on the knowledge gained from our DSR. These DPs aim to provide structured guidelines for implementing DTs in food heritage contexts, supporting traditional processes' preservation, optimization, and continuity. Following the anatomy proposed by Gregor et al. [47] (*"DP Name: For Implementer I to achieve or allow for Aim A for User U in Context C, employ Mechanism M1, M2, ..., Mn involving Enactors E1, E2, ..., En because of Rationale R."*), the DPs are formulated as follows:

- *DP1. Authenticity Preservation:* For DT developers to preserve the authenticity of traditional food-making processes for cultural heritage experts in the context of intangible cultural preservation, employ accurate digital replication, continuous community engagement, and iterative validation with domain experts, involving local artisans, cultural historians, and anthropologists, because maintaining the integrity of traditional practices ensures cultural authenticity.
- *DP2. Sustainability Monitoring:* For system architects to optimize resource use and ensure sustainable production for cheesemakers in the context of artisanal industries, implement real-time monitoring of resources, predictive analysis for resource optimization, and feedback loops for process improvement involving environmental scientists and supply chain managers because proactive resource management contributes to environmental and economic sustainability.
- *DP3. Compliance Assurance:* For quality assurance teams to validate adherence to certification standards for certification bodies in the context of food heritage products, apply automated compliance checks, traceability systems, and certification workflows involving compliance officers and regulatory authorities because systematic and transparent validation process ensure product integrity and trust.
- *DP4. Cultural Continuity:* For preservation specialists to ensure the continuity of food heritage practices for future generations in the context of cultural conservation, establish digital archiving, knowledge transfer initiatives, and community-driven content creation, involving archivists, cultural practitioners, and digital librarians, because preserving knowledge and practice contributes to ensuring the legacy of food heritage.
- *DP5. Seamless Integration:* For technology integrators to maintain the continuity of cheesemakers' daily tasks without introducing new barriers for artisanal producers in the context of traditional cheesemaking, employ intuitive user interface design, minimal disruptive technology implementation, and user-centered training programs, involving user experience designers, process engineers, and educational specialists, because facilitating a seamless transition to digital aids preservers operational efficiency and user acceptance.
- *DP6. Two-Stage Evaluation Approach:* For implementers to achieve a comprehensive understanding of system impact on cultural heritage stakeholders in the context of DT implementation, employ a two-stage evaluation process consisting of an initial diagnostic assessment and a final impact evaluation involving system designers, local stakeholders, and evaluation experts, because conducting evalua-

tions at key stages ensures informed design decisions, contextual awareness, and measurable outcomes.

- *DP7. Knowledge Formalization:* For system developers to capture and codify tacit knowledge for local cheesemakers in the context of traditional cheesemaking, employ knowledge formalization techniques such as process documentation, multimedia records (videos, images), and collaborative platforms involving local artisans, food historians, and digital knowledge experts because formalizing tacit knowledge ensures its transferability and accessibility.
- *DP8. Digital Literacy Enhancement:* For system designers to promote the adoption of DT systems among cheesemakers with varying digital literacy levels in the context of artisanal production, employ user-friendly interfaces, simplified workflows, and continuous digital training involving user experience designers, educators, and local training facilitators, because improving digital skills and reducing system complexity enhances user engagement and acceptance.
- *DP9. System Customization:* For developers to adapt the DT to diverse operational environments for cheesemakers in different regions within the context of food heritage production, implement customized system features, adjustable monitoring parameters, and local options involving system architects, local producers, and regional experts, because allowing context-specific customization supports better system alignment with local practices and constraints.

These DPs form the foundation for developing food heritage DTs responsible for the cultural, environmental, and operational contexts in which they are implemented. These DPs offer a roadmap for future DT efforts to preserve ICH while optimizing production practices by addressing authenticity, sustainability, compliance, and user adoption challenges.

## 8 Conclusions

This research adopted a DSR approach to create a heritage DT for the artisanal production of Serra da Estrela cheese, preserving centuries-old cheesemaking practices while integrating modern digital technologies. The key achievement of this study was the design of a dynamic digital replica of the cheesemaking process. This DT allows for real-time simulation, monitoring, and optimization of the production process in a virtual environment, ensuring compliance with traditional methods while promoting resource optimization for sustainability.

For theory, our work extends the application of DTs beyond physical manufacturing into the preservation of ICH. The HKSM provides a framework for understanding the intersection of digital technologies and traditional knowledge preservation. For practitioners, the Heritage DT offers a blueprint for leveraging digital technologies to preserve cultural practices and ensure their transmission to future generations. It underscores the importance of engaging local communities in the evaluation and development process, ensuring that the DT reflects the technical and cultural dimensions of traditional production.

One of this study's key strengths lies in its comprehensive, user-centered design approach. The needs and feedback of local stakeholders (cheesemakers, certification bodies, ICH experts, and regional authorities) were central to the development of the DT. This ensured the artifact's relevance to real-world applications and increased its potential for practical adoption. Additionally, using theoretical frameworks, such as SST, CoP, and PBKM, strengthened the conceptual grounding of the research.

Some limitations must also be stated. The complexity of the DT system and varying levels of digital literacy among cheesemakers presented challenges to broader adoption. While the DT is designed to optimize production and ensure compliance, its usability for craftspeople with limited technical skills remains a concern. Moreover, the iterative nature of the DSR approach, which relies heavily on stakeholder feedback, may slow down the wider deployment and adaptation of the DT across different regions or other ICH practices. The first complete DSR design cycle has been completed, but scaling this solution requires further refinement.

Future research should focus on enhancing the usability of the DT interface to ensure it is accessible to users with different levels of digital proficiency. Improving the user experience is crucial for wider adoption among artisanal producers. Future development could also broaden the application of DT to other forms of ICH, expanding the scope of preservation efforts beyond cheesemaking. Integrating advanced analytics and machine learning within the DT could further enhance its capabilities, offering deeper insights into optimizing traditional practices and supporting the sustainability and resilience of cultural heritage in the digital era. These advancements can contribute to preserving valuable knowledge and empower cultural practices to adapt and thrive in the future.

**Declaration of Competing Interests**

The authors declare that they have no known competing financial interest or personal relationships that could have appeared to influence the work reported in this paper.

**Acknowledgements** This work is partially financed through national funds by FCT – Fundação para a Ciência e a Tecnoloiga, I.P., in the framework of the Project UIDB/00326/2025 and UIDP/00326/2025. The second author is funded by FCT under the Ph.D. grant 2022.09950.BD.

## References

1. Blake, J. (2008). UNESCO's 2003 convention on intangible cultural heritage: The implications of community involvement in 'Safeguarding'. In L. Smith & N. Akagawa (Eds.), *Intangible heritage*. Routledge.
2. Kurin, R. (2007). Safeguarding intangible cultural heritage: Key factors in implementing the 2003 convention. *Intangible Heritage., 9*.
3. Smith, L. (2006). *Uses of heritage*. Routledge.
4. UNESCO. (2003). *Convention for the safeguarding of the intangible cultural heritage*.
5. Inácio, R. S., Gomes, A. M. P., & Saraiva, J. A. (2020). Serra da Estrela cheese: A review. *Journal of Food Processing & Preservation, 44*(5).

6. Tao, F., Zhang, H., Liu, A., & Nee, A. Y. C. (2019). Digital twin in industry: State-of-the-art. *IEEE Transactions on Industrial Informatics, 15*(4), 2405–2415.
7. Li, L., Lei, B., & Mao, C. (2022). Digital twin in smart manufacturing. *Journal of Industrial Information Integration, 26*, 100289.
8. Lu, Y., Liu, C., Wang, K. I.-K., Huang, H., & Xu, X. (2020). Digital twin-driven smart manufacturing: Connotation, reference model, applications and research issues. *Robotics and Computer-Integrated Manufacturing, 61*, 101837.
9. Xin, L., Hongyu, G., Kyeong, S. E., Qitao, W., Guojun, Y., & Bangkun, D. (2023). Towards cultural heritage digital twin: Concept, characteristics, framework and applications. In *2023 9th International Conference on Virtual Reality (ICVR)* (pp. 549–557). IEEE.
10. Mendes, I., Monteiro, J., & Barata, J. (2024). A heritage digital twin for Serra da Estrela cheese production. In B. Marcinkowski, A. Przybyłek, A. Jarzębowicz, N. Iivari, E. Insfran, M. Lang, H. Linger, & C. Schneider (Eds.), *Harnessing opportunities: Reshaping ISD in the post-COVID-19 and generative AI era (ISD2024 proceedings)*. University of Gdańsk.
11. Gregor, S., & Hevner, A. R. (2013). Positioning and presenting design science research for maximum impact. *MIS Quarterly., 37*(2), 337–355.
12. Vieira, G., de Castro, E., Gomes, H., Loureiro, F., Fernandes, M., Patrocínio, F., Firmino, G., & Forte, J. (2020). *The Estrela Geopark–from planation surfaces to glacial erosion*. Springer International Publishing.
13. Stones, R. (2005). *Structuration theory*. Palgrave Macmillan.
14. Wenger, E. (1998). *Communities of practice*. Cambridge University Press.
15. Orlikowski, W. J. (2002). Knowing in practice: Enacting a collective capability in distributed organizing. *Organization Science., 13*(3), 249–273.
16. Glaessgen, E., & Stargel, D. (2012). The digital twin paradigm for future NASA and U.S. air Force vehicles. In *53rd AIAA/ASME/ASCE/AHS/ASC Structures, Structural Dynamics and Materials Conference, 20th AIAA/ASME/AHS Adaptive Structures Conference, 14th AIAA*. American Institute of Aeronautics and Astronautics.
17. Jones, D., Snider, C., Nassehi, A., Yon, J., & Hicks, B. (2020). Characterising the digital twin: A systematic literature review. *CIRP Journal of Manufacturing Science and Technology, 29*, 36–52.
18. Tao, F., Cheng, J., Qi, Q., Zhang, M., Zhang, H., & Sui, F. (2018). Digital twin-driven product design, manufacturing and service with big data. *The International Journal of Advanced Manufacturing Technology., 94*(9–12), 3563–3576.
19. Fuller, A., Fan, Z., Day, C., & Barlow, C. (2020). Digital twin: Enabling technologies, challenges and open research. *IEEE Access, 8*, 108952–108971.
20. Wurm, B., Becker, M., Pentland, B. T., Lyytinen, K., Weber, B., Grisold, T., Mendling, J., & Kremser, W. (2023). Digital twins of organizations: A socio-technical view on challenges and opportunities for future research. *Communications of the Association for Information Systems., 52*, 552–565.
21. Ali, S., Abdallah, S., & Pervaiz, S. (2022). A review of the design and implementation of digital twins for smart manufacturing. In *Volume 2B: Advanced Manufacturing*. American Society of Mechanical Engineers.
22. Tao, F., & Zhang, M. (2017). Digital twin shop-floor: A new shop-floor paradigm towards smart manufacturing. *IEEE Access, 5*, 20418–20427.
23. Gallego-García, S., Gallego-García, D., & García-García, M. (2023). Sustainability in the Agri-food supply chain: A combined digital twin and simulation approach for farmers. *Procedia Computer Science, 217*, 1280–1295.
24. Singh, G., Rajesh, R., Daultani, Y., & Misra, S. C. (2023). Resilience and sustainability enhancements in food supply chains using digital twin technology: A Grey causal modelling (GCM) approach. *Computers and Industrial Engineering, 179*, 109172.
25. Melesse, T. Y., Bollo, M., Di Pasquale, V., Centro, F., & Riemma, S. (2022). Machine learning-based digital twin for monitoring fruit quality evolution. *Procedia Computer Science, 200*, 13–20.

26. Wang, B., Zhou, H., Li, X., Yang, G., Zheng, P., Song, C., Yuan, Y., Wuest, T., Yang, H., & Wang, L. (2024). Human digital twin in the context of industry 5.0. *Robotics and Computer-Integrated Manufacturing, 85*, 102626.
27. Shi, H., Duan, T., Yu, X., & Dong, Q. (2023). Digital inheritance of traditional Mongolian robes of the Nayman tribe. *Fibres & Textiles in Eastern Europe., 31*(6), 1–14.
28. Wen, Y., & Xu, K. (2024). Dissemination of intangible cultural heritage based on digital twin technology. In *2024 International Conference on Culture-Oriented Science & Technology (CoST)* (pp. 94–98). IEEE.
29. Stacchio, L., Garzarella, S., Cascarano, P., De Filippo, A., Cervellati, E., & Marfia, G. (2024). DanXe: An extended artificial intelligence framework to analyze and promote dance heritage. Digital applications in archaeology and cultural. *Heritage, 33*, e00343.
30. Wang, M., & Lau, N. (2023). NFT digital twins: A digitalization strategy to preserve and sustain Miao silver craftsmanship in the Metaverse era. *Heritage, 6*(2), 1921–1941.
31. Li, M., Xu, S., Tang, J., & Chen, W. (2024). Design and research of digital twin platform for handicraft intangible cultural Heritage–Yangxin Cloth paste. *Heritage Science, 12*(1), 43.
32. Giddens, A. (1984). *The constitution of society*. University of California Press.
33. Greenhalgh, T., & Stones, R. (2010). Theorising big IT Programmes in healthcare: Strong structuration theory meets actor-network theory. *Social Science & Medicine, 70*(9), 1285–1294.
34. Coad, A. F., & Herbert, I. P. (2009). Back to the future: New potential for structuration theory in management accounting research? *Management Accounting Research., 20*(3), 177–192.
35. Lave, J., & Wenger, E. (1991). *Situated learning*. Cambridge University Press.
36. Amin, A., & Roberts, J. (2008). Knowing in action: Beyond communities of practice. *Research Policy, 37*(2), 353–369.
37. Cook, S. D. N., & Brown, J. S. (1999). Bridging epistemologies: The generative dance between organizational knowledge and organizational knowing. *Organization Science., 10*(4), 381–400.
38. Brown, J. S., & Duguid, P. (2001). Knowledge and organization: A social-practice perspective. *Organization Science., 12*(2), 198–213.
39. Carlile, P. R. (2002). A pragmatic view of knowledge and boundaries: Boundary objects in new product development. *Organization Science., 13*(4), 442–455.
40. Hevner, A. R., March, S. T., Park, J., & Ram, S. (2004). Design science in information systems research. *MIS Quarterly., 28*(1), 75–105.
41. March, S. T., & Smith, G. F. (1995). Design and natural science research on information technology. *Decision Support Systems, 15*(4), 251–266.
42. Peffers, K., Tuunanen, T., Rothenberger, M. A., & Chatterjee, S. (2007). A design science research methodology for information systems research. *Journal of Management Information Systems., 24*(3), 45–77.
43. vom Brocke, J., & Maedche, A. (2019). The DSR grid: Six Core dimensions for effectively planning and communicating design science research projects. *Electronic Markets., 29*(3), 379–385.
44. Venable, J., Pries-Heje, J., & Baskerville, R. (2016). FEDS: A framework for evaluation in design science research. *European Journal of Information Systems., 25*(1), 77–89.
45. Brown, S. (2023). *The C4 model for Visualising software architecture*. Leanpub.
46. Monteiro, J., & Barata, J. (2024). An evaluation method for digital twin development platforms. In *Lecture notes in computer science* (pp. 425–434).
47. Gregor, S., Kruse, L., & Seidel, S. (2020). Research perspectives: The anatomy of a design principle. *Journal of the Association for Information Systems, 21*, 1622–1652.

# Beyond Agile Methodologies: Exploring the Business Analyst's Role in Agile Software Development

**Mateusz Kwiatkowski and Aleksander Jarzębowicz**

**Abstract** **Context:** Agile methodologies are now used in the majority of software projects, but the definitions of such methodologies rarely include the role of a business analyst (BA). **Objective:** This paper investigates the responsibilities assigned to BAs participating in agile software projects. **Method:** We identified potential responsibilities through a systematic literature review (3 databases) and interviews with 6 practitioners. The most commonly mentioned responsibilities were further evaluated in an international questionnaire survey study with 72 respondents. **Results:** The combined findings from the SLR and interviews resulted in 89 unique responsibilities grouped into 7 areas. A subset of 49 responsibilities were ranked according to the frequency with which they were assigned to BAs in the survey respondents' organizations. **Conclusions:** Our findings show that BAs typically support Product Owners (rather than taking on that role) and focus on requirements engineering, business needs, and working closely with development teams. Based on our findings, we propose a framework of agile BA responsibilities.

## 1 Introduction

Agile software development (ASD) is an approach commonly used in software projects today. It is a term that describes a way of thinking and working that follows the principles and values summarized in the Agile Manifesto [10]. ASD encompasses a number of specific agile methodologies, some of which predate the Manifesto (e.g. [6]), while the others were proposed after the agile approach gained more recognition. One of the core elements of any agile methodology is the definition of project roles and their responsibilities. Agile methodologies, however, usually do not recognize a role of business analyst (BA) or similar. There are some exceptions, e.g. OpenUP and AgilePM, but the most popular ones (according to e.g.

M. Kwiatkowski · A. Jarzębowicz (✉)
Department of Software Engineering, Gdańsk University of Technology, Gdańsk, Poland
e-mail: s174159@student.pg.edu.pl; olek@eti.pg.edu.pl



B. Marcinkowski et al. (eds.), *Advances in Information Systems Development*,
Lecture Notes in Information Systems and Organisation 77,
https://doi.org/10.1007/978-3-031-87880-0_11

State of Agile Survey [41]) like Scrum, Kanban, Scrumban and XP, as well as SAFe (Scaled Agile Framework) do not include a BA role. At the same time, the number of BAs and the industry's demand for them is growing, as evidenced by job postings (e.g., a search on LinkedIn on June 26, 2024 returned 7508 job postings for BAs in the EU and 9180 in the US). It is also confirmed by job market trends [7], and the number of certificate holders [18, 19]. Thus, given the current level of adoption of ASD in the IT industry [41], it is very likely that BAs are being utilized in agile projects, although it is not clear how exactly.

It is widely recognized that business analysis and requirements engineering activities affect agile projects. This fact is reflected in industry guides [14, 15, 17] and academic works [32, 44] to the extent that a term of Agile Requirements Engineering (ARE) was coined [33]. ARE focuses on practices and techniques that fit well with agile processes and values, and on addressing the specific challenges of requirements engineering in projects using team-level agile methodologies [21, 42] or agile scaling frameworks [22, 36]. Despite the substantial body of knowledge available, there is no established guidance on the role and responsibilities of the BA in an agile project, especially in relation to other roles defined in Scrum such as Product Owner (PO) or Scrum Master (SM). While there are several studies dedicated to standard agile roles, such as Product Owner [34] and Scrum Master [28], as well as proposals for new roles to be performed in agile teams, such as UX Designer [31] and Product Manager [37], no such proposal could be found for a BA. As for a more general approach, some sources suggest that the BA should act as a PO [17], while others suggest that the BA should rather support the PO and/or the development team [14]. While there is no consensus on this issue, the IT industry seems to be finding appropriate ways to employ BAs in software projects, as evidenced by the growing number of BA positions. We found that while this issue is discussed in thematic forums [27] and blogs [1], it is difficult to identify any scientific works dedicated to the role of BA in an agile environment. We decided to fill this research gap by investigating what constitutes the role of the BA in agile projects, i.e. what responsibilities are assigned to BAs. We define the following research questions:

- **RQ1**—What are the potential responsibilities of BAs working in agile software projects?
- **RQ2**—What responsibilities are most frequently assigned to BAs in industrial practice?

To answer RQ1, we conducted a systematic literature review (SLR) and a series of interviews with practitioners, which resulted in a list of potential BA responsibilities. We then selected the most frequently mentioned responsibilities and conducted a questionnaire-based survey. Respondents were asked to select responsibilities performed by BAs in agile projects in which they participated. We used the survey results to answer RQ2.

This paper is an extended version of a conference paper [26] presented at the 32nd International Conference on Information Systems Development held in 2024 in Gdańsk, Poland. Given that information systems are nowadays mostly developed using agile methodologies [41], the research reported in [26] is well-aligned with conference profile and in particular with its Lean and Agile Software Development track. In this paper the following additional contributions are included: (1) The presentation of survey respondents' characteristics (answers to demographic questions); (2) The analysis of responses with respect to the selected characteristics (respondent's company size, respondent's experience); (3) The proposal of a framework summarizing key responsibilities of agile BA.

The paper is organized as follows. The next three Sects. 2–4 are dedicated to the subsequent steps of the research study conducted: a systematic literature review (Sect. 2), a series of interviews (Sect. 3), and a questionnaire-based survey (Sect. 4). Each of these sections describes the design, execution, and results of a particular step. We discuss the results in Sect. 5. On the basis of our findings we propose a framework of agile BA key responsibilities in Sect. 6. Threats to validity are reported in Sect. 7 and the paper is concluded in Sect. 8.

## 2 Systematic Literature Review

The first step was dedicated to RQ1 and involved a review of the current literature using the Systematic Literature Review method [23]. We selected several independent scientific literature databases relevant to software engineering and information systems, namely Elsevier Scopus, IEEExplore, and SpringerLink. We designed the search string based on RQ1, but also considering synonyms and different expressions used in the community. After initial searches and analysis of the results, we found that the queries returned very few results. This confirmed our initial suspicion, based on non-systematic searches, that the topic is not widely covered in the scientific literature. However, in order to obtain a more comprehensive set of sources to review, we decided to include the keyword "product owner" in our search string. The reason is that several sources indicate that the BA assumes the position of the PO in an agile project and performs the responsibilities of the PO. Being aware that this might introduce some bias, we planned to treat BA and PO responsibilities separately in the data extraction phase. The generic search string below was later adapted to specific search engines used in scientific databases.

```
A: (("business analysis" OR "business analyst" OR "product owner"
OR "requirements engineering")
B: ("agile" OR "scrum" OR "kanban" OR "XP" OR "FDD" OR "DSDM" OR "lean")
C: ("role" OR "roles" OR "responsibilities" OR "activities" OR "duties"
OR "job" OR "work" OR "tasks"))

Final search string: A AND B AND C
```

**Table 1** SLR results

| Database | All sources | Titles | Abstracts | Full texts |
|---|---|---|---|---|
| Scopus | 507 | 73 | 38 | 17 |
| IEEEXplore | 159 | 39 | 6 | 1 |
| SpringerLink | 341 | 42 | 1 | 0 |
| Total | 1007 | 154 | 45 | 18 |

Inclusion criteria were defined as follows: (IC1) sources in English; (IC2) peer-reviewed sources; (IC3) sources relevant to the defined search terms; (IC4) sources related to industry practice (empirical research, experience reports). We excluded articles that met the following criteria: (EC1) sources closely related to other sources (e.g. basic and extended versions of the same paper); (EC2) sources not referring to industry experience. The SLR study was conducted from March 2022 to May 2022 and involved both authors of this paper. The results of the search are shown in the "All sources" column of Table 1. The Scopus database was used first in the search process. The search in the IEEEXplore and SpringerLink databases therefore resulted in many duplicates, which were discarded from further processing and are not shown in Table 1. The sources returned by the database search engines were checked in three steps by examining: (1) titles; (2) abstracts; (3) full texts. Table 1 provides details on how many sources were qualified after each step. The final number of qualified sources was 18.

The data extraction process focused on the responsibilities (tasks, duties) listed by the reviewed source as assigned to the BA or PO (recorded separately for each of these roles). In addition, the basic information about the paper and its venue, research methodology used and the relevance to the search topic were recorded. The extracted responsibilities were analyzed in order to identify identical or very similar items and thus to create a unified list summarizing all qualified sources. Each such decision was agreed upon by both authors in a consensus-based manner. To structure the results, we decided to divide the responsibilities into 7 work areas: Product Backlog, Requirements, Project, Product, Business, Team and Development. These work areas have been adopted from the classification proposed by Remta [34] on the basis of reviewing several sources. However, we have introduced two additional areas (namely Requirements and Product) due to the fact that such topics are emphasized as the core of BA's work [14].

The partial results of the SLR study are summarized in Tables 2, 3, and 4 in "SLR: PO" and "SLR:BA" columns. The full results could not be included here due to page limitations and are available online [25]. Separate columns for BA and PO allowed us to retain PO responsibilities as candidate items for use in the planned quantitative study (questionnaire-based survey), but without mixing them with BA responsibilities. The decision process regarding the questionnaire design and its content is described in Sect. 4. As an additional contribution, such a presentation makes it possible to compare how such two roles are considered in the literature.

**Table 2** Product backlog-related responsibilities

| ID | Responsibility | SLR: PO | SLR: BA | Interviews |
|---|---|---|---|---|
| R1 | Managing the product backlog (PB) | [4, 29, 30, 34, 38], [3, 12, 13, 35] | [8, 9, 11, 20] | A, B, C, E |
| R2 | Accepting user stories to the PB | [34, 39] | [8] | A |
| R3 | Refining the product backlog | [34] | [9, 11, 43], | B, C |
| R4 | Story mapping | | [43] | |
| R5 | Prioritizing the product backlog | | | C |

**Table 3** Requirements-related responsibilities

| ID | Responsibility | SLR: PO | SLR: BA | Interviews |
|---|---|---|---|---|
| R6 | Analyzing use cases | | | A, B, D |
| R7 | Gathering requirements | [3, 4, 12, 30, 34] | [8, 43] | A, E |
| R8 | Prioritizing requirements | [3, 12, 13, 35, 38–40] | [8, 11, 43] | A, B, C |
| R9 | Creating user stories | [13, 34, 39, 40] | [11, 20, 43] | B, C, D |
| R10 | Documenting requirements | [12, 30, 34] | [20] | A, B, D, E, F |
| R11 | Requirements completion verification | [4, 12, 34] | | |
| R12 | Managing agile sample documentation repository | | [11] | |
| R13 | Explaining requirements to developers | | [20] | A, B, C, E |
| R14 | Requirements refinement | | [20, 43] | A, B, C |
| R15 | Acceptance test criteria definition | [12, 34] | [9, 11, 20, 43] | F |
| R16 | Creating epics | [13] | [20] | B |
| R17 | Designing workshops | [30] | [9] | |
| R18 | Collaboration with stakeholders | [12, 34, 39] | [43] | A, B |
| R19 | Prototyping requirements | | [20] | |
| R20 | Analyzing requirements | | | A |
| R21 | Collaboration with Product Owner on creating requirements | | | B |
| R22 | Creating UML models | | | D |
| R23 | Checking if requirements are met | | | F |

**Table 4** Project-related responsibilities

| ID | Responsibility | SLR: PO | SLR: BA | Interviews |
|---|---|---|---|---|
| R24 | Release management | [3–5, 34, 35, 38, 39] | [11] | B |
| R25 | Managing the project | [29, 34] | | B |
| R26 | Ensuring corporate guidelines and policies | [3, 5, 34] | | |
| R27 | Risk assessment | [3, 5, 34, 35, 38–40] | | A, B, C, D |
| R28 | Improving project processes | [34] | | |
| R29 | Tracking status of the project | | [43] | D, F |
| R30 | Creating specification document | | | A |
| R31 | Prioritizing tasks | | | A |
| R32 | Creating project roadmap | | | B |
| R33 | Organizing other employees' work | | | D |
| R34 | Adding project tasks to Jira | | | D, F |
| R35 | Managing Sprints | | | F |

## 3 Interviews

The second research step also aimed to answer RQ1 with qualitative research. As the findings from the literature turned out to be not very complete (especially considering the tasks explicitly mentioned as responsibilities of BAs), we decided to apply a triangulation approach and collect additional information using another research method. We chose semi-structured moderated interviews with industry practitioners as the most appropriate method to facilitate the free identification of responsibilities. The target population in this case consisted of BAs and other practitioners directly involved in business analysis tasks in agile projects.

An interview guide was prepared beforehand to ensure that, despite the open nature of the interviews, the essential information was collected. The interview included a formal introduction: informing the interviewee about the purpose of the interview, guarantee of confidentiality and use of the information collected for scientific purposes only; asking for permission to record the interview. It also listed a number of demographic questions about the interviewee's background and experience, as well as their work environment (organization and its structure, agile methodologies used, team structure and roles) to provide some context. The main part of the guide started with an open question about the responsibilities of BAs in the interviewee's organization. This was followed by questions about the BA's responsibilities in each of the 7 BA work areas (explained in Sect. 2) to provide better coverage.

We identified potential interviewees primarily through thematic groups on LinkedIn and other social media, and to some extent through personal contacts. We took care to include practitioners from organizations of different sizes and business sectors. However, it was not possible to use systematic sampling, so the method used was purposive sampling. The basic characteristics of the 6 practitioners

 

**Table 5** Characteristics of the practitioners interviewed

| ID | Position(s) | Pos. exp. | Agile exp. | Total exp. | Sector | Org. size |
|---|---|---|---|---|---|---|
| A | Senior manager of software, system design architect, product owner | 6 | 10 | 16 | Telecommuni-cations | 2000 |
| B | Business analyst | 8 | 6 | 22 | Software house | 200 |
| C | Business analyst | 4 | 4 | 15 | Leasing | 150 |
| D | Technical advisor, business analyst, DevOps | 10 | 15 | 20 | Software house | >10000 |
| E | Business and system analyst | 1,5 | 3 | 3,5 | Finances | >10000 |
| F | Business analyst | 0,5 | 0,5 | 1 | Insurance | 850 |

interviewed are summarized in Table 5. The interviews were conducted by the first author between July 2022 and November 2022. In each case, a videoconferencing tool was used and the interview was recorded with the consent of the interviewee.

We reviewed the recordings to extract the responsibilities mentioned by the interviewees and processed them by performing open coding [2] based on the qualitative data available (interviewee responses). As a result, complex sentences were converted into codes. Next, the coded responsibilities were assigned to areas (in many cases the interviewees mentioned them in the parts of the interview dedicated to another topic) and reviewed to identify duplicates and similarities. Finally, a comparative analysis was conducted between the results of the two research studies (SLR and interviews). The partial results are presented in Tables 2, 3, and 4, while all of them are included in the online appendix [25]. The interview results are included in the "Interviews" columns and juxtaposed with the corresponding SLR results.

## 4 Survey

The third research step was dedicated to RQ2 and involved a quantitative approach—a survey of industry practitioners conducted using the guidelines of Kitchenham and Pfleeger [24]. We wanted to assess the frequency with which certain responsibilities are confirmed by practitioners as carried out by BAs in their working environment. We decided to use a questionnaire with closed questions dedicated to specific responsibilities identified in the previous steps. However, the number of responsibilities was too high (89) to include them all. We decided to make a selection to minimize the risk of potential respondents becoming tired or overwhelmed and dropping out.

The following selection criteria were used. The questionnaire items were selected from the results of the interviews and the literature review. They included all the responsibilities that were mentioned by at least two interviewees. For each of the remaining items, a score was calculated using the following values: (a) A responsibility mentioned in an interview: +3 points; (b) A responsibility listed in the SLR findings as assigned to BA: +2 points; (c) A responsibility listed in the SLR findings as assigned to PO (SLR results): +1 point.

For each of the 7 areas (described in Sect. 2), two additional responsibilities with the highest scores were included in the questionnaire (more in case of equal top scores). The values used to calculate the score reflect our attitude—we treated interview results as the most reliable and up-to-date. As for the literature, we again distinguished the results related to BAs and POs. The selection of additional responsibilities from each area results from the intention to cover all aspects of the BA's job. A total of 49 responsibilities were included.

We created the online questionnaire in English using the Google Forms service. The questionnaire included a number of demographic questions about the respondent (job position, job experience, experience with agile methodologies) and their current organization (size, industry, agile methodologies used). We also asked an explicit question about the name of the position within the organization given to people who work on business analysis tasks in agile projects. The reason for this was our curiosity whether the BA position is still recognized in agile organizations or whether a different name is used. The main part of the questionnaire was divided into 7 parts, corresponding to the identified work areas. In each part, the respondent was asked the question: "What are the responsibilities of the business analyst in (...) area in your company?", followed by a list of responsibilities. We used closed-ended, multiple-choice questions—a respondent was asked to select any number of responsibilities from those presented. To ensure the accuracy of the questionnaire, a pilot study was conducted with individuals who matched the profile of the target respondent.

The questionnaire was published online on February 24, 2023. Invitations were posted in several international IT related forums (for BAs, Product Owners, Scrum Masters and developers) and sent to a few IT companies through personal contacts. The survey was closed on March 20, 2023 with 72 complete and valid responses.

We processed the results to uncover the demographics of the respondents as well as the responses that contributed to RQ2 (about the BA's responsibilities). The majority of respondents identified themselves as business analysts (63.5%). The others were mostly: Product Owners (6.9%), developers (6.9%), testers (5.6%), project managers (4.2%) and Scrum Masters (4.2%). Most of the respondents had 2–5 years of experience in their current position (34.7%), followed by 10+ years (22.2%), 1–2 years (19.4%) and 5–10 years (15.3%), while inexperienced practitioners (less than 1 year of experience) made up only 8.3% of the population. Respondents were also quite experienced in using agile methodologies, with most reporting between 2 and 5 years (45.8%), followed by 1–2 years (22.2%) and 5–10 years (15.3%). Respondents tended to work for larger organizations: 1000+ employees (59.7%), 100–500 employees (18.1%), 500–1000 employees (12.5%). This means that the proportion of practitioners working in smaller organizations (less than 100 employees) was less than 10%. The organizations in which the respondents worked represented a very wide range of business sectors, with the most common being Services (19.4%), Telecommunications (16.7%), Finance

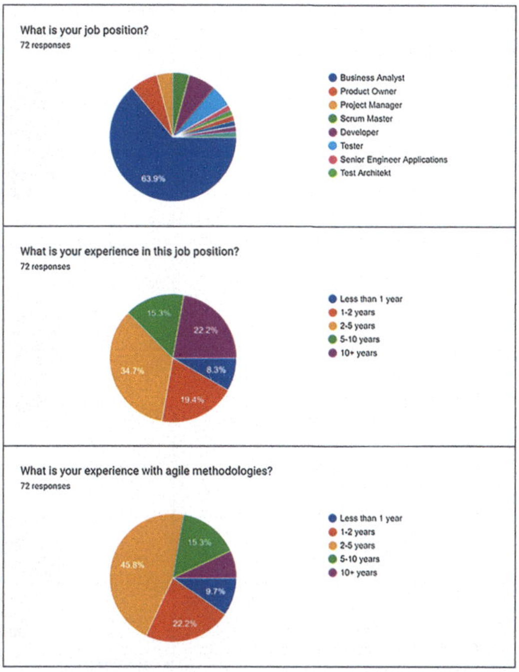


**Fig. 1** Survey demographics—respondents

(11.1%), and Insurance (8.3%). When it comes to agile methodologies, Scrum dominates the landscape, with 79.2% of respondents reporting that it is used in their organizations. The other most frequently cited methodologies are Kanban (5.5%) and Scrumban (4.2%). The majority of respondents' organizations (77.8%) recognize the job position of Business Analyst. None of the alternative job titles provided by respondents was mentioned by more than 1 person, they seem to depend on the nomenclature used by a particular organization. Unfortunately, we did not ask about the country in which the respondent works, so this characteristic is not available. The demographics of the respondents are visualized in Figs. 1 and 2.

The main result of the survey is shown in Fig. 3. Each of the responsibilities listed in the questionnaire was selected at least 5 times (6.9%) and at most 66 times (91.7%). We believe that this confirms the validity of the results of the previous research steps (SLR and interviews).

We conducted additional analyses of the distributions we obtained for the influence of certain respondent characteristics. In some cases the distribution was too dispersed (e.g., business sector) or too unbalanced (e.g., agile methodologies used in the respondent's organization), but we were able to analyze the differences in terms of organization size and respondent experience.

We considered companies with less than 1000 employees (29 responses, 40.3%) and 1000+ employees (43 respondents, 59.7%). The most significant differences are reported as follows. In Product Backlog area, BAs from smaller companies are more often responsible for managing Product Backlogs (R1), while in smaller companies

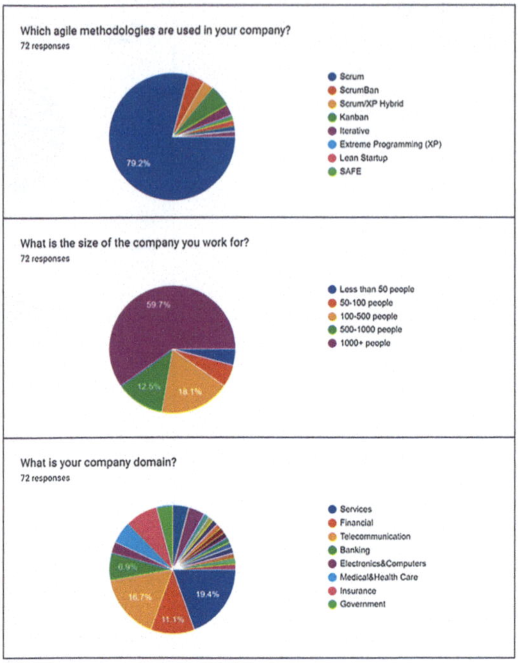


**Fig. 2** Survey demographics—respondents' companies

they rather tend to refine PBs (R3). This is also reinforced by the responses from the Requirements area—prioritizing requirements (R8) is more common in larger companies. In turn, virtually all BAs from smaller companies are responsible for gathering requirements (R7), while only about 80% of their colleagues from 1000+ organizations have such responsibility assigned. As for Project area, project-related risk assessment (R27) and tracking the project status (R29) are more frequently performed by BAs from smaller organizations. In addition, smaller organizations are more likely to assign BAs additional responsibilities related to management tasks—particularly release management (R24) and overall project management (R25). The main difference in Product area is that BAs from smaller companies are often responsible for developing product vision (R37), while in 1000+ organizations this seems to be someone else's job, but instead BAs focus on maximizing the value of the product (R36). In addition, a higher proportion of BAs from larger organizations are responsible for analyzing the product (R41) and providing input for management's product-related decisions (R42). In Team area, the participation in Daily meetings is more likely to be part of the workday for BAs from smaller organizations. No significant differences were found in Business and Development areas. We also examined whether the experience of the respondents in their positions might influence the results by comparing the less experienced (up to 2 years—20 respondents, 27.8%) and more experienced (more than 2 years—52 respondents, 72.2%) practitioners who participated in the survey. We report the differences found in order to provide the full picture, including the potential biases. The less

**Fig. 3** Responsibilities of BAs in respondents' organizations—distribution of survey responses

experienced respondents tended to assign the tasks of prioritizing the PB (R5) and prioritizing the requirements (R8), from Product Backlog and Requirements areas, respectively, to BAs. They also claimed that epics technique used for requirements specification (R16) is commonly used by BAs in Requirements area. Other answers they selected more often are: analyzing the product (R41) from Product area as well as participation in Daily meetings (R73) and consultations provided to team members (R75)—both belonging to Team area. In the remaining areas, no significant differences were found.

## 5 Discussion

The results from the literature suggest that the BA's involvement in an agile project is mostly focused on requirements development (R7-R10; R12-R19) and on Product Backlog maintenance (R1-R4). Other responsibilities are rather single, selected activities from the remaining areas: communicating with business stakeholders and sharing the product vision with them (R58) and participating in Scrum ceremonies (R68; R73-R74). If we compare the SLR results for BA and PO, we see that there are many similarities in the tasks that deal with Product Backlog and requirements. Interestingly, POs have many more tasks listed in the literature, especially those related to business aspects, project management and team cooperation. The possible reason is that the original distinction of three roles in Scrum implies more responsibilities for each of them, while the introduction of additional roles like BA or Design Architect allows to narrow their work focus.

The interviews resulted in some changes to the overview provided by the literature review. The results regarding the responsibilities from Product Backlog and requirements areas confirmed the SLR results, although the interviewees listed some additional tasks (R20-R23). However, they implied much more responsibilities of BAs in project-related (especially risk assessment—R27) and product-related (especially product vision development—R37) areas. The BAs in the interviewees' organizations are also much more active in the business-related area (which had almost no coverage in the literature), the most frequently mentioned responsibilities include: identification of business needs (R55) and their further analysis (R66), providing business expertise to the rest of the team (R49) and using advanced techniques such as financial analysis (R64). A similar situation can be observed in the development area—most respondents confirmed the involvement of BAs in verification testing to determine whether the developed software meets the established requirements (R87). In addition, BAs may participate in acceptance testing (R86) and even act as developers and write the source code (R85). The most significant differences, however, are in team-related responsibilities. Contrary to the findings from the literature, the interviews revealed numerous tasks for which BAs are responsible, including participating in various meetings and activities (R73-R74, R76-R77), supporting team members on technical issues (R80), and supporting POs (R79). However, the main team-related responsibilities of the BA include facilitating communication between teams and customers (R78), working closely with teams (R69), and, in particular, providing answers and explanations to team members when they have doubts about product requirements (R75). This last task was mentioned in all 6 interviews.

The survey study examined only a subset of the responsibilities identified through the SLR and interviews. Unsurprisingly, the greatest involvement of BAs is reported in the requirements area and consists mainly of typical requirements engineering activities such as collaborating with stakeholders (R18), gathering (R7), refining (R14) and documenting (R10) requirements. BAs also create and analyze specific requirements representations, such as use cases (R6), user stories (R9), and epics (R16). Defining acceptance test criteria (R15) is closely related to requirements (testability/verifiability is a key quality characteristic of requirements) and is also often performed by BAs. Their tasks also include communicating the requirements to the developers and explaining the features to be implemented (R13). All these activities are defined in standards and guides on business analysis and requirements engineering, and it seems natural that a BA is responsible for them in software projects, including agile ones.

Significant BA involvement is also reported in the team-related area, although the proportion of responses is lower than in the requirements-related area. BAs work closely with development teams (R69, R75, R78) and participate in meetings (R68, R73, R76, R77). They are not expected to be team leaders (R72). Interestingly, a very high number of responses (80.6%) for providing support to the PO (R72) suggests that the positions of BA and PO are distinct in industrial practice, contrary to the ideas found in the literature. This seems to be confirmed by the responses from the Product Backlog area—BAs are more often involved in PB management (R1) and refinement (R3) than in making decisions about PB contents (R2) or their priorities (R5). It seems that the PO is the keeper of the Product Backlog (as defined in Scrum), while the BA interacts with stakeholders, performs requirements engineering activities, and provides expertise in maintaining the Backlog.

The involvement of BAs in product-related responsibilities is rather average, and they are expected to analyze (R41) and improve (R36) the product as well as provide information necessary for management decisions (R42). They rarely have primary responsibility for the long-term vision of the product (R37, R40). The possible reason is that this responsibility is taken by someone else (e.g. PO, product manager). In addition, product vision is not so important in the case of custom software for a particular customer, and some respondents may work on such projects. As for the business-related area, the responsibilities of BAs seem to focus on the core business analysis activities, i.e. identifying business needs (R55), analyzing them to introduce the necessary changes (R66), and working with stakeholders to establish a shared vision of the solution (R58). Neither the specific techniques/tools such as business plan development (R43) or financial analysis (R64) nor working with other parties (R48-R52) are as common in respondents' organizations.

BAs are not expected to perform project management activities (R24-R27), except for tracking the status of the project (R29) and defining additional tasks as needed (R34). As the BA interacts with customer representatives and other stakeholders, he/she may be informed about discovered defects and change requests, so it is natural that such information is translated into tasks to be performed. In terms of development-related responsibilities, BAs are quite often involved in testing (R86, R87), but very rarely in typical developer tasks (R85, R89).

Among the potential differences that can be attributed to the size of the organization are the BAs' responsibilities related to project and product management, such as: managing the Product Backlog, release management (R24), project management (R25), project-related risk assessment (R27) and tracking the project status (R29), which are more likely to be assigned to BAs in smaller organizations. The possible explanation is that in such organizations there are fewer project roles defined and consequently the existing roles have to cover a wider range of tasks that need to be performed in any IT project.

## 6 Agile Business Analyst Responsibilities Framework

This section translates the results of our study into a proposed framework that lists the expected responsibilities of a BA working in an agile project. We avoid the terms like "competency model" or "competency framework" that are used in the literature (e.g. [16]), because our results only concern responsibilities/tasks, while a complete competency model should also consider other aspects like soft skills, underlying skills and desired personality traits. It would be possible to treat them as implicit characteristics necessary to effectively perform the identified BA's tasks and extract them from the task descriptions. However, we believe this is too far-fetched and lacks sufficient evidence. In our opinion, the identification of such competencies requires additional dedicated research. For this reason, we will limit the content of this section to the BA responsibilities identified as a result of our study. A BA in an agile project is expected to:

1. Address the business aspects of the project by:
   (a) Identifying and analyzing business needs;
   (b) Using the knowledge about business needs to maximize the value of the product;
2. Perform core requirements engineering tasks, including:
   (a) Collaborating with the stakeholders and eliciting the requirements;
   (b) Analyzing and refining the elicited requirements;
   (c) Documenting the requirements using a variety of specification techniques e.g., user stories, acceptance criteria, use cases, epics;
3. Participate in the maintenance of the Product Backlog:
   (a) Supporting the Product Owner (considered a separate role);
   (b) Alternatively, as a less likely option, but still possible in smaller organizations, the BA may take over all PB management;
   (c) Providing the skills needed to refine and prioritize the Product Backlog;
4. Work closely with the development team by:
   (a) Attending team meetings, e.g. Scrum ceremonies;

   (b) Consulting with developers and explaining requirements to them;
   (c) Facilitating effective communication between developers and stakeholders representing the customer;

5. Participate in testing activities by:

   (a) Defining acceptance criteria to be used in testing;
   (b) Verifying the implementation of requirements through verification and acceptance testing;

6. Support management through:

   (a) Tracking the status of the project and documenting additional tasks so that they are available along with the requirements (e.g. in Jira or a similar tool);
   (b) Providing the necessary business knowledge for management decisions, especially those related to the developed product.

## 7 Threats to Validity

We discuss the threats to each of the research steps presented (SLR, interviews, survey) separately.

In an SLR study, it is crucial to minimize the risk of omitting relevant sources. In our study, a possible limitation is that we restricted the search to three databases, but we deliberately chose databases that are provided by the main publishers and that are diverse, i.e. their content does not overlap significantly (such as e.g. Scopus and ScienceDirect). It was a trade-off between the coverage of the databases and the effort required. We believe that the threat of insufficient size and number of samples is not applicable, as the search resulted in over 1000 records to be reviewed, which is a considerable size for a small number of researchers. The threat of an incorrect or suboptimal search string was mitigated by careful selection of keywords and construction of the search string, including synonyms, and by conducting initial searches (e.g., PO-related keywords were added as a result). The threat of selection bias was mitigated by explicit inclusion/exclusion criteria and a shared, consensus-based decision-making process.

In the case of the interview study, selection of participants can be considered a threat, especially given the purposive sampling method used. However, we are not aware of any means of systematic sampling of the target population. The number of interviewees (6) is a limitation that we acknowledge—it was difficult to persuade busy professionals to participate, especially as we were unable to offer them any bonuses. We did, however, attempt to diversify the interviewees in terms of organization size and industry. The inclusion of an interviewee with little experience (participant F) can be seen as a threat. However, the analysis of the recorded interview convinced us that the interviewee was able to answer all the questions and demonstrated substantial knowledge about his responsibilities and about the software development processes of his company. Therefore, there was no reason to doubt the information gathered in this interview and we decided to process and use it in the next research step. The risk of not covering important aspects relevant to the research objective was mitigated by preparing an interview guide based on the results of the SLR and by asking open-ended questions without restricting the interviewees. The threat of researcher confirmation bias was mitigated by collecting data through open-ended questions, while the threat of bias during data analysis was mitigated by recording all interviews and following a coding process applied to the collected data.

Questionnaire-based surveys are highly dependent on the quality of the questionnaire. Therefore, we paid attention to the questionnaire design process and the wording used in the questions. The design process included several iterations and a pilot study with representatives of the target population. A non-systematic sampling method was used (personal and group invitations, mainly through social media), which can be considered a threat (a sample that is not representative of the population), but we were not able to apply systematic sampling. The results of the survey show that very few respondents worked for smaller organizations (<100 employees), which could also introduce a bias. Another threat can be introduced by less experienced respondents with possibly limited knowledge of the responsibilities and tasks in their teams/organizations. We have analyzed the notable differences in their responses (compared to the more experienced respondents) and listed them explicitly so that the reader is aware of where such bias may be present. The limited number of respondents (72) is also a threat to external validity. We assess the threat related to the trustworthiness of the respondents as very low—although we cannot exclude the possibility of their being dishonest (e.g., giving false answers, completing the questionnaire multiple times), we are not able to find any evidence of such behavior.

## 8 Conclusions

The aim of the research reported in this paper was to identify the potential responsibilities of BAs working in agile software projects (RQ1) and to evaluate which responsibilities are assigned to them in industrial practice (RQ2). The main contributions of this paper are: the list of 89 responsibilities identified through an SLR and a series of interviews (answer to RQ1), the results of a survey in which practitioners selected from 49 items the responsibilities performed by BAs in their organizations (answer to RQ2) and the framework of agile BA responsibilities. Since we were not able to find any related work that provides a comprehensive overview of the responsibilities of BAs in agile projects, there is no way to compare the results with those reported by others. Moreover, to the best of our knowledge, it is the first systematic attempt to address the topic we identified as a research gap.

Our work has several implications for research and practice. The list of identified responsibilities and the evaluation of their subset can be used in future research studies, for example, involving a larger group of practitioners or focusing on a more concrete context (organization size, project type, software development processes). It may also be interesting to investigate whether there are differences in agile BA roles across countries or parts of the world. Another possibility is to analyze which responsibilities are shared with other roles or to investigate the reasons why certain responsibilities are assigned to the BA or not in a given context. We plan to work on such further studies ourselves. It is also worth noting that our research focused on BA responsibilities, and as such includes "hard skills" rather than "soft skills" and desired personality traits. In order to develop a complete agile BA competency model, such additional aspects (not covered in this research study) would also need to be included, which implies another possible direction of future work. Implications for practice include the possibility for BAs to review the possible competencies required to work in agile projects, and for managers to review the definitions of roles (and their responsibilities) in their projects/organizational units.

**Acknowledgments** We would like to express our gratitude to all practitioners, who contributed to the presented research by participating in interview and survey studies. We also thank the reviewers for their helpful comments and suggestions.

## References

1. Ambler, S. (2024). Agile business analysts: Rethinking the role of business analysts. Retrieved June 26, 2024, from https://agilemodeling.com/essays/businessanalysts.htm
2. Baskerville, R., & Pries-Heje, J. (1999). Grounded action research: A method for understanding IT in practice. *Accounting, Management and Information Technologies, 9*(1), 1–23.
3. Bass, J. M. (2015). How product owner teams scale agile methods to large distributed enterprises. *Empirical Software Engineering, 20*, 1525–1557.
4. Bass, J. M., Beecham, S., Razzak, M. A., Canna, C. N., & Noll, J. (2018). An empirical study of the Product Owner role in Scrum. In *Proceedings of the 40th International Conference on Software Engineering: Companion Proceeedings* (pp. 123–124)
5. Bass, J. M., & Haxby, A. (2019). Tailoring product ownership in large-scale agile projects: Managing scale, distance, and governance. *IEEE Software, 36*(2), 58–63.
6. Beck, K. (1999). Embracing change with Extreme Programming. *Computer, 32*(10), 70–77.
7. CareerExplorer. (2024). The job market for business analysts in the United States. Retrieved June 26, 2024, from https://www.careerexplorer.com/careers/business-analyst/job-market/
8. Diebold, P., Ostberg, J.-P., Wagner, S., & Zendler, U. (2015). What do practitioners vary in using Scrum? In *Agile Processes in Software Engineering and Extreme Programming: 16th International Conference, XP 2015, Helsinki, Finland, May 25–29, 2015, Proceedings* (vol. 16, pp. 40–51). Springer.
9. Forowicz, P. (2020). Approaches to business analysis in Scrum at Stepstone—case study. In *Data-Centric Business and Applications: Towards Software Development* (vol. 4, pp. 211–223). Springer.
10. Fowler, M., & Highsmith, J. (2001). The agile manifesto. *Software Development, 9*(8), 28–35.
11. Gregorio, D. (2012). How the business analyst supports and encourages collaboration on agile projects. In *International Systems Conference SysCon 2012* (pp. 1–4). IEEE.
12. Gupta, R. K., Jain, S., & Singh, B. (2018). Challenges in scaling up a globally distributed legacy product: A case study of a matrix organization. In *Proceedings of the 13th International Conference on Global Software Engineering* (pp. 77–81).

13. Heikkilä, V. T., Paasivaara, M., Lasssenius, C., Damian, D., & Engblom, C. (2017). Managing the requirements flow from strategy to release in large-scale agile development: A case study at Ericsson. *Empirical Software Engineering, 22*, 2892–2936.
14. International Institute of Business Analysis. (2015). *A guide to the business analysis body of knowledge (BABOK Guide) version 3.*
15. International Institute of Business Analysis. (2017). *Agile extension to the BABOK guide version 2.*
16. International Institute of Business Analysis. (2017). *Business analysis competency model version 4.*
17. International Requirements Engineering Board. (2023). *CPRE advanced Level RE@Agile - hand - book version 2.0.1.*
18. International Institute of Business Analysis. (2024). *Digital badges membership and certifications.* Retrieved June 26, 2024, from https://www.iiba.org/business-analysis-certifications/certification-digital-badge-program-and-directory/
19. International Requirements Engineering Board. (2024). *CPRE - development and spread.* Retrieved June 26, 2024, from https://www.ireb.org/en/service/statistics
20. Jarzębowicz, A., & Sitko, N. (2019). Communication and documentation practices in agile requirements engineering: A survey in Polish software industry. In *Information Systems: Research, Development, Applications, Education: 12th SIGSAND/PLAIS EuroSymposium 2019* (pp. 147–158). Springer.
21. Jarzębowicz, A., & Ślesiński, W. (2018). Assessing effectiveness of recommendations to requirements-related problems through interviews with experts. In *2018 Federated Conference on Computer Science and Information Systems (FedCSIS)* (pp. 959–968). IEEE.
22. Joskowski, A., Przybyłek, A., & Marcinkowski, B. (2023). Scaling Scrum with a customized Nexus framework: A report from a joint industry-academia research project. *Software: Practice and Experience, 53*(7), 1525–1542.
23. Kitchenham, B., & Charters, S. (2007). Guidelines for performing systematic literature reviews in software engineering. Technical Report EBSE-2007-01.
24. Kitchenham, B. A., & Pfleeger, S. L. (2008). Personal opinion surveys. In *Guide to advanced empirical software engineering* (pp. 63–92). Springer.
25. Kwiatkowski, M., & Jarzębowicz, A. (2024). Appendix 1 - Complete SLR and interview results. Retrieved June 26, 2024, from https://doi.org/10.5281/zenodo.12552192
26. Kwiatkowski, M., & Jarzębowicz, A. (2004). On the business analyst's responsibilities in an agile software project - A multi-method study. In B. Marcinkowski, A. Przybyłek, A. Jarzębowicz, N. Iivari, E. Insfran, M. Lang, H. Linger, & C. Schneider (Eds.), *Harnessing Opportunities: Reshaping ISD in the post-COVID-19 and Generative AI Era (ISD2024 Proceedings).* University of Gdańsk.
27. Modern Analyst. (2024). What is an agile business analyst? Retrieved June 26, 2024, from https://www.modernanalyst.com/Careers/InterviewQuestions/tabid/128/ID/6405/What-is-an-Agile-Business-Analyst.aspx
28. Noll, J., Razzak, M. A., Bass, J. M., & Beecham, S. (2017). A study of the Scrum Master's role. In *Product-Focused Software Process Improvement: 18th International Conference, PROFES 2017, Innsbruck, Austria, November 29–December 1, 2017, Proceedings 18* (pp. 307–323). Springer.
29. Oomen, S., De Waal, B., Albertin, A., & Ravesteyn, P. (2017). How can Scrum be succesful? Competences of the Scrum Product Owner. In *Proceedings of the 25th European Conference on Information Systems, ECIS 2017* (pp. 131–142).
30. Paasivaara, M., Heikkilä, V. T., & Lassenius, C. (2012). Experiences in scaling the product owner role in large-scale globally distributed Scrum. In *2012 IEEE Seventh International Conference on Global Software Engineering* (pp. 174–178). IEEE.
31. Plonka, L., Sharp, H., Gregory, P., & Taylor, K. (2014). UX design in agile: A DSDM case study. In *Agile Processes in Software Engineering and Extreme Programming: 15th International Conference, XP 2014* (pp. 1–15). Springer.

32. Przybyłek, A., & Zakrzewski, M. (2018). Adopting collaborative games into agile requirements engineering. In *13th International Conference on Evaluation of Novel Approaches to Software Engineering* (pp. 54–64).
33. Ramesh, B., Cao, L., & Baskerville, R. (2010). Agile requirements engineering practices and challenges: An empirical study. *Information Systems Journal, 20*(5), 449–480.
34. Remta, D. (2020). Has Product Owner's role changed with Agile development expansion? In *Proceedings of IDIMT 2020: Digitalized economy, society and information management* (pp. 443–450). IEEE.
35. Remta, D., Doležel, M., & Buchalcevová, A. (2020). Exploring the Product Owner role within safe implementation in a multinational enterprise. In *International Conference on Agile Software Development, XP 2020* (pp. 92–100). Springer.
36. Saeeda, H., Ahmad, M. O., & Gustavsson, T. (2023). Challenges in large-scale agile software development projects. In *Proceedings of the 38th ACM/SIGAPP Symposium on Applied Computing* (pp. 1030–1037).
37. Tkalich, A., Ulfsnes, R., & Moe, N. B. (2022). Toward an agile product management: What do product managers do in agile companies? In *International Conference on Agile Software Development* (pp. 168–184). Springer.
38. Unger-Windeler, C., & Klünder, J. (2018). On the tasks and characteristics of Product Owner: A case study in the oil and gas industry. In *Product-Focused Software Process Improvement: 19th International Conference, PROFES 2018* (pp. 3–11). Springer.
39. Unger-Windeler, C., Klünder, J. A.-C., Reuscher, T., & Schneider, K. (2021). Are Product Owners communicators? A multi-method research approach to provide a more comprehensive picture of Product Owners in practice. *Journal of Software: Evolution and Process, 33*(1), e2311.
40. Unger-Windeler, C., & Schneider, K. (2019). Expectations on the Product Owner role in systems engineering-a Scrum team's point of view. In *2019 45th Euromicro Conference on Software Engineering and Advanced Applications (SEAA)* (pp. 276–283). IEEE.
41. VersionOne. (2024). 16th annual state of agile report. Retrieved June 26, 2024, from https://stateofagile.com/.2022
42. Wagner, S., Fernández, D. M., Felderer, M., & Kalinowski, M. (2017). Requirements engineering practice and problems in agile projects: Results from an international survey. In *Iberoamerican Congress of Software Engineering (CibSE)*.
43. Zajac-Woodie, D. (2013). Beyond requirements dictator: How agile helped a business analyst discover her real value. In *2013 Agile Conference* (pp. 88–93). IEEE.
44. Zakrzewski, M., Kotecka, D., Ng, Y. Y., & Przybyłek, A. (2019). Adopting collaborative games into agile software development. In *ENASE 2018 Conference, Revised Selected Papers* (vol. 8, pp. 119–136). Springer.

# Assessing Operational Business-IT Alignment for Architecture Improvement

**Pascal André, Ali Benjilany, Hugo Bruneliere, and Dalila Tamzalit**

**Abstract** Business-IT alignment (BITA) remains a challenging topic for enterprise architects. This is notably the case of operational BITA that focuses on the alignment between business processes and IT applications. In this context, a major challenge is to determine the level of alignment between these Business and IT layers. Existing approaches already propose to assess this alignment, but they are often context-specific. Moreover, no approach intends to combine various assessment means for a more in-depth evaluation of the alignment. As a solution, we propose an alignment assessment approach combining different means (metrics, consistency rules, and anti-patterns). We also provide a methodology that integrates this approach by relying on an established cartography (expressing the current state of alignment) and proposes a corresponding redress step. This cartography is composed of Business and IT models, and of explicit links between them. Both the proposed methodology and assessment approach are illustrated on two case studies for validation purposes. In the reported experiments, we considered six metrics, two consistency rules, and four anti-patterns.

This article is a revised and extended version of the ISD 2024 paper untitled "An Approach to Assess Operational Business-IT Alignment" [7].

P. André (✉) · A. Benjilany · D. Tamzalit
Nantes University - CNRS/LS2N, Nantes, France
e-mail: pascal.andre@ls2n.fr; ali.benjilany@etu.univ-nantes.fr; dalila.tamzalit@ls2n.fr

H. Bruneliere
IMT Atlantique - CNRS/LS2N, Nantes, France
e-mail: hugo.bruneliere@imt-atlantique.fr

 
B. Marcinkowski et al. (eds.), *Advances in Information Systems Development*, Lecture Notes in Information Systems and Organisation 77,
https://doi.org/10.1007/978-3-031-87880-0_12

## 1 Introduction

Business-IT alignment aims to efficiently integrate business goals and underlying IT operations within the information system of an organisation. The ultimate goal is to reduce the technical debt, limit the related costs, and improve agility in order to be able to respond to evolving customers' or partners' expectations. As a consequence, Business-IT alignment (BITA) is a crucial challenge in the field of Information Systems (IS) [4]. In this context, several definitions have been associated to the notion of *alignment* since this term was coined in the 1990s, for example *fitness* [14] or *congruence* [15]. Notably, the Strategic Alignment Model (SAM) [19] proposes a common definition that has already been adopted in several approaches [6, 16].

In this context, the integration of the Business and IT domains is a fundamental need. We target a functional integration called *Operational BITA* [2, 18, 26]. Existing Enterprise Architecture (EA) frameworks already allow to express the different abstraction levels (strategic and functional/operational) through a layered representation of the IS [30, 32]. *Operational alignment* is thus a dynamic process that aims to align, sometimes continuously, these Business and IT layers [29]. To this end, it is first required to be able to properly assess the current state of alignment. Recent literature reviews on operational alignment [2, 18, 26] highlight the lack of assistance provided to the enterprise architects in charge of the alignment process [15]. More specifically, there is a lack of methodologies and tools to practically assess the current level of operational alignment. A few approaches propose to assess the alignment level through assessment means which are often specific to a given context (for example agility metrics [20] or metrics for all the SAM alignment types [13]). However, no approach intends to combine different assessment means to obtain a more thorough appreciation of the alignment level.

To overcome these limitations, we propose an approach to assess the level of alignment between the Business (process) layer and the Application layer for any given IS. We consider two main phases: *(1) Cartography establishment* for representing the current alignment state, including the Business and IT models as well as the explicit links between them. *(2) Alignment assessment* for using this alignment state in order to assess the current level of alignment. Our first contribution is an alignment assessment approach that relies on the combination of several different assessment means (metrics, consistency rules, and anti-patterns). Our second contribution is a global methodology that integrates this alignment assessment approach along with the previous cartography establishment phase and a next redress phase. We applied in practice this methodology and assessment approach on two case studies, namely SOFTSLATE (an open-source Java E-commerce solution) and ARCHIMETAL (a standard example of modeled IS). To this end, we established in both cases a cartography of the concerned IS that we then assessed by relying on six metrics, two consistency rules and four anti-patterns (in total).

The remainder of this paper is structured as follow. Section 2 presents the existing works related to operational alignment and the required background in terms of corresponding assessment means. Section 3 details the alignment assessment approach we propose in terms of structure and computation method. Section 4 describes the global methodology we provide in order to integrate this alignment assessment approach with a previous cartography establishment phase and next redress phase. Section 5 demonstrates the practical application of the proposed methodology and assessment approach in the context of our two case studies. Section 6 discusses the obtained results, current limitations, and overall applicability of our contributions. Finally, Sect. 7 concludes the paper and opens on future perspectives.

## 2 Background and Related Work

Recent surveys [2, 26] highlighted the limitations of existing approaches regarding the provided support for operational alignment. Indeed, only 20% of the studied approaches reach the point of assessing the alignment while most of them focuses only on establishing the alignment cartography. Among them, the framework of Aversano et al [5] is a major reference because it covers most of the alignment process. It starts with alignment links establishment, then alignment assessment via metrics computation, and finally evolution recommendations to improve the alignment quality. The framework comes with some tool support and has been validated on a single case study. Another reference work [14] provides metrics to quantify the fitness level between the business and the IT system supporting it. Business and IT domains are represented using dedicated ontologies on which these metrics are applied. Therefore, the proposed metrics are independent from specific languages and can be adapted to specific context (e.g. to UML). However, to our knowledge, no corresponding tool support is provided yet. Another recent approach [13] aims at generalizing the alignment assessment by defining a dedicated metamodel. To the best of our knowledge, this approach has not been applied on any case study. Very recently, two new types of links have been proposed to establish a cartography [1]. These links are also used to compute various metrics and verify a few consistency rules. This last approach already provides a basic tool support but does not combine different assessment means together.

We generally observed that most existing works rely on quantitative assessment means, namely metrics. A reference work [4] defines two main alignment criteria that led to metrics: Technological Coverage (TC) for the percentage of process activities adequately supported by an IT system, and Technological Adequacy (TA) for the similarity between linked concepts. Based on this, 5 metrics for TC and 4 metrics for TA have been proposed [5]. The results of single metrics are then aggregated across several linked concepts. Another work [14] provides 10 metrics for 10 alignment criteria grouped in 4 different alignment factors, for example the functional factor addressing functional integration. However, the proposed metrics are not combined in practice and a weighted aggregation is just discussed as future work. A more recent work provides a catalog of 25 metrics [13]. It proposes a reinterpretation of 9 metrics coming from previous works [5, 14]. In addition,

16 new metrics are proposed at different levels, including 2 metrics to assess functional integration at the operation level (namely *Business function automation rate & Business interaction automation rate*). These 2 metrics targeting operational alignment have been recently generalized to *Business functional concepts' support rate* and complemented with 5 other metrics [1]. Complementary to the use of metrics, consistency rules have also been considered as another suitable assessment mean. For instance, they can allow for the verification of the consistency between functional and data concepts in Archimate [1] or between functions and data in the more general case [28]. In an other approach, rules are defined by model transformations from business to IT allowing to check consistency by verifying few conditions [8]. Consistency heuristics can also be defined by querying such a mapping, for example with the Kalcas Query Language [10]. In this approach, an alignment Query and a Redundancy Query are specified to detect a potential misalignment on specific objects. Another tool-supported approach aims to consistently synchronize related Business and IT process models, and to propagate changes to the other views [23]. Patterns can also represent a relevant assessment mean in many cases. For instance, common misalignment patterns between the Business and IT layers have been identified from the study of 30 different ISs [17].

Overall, we observed that most of the existing metrics have never been combined together in order to provide a general assessment of a current level of operational alignment. Moreover, other complementary assessments means, such as consistency rules and anti-patterns, are either not implemented yet nor combined together (along with metrics). We consider that these different assessment means, each one targeting a specific aspect of the system, would benefit from being aggregated together in order to target a more thorough alignment assessment. We explore this idea by proposing a corresponding alignment assessment approach in Sect. 3.

Complementary to assessing the alignment, it appears useful to also offer correction actions in order to redress a potentially incorrect alignment. However, according to a recent survey [2], only few works (8/44) discuss such corrective changes (propagation, impact, migration). Among these few works, only three of them explicitely mention re-alignment. In a first work [31], business process re-engineering is addressed using i*, but the support for the IT layer remains ad-hoc. In a second work [5], the authors mention that increasing the alignment level cannot be performed without the experience and knowledge of the process stakeholders and software engineers. As a result, they only introduce two automated evolution actions in the context of a particular case study. In a third work [14], the Alignment Correction and Evolution Method (ACEM) performs the change operations on a pivot model that reflects alignment refinements from intention to implementation. More generally, the term *redress* is often associated to the notion of "misalignment" [26]. A prior study on addressing strategic alignment [3] already made the same observation we did: "*most of the current research efforts investigate IT-business alignment/misalignment in terms of detection, but they are not targeted a specific set of actions to solve this issue.*" As a possible solution, these efforts envision different algorithms for IT-business misalignment redress, e.g. by identifying symptom/therapy actions [9, 24]. Still, these are currently mostly ideas and few of the proposed actions are directly applicable to our context of operational BITA. For instance, BITAM [12] proposes 12 steps to address the management of misalignment, including the realignment of both business and architectural strategies, which are outside the scope of operational BITA. However, no concrete application guidelines are provided. Another approach proposes 28 symptoms [25] but its implementation is actually left to the readers. Also, a misalignment correction framework was proposed to analyses the cause and effect of misalignment symptoms [33]. Nevetheless, it remains relatively incomplete. Based on these efforts, we notably propose a process for *Alignment Redress* as part of our global methodology in Sect. 4.

## 3 An Alignment Assessement Approach Combining Different Evaluation Means

One of our main goals is to propose an assistance to enterprise architects through an assessment dashboard allowing the combination of different assessment means: metrics, consistency rules and anti-patterns. According to her (mis)alignment assessment needs, architects can (1) select the most suitable means and (2) combine them by attaching appropriate weights to indicate their importance. These selected means, along with their weights, are then combined within a single formula. In order to ease their definition and selection, these means are structured based on specific criteria and according to identified factors.

### *3.1 Alignment Assessment Structure*

The structure of our alignment dashboard is adapted from the hierarchical structure of the Cavano and McCall's framework [11] proposing *Factors*, *Criteria* and *Metrics*. *Factors* present qualitative attributes referring to different alignment perspectives, e.g. intentional-functional-informational-dynamic [14] or functional-data [1]. In our context, we call them *Alignment Factors.* Factors of the Cavano and McCall's framework are then broken down into *Criteria*, e.g. Technological Adequacy and Technological coverage [5]. In our context, we call them *Alignment Criteria.* Finally, while the Cavano and McCall's framework only relies on *Metrics*, we consider more assessment means. Thus, in our context, we call them *Alignment Assessment Means*: metrics, consistency rules and anti-patterns. For example, metrics and consistency rules can be defined on Operational BITA links between the business and the application layers [1]. Anti-patterns can also be based on such links, as core elements allowing to assess alignment and conduct an alignment process [17].

**Assessment Means Selection** In our approach, alignment factors are selected according to the architect's objectives. For example, an architect could prioritise the support for all the business processes while another could favor the performance of corresponding applications. Each factor is then broken-down into different underlying alignment criteria chosen by the architect. Finally, each alignment criteria can be evaluated by relying on one or several corresponding alignment assessment means. Overall, selecting alignment factors, criteria, and assessment means strongly depends on the IS objectives and business priorities.

**Assessment Means Weighting** After selection, the architect has to assign weights to each assessment mean. A weight reflects the importance of a given assessment mean compared to the others. We introduce two different types of weights: **specific weights** relate to individual assessment means while **aggregated weights** are associated to types of assessment mean. Thus, the weight associated to metrics can differ from the weight associated to consistency rules or anti-patterns. For instance, metrics can be considered for 20% of the whole weight while consistency rules and anti-patterns can be respectively considered for 40%, if more relevant in terms of coverage in a particular case.

## *3.2 Alignment Assessment Score Calculation*

Alignment assessment is complex because some alignment/misalignment means are hardly quantifiable, and sometimes difficult to analyse. Moreover, such means can provide different kinds of results (numerical values, rates, etc.) and require an harmonisation step before combining them in aggregate factors. To overcome this, we propose a scoring approach calculating an overall alignment score from heterogeneous assessment means: metrics, consistency rules and anti-patterns. In practice, we started with an initial catalog of assessment means we selected from the literature. Table 1 shows different assessment factors, criteria and means we currently consider. Note that providing a complete catalog is beyond the scope of this chapter, and would require extra-work with expert architects.

**Assessment Means: Harmonisation** The results obtained from different types of assessment means first need to be harmonised in a unified scale so that they can be combined and interpreted correctly. For example, if a given mean gives a result within a scale between 0 and 10, and another mean gives a percentage or a rate, the latter can be transformed to a number using the same predefined scale. Also, similar results for different assessment means should be considered carefully. For example, the value of "80%" of aligned concepts and of "80%" of misaligned concepts does not provide the same information about the alignment. Instead, a harmonised result would allow a more uniform appreciation of the current alignment level.

**Weighted Score Calculation per Type of Assessment Mean** Before aggregating all the harmonised results, we first group the results by type of means. We calculate

**Table 1** Catalog of assessment means

| Category | Assessment means | Factor | Criteria | Mean name in related works |
|---|---|---|---|---|
| Metrics | Ratio of BU concepts per IT concepts | Functional | Coverage | M2 in [1], TC Metrics in [5] |
| | Ratio of IT concepts used per BU concepts | Functional | Coverage | M5 in [1] |
| | Over used IT concepts | Functional | Overload | M6 in [1] |
| | Over implemented business concepts | Functional | Overload | M3 in [1] |
| | Number of links for a fun BU concept | Functional | Coverage | M1 in [1] |
| | Number of links for a fun IT concept | Functional | Coverage | M4 in [1] |
| | Ratio of BU data concepts per IT data concept | Data | Coverage | Infor. completeness in [14] |
| | Ratio of IT data concepts per BU data concept | Data | Coverage | Infor. completeness in [14] |
| | Number of links per BU data concept | Data | Coverage | M7 |
| | Number of links for an IT data concept | Data | Coverage | M8 |
| | Similarity between linked concepts | All | Consistency | TA Metrics in [5] |
| Consistency rules | Existence of functional links | All | Consistency | CR1 in [1] |
| | Existence of data links | All | Consistency | CR2 in [1] |
| | Symmetry of data (resp. functional) links | All | Consistency | CR3, CR4 |
| | Transitivity of functional/data links | All | Consistency | CR5, rules 6.32 to 6.34 in [28] |
| Anti-patterns | Pure technical integration | Functional | Consistency | AP1 in [17] |
| | Functional SILO | Functional | Consistency | AP2 in [17] |
| | Monolith application | Functional | Coverage | AP3 in [17] |
| | Multiple functional implementation | Functional | Coverage | AP4 in [17] |

the aggregated weight score from specific weights as follow: (I) *Metrics weighted.* Let *Mi* the i-est metric, *rMi* its result and *wMi* its weight with $\sum wMi = 1$. To calculate a combined score of selected metrics, we use the formula: $rM = \sum wMi \times rMi$. (II) *Consistency Rules.* Let *CRi* the i-est consistency rule, *rCRi* its result and *wCRi* its weight with $\sum wCRi = 1$. The weighted score of consistency rules score equals: $rCR = \sum wCRi \times rCRi$. (III) *Anti-patterns.* Let *APi* the i-est anti-pattern, *rAPi* its result and *wAPi* its weight with $\sum wAPi = 1$. Then, the weighted score of anti-patterns score equals: $rAP = \sum wAPi \times rAPi$. (IV) *Other assessment means.* The enterprise architect in charge of the alignment process has the possibility of adding new assessment means or new types of assessment means. To integrate them, she needs to respect the harmonised format already used for the other assessment means.

**Overall Alignment Score Calculation** The calculation of the aggregated weighted scores for each type of assessment means, in addition to the associated aggregated weights, enables the calculation of an overall score of alignment. Thus, the alignment overall score *S* is calculated by aggregating the results of the previous step: $S = \omega M \times rM + \omega CR \times rCR + \omega AP \times rAP$ where *wM*, *wCR* and *wAP* are respectively the aggregated weights allocated to metrics overall score *rM*, consistency rules overall score *rCR* and anti-patterns overall score *rAP*.

# 4 A General Methodology for Cartography Establishment, Alignment Assessment, and Alignment Redress

In order to perform the previously presented alignment assessment approach, we propose a general methodology for cartography establishment, alignment assessment, and alignment redress. We summarise the corresponding process in BPMN[1] as shown in Fig. 1. The main actor is the enterprise architect as she is usually responsible for dealing with the alignment-related issues [15]. Throughout the process, she also has to communicate and collaborate with other stakeholders from the business side (e.g. Business Architects) or the IT side (e.g. Solution Architects or Software Architects). The overall process starts when the need for alignment assessment is expressed, and ends when the IS is (sufficiently) realigned. It is composed of three sub-processes dedicated to cartography, assessment and redress. As indicated in previous work [21], BITA alignment is an iterative process that often requires several consecutive applications over time. This is also the case of the process we propose in this chapter.

## *4.1 Cartography Establishment*

The first sub-process, depicted in Fig. 2, is called **"Establish Cartography"** and provides the steps needed to establish the cartography. This is realised by setting up the Business and IT models, providing their concepts, and specifying the links between them (*cf.* Sect. 2). The initial step is to check the existence of the required Business and IT models: (i) When available, the architect needs to check if the used

[1] https://www.omg.org/spec/BPMN/2.0/PDF.

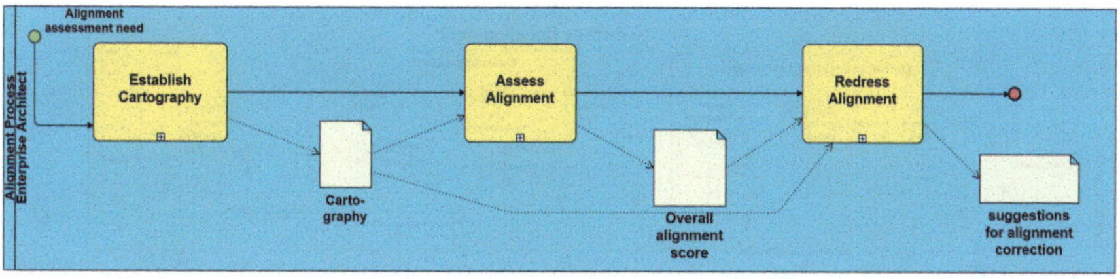


**Fig. 1** A process for cartography establishment, alignment assessment, and alignment redress

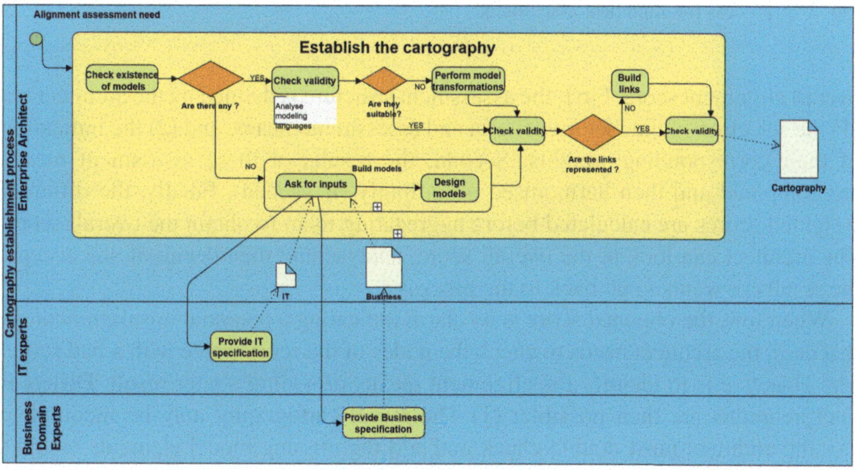


**Fig. 2** A process for cartography establishment

modelling languages allow to represent all the required Business and IT information. If this it not the case, she can perform corresponding transformations from the used modelling languages to more suitable ones (manually or in an automated way). (ii) If not available, the models need to be built from scratch using suitable modelling languages. To do so, the enterprise architect requests both Business Architects (for collecting the Business requirements) and IT architects (for getting the IT specification). The objective is that they build together the necessary models and further elaborate on the links between these models (*cf.* Sect. 2). The result of this sub-process is the obtained cartography that will be assessed in the following sub-process.

## 4.2 Alignment Assessment

The second sub-process, depicted in Fig. 3, is called **"Alignment assessment"** and corresponds to the Alignment Assessment approach we presented in Sect. 3. This sub-process describes the two main steps going from the obtained cartography to the

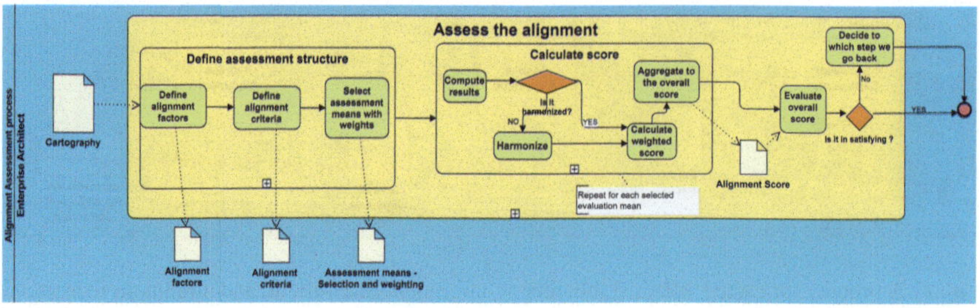


**Fig. 3** A process for alignment assessment

overall alignment score. First, the assessment structure is defined by the architect via (1) the selection of the factors, criteria and assessment means, and (2) the indication of their corresponding weights. Second, the results of these assessment means are computed and then harmonised accordingly (if needed). Finally, the different weighted scores are calculated before aggregating them to obtain the overall score. The architect can look at the overall score, analyse and then decide if she accepts the results or wants to go back to the process.[2]

When low, the obtained score is an alarm indicating a potential misalignment. In that case, the architect needs to check the nodes of the scoring tree with a bad score. The objective is to identify the alignment means providing a poor result. Different interpretations are then possible: (1) The initial cartography may be incomplete → the architect must double-check and add the missing model elements or links between these elements. (2) The implementation of the assessment means may be incomplete → the architect needs to revise the used algorithms, e.g. to take into account all the links between model elements. (3) The weights may be wrongly allocated → the architect has to revise the considered weights, e.g. a (minor) factor can have an exceeding weight compared to others. (4) The alignment criteria may be complex to assess → the architect must perform a deeper analysis of some criteria such as coverage and consistency.

## 4.3 Alignment Redress

Once the overall alignement score is consolidated, alignment correction actions may have to be considered according to the obtaine result. To this end, we propose a third and last sub-process, depicted in Fig. 4 and called **"Alignment redress"**. Based on common Operational BITA practices, and according to the assessment structure

[2] The covered assessment means and associated tooling are presented in detail in a previous work [1].

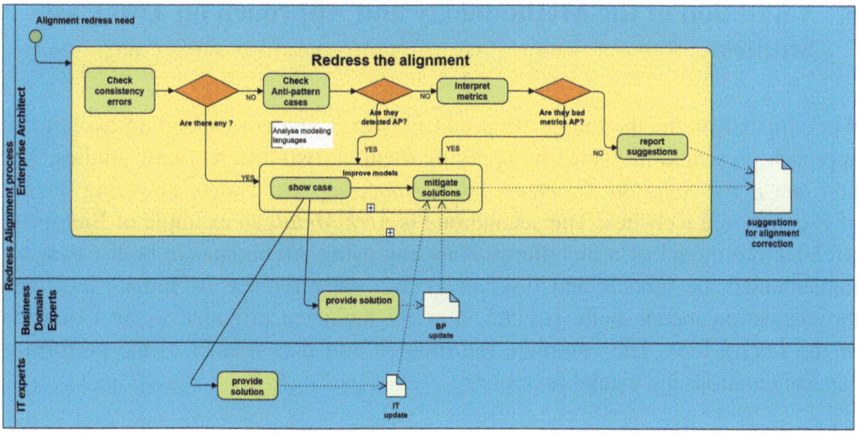


**Fig. 4** A process for alignment redress

used in our approach, we propose to follow three consecutive steps: (1) correct the misalignments detected by consistency rules; (2) refactor the misalignments detected by anti-patterns; (3) re-align the models to improve the metrics values and overall assessment score. Indeed, in order to properly redress, we must look deeper into each "bad" result of assessment mean, find the symptoms, and look for a cure. To start with, related "bad" values can be grouped together by families of symptoms: one single problem may concern several different means. A given symptom can denote two main kinds of issues (i) modelling issues (missing business or IT concepts, missing links, redundancy, inadequate representation, name mismatch, etc.) and (ii) real-world issues (legacy debt, inadequate processes, missing digitalised data, etc.). Both kinds of issues require that the architects, business and IT stakehoders work in collaboration and discuss possible solutions for improvement. To allow this, they must converge on common, consensual definitions and terminology, in order to avoid contradictions, redundancies, ambiguities, etc. In this context, another interesting aspect to consider is the notion of **dimension** as a point of view on the alignment [1]. Dimensions have to play a role in the organisation of the alignment redress since they target the possible concerns of the different stakeholders, e.g. functions, data, urbanisation, actors, security, privacy. For example, in IS modelling, we usually make a distinction between the structure, the functional behavior and the dynamic behaviour. As a consequence, we propose to operate first on individual dimensions (only the data and function dimensions are taken into account in this chapter) and then later on cross dimensions for broader consistency and completeness.

# 5 Validation of the Methodology and Approach on Two Case Studies

We validated the methodology proposed in Sect. 4 and corresponding assessment approach presented in Sect. 3 by applying them on two different case studies. The first one is the *SoftSlate Commerce Java shopping cart system* powering dozens of E-commerce websites. The second one is *ArchiMetal*, an example of Enterprise Architecture model of a metallurgy company using Archimate. In both cases, we implemented the models and links in `Archi`, the reference Archimate tool, and the evaluation means with `jArchi`, a script language provided as an extension of the `Archi` tool. The complete information and data related to the performed experimentations are available online.[3]

## 5.1 *SoftSlate*

We opted for this case study in our first experiment because it is (i) realistic since *SoftSlate Commerce* actually exists,[4] (ii) challenging since business and application models are not provided (we designed them from scratch, simulating the case where an IS would not come with such models), (iii) reasonably complex in terms of structure and relatively large in terms of number of lines of code, (iv) provided with an implementation available online, including its complete source code and documentation.[5]

### (A) Setting the Cartography of SoftSlate

**Check the Existence of Models** Models representing the business and application layers are not available in this case study. The only directly exploitable assets to build the needed models are the user guide, source code, and MVC pattern architecture description provided with the system.

**Design Models** We exploit the user guide as a business specification to design a business process model. Then, we rely on the source code and MVC pattern architecture description (as IT documents) to design an (IT) application model. Once these models are designed, the next step is to check their validity. In this case study, we do not have a direct contact with SoftSlate's business domain experts or developers. Thus, we validated the models ourselves by cross-checking them.

[3] https://uncloud.univ-nantes.fr/index.php/s/wMQ6NPgbpkgRgWa.

[4] https://www.softslate.com/.

[5] The *SoftSlate web application*—https://www.softslate.com/category/archivedDocs.

**Create Links** We use a simple typology of links [1] to create alignment links between the designed models, resulting in a cartography of the SoftSlate system. Due to the available resources, we elaborated on a partial cartography that only details the administrator part of the system. However, this cartography is already rich enough in terms of concepts and links.

### (B) Alignment Assessment Structure for SoftSlate

**Alignment Factors** For this first case study, we consider mainly the functional assessment factor. Other factors could be integrated later in the context of more advanced experiments.

**Alignment Criteria** Our alignment assessment structure for SoftSlate relies on two main assessment criteria corresponding to the functional assessment factor: **Coverage and Overload.** Coverage consists in verifying that one business layer concept is at least implemented by one application layer concept. Overload consists in verifying that no business concept is over-implemented (e.g. many applications for one business process) and/or no application concept is over-used (e.g. one application for many business processes). **Consistency.** In this case study, consistency consists in avoiding a misalignment between different alignment factors and layers.

**Assessment Means: Selection** According to the defined alignment criteria, we select the following assessment means from the catalog displayed in Table 1: We consider **Metric 2** & **Metric 5** for functional coverage, **Metric 3** & **Metric 6** for functional overloading and **Metric 7** & **Metric 8** for data coverage. We implement consistency rules **CR1** and **CR2** for consistency verification. We develop algorithms supporting the detection of anti-patterns **AP1, AP2, AP3, AP4** also for consistency and coverage verification. The two first columns on the left in Table 2 shows these selected assessment means.

**Assessment means: Weighting** We apply the weighting system proposed in Sect. 3.2:

- *Specific weights.* The column ***w*** in Table 2 reports on the specific weights allocated to each assessment mean. For the six metrics, we allocate the same weight as we consider them of equal importance. As a result, we have $wMi = 1/\text{number of metrics} = 0.165$. For the two consistency rules, we also allocated the same weight as well. As a result, we have $wCRi = 0.5$. Finally, we allocated the same weight to the four anti-patterns. As a result, we have $wAPi = 0.25$. Note that it is possible to customise the different specific weights for the metrics, consistency rules, or anti-patterns, depending on how important they are for the architect.
- *Aggregated weights.* The third column of Table 2 shows the aggregated weights per type of assessment means. We consider that consistency rules and anti-patterns represent more powerful indicators of the alignment level than metrics,

**Table 2** SOFTSLATE score calculation

| Assessment means | Computation & results | | Weight [0,1] | Harmonisation of results | Score (r) | Aggregation weight [0,1] | Alignment score (s) |
|---|---|---|---|---|---|---|---|
| Metrics | M2 | 41.60% | 0.165 | 58.40% | 76.50% | 0.2 | 94.30% |
| | M3 | 0 | 0.165 | 100% | | | |
| | M5 | 53.80% | 0.165 | 46.20% | | | |
| | M6 | 1 | 0.165 | 90% | | | |
| | M7 | 16.66% | 0.165 | 83.33% | | | |
| | M8 | 14.28% | 0.165 | 85.72% | | | |
| Consistency rules | CR1 | 0 | 0.5 | 100% | 100% | 0.4 | |
| | CR2 | 0 | 0.5 | 100% | | | |
| ANTI-pattern detection | AP1 | 0 | 0.25 | 100% | 97.5% | 0.4 | |
| | AP2 | 0 | 0.25 | 100% | | | |
| | AP3 | 1 | 0.25 | 90% | | | |
| | AP4 | 0 | 0.25 | 100% | | | |

as they allow validating advanced constructs in the cartography (notably in terms of coverage). For example, a detected inconsistency may be critical for the system whereas an unimplemented business process does not necessarily implies an error. Therefore, we allocated a smaller weight to metrics ($wM = 0.2$) than to consistency rules and anti-patterns ($wCR = wAP = 0.4$).

### (C) Alignment Score Calculation for SOFTSLATE

**Compute Results** The results are shown in the column **Computation & Results** in Table 2.

**Harmonisation** These results need to be harmonised as explained in Sect. 3.2.

(a) *Harmonisation of metrics results.* We propose to use an unified format as follows.

- Metric `M2` refers to the rate of unimplemented business processes, i.e. not related to any implementation link. The harmonised rate *rM2* of `M2` becomes the rate of implemented business processes. The higher is *rM2* the better is the appreciation of the alignment level.
- Metric `M3` refers to the list of the most implemented business processes, *i.e.* implemented by more than a given number of implementation links. The harmonised rate *rM3* of `M3` becomes calculated as $rM3 = 100\% - (N * 10\%)$ with $N$ the number of elements in the list. The higher is *rM3* the better is the appreciation of the alignment level.
- Metric `M5` refers to the rate of unused application functions, i.e. not related by any implementation link. The harmonised rate *rM5* of `M5` becomes the rate of

used application functions. The higher is *rM5* the better is the appreciation of the alignment level.

- Metric `M6` refers to the most used application functions, i.e. having more than a given number of implementation links. The harmonised rate *rM6* of `M6` is calculated as $rM6 = 100\% - (N * 10\%)$ with $N$ the number of elements in the list. The higher is *rM6* the better is the appreciation of the alignment level.
- Metric `M7` (respectively `M8`) counts the number of links per data business (respectively IT) concept. The harmonised rate *rM7* (respectively *rM8*) denotes the rate of unlinked concepts. The higher are *rM7* or *rM8* the better is the appreciation of the alignment level.

(b) *Harmonisation of consistency rules results.* We set $rCRi = 100\% - (N * 10\%)$ where N is the number of occurrences when consistency rule $i$ is not verified. For instance, if there is 1 occurrence of the non-verified consistency rule $k$ and 2 occurrences of the non-verified consistency rule $l$, then the harmonised results are:

$rCRk = 100\% - (1 * 10\%) = 90\%$ and $rCRl = 100\% - (2 * 10\%) = 80\%$.

(c) *Harmonisation of anti-patterns results.* For anti-patterns we set $rAPi = 100\% - (N * 10\%)$ where N is the number of occurrences when Anti-Pattern $i$ is detected. For instance, if there is 0 occurrence of Anti-Pattern $p$ then $rAPp = 100\% - (0 * 10\%) = 0\%$.

All these results are reported in Table 2 in the column **Harmonisation of results**.

**Weighted Score Calculation per Type of Assessment Mean** By combining the harmonised results and specific weights as explained in Sect. 3, we obtained the aggregated weighted score for each assessment mean's type. The results are given in column **SCORE (r)** of Table 2.

- For metrics, we have: $rM = \sum_{i=2}^{6} \omega M_i \times rM_i = \omega M_2 \times rM_2 + \omega M_3 \times rM_3 + \omega M_5 \times rM_5 + \omega M_6 \times rM_6 = 73.65\%$
- For consistency rules, we have: $rCR = \sum_{i=1}^{2} \omega CR_i \times rCR_i = \omega CR_1 \times rCR_1 + \omega CR_2 \times rCR_2 = 100\%$
- For anti-patterns, we have: $rAP = \sum_{i=1}^{4} \omega AP_i \times rAP_i = \omega AP_1 \times rAP_1 + \omega AP_2 \times rAP_2 + \omega AP_3 \times rAP_3 + \omega AP_4 \times rAP_4 = 97.5\%$

**Overall Alignment Score Calculation** Based on the calculation of the aggregated weighted scores, and on the associated aggregated weights, we can now calculate the overall alignment score. Thus, we have: $S = \omega M \times rM + \omega CR \times rCR + \omega AP \times rAP = 0,2 \times 73,95\% + 0,4 \times 100\% + 0,4 \times 97,5\% = 93.73\%$

In the general case, the obtained alignment score must always be carefully considered and analysed according to the architect's knowledge and experience. For instance, in this case study, the alignment score is high (93.73 %) but only two business processes have been modelled so far. We can mitigate this good score since the input models are directly inspired from the source code, they are quite small compared to large enterprise ISs, and we paid a particular attention when linking the business and application layers (which is not always the case in companies).

#### (D) Alignment Redress for SoftSlate

We apply the general guidelines we proposed in Sect. 4.3. In this case study, the redress step notably aims to correct the low values of the means displayed in Table 2: `M2`, `M5` and `AP3`. Thus, we suggest the following corrections in this SoftSlate case study: (i) To improve `M2`, we should fix the case of business functions and activities that are parts of composite activities, and vice-versa. For instance, corresponding links could be added automatically by a dedicated model transformation applied to the business model. (ii) Due to our initial assumption of partial business modelling, we should cover a wider range of business processes models. This should allow to reduce the value of `M5` because more application functions will be (correctly) linked. (iii) `AP3` raised a warning because the application concept `Add Shipping Rate` is linked to three different business concepts which correspond to three alternatives. Thus, we should factorise the common parts in one business function only. Moreover, we observed that `M7` and `M8` do not present any significant shortcomings. The related issue simply comes from a missing link for the `Payment` data object. This should be addressed by adding a corresponding business object in the business layer.

## 5.2 *ArchiMetal*

We opted for this complementary case study in our second experiment because it (i) is a representative example or EA modelling as provided by *TheOpenGroup*,[6] (ii) presents a ready-to-study mapping, and therefore a different context than for SoftSlate, (iii) comes with an EA model than can be easily integrated into `Archi` thanks to The Open Group library.

#### (A) Setting the Cartography of ArchiMetal

**Check the Existence of Models and Design Models** Models representing the business and application layers are already available in the ArchiMate®Model Exchange File Format.[7] The given models are quite detailed since the objective

[6] https://pubs.opengroup.org/architecture/case-study-models/Archimetal-html/.

[7] https://github.com/archimatetool/ArchiModels/tree/master/Archimetal.

**Table 3** ARCHIMETAL score calculation

| Assessment means | Computation & results | | Weight [0,1] | Harmonisation of results | Score (r) | Aggregation weight [0,1] | Alignment score (s) |
|---|---|---|---|---|---|---|---|
| Metrics | M2 | 45.68% | 0.165 | 54.32% | 68.075% | 0.2 | 91.615% |
| | M3 | 0 | 0.165 | 100% | | | |
| | M5 | 35.52% | 0.165 | 67.60% | | | |
| | M6 | 0 | 0.165 | 100% | | | |
| | M7 | 66.66% | 0.165 | 33.33% | | | |
| | M8 | 46.80% | 0.165 | 53.20% | | | |
| Consistency rules | CR1 | 0 | 0.5 | 100% | 100% | 0.4 | |
| | CR2 | 0 | 0,5 | 100% | | | |
| ANTI-pattern detection | AP1 | 0 | 0.25 | 100% | 95% | 0.4 | |
| | AP2 | 0 | 0.25 | 100% | | | |
| | AP3 | 2 | 0.25 | 80% | | | |
| | AP4 | 0 | 0.25 | 100% | | | |

of their authors is to demonstrate the full capabilities of ArchiMate in terms of modelling.

**Create Links** Archimate provides a rich set of inter-layer relations. However, "many" is not the best for every case. Applying the Occam's razor principle, we restrict to two kind of association (implementation, representation) [1]. As a consequence, we *transformed* the other kinds of ArchiMate relationships (e.g. *Realization*, *Serving*) in the two above-mentioned types.

### (B) Alignment Assessment Structure for ARCHIMETAL

We keep the same choices than those of the SOFTSLATE case study (cf. Sect. 5.1-B).

### (C) Alignment Score Calculation for ARCHIMETAL

The results we obtained for this second case study are provided in Table 3. The harmonisation and score calculation steps are computed in the same way than for SOFTSLATE. The overall alignment score is good (91.615%). We can explain that by the fact that the ARCHIMETAL model designers are Archimate experts and thus focused on rigorous modelling of functions/services. Indeed, the enterprise application integration is modelled by application functions that map to business functions (cf. the `01. Functional enterprise-control model` view in the `Archi` model for instance). However, the provided application models are rather high level (ERP, CRM, control application) and are missing/hidding some details that lead to uncovered links. Moreover, not all inter-layer links are represented, especially for data as illustrated by `M7` and `M8`. As a result, the data dimension is not very well covered in the used ARCHIMETAL models. Overall, this case study does not really allow to reflect on complex situations where many defaults and misalignment exist. In this sense, it is quite complementary to the previous SOFTSLATE case study.

#### (D) Alignment Redress for ARCHIMETAL

Once again, we apply the general guidelines we proposed in Sect. 4.3. In this case study, the redress step notably aims to correct the low values of the means displayed in Table 3: `M2`, `M5`, `M7`, `M8` and `AP3`. Thus, we suggest the following corrections in this ARCHIMETAL case study: (i) To improve `M2`, we should fix the missing details in the application model and, for each application concept, find the link to its business counterpart. Still, we do not have the same problem as in SOFTSLATE because the ARCHIMETAL business model already follows best practice in terms of modelling (e.g. layered ordering of functions and activities). (ii) Due to hidden details, we should cover a wider range of application models. This should allow `M5` to better reflect the reality because more application functions will be linked. (iii) `M7` and `M8` should be improved by making the data dimension more explicit in the models. This would require enriching them with business objects and data objects. (iv) `AP3` raised two warnings because the application concepts are high-level and gather several application functions. To overcome this, we should be more precise and set representative, and atomic enough, interlayer links (e.g. for the ERP and CRM applications).

## 6 Discussion

Following the validation of our methodology and approach on two complementary case studies, we now discuss the current limitations of the work presented in this chapter. We also explain how we intend to possibly tackle these limitations in the future. Finally, we discuss the relevance and novelty of our work according to the current state-of-the-art.

### *6.1 Considering Threats to Validity*

The proposed methodology and approach have been empirically validated thanks to their practical application in the context of two case studies. Still, they should be experimented further by considering additional case studies in order to demonstrate their relevance in more different realistic scenarios. For example, we cannot completely ensure at this stage that (i) the alignment score fully reflects the real alignment level of the IS (*conclusion validity*); (ii) each assessment means value adequately captures the targeted symptom (*internal validity*); (iii) the set of provided assessment means is sufficiently consistent and complete (*construction validity*); (iv) the cartography covers a majority of the common enterprise situations (*external validity*).

## 6.2 Performing More Validation on Different Case Studies

As introduced before, we still need to experiment with both our methodology and approach in the context of other case studies. Moreover, these case studies must also be evaluated by integrating more alignment assessment factors than the functional assessment ones we considered so far. The realisation of these additional experiments will require to have access to the Business and IT models of more IS, which is a major obstacle since companies do not usually share them. Otherwise, it will require to build the appropriate models and corresponding links manually, which is time consuming and error prone without the business knowledge. If IS are made available, our work could gain strength by using AI [22] in order to automatically exploit the huge amount of information within the IS. This could also help to propose a maturity model [27] dedicated to the aligment.

## 6.3 Working on Alignment Objectives and Their Specification

As mentioned in Sect. 3.2, the proposed overall alignment score can be an interesting indicator of the current alignment level. However, its interpretation may differ from one architect to another, or between the Business and IT actors. To prevent from such a situation, it is important to define explicit alignment objectives as a formal contract. This could be done by specifying a set of alignment clauses to be checked, an associated set of thresholds integrated into an interactive dashboard, etc. The defined objectives could notably include corresponding specific weights or thresholds for particular factors/criteria. This way, the architect could more easily specify her alignment strategy.

## 6.4 Improving the Catalogue/Repository of Evaluation Means

In addition, our current catalogue of assessment means could be complemented with more implementations of metrics, consistency rules, anti-patterns, and eventually other means. In this paper, we started by collecting from the literature some existing assessment factors, criteria and means. In the long term, the development of a richer open repository dedicated to operational Business-IT alignment would be beneficial for enterprise architects. This will notably imply a direct collaboration between researchers and architects from different companies. The ultimate goal is to classify the application architectural styles (up to the notation, the business process styles remain very similar), and to provide a catalogue of pertinent assessment means for each style.

## *6.5 Proposing Different Calculation Methods*

Another area for improvement would be to provide alternative calculation methods for alignment assessment. The proposed variations should concern not only the weighting system but also the formulas themselves. This way, we could build and provide a library of calculation methods that could be shared across different alignment processes in the context of various IS. Going one step further, different calculation methods could be considered depending on the selected factors/criteria (e.g. a coverage-specific method), and then eventually combined together whenever relevant in the context of a same IS.

## *6.6 Adapting the Approach and Corresponding Tooling*

Overall, the already provided alignment objectives, assessment means, and calculation methods, can be adapted to different contexts. Our current implementation already supports by default a given set of objectives, means, and methods. It also allows developing and integrating new ones, in order to replace and/or complement the existing ones. For instance, a challenge is to tackle the complexity of contemporary software architectures (multi-layer architectures, micro-services, etc.) by proposing appropriate assessment factors, criteria and means. In any case, a finer-grained definition and selection process could be specified to better guide the architect while expressing her alignment needs. To go further in terms of tooling, a deeper integration within the `Archi` tool (or any other suitable open source CASE tool) can also be envisioned, in collaboration with a company for example.

## *6.7 Diagnosing and Repairing Operational BITA*

Identified symptom/cure actions (cf. Sect. 2) are interesting from the management point of view (strategy, organisation, performance) or deployment point of view (distribution and quality). However, only few of these actions address our requirements for Operational BITA. Among them, we notably found (i) S.13 (ambiguity), S.19 (duplicates), S.23 (data redundancy), S.24 (discontinuity), S.26 (function redundancy), S.30 (integrity) [9], (ii) LF.6 (redundancy) [3], (iii) OS.14 (CRUD requirement), OS.15 (unused data), OS.16 (unused functions), OS.18 (S.23), OS.19 (part of LF.6), OS.20 (S.26), OS.27 (S.19) [25]. We already address a significant number of them in our current assessment means (S.13, S.19, S.26, OS.15, OS.16), while others remain to be studied as targeting other quality factors (S.23, S.24, S.30, LF.6, OS.14). Morevoer, misalignment corrections in those approaches often refer to general guidelines and actions rather than concrete and practical tasks.

### *6.8 Summarizing the Relevance of Our Work*

Despite the discussed limitations, we already showed that the proposed alignment assessment approach and corresponding methodology are applicable in practice on realistic case studies. Thus, they are potentially also relevant in the context of any other IS sharing similar characteristics than *SoftSlate*. Moreover, our assessment approach is quite novel since combining different types of assessment means to provide aggregated alignment indicators (cf. Sect. 2). Furthermore, our methodology integrates three important consecutive steps of the alignment process, namely cartography establishment, alignment assessment, and alignment redress. Except from a few works also proposing some directives for alignment evolution based on previous assessment results [5, 28], a large majority of the other existing approaches only address one step of the process (often cartography establishment) [2, 26].

## 7 Conclusion

Enterprise architects need more methods and tools in order to assist them in their Business-IT alignment activities. Despite various research efforts, there is still no global solution to fully support Operational BITA, nor to assess the current state of operational alignment and derive correction actions accordingly. To go a step further in this direction, we proposed in this chapter an alignment assessment approach that rely on the combination of several different assessment means (metrics, consistency rules, anti-patterns). Thanks to this approach, the architects can compute an overall alignment score and globally assess the current alignment level in the context of a given IS. In addition, we also proposed a global methodology that integrates this alignment assessment approach along with a previous cartography establishment phase and a next alignment redress phase. Such a cartography is composed of both Business and IT models, interrelated via different types of alignment links. To illustrate the applicability of these approach and methodology, we experimented with them on two complementary case studies named SOFTSLATE and ARCHIMETAL. In both cases, we established a cartography of the concerned IS, that we then assessed by considering six metrics, two consistency rules and four anti-patterns (in total). Based on the obtained results, we were able to propose some actions in order to improve the current IS architecture.

Among the different possible future works we discussed earlier in the paper, we can notably mention additional experiments in the context of other case studies and IS. Additional tool support can also be provided to the enterprise architects by offering them an explicit way of specifying their alignment objectives. Moreover, we can mention the enrichment of the proposed catalog of assessment means, in parallel to the work on alternative calculation methods for improving the quality of the overall alignment score. As mentioned before, the extended tool support could rely on an open repository dedicated to operational Business-IT alignment. This support could also include the provisioning of detailed recommendations to assist enterprise architects on how to achieve in practice the operational Business-IT alignment they target. Last but not least, we believe that our methodology and approach can help to more efficiently work on the implementation of existing misalignment methodologies [9, 12, 24, 25].

## References


1. André, P., Benjilany, A., Bruneliere, H., & Tamzalit, D. (2024). A practical approach to evaluate operational business-IT alignment. In J. Filipe, M. Smialek, A. Brodsky, & S. Hammoudi, S. (Eds.), *26th International Conference on Enterprise Information Systems, ICEIS, Angers, France, April 28–30, 2024*. Revised Selected Papers. LNBIP. Springer.
2. André, P., Bruneliere, H., Tamzalit, D., & Benjilany, A. (2024). *Core operational business-IT alignment: Current trends and open challenges* (pp. 41–62). Springer.
3. Aseeva, N., Babkin, E., Malyzhenkov, P., & Masi, M. (2022). Strategic integration of alignment models for the IT-business misalignment detection and redress. In *Digitalization of society, economics and management: A digital strategy based on post-pandemic developments* (pp. 97–113). Springer.
4. Aversano, L., Bodhuin, T., & Tortorella, M. (2005). Assessment and impact analysis for aligning business processes and software systems. In *Proceedings of the 2005 ACM symposium on Applied computing* (pp. 1338–1343).
5. Aversano, L., Grasso, C., & Tortorella, M. (2016). Managing the alignment between business processes and software systems. *Information and Software Technology, 72*, 171–188.
6. Avila, O., Goepp, V., & Kiefer, F. (2018). Addressing alignment concerns into the design of domain-specific information systems. *Journal of Manufacturing Technology Management, 29*(5), 726–745.
7. Benjilany, A., Bruneliere, H., André, P., & Tamzalit, D. (2024). An approach to assess operational business-IT alignment. In *Proceedings of the 32nd International Conference on Information Systems Development. ISD 2024* (vol. 72). University of Gdańsk. http://dx.doi.org/10.62036/ISD.2024.13
8. Buchwald, S., Bauer, T., & Reichert, M. (2012). Bridging the gap between business process models and service composition specifications. In *Service life cycle tools and technologies: Methods, trends and advances* (pp. 124–153). IGI Global Scientific Publishing.
9. Carvalho, R., & Sousa, P. (2008). Business and information systems misalignment model (bismam): An holistic model leveraged on misalignment and medical sciences approaches. *Proceedings of BUSITAL, 8*, 105.
10. Castellanos, C., & Correal, D. (2012). KALCAS: A framework for semi-automatic alignment of data and business processes architectures. In *Advances in databases and information systems*. Lecture Notes in Computer Science (pp. 111–124). Springer.
11. Cavano, J. P., & McCall, J. A. (1978). A framework for the measurement of software quality. In *Proceedings of the Software Quality Assurance Workshop on Functional and Performance Issues* (pp. 133–139). ACM.

12. Chen, H. M., Kazman, R., & Garg, A. (2005). Bitam: An engineering-principled method for managing misalignments between business and it architectures. *Science of Computer Programming, 57*(1), 5–26. System and Software Architectures.
13. Darii, H., Laval, J., Botta-Genoulaz, V., & Goepp, V. (2020). Measurement of the business/it alignment of information systems. In *ILS 2020-8th International Conference on Information Systems, Logistics and Supply Chain* (pp. 228–235)
14. Etien, A., & Rolland, C. (2005). Measuring the fitness relationship. *Requirements Engineering, 10*(3), 184–197.
15. Gellweiler, C. (2022). It architects and it-business alignment: A theoretical review. *Procedia Computer Science, 196*, 13–20. International Conference on ENTERprise Information Systems 2021.
16. Gerow, J. E., Thatcher, J. B., & Grover, V. (2015). Six types of it-business strategic alignment: An investigation of the constructs and their measurement. *European Journal of Information Systems, 24*(5), 465–491.
17. Gouigoux, J. P., & Tamzalit, D. (2021). Business-it alignment anti-patterns: A thought from an empirical point of view. In *ISD 2021, Valencia.*
18. Habba, M., Fredj, M., & Benabdellah Chaouni, S. (2019). Alignment between business requirement, business process, and software system: A systematic literature review. *Journal of Engineering, 2019*, 6918105.
19. Henderson, J. C., & Venkatraman, H. (1999). Strategic alignment: Leveraging information technology for transforming organizations. *IBM Systems, 38*(2–3), 472–484.
20. Imgharene, K., Doumi, K., & Baina, S. (2020). Agility metrics model for business IT alignment. In *2020 7th International Conference on Control, Decision and Information Technologies (CoDIT)* (vol. 1, pp. 662–667).
21. Kassahun, A., & Tekinerdogan, B. (2016). Collaboration viewpoint for modeling cross-organizational business concerns. In *ICST International Conference on Software Technologies* (pp. 3–21). Springer.
22. Kojima, T., Gu, S. S., Reid, M., Matsuo, Y., & Iwasawa, Y. (2022). Large language models are zero-shot reasoners. *Advances in Neural Information Processing Systems, 35*, 22199–22213.
23. Küster, J. M., Völzer, H., Favre, C., Branco, M. C., & Czarnecki, K. (2016). Supporting different process views through a shared process model. *Software and Systems Modeling, 15*(4), 1207–1233.
24. Luftman, J. N. (2003). *Competing in the information age: Align in the sand*. Oxford University Press.
25. Őri, D. (2014). Misalignment symptom analysis based on enterprise architecture model assessment. *IADIS International Journal on Computer Science & Information Systems, 9*(2), 146–158.
26. Őri, D., & Szabó, Z. (2024). A systematic literature review on business-IT misalignment research. *Information Systems and e-Business Management, 22*, 139–169.
27. Paulk, M. C., Curtis, B., Chrissis, M. B., Weber, C. V. (1993). Capability maturity model, version 1.1. *IEEE Software, 10*(4), 18–27.
28. Pepin, J., André, P., Attiogbé, J. C., & Breton, E. (2016). An improved model facet method to support EA alignment. *Complex Systems Informatics and Modeling Quarterly, 9*, 1–27.
29. Tarafdar, M., & Qrunfleh, S. (2009). IT-business alignment: A two-level analysis. *Information Systems Management, 26*(4), 338–349.
30. The Open Group. (2013). *Archimate 2.1 specification*. Van Haren Pub.
31. Ullah, A., & Algarni, F. (2017). Business and information technology re-alignment through managing business process. *Journal of Software 12*(9), 695–707.
32. Zachman, J. A. (1987). A framework for information systems architecture. *IBM Systems Journal, 26*(3), 276–292.
33. Zhang, M., Chen, H., & Liu, J. (2019). Cause–effect analysis for multiple misalignment symptoms in misalignment correction stage. *Arabian Journal for Science and Engineering, 44*, 2729–2735.

# An EBNF-Based Grammar for Use Case Specification

**Marinos Georgiades**

**Abstract** This paper presents a use case grammar for specifying functional requirements, providing syntactic and semantic rules that integrate with a specific yet extensible vocabulary to form a semi-formal language for use case specification. Built on EBNF and implemented in ANTLR, the grammar ensures well-formedness and facilitates validation of such specifications. Core elements of the grammar include (i) use case patterns, which define structured sequences of action blocks to achieve specific functionalities; (ii) action blocks, serving as fundamental units of user or system actions, further categorized into atomic blocks for main scenarios and composite blocks for alternate scenarios; (iii) support for both design-free and design-augmented functional specifications; (iv) a hierarchical grammar structure that promotes modularity and traceability; and (v) mechanisms to identify and specify actors, related use cases, and alternate scenarios. This structured approach reduces redundancies, inconsistencies, and omissions while facilitating the validation of requirements; it also provides a foundation for generating automatically diagrammatic notations, such as use case and sequence diagrams, in future implementations. Ultimately, it accelerates requirements engineering and enhances the overall quality of functional requirements.

## 1 Introduction

*Use case modeling is a widely adopted approach for describing functional requirements in software engineering.* One reason for its popularity is that a well-written use case is relatively easy to read, *as it employs natural language and scenario-based narratives.* However, easy-to-read does not also mean easy-to-write. The application of use case driven analysis (UCDA) often results in poorly defined use case models for the following reasons: (i) insufficient syntactic and semantic

M. Georgiades (✉)
University of Tartu, Tartu, Estonia
e-mail: marinos.georgiades@ut.ee

 
B. Marcinkowski et al. (eds.), *Advances in Information Systems Development*, Lecture Notes in Information Systems and Organisation 77,
https://doi.org/10.1007/978-3-031-87880-0_13

**Table 1** Omission of actors

| Deficient Specification | Good Specification | Issue Addressed |
|---|---|---|
| 3. Input ID. | 3. Doctor inputs Patient's ID. | Omission of primary actor: The primary actor (doctor) is unknown. |
| 7. System notifies about prescription approval. | 7. System notifies pharmacist about prescription approval. | Omission of secondary actor: The recipient (pharmacist) is not specified. |

rigor for specifying the main elements of the use case model, such as use cases, actors, scenario actions, and relationships [1]; (ii) over-reliance on free-form natural language, which introduces ambiguities, inconsistencies, and jargon that complicate requirements maintenance and customer understanding [2]; (iii) limited support of dedicated software tools, which makes UCDA a time-consuming and error-prone activity. The lack of a formal semantics hinders the use of automated tools for use case modelling, refinement, verification and transformation, since informal natural language (NL) is inherently complex, vague and ambiguous.

Specifically, common issues in use case writing include omission of actors, related use cases and actions, use of combined instead of atomic actions, and mixing design with functional specifications. Table 1 shows an example of omission of actors, which leads to ambiguity about responsibilities and interactions.

The absence of the primary actor (Doctor) in step 3 of the deficient specification leaves it unclear who is performing or who is responsible for the action. Similarly, step 7 omits the secondary actor Pharmacist, who is the intended recipient of the system notification. These omissions make it difficult to assign responsibilities and understand the system's intended behavior. The good specifications rectify these issues by explicitly identifying both the primary and secondary actors, ensuring clarity and completeness.

Omitting related use cases often leads to redundancy and inefficiency. For instance, patient identification steps may unnecessarily be specified in the "Create Prescription" use case instead of being specified in a reusable "Create Patient Identification" use case. Similarly, possible extending functionality, such as providing medication advice, during the prescription process, is often overlooked. Table 2 highlights these issues and their resolutions with the utilization of an included and an extending use case.

Validation, notification, confirmation, and save actions are sometimes neglected in use case specifications, leading to incomplete and error-prone models. This is what is depicted in the example of Table 3 below.

The deficient specification includes only the submission step, omitting essential following actions like validation, confirmation, and notifications. These omissions compromise the specification's clarity and integrity. The improved version adds these missing actions in a logical sequence, ensuring a comprehensive and systematic definition of the use case. Additionally, this example illustrates how the lack of guidance in sequencing actions can leave specifications vulnerable to such omissions.

**Table 2** Omission of related use cases

| Deficient Specification | Good Specification | Issue Addressed |
|---|---|---|
| 3. User inputs ID. 4. User input name. | 3. User identifies patient [via UC Create Patient Identification*]. Note: Or as a precondition. | The "Create Patient Identification" use case is reusable and avoids redundancy. |
| 5. Doctor selects medicines and quantities. | 5. Doctor selects medicines and quantities. [extension point: Medication advice required; UC Present Medication Report**]. | Extension point for advice is ignored, reducing extensibility. |

Note: *Identifying a patient in a healthcare system can be a complex process, as it may involve different types of identification (e.g., use of barcode, manual input) as well as exceptional scenarios, such as emergency situations during which the patient identification is not possible; therefore, it can be a separate use case. **Similarly, the process of presenting a medication report can have sufficient complexity and include a rich set of actions, especially if it involves dynamic, context-sensitive advice based on the patient's medical data, prescribed medications, and potential interactions

**Table 3** Missing actions

| Deficient Specification | Good Specification | Issues Addressed |
|---|---|---|
| 6. Doctor submits prescription. | 6. Doctor submits prescription.<br>7. System validates medication availability and quantity.<br>8. System saves prescription.<br>9. System confirms prescription creation.<br>10. System notifies pharmacist about the prescription. | Missing actions: Steps such as validation and notification are omitted.<br>Lack of guidance in action sequencing. |

Another common issue is the lack of a clear distinction between design-free and design-related specifications. Embedding design choices in requirements may prematurely constrain potential technical implementations, limiting flexibility in solution design. Additionally, non-technical stakeholders may struggle to understand requirements that are laden with technical design details, hindering effective communication and collaboration. Table 4 shows an example of mixing requirements and design in a use case step.

In the deficient specification, functional requirements are originally intertwined with specific interface design choices, such as dropdown menus and text boxes. This approach assumes in advance a particular design choice (dropdown menu and text box) and doesn't account for alternatives, such as voice commands. The improved specification separates design-free functionality from design-related details, focusing on clear functionality while allowing interface designs to evolve independently.

Lastly, combined actions in a single step are another common pitfall in use case modeling. Such conflation obscures the granular responsibilities of the system and actors, making validation, error handling, and modularity more challenging. Considering the same example as in Table 4, in the deficient specification, selecting

**Table 4** Design-free and design-related specification

| Deficient Specification | Good Specification | Issues Addressed |
|---|---|---|
| 6. The user selects the medication using a dropdown menu and enters the dosage in a text box. | **Design-free:**<br>6. Doctor provides medication.<br>7. Doctor provides dosage of medication. | Combines functional actions with interface-specific design details.<br>Combined actions: Conflating multiple actions into a single step makes validation and error handling challenging. |
| | **Design-augmented:**<br>6. Doctor provides medication using keyboard, a dropdown menu, or voice commands.<br>7. Doctor provides dosage using keyboard or voice input. | |

the medication and entering the dosage are combined into one step, which limits the flexibility of the specification. The good specification breaks these into atomic actions, enabling each step to be validated and managed independently. For instance, after Step 6, the system can validate that the selected medication is available in the database before proceeding to dosage input. This atomicity promotes clearer specifications, systematic validation, and enhanced maintainability.

This paper presents an Extended Backus–Naur Form (EBNF)-based grammar that defines syntactic and semantic rules for writing use case specifications in a semi-formal natural language, combining structured rigor with human readability. Core features of the grammar include the categorization of each use case under a specific pattern and the precise sequencing of scenario actions. These patterns are built around fundamental information system functions—such as creating, modifying, storing, presenting—that are applied to domain objects. Additionally, the grammar distinguishes between design-free and design-augmented specifications and provides a robust mechanism for integrating related use cases and alternate scenarios into the base use case. The presented grammar is defined and tested using the EBNF-like syntax provided by Another Tool for Language Recognition (ANTLR). Using this syntax allows the validation of key properties, such as well-formedness and closure. Well-formedness ensures that the use case specifications adhere to the grammar's syntactic rules, while closure guarantees that all referenced elements, such as alternate scenarios and related use cases, are properly defined and self-contained. ANTLR serves as both a parser and translator generator, enabling the definition of language grammars, the execution of concrete examples, and the isolation of mistakes during testing. In summary, the proposed grammar not only makes the expression of use case-based requirements more disciplined, understandable, and organized but also facilitates their conversion into diagrammatic notations, such as use case and sequence diagrams.

The rest of this paper is structured as follows: sect. 2 summarizes related work, sect. 3 elaborates on the proposed grammar and its fundamentals, sect. 4 provides a use case example implemented and tested in ANTLR, and sect. 5 presents conclusions and future goals.

## 2 Related Work

A number of structured techniques for the description of use cases have been proposed. In Eriksson et al.'s work [3], a tabular representation is used, and in Leite et al.'s [4], a structured natural language is presented for use case description. These structured representations provide a generic formalization of the use case (UC) specification template, hence not a clear formalism of the use case specification elements, and especially the basic and alternative flow actions. Osaki et al. [5] provide some textual statements representing actor and system behavior, however, in addition to the lack of action types included in their work as well as of other use case elements, the proposed actions are not placed in any order or sequence, and they also lack the well-formedness of a grammar with syntactical and semantic rules. Moreover, some formal techniques such as formal grammars [6], statecharts [7, 8] and scenario trees [8] were introduced for the description of use cases or their scenarios. Although such formal representations facilitate formal analysis, they are difficult for analysts and users to understand and use.

Savi et al. [9, 10] have developed a grammar in BNF that covers only three types of actions; these actions are "Actor (user) prepares data for system operation execution", "Actor call system to execute system operation", and "System returns results of system operation execution". In addition to the lack of action types included in their grammar, user actions are placed as a separate group from system actions within their use case specification; contrary to their approach, the grammar proposed by Georgiades [11] associates a use case with a specific pattern, and according to this pattern (e.g., Create, Alter, Erase, Read), specific user and system actions, combined in a specific sequence, are used to form the main flow of the use case. Yet, this grammar lacks rules for specifying and differentiating between design-free and design-augmented scenarios, as well as mechanisms for integrating alternate scenarios—key features of the grammar proposed in this paper. Golbaz et al. [12] also propose a use case grammar which is defined in XML, but their work lacks covering any specific types of actions. However, their XML grammar and the fact that they use XSLT to transform their use cases from a concrete syntax expressed in semi-formal language to that of a natural language-like form provide useful insights for future work related to the grammar proposed in this paper.

Jacobson [13] has also suggested the following well-known combination of use case actions:

- The primary actor sends request and data to the system
- The system validates the request and the data
- The system alters its internal state
- The system responds to the actor with the result.

This is a generic approach, lacking, on the one hand, the well-formedness of a grammar with syntactical and semantic rules, and, on the other hand, of additional and more specific user and system actions together with the rest of the elements of a use case specification, all defined under a use case grammar.

# 3 The Proposed Grammar

The proposed EBNF-based grammar has been developed with the Another Tool for Language Recognition (ANTLR) parser generator. ANTLR is a parser and translator generator tool that lets one define language grammars in EBNF-like syntax. In particular, this work has used ANTLRWorks, which is a grammar development GUI environment for ANTLR grammars. It combines a grammar-aware editor with an interpreter for rapid prototyping and a language-agnostic debugger for isolating grammar errors [14].

The following paragraphs elaborate on the abstract syntax of the most important rules of the proposed grammar as well as on the concrete syntax of several rules. Through the presentation of these rules, the various fundamentals of the grammar will be discussed, including (i) use case patterns which are structured sequences of action blocks tailored to achieve specific system functionalities, such as creating, reading, or modifying a domain object (referred to as an *information object* in this work, as defined later). Each pattern defines the logical sequence of actions, such as Input → Validate → Save → Confirm in a *Create* pattern, and their relationships, such as the use of an *Extend* action block to trigger an extending use case. (ii) action blocks, serving as fundamental units of user or system actions, further categorized into atomic blocks for main scenarios and composite blocks for alternate scenarios (iii) support for design-free and design-augmented specifications for action blocks, (iv) the hierarchical structure of the grammar, (v) mechanisms to identify actors, related use cases, preconditions and alternate scenarios.

## *3.1 Hierarchical Structure*

The proposed grammar starts with defining the root parser rule *UseCaseSpecification* (Table 5). It defines the main elements of a use case specification including the use case identification through the parser rule *useCase*, the use case description through the parser rule *description*, the primary and secondary actors through the parser rule *actors*, preconditions and postconditions through the parser rules *preconditions* and *postconditions*, respectively, the main flow through the parser rule *mainFlow*, and the alternate scenarios through the parser rule *alternateScenario*.

The *useCase* parser rule defines a use case with a unique identifier and a use case name (Table 6). The question mark symbol (?) denotes optional behavior that may happen only once, so the use of the unique identifier is optional.

**Table 5** Abstract syntax of the parser rule *useCaseSpecification*

```
useCaseSpecification
        :       useCase
                description
                preConditions
                actors
                mainFlow
                alternateScenario*
                postConditions ;
```

**Table 6** Abstract syntax of the parser rule *useCase*

```
useCase
        : ucID? ucName
        ;

ucID
        : 'UC' INTEGER ;
```

**Table 7** Abstract syntax of the parser rule *ucName*

```
ucName
        :       ucType io       ;
```

Note: The parser rules *ucType* and *io* are presented in Tables 9 and 8, respectively.

Each use case is related to one domain concept, namely the **Information Object (IO),** and it also falls under a use case type; these two (IO, type) make up the use case name which is defined by the parser rule below (Table 7).

According to Georgiades and Andreou [15]:

> An information object (IO) is a digital representation of a tangible or intangible entity—described by a set of attributes—which the users need to manage through creating, modifying, reading, and erasing its instances, and be notified by the messages each instance (IOi) can trigger.[1] [p. 269]

Information objects are distinguished into the following categories: business role (as a type of animate [supertype] entity, e.g., doctor), inanimate entity (e.g., car), procedure (e.g., translation), document (e.g., book), event (e.g., appointment), site (e.g., country, hospital), and state (e.g., disease). This distinction makes easier the identification and organization of the basic elements of an information system and their association with use case elements (e.g., business roles[people]➔actors, *ucType* + IO [function]➔use case), their relationships, and the identification of the attributes of an IO, which (viz. the attributes) have to be processed by use cases. It is worth noting that by specifying the type of an IO, the analyst will be able to identify its attributes more easily (more information on this is out of the scope of this paper). Table 8 below presents the abstract syntax of the parser rule *io* for the Information Object.

The parser rule *ucType* (Table 9) indicates the types of functions which are applicable to an information object. *ucType* use cases follow the nine **use case patterns** proposed by Georgiades and Andreou [15], namely (a) Create information

[1] An IO is conceived and processed at an abstraction level, while an IOi is conceived and processed at a factual level; instances of the same IO differ only in the values of their attributes.

**Table 8** Abstract syntax of the parser rule *io*

```
io
        :       ioName ioType?
        ;

ioName
        :       CAPITALIZED_NOUN | 'Authentication'
        ;

ioType
        :       'type' '"' IO_TYPE '"'
        ;

Where

IO_TYPE : 'business role' | 'inanimate'| 'procedure'| 'document'| 'event'| 'site'|
'state';

CAPITALIZED_NOUN : ('A'..'Z') ('a'..'z'|'A'..'Z'|'_')*;
```

Note: Concrete syntax examples of the parser rule *io* could be "Prescription" and "Examination", or "Prescription type document" and "Examination type procedure".

**Table 9** Abstract syntax of the parser rule *ucType*

```
ucType
        :       'create' | 'creates' | alter | read | 'erase' | 'erases' | notify
        ;

alter
        :       'correct' | 'corrects' | alter_expanded
        ;

alter_expanded
        :       'cancel' | 'cancels' | 'archive' | 'archives' | 'complete' |
'completes' | VERB
        ;


read
        :       'read' | ('read' 'report' 'about') | 'reads' | ('reads' 'report'
'about')
        ;

notify
        :       ('send' | 'sends') 'Notification' ('about' 'the' ('creation' |
'altering' | 'reading' | 'erasing'))? 'of'
        ;
```

object (IO), (b) Correct IO, (c) Alter IO state, which leads to the more specialized patterns Cancel IO, Archive IO, and Complete IO, (d) Erase IO (e) Read IO, (f) Read IO intra-report | inter-report, (g) Read supporting information, (h) Notify, and (i) Authorize. It is worth noting that as *ucType* use cases are applied to electronic information following the abovementioned nine patterns, strong verbs of the domain vocabulary, such as "enroll" and "register", should be examined if they can be transformed to information objects in the form of their corresponding nouns. For example, "enroll" derives the noun "enrolment", and "register" derives the noun "registration". As a result, a use case titled "Enroll in Seminar" by conventional approaches (e.g., [16]), leads to the use of the IOs Enrolment and Seminar, under the proposed grammar, as well as to the use of the relevant *ucType* use cases for each IO. For example, for the IO *Enrolment*, there are the use cases *Create Enrolment, Correct Enrolment, Cancel Enrolment, Archive Enrolment, Complete Enrolment,*

**Table 10** Abstract and a concrete syntax of the parser rule *description*

```
description
        :       'Description' ':' primaryActor ucName '.' (((secondaryActor) ('and'
secondaryActor)*) (('provides' 'or' 'verifies') | ('provide' 'or' 'verify'))
'relevant' 'information.')? (secondaryActor ('and' secondaryActor)* ('is an intended
recipient' | 'are intended recipients') 'of' io '.')?

Description: Doctor creates Prescription. Patient and Medical_system provide or verify
relevant information. Pharmacist is an intended recipient of Prescription.
```

**Table 11** Abstract syntax of the parser rule *actors*

```
actors
        :       'Actors' ':' primaryActor (',' secondaryActor)*
        ;
```

**Table 12** Abstract syntax of the parser rules *primaryActor* and *secondaryActor*

```
primaryActor
        :       actorName paType?
        ;

actorName
        :       CAPITALIZED_NOUN
        ;

paType
        :       '(' 'type:' PA_TYPE ')'
        ;

secondaryActor
        :       actorName saType?
        ;

saType
        :       '(' 'type:' SA_TYPE ')'
        ;

Where

PA_TYPE :       'creator' | 'alterer' | 'experiencer';

SA_TYPE :       'accompaniment' | 'intended recipient' | 'notifiee';

CAPITALIZED_NOUN : ('A'..'Z') ('a'..'z'|'A'..'Z'|'_')*;
```

etc., and for the IO Seminar, there are the use cases *Create Seminar, Correct Seminar, Cancel Seminar, Archive Seminar, Complete Seminar*, etc. Similarly, from the conventional and widely used use case "Withdraw Money", we can derive the IO "Withdrawal".

Table 10 below shows the abstract parser rule *description* and its concrete syntax for the use case *Create Prescription.*

Actors are defined through the *actors* parser rule, as depicted below (Table 11). Specifically, the rule allows the definition of one primary actor and zero or more secondary actors.

Primary actors fall into three categories, and secondary actors fall into two categories, as defined by the rules below (Table 12).

The sect. 4 complete concrete syntax of use case *Create Prescription* presents the concrete syntax of the actors *doctor*, *patient* and *pharmacist*, based on the corresponding abstract rules depicted in Tables 11 and 12 above. For clarification purposes, the same concrete syntax is depicted here, too:

```
Actors: Doctor (type: creator), Patient (type: accompaniment),
    Pharmacist (type: intended recipient)
```

To identify the actors involved in each use case, the functional roles provided by Georgiades and Andreou [17] are utilized. Indicatively, a *Create* use case involves the functional roles *creator*, *accompaniment*, *intended recipient*, and *notifiee*. The creator is played by a primary actor, while the accompaniment, intended recipient and notifiee are played by secondary actors. The creator is responsible for setting (or confirming) the values of a number of particular attributes (required and optional) of an IOi (e.g., *Doctor* is the creator of prescriptions in the UC *Create Prescription*). The accompaniment participates in close association with the creator to help in the creation of an instance of the IO (e.g., *Patient* provides to the *Doctor* information about his/her physical condition/pain so that an examination is created through the *UC Create Examination*. Another accompaniment in this use case could be the *Nurse* that provides help during the examination, including the completion of the relevant examination form. The intended recipient (IR) takes action after being notified about the creation of an IOi. The action to be taken needs to fulfil the purpose of having/using the IO, and the fulfilment is achieved by creating or altering instances of other related IOs. For example, in the UC *Create Prescription, Pharmacist* is one IR of the *Prescription* IO, because after the creation of a *Prescription* IOi, the pharmacist will fulfil the purpose of having/using the prescription (the purpose is to provide medicines to the patient) by altering the relevant *Medicine* IOi (since the medicine handed to the patient must be removed electronically from the system, by reducing its quantity).

To derive the actors from their functional roles, specific questions need to be made. The following are indicative question patterns for identifying (i) the creator: Who should create an <IO>? Who has the responsibility for the creation of a(n) < IO>?; and (ii) the accompaniment: Who should assist the <Creator> to create an <IO>? How does the <Accompaniment> help the <Creator> during the creation of an <IO>?

Additionally, the collaboration between a primary actor and an accompaniment can derive both *include* and *extend* relationships, where extending or included use cases are invoked by their base use cases and involve the accompaniments. For example, during the creation of a prescription, the doctor may need to ask for the assistance of another doctor/counsellor or of a medical database system, in order, for example, to choose between two medicines for the treatment of a patient. In this case the counsellor and the medical system are accompaniments that provide feedback, and the use cases *Read Counsellor* and *Read Medical System Report* extend the behaviour of the use case *Create Prescription*.

Moreover, the use of the intended recipient helps in identifying preconditions by checking if the primary actor of one use case is an IR in another related (preceding, specifically) use case. For example, the primary actor of *UC Create Examination* is *Doctor; Doctor* is also an IR in the latter use case, as a doctor will be notified about the creation of an examination and take some action by creating or altering instances of another IO, that is, *Prescription;* therefore, in this example, a precondition of

**Table 13** Abstract syntax of the parser rule *preConditions*

```
preConditions
        :       'Pre-conditions' ':' (INTEGER '.' precondition)*
        ;

precondition
        :       statePre | authe_pre | autho_pre | other_pre
        ;
statePre
        :       io 'is at' state 'state' '.' 'Triggered by' useCase (',' useCase)* '.'
//useCase is an essentially preceding use case which causes the initiation of the
state.
        ;
state
        :       'Cancelled' | 'Pending' | 'Complete' | SMALL_NOUN
        ;
authe_pre
        :       primaryActor 'is authenticated' '.'
        ;

autho_pre
        :       primaryActor 'is authorized' '.'

other_pre
        : TEXT
        ;
SMALL_NOUN : ('a'..'z') ('a'..'z'|'_')*;
```

**Table 14** Abstract syntax of the parser rule *postConditions*

```
postConditions
        : 'Post-conditions' ':' (INTEGER '.' postCondition)*
        ;

postCondition
        :       io 'is at' state 'state' '.'
        ;
```

the UC *Create Prescription* is "Examination is in Complete state (from the related [preceding] use case UC *Create Examination*)."

Another type of precondition refers to the primary actor (e.g., the *Creator*) that initiates the use case. Normally, the system must check that the primary actor is authenticated or authorized to initiate the use case. For example, for the UC *Create Prescription*, "Doctor is authorized" is a precondition. The abstract syntax of preconditions is depicted in Table 13 below. Similarly, the abstract syntax of postconditions is depicted in Table 14.

## 3.2 Main Flow - Patterns - Action Blocks

The parser rule *mainFlow* defines the actual execution of the use case. According to the use case type, the corresponding action pattern will take place; for example, if the use case type is "Create", then *PatternCreate* will take place. Below (Table 15) is the abstract syntax of the main flow parser rule including all the possible patterns.

As aforementioned each pattern rule is composed of a sequence of **action blocks**. Action blocks are the building units of the use case scenarios of use case patterns, categorized into atomic and composite types. Atomic action blocks define

**Table 15** Abstract syntax of the parser rule *mainFlow*

```
mainFlow
        :       'Main' 'Flow' ':' patternCreate | patternCorrect | patternRead |
patternErase | patternCancel | patternArchive | patternComplete | patternReadReport |
patternReadInfo | patternNotify
        ;
```

Note: Possible expansions of the patterns may include functionalities such as searching and sorting. Depending on the context, these functionalities can be applied to an IOi (e.g., searching for a specific prescription) or to a list/collection of IOis, with the latter often considered a temporary IO (e.g., a *List of Prescriptions* meeting specific search or sort criteria).

**Table 16** Abstract syntax of the parser rule *patternCreate*

```
patternCreate
        :       initialUA
                promptInputSA
                (inputUA validate_inputSA?)+
                submitUA
                validateSA
                saveSA
                (notifySA includes?)?
                extended_by*
                includes*
                cancellationSteps*;
```

**Table 17** Abstract syntax of the parser rule *initialUA*

```
initialUA :     'UA' INTEGER '.' primaryActor 'requests to' ucName   '.';
```

Note: For *patternCreate*, the *ucType* (part of *ucName*) value is "Create".

**Table 18** A concrete syntax of the parser rule *initialUA*

```
UA 1. Doctor requests to create Prescription.
```

indivisible system or user actions and are primarily used in main scenarios, ensuring clarity and modularity. Composite action blocks, on the other hand, are constructed by grouping multiple atomic actions, commonly employed in alternate scenarios to encapsulate more complex behaviors and deviations from the main flow. Together, these action blocks enable the precise and reusable specification of functional requirements. As already mentioned, each block defines a specific type of user or system action, such as input, validation, or notification. Currently, 18 action blocks have been defined by the proposed grammar, and this number can be increased in the future. The parser rules of some of these action blocks are provided in this paper.

Below (Table 16), pattern*Create* is presented, consisting of several action blocks to be discussed in this section.

The parser rule *patternCreate* starts with an initial user action, that is, a request to create a new information object (Table 17). Table 18 depicts a concrete syntax validated in ANTLR.

Subsequently, the parser rule *promptInputSA* involves another system action, that is, the system will prompt the user to input the values of the required and optional attributes, and, thus, create an instance of the IO. The abstract syntax of this rule is depicted in Table 19, while a concrete syntax is presented in Table 20.

Before proceeding to the next parser rule, it is important to note that the action blocks encompass both **design-free and design-augmented specifications**. Design-

**Table 19** Abstract syntax of the parser rule for prompting a user to input attribute values

```
promptInputSA : 'SA' INTEGER '.' 'The system prompts' primaryActor 'to
input ('the required and optional attribute values of the' io | ioAttribute |
            specificInput) '.' ;
specificInput: TEXT;
```

**Table 20** A concrete syntax of the parser rule for prompting a user to create an IOi

```
SA 2. The system prompts Doctor to input the required and optional attribute values of
the Prescription.
```

**Table 21** Abstract syntax of *inputUA* for design-free and design-augmented specifications

```
inputUA
      : 'UA' INTEGER '.' primaryActor (designFreeInputAction |
      designSupplementedInputAction) ioAttribute ('(' attributeType ')')?'.'
      secondaryActor ('provides' | 'verifies') 'this information' '.')?
      ;
designFreeInputAction
                      : 'provides' | 'inputs' | 'enters' | 'adds';
designFreeInputAction
                      : ('selects' | 'types' | 'uploads' | 'chooses') uiElement?;
uiElement : 'from a dropdown menu' | 'in a text box' | 'in a file upload dialog' | 'on
a slider';
```

**Table 22** Concrete syntax of *inputUA*, for design-free and design-augmented specifications

```
Design-free:
UA 4. Doctor inputs Medication of Prescription (required).
UA 5. Doctor inputs Dosage(required).
Design-augmented:
UA 4. Doctor selects Medication of Prescription from a dropdown menu (required).
UA 5. Doctor enters Dosage in a text box (required).
```

free specifications focus solely on system functionality, avoiding constraints related to design or technical considerations, thereby ensuring flexibility for various design implementations. In contrast, design-augmented specifications build upon design-free specifications by incorporating details about how the functionality is realized in terms of user interface, data model, or other design aspects. They supplement the functional steps with specific design elements or constraints, offering clearer implementation guidance while maintaining alignment with the underlying functionality.

Following, the parser rule *inputUA* (in Table 21) refers to the user's action of inputting data for the creation of the IOi, covering both design-free and design-augmented specifications; Table 22 depicts the concrete syntax of two actions from the use case *Create Prescription*.

*inputUA* is also followed by the optional rule *validate_inputSA?* denoting that inputting data could be validated. System action 4 "The System validates Medicine1 of Prescription." of the full concrete example of sect. 4 is such a validation action. It is worth noting that the plus sign (+), appearing in Table 16, indicates one or more occurrences of *inputUA* followed optionally by *validate_inputSA*. Also, it is important to distinguish between this optional validation action that can take place after an input action and the overall validation action that takes place after submitting all the data. An example of application of the former rule is in the case

**Table 23** Abstract syntax of the parser rule for defining an attribute

```
ioAttribute
        :       CAPITALIZED_NOUN ('of' io)?
        ;
CAPITALIZED_NOUN : ('A'..'Z') ('a'..'z'|'A'..'Z'|'_')*;
attributeType: 'required' | 'optional';
```

**Table 24** Abstract syntax of the parser rule *saveSA*

```
saveSA  : 'SA' INTEGER '.' 'The System saves' io (saveDesignDetails)? '.' ;
saveDesignDetails : recordLocation | fileLocation ;
recordLocation : 'to database' ('with reference from' io 'to' associatedRecords)? ;
associatedRecord :associatedRecord (',' associatedRecord)* ;
fileLocation: 'to' storageType ('with reference from' io 'to' fileAssociatedRecords)?;
fileAssociatedRecords : fileAssociatedRecord (',' fileAssociatedRecord)* ;
storageType : 'local storage' | 'cloud storage' | 'external drive' ;
associatedRecord: TEXT ;
fileAssociatedRecord: TEXT ;
```

**Table 25** Concrete syntax of *saveSA*, for design-free and design-augmented specifications

```
Design-free:
SA 11. The system saves Prescription.
Design-augmented:
SA 11. The system saves Prescription to database with reference from Prescription to
Patient record, Doctor record.
```

**Table 26** Abstract syntax of the parser rule *notifySA*

```
notifySA :      'SA' INTEGER '.' 'The System' notificationAction notificationContext?
                'to the following' actors designAugmentedNotificationDetails? '.';

notificationAction :
        :       'sends' ('Notification' | 'Alert' | 'Information' | 'Reminder';
notificationContext :
                        'about the' ('creation' | 'altering' | 'deletion' |
'cancellation' | 'archiving'))? 'of' io;
designAugmentedNotificationDetails :
                                ', via' notificationMethod (',' notificationMethod)*
'.';
notificationMethod:
                        'in-app message' | 'email' | 'SMS' | TEXT ;
```

that inputting data for one attribute, firstly requires inputting data for a preceding attribute.

*ioAttribute* determines the value added for an attribute of the IOi. Iteration of this addition may take place as depicted in Table 16 and in the example of sect. 4. Table 23 below presents the abstract syntax of the IO attribute.

Subsequently, according to the *mainFlow* rule of Table 16, the *submitUA* user action parser rule denotes that the user submits the data, while the next rule *validateSA* defines a system action denoting that the system checks the values of the attributes, and if everything is correct, it saves the new information object instance through the parser rule *SaveSA*. Tables 24 and 25 show the abstract and a concrete syntax of SaveSA.

Next, the system, through the parser rule *notifySA* (Tables 26 and 16), notifies the primary actor and any interested secondary actors about the creation of the information object. Table 27 depicts examples of concrete syntax for both design-free and design-augmented specifications.

**Table 27** Concrete syntax of *notifySA*, for design-free and design-augmented specifications

```
Design-free:
SA 10. The System sends Notification about the creation of Prescription to the
following Actors: Doctor, Patient, Pharmacist.
Design-augmented:
SA 10. The System sends Notification about the creation of Prescription to the
following Actors: Doctor, Patient, Pharmacist, via in-app message, email, SMS.
```

**Table 28** Abstract and concrete syntax of *extended_by*, *includes* and *cancellationSteps*

```
//Abstract syntax:
extended_by
        :       '[' 'Extension point:' TEXT; useCase '];' 'at step' INTEGER '.'
        ;
includes
        :       '[' 'Include' useCase '];' 'between steps' INTEGER 'and' INTEGER '.'
        ;
cancellationSteps
        :       'Cancellation allowed during steps INTEGER'..'INTEGER'.'
        ;
//Concrete syntax:
        [ Extension point: Guidance required; UC3 Read Counsellor Report ]; at step 4.
        [ Include UC1.5 Create Patient Identification ]; between steps 1 and 2.
        Cancellation allowed during steps 3..5.
```

Finally, the optional parser rule *extended_by** (in Tables 16 and 28) denotes that the *Create IO* use case can be extended by zero or more use cases at specific steps of the scenario, based on defined extension points. Some input actions can often be extended by other use cases that provide supplementary information, such as reports or documents. For instance, during the execution of the *UC Create Prescription*, the "Input medicine" step may invoke *UC Read Counsellor Report* or *UC Read Examination Report* to provide necessary guidance to the doctor (see the complete example in Sect. 4). Similarly, the optional parser rule *includes** defines how the base use case invokes an included use case.

As it cannot be predefined which step of a scenario relates to an included or extending use case, the proposed syntax offers flexibility by allowing explicit referencing of the relevant step. Additionally, the syntax supports cases where the user opts to cancel the creation of an IOi during a scenario. This simple cancellation action is distinct from the *Cancel IO Pattern* which modifies the state of an IOi and is treated as a separate use case.

The full example presented in sect. 4 includes the concrete syntax of one extending use case and one included use case.

## *3.3 Alternate Scenarios*

Alternate scenarios in use case modeling describe deviations or exceptions from the main flow, ensuring that the system's behavior is robust and comprehensive. Despite their importance, alternate scenarios are often overlooked or vaguely defined, leading to incomplete and ambiguous specifications. This paper's grammar provides

**Table 29** Abstract syntax of the parser rule *alternateScenario*

```
alternateScenario : 'Alternate Flow' ':' scenarioID 'Triggered by' primaryFlowStep
                    'Condition:' condition alternateSequence rejoinPoint? ;

alternateSequence : (missingInputSequence | validationFailureSequence |
              approvalSequence | systemErrorSequence | externalActionSequence)+ ;

missingInputSequence : promptInputSA inputUA ; //Already defined in this paper
validationFailureSequence : validationSequence notifySA inputUA ;
approvalSequence : requestApprovalAction? approvalAction approvalOutcomeAction? ;
systemErrorSequence : systemErrorNotification userRetryAction ;

requestApprovalAction : 'UA' INTEGER '.' actor 'requests approval from' actor '.' ;
approvalAction : 'UA' INTEGER '.' actor ('approves' | 'rejects' | 'denies' |
'authorizes') TEXT '.' ;
approvalOutcomeAction : 'SA' INTEGER '.' 'The system records' ('approval' |
'rejection') 'by' actor '.' ;
//not all the rules are specified here.
```

a structured approach to modeling alternate scenarios, ensuring accuracy and clarity through dedicated syntax rules and composite action blocks.

The grammar's core rule for alternate scenarios, *alternateScenario*, captures necessary elements of an alternate flow, as depicted in Table 29.

This rule enforces the structured representation of alternate scenarios by including:

1. Triggering Point: The step in the main flow that leads to the alternate scenario (e.g., "Triggered by Step 2").
2. Condition: The specific condition or exception that initiates the alternate scenario.
3. Alternate Sequence: A sequence of actions (e.g., missingInputSequence or validationFailureSequence) that define how the system handles the deviation.
4. Rejoin Point (optional): Where the alternate scenario rejoins the main flow

For example, for the "Create Patient Identification" use case, one alternate scenario occurs when a patient cannot provide an ID. This scenario involves prompting the *Doctor* to proceed with a temporary *Patient ID* and handling its input. Using the proposed grammar, this alternate flow is defined as:

```
Alternate Flow: AS 1
Triggered by Step 2
Condition: Patient cannot provide ID.
SA 1. The system prompts Doctor to input TemporaryID of
Patient. // promptInputSA
UA 2. Doctor inputs TemporaryID of Patient. // inputUA
Rejoins Main Flow at Step 5.
```

In the "Create Prescription" use case, a validation failure during prescription submission triggers an alternate scenario. For example, if the dosage exceeds allowable limits, the system must initiate an approval sequence before continuing. Using the grammar in Table 29 (see mainly the rule *approvalSequence*), this alternate flow is defined as:

```
Alternate Flow: AS 2
```

```
Triggered by Step 5
Condition: Dosage exceeds allowable limits.
UA 1. Doctor requests approval from Pharmacist.
                        // requestApprovalAction
UA 2. Pharmacist approves Dosage. // approvalAction
Rejoins Main Flow at Step 8.
```

This modular structure ensures that approvals, rejections, and other outcomes are consistently modeled across different use cases.

# 4 Grammar Validation and Implementation: Create Prescription Use Case

To validate the robustness of the proposed grammar, the latter was implemented and tested using ANTLR. This process involved parsing use case specifications against the EBNF-like rules, verifying syntax correctness, and refining the grammar to address ambiguities. Sample use cases were used to confirm that each rule functioned as intended, with error reporting from ANTLR facilitating the identification and resolution of ambiguities. A key example is the *Create Prescription* use case, which was tested using the *createPattern*. Both design-free and design-augmented versions of the use case were specified to demonstrate the grammar's flexibility in transitioning from functional requirements to design. Below the concrete syntax of the design-free version is presented:

```
UC 1 create Prescription =
Description: Doctor creates Prescription. Patient and Medical_system
provide or verify relevant information. Pharmacist is an Intended Recipient
of Prescription.
Pre-conditions:     1. Examination is at Complete state. Triggered by UC 11
create Examination.
        2. Doctor is authorized.
Actors: Doctor (type: creator), Patient (type: accompaniment), Pharmacist
(type: intended recipient)
Main Flow:     UA 1. Doctor requests to create Prescription.
SA 2. The system prompts Doctor to input the required and optional
attribute values of Prescription.
UA 3. Doctor inputs Medicine1 of Prescription.
SA 4. The System validates Medicine1 of Prescription.
UA 5. Doctor inputs Dosage of Medicine1.
SA 6. The System validates Dosage of Medicine1.
UA 7. Doctor inputs Notes of Prescription.
UA 8. Doctor submits Prescription.
SA 9. The System validates Prescription, checking required and optional
field entries.
SA 10. The System saves Prescription.
SA 11. The System sends Notification about the creation of Prescription to
the following Actors: Doctor, Patient, Pharmacist.
[Extension point: Guidance required; UC 12 Read Examination report]; at
step 5
```

```
[Extension point: Guidance required; UC 12 Read Examination report]; at
step 6
[Include UC 15 Create Patient Identification]; between steps 1 and 2.
                          //this could, alternatively, be a precondition.
Cancellation allowed during steps 3..5.
Alternate Flow: AS 1
Triggered by Step 6
Condition: Dosage exceeds allowable limits.
UA 1. Doctor requests approval from Pharmacist.
UA 2. Pharmacist approves Dosage.
Rejoins Main Flow at Step 7.
Post-conditions: 1. Prescription is at Pending state.
```

# 5 Conclusions and Future Work

This paper presented a grammar for the formalization of the use case model. The proposed grammar, which has been defined in EBNF and developed and tested in ANTLR, provides syntactic and semantic rules for writing use case specifications in semi-formal natural language. Use cases can be written in ANTLR, in the form of concrete syntax, and are validated against the already defined abstract syntax, which has been described in this paper. Core elements of the grammar include (i) use case patterns, which define structured sequences of action blocks tailored to achieve specific functionalities; (ii) action blocks, which are fundamental units of user or system actions, categorized into atomic blocks for main scenarios and composite blocks for alternate scenarios; (iii) support for both design-free and design-augmented specifications, enabling flexibility in varying levels of detail; (iv) a hierarchical grammar structure that ensures modularity, traceability, and reusability; and (v) mechanisms to identify and specify actors, related use cases, and alternate scenarios. Conclusively, the proposed grammar, within its powerful development and testing environment, helps to make expression of use case-based requirements more disciplined, understandable, well-formed, correct and complete, and it also makes easier their conversion into diagrammatic notations.

Despite its contributions, the proposed grammar has some limitations. Currently, it supports a predefined set of use case patterns and action blocks, which may require extensions to handle highly domain-specific actions or alternate scenarios involving concurrent actions and conditional dependencies. Additionally, while the current grammar includes various rules for the design-augmented specification of use case action blocks, it can be further enhanced with additional rules to enrich use case specifications with supplementary details about user interface and data model elements—key aspects critical to the implementation of use cases. Moreover, although the grammar facilitates structured representation, it does not yet integrate built-in capabilities for generating diagrams or querying specifications. Addressing these gaps will form a key focus of future work. Furthermore, other platforms or languages will be explored for the representation and transformation of the proposed grammar, such as XML and XSLT. Also, XQuery could be used for querying and processing use case data, in order to come to useful conclusions, especially about metrics such as the number of actors and use cases of a project, or the average number of actions or steps regarding various projects. When these measurements are taken on a regular basis, they can be used for project estimation purposes. Additionally, the proposed grammar will be utilized and tested in several real-world projects, and the resulting use cases will be evaluated for correctness, completeness and consistency. Finally, a tool is expected to be developed to enhance the usability of the proposed grammar. It will streamline grammar validation by parsing specifications, ensuring conformance, and providing precise error feedback. The tool will incorporate a database to store specifications, track changes, and enable advanced queries for analyzing project metrics. It will also support the customization of action blocks and grammar rules, allowing for broader requirements coverage and adaptation to domain-specific needs. Additionally, the tool may include the capability to automatically generate use case and sequence diagrams from validated specifications.

## References


1. Sinnig, D., Chalin, P., & Khendek, F. (2009). *LTS semantics for use case models*. ACM Symposium on Applied Computing.
2. El-Attar, M., & Miller, J. (2006). Matching Antipatterns to improve the quality of use case models. In *Proceeding of the 14$^{th}$IEEE International Requirements Engineering Conference (RE'06)* (pp. 99–108).
3. Eriksson, M., Börstler, K., & Borg, K. (2004). Marrying features and use cases for product line requirements modeling of embedded systems. In *Proceedings of the fourth conference on software engineering research and practice (SERPS'04)* (pp. 73–82).
4. Leite, J., Rossi, G., Balaguer, M., Kaplan, G., Hadad, G., & Oliveros, A. (1997). Enhancing a requirements baseline with scenarios. In *Proceedings of requirements engineering* (Vol. 2, pp. 184–198).
5. Osaki, T., Kobayashi, A., & Kato, T. (2006). Writing use-case with a minimal set of words. In *Proceedings of the 5th IEEE/ACIS International Conference on Computer and Information Science* (pp. 393–398).
6. Hsia, P., Samuel, J., Gao, J., Kung, D., Toyoshima, Y., & Chen, C. (1994). Formal approach to scenario analysis. *IEEE Software, 11*, 2.
7. Glinz, M. (1995). An integrated formal model of scenarios based on Statecharts. In *Proceedings of 5th European Software Engineering Conference* (pp. 254–271). Springer (Lecture Notes in Computer Science 989).
8. Seybold, C., Meier, S., & Glinz, M. (2006). Scenario-driven modeling and validation of requirements models. In *5th ICSE International Workshop on Scenarios and State Machines: Models* (pp. 83–89). Algorithms and Tools.
9. Savic, D., Antovic, I., Vlajic, S., Stanojevic, V., & Milic, M. (2011). Language for use case specification. In *2011 IEEE 34th Software Engineering Workshop* (pp. 19–26). https://doi.org/10.1109/SEW.2011.9
10. Savic, D., Vlajic, S., Lazarevic, S., Antović, I., Stanojevic, V., Milic, M., & Silva, A. R. (2015). Use case specification using the SILABREQ domain specific language. *Computing and Informatics, 34*, 877–910.

11. Georgiades, M. (2024). A use case grammar for requirements specification. In B. Marcinkowski, A. Przybylek, A. Jarzębowicz, N. Iivari, E. Insfran, M. Lang, H. Linger, & C. Schneider (Eds.), *Harnessing opportunities: Reshaping ISD in the post-COVID-19 and generative AI era (ISD2024 proceedings)*. University of Gdańsk.
12. Golbaz, M., Hasheminasab, A., & Daneshpour, N. (2008). An XML definition language to support use case-based requirements engineering. In *Proceeding of the international Multiconference of Engineers and Computer Scientists 2008(IMECS 2008)* (Vol. 1).
13. Jacobson, I., Christerson, M., Johnsson, P., & Overgaard, G. (1992). *Object-oriented software engineering: A use case driven approach*. Addison-Wesley.
14. ANTLRWorks: The ANTLR GUI Development Environment. Accessed Feb 2, 2024., from https://www.antlr3.org/works/
15. Georgiades, M., & Andreou, A. (2013). Patterns for use case context and content. In J. Favaro & M. Morisio (Eds.), *Safe and secure software reuse. ICSR 2013* (Lecture notes in computer science) (Vol. 7925). Springer. https://doi.org/10.1007/978-3-642-38977-1_18
16. Cockburn, A. (2000). *Writing effective use cases*. Addison-Wesley.
17. Georgiades, M., & Andreou, A. (2012). Formalizing and automating use case model development. *The Open Software Engineering Journal, 6*, 21–40.

# Changes in Node.js Server-Side Application Performance Characteristics Over Time Under Load

**Pawel Kuffeł and Bartosz Walter**

**Abstract** Application frameworks based on Node.js are commonly used in developing modern web systems. They differ not only in terms of the abstractions that they introduce but also in their underlying architecture, which intuitively should affect the performance characteristics of applications using them as a dependency. In this work, we extend our empirical comparative analysis of the selected frameworks, present a purpose-built tool for tracking changes in application performance characteristics over the duration of load tests, and formulate additional practical recommendations for developers of server-side Node.js applications.

## 1 Introduction

Node.js is a popular cross-platform runtime environment that enables JavaScript execution outside of a web browser. It is commonly employed for server-side scripting and running backend applications. Since its 2009 release, Node.js's popularity has soared, largely due to its utilization of JavaScript, easing the transition into backend development for frontend developers. The Stack Overflow Annual Developer Survey found Node.js as the most popular technology in its category since 2017 [30]. Also the number of modules managed by Node.js's package manager, `npm`, confirms its popularity. As of November 2024, it hosted over 3 million modules, surpassing the combined offerings of Maven Central (Java), Nuget (.NET), Packagist (PHP), and Python Package Index.

Node.js has become a foundation for developing various customized backend frameworks that allow for developing large and complex web systems. Such frameworks typically offer ready-to-use implementations for common server-side functions, such as request routing, user authentication, and error handling. They differ in terms of the development style, expressiveness, but also community support

P. Kuffeł (✉) · B. Walter
Poznan University of Technology, Poznan, Poland
e-mail: pawel@kuffel.io; bartosz.walter@cs.put.poznan.pl

 
B. Marcinkowski et al. (eds.), *Advances in Information Systems Development*,
Lecture Notes in Information Systems and Organisation 77,
https://doi.org/10.1007/978-3-031-87880-0_14

and the performance. As a result, software engineers face a difficult choice, being confronted with a plenitude of solutions offering diverse features and characteristics that need to be matched to the specific requirements.

The following paper extends our previous results of Node.js application performance tests [20] by elaborating on the development, usage and performance analysis of Gocannon, a custom, purpose-built tool for measuring changes in HTTP application performance over time under load, which has been developed to address the limitations of other popular testing utilities. Secondly, we present a more comprehensive analysis of selected Node.js backend application frameworks, discussing the observed variations in the performance characteristics under sustained load and explaining them by analyzing Node.js internals. Lastly, following feedback received when presenting the original conference paper, we formulate additional practical recommendations for performance testing of Node.js applications.

## 2 Background

Certain aspect of Node.js internal implementation may be relevant to the performance characteristics of applications executed in that runtime environment. This section describes selected details of the Node.js's architecture that may have a direct or indirect impact on performance. Specifically, we focus on the event loop concurrency model, hidden classes, inline caching and selective machine code generation.

At a higher level, Node.js uses Google's V8 JavaScript engine initially developed for Chrome and Chromium web browsers, supplemented by a standard library and an event loop implementation. The following subsections discuss selected components and optimization techniques used within Node.js.

### *2.1 Event Loop Concurrency Model*

Traditional web servers employ a *thread-per-connection model*, in which the main thread listens for incoming connections, and each connection is off-loaded to a separate thread for processing. This approach allows the developer for writing sequential, blocking operations, which are isolated per connection, making code easier to develop and debug. However, this model may not scale under load, as each active connection requires a separate thread to be managed by the operating system.

The event loop concurrency model addresses the shortcomings of the thread-per-connection model. Instead of spawning a separate thread per connection, this model awaits for changes across all connections and processes them in a single thread. This requires a different set of OS-level primitives for I/O multiplexing, such as `epoll` in Linux, `kqueue` in MacOS or I/O Completion ports in Windows.

Using `epoll`, a server can replace all connection threads with a single thread. Any operation that would otherwise be a blocking call (such as a database query) is executed asynchronously and once it is completed, its results are processed sequentially in an event loop iteration.

However, the event loop model increases implementation complexity due to the need for tracking the execution state of each asynchronous operation. This is especially true for runtime environments like Node.js, which execute arbitrary code and need to maintain the execution context of each asynchronous operation.

In Node.js, the event loop implementation is provided by Libuv. This library written in C abstracts platform-specific asynchronous I/O operations, reducing OS-specific branching within Node.js source code [13]. Libuv employs two main abstractions: *handles* and *requests*. Handles represent long-lived resources, like TCP sockets or child processes, while requests denote short-lived operations like file I/O and DNS resolution.

The libuv event loop runs in seven phases [4]. Each iteration begins with updating the loop timestamp and processing callbacks scheduled by JavaScript timeouts and intervals. Then, three groups of callbacks and handles are executed, which are predominantly used by low-level code in an Aspect-Oriented-Programming manner. The fifth phase involves waiting for I/O operations through `epoll_wait`, after which corresponding JavaScript callbacks are executed. This is followed by invoking check handles and close callbacks. If no active handles or requests remain, the program exits; otherwise, the next event loop iteration begins.

## 2.2 The V8 JavaScript Engine

The V8 JavaScript engine is embedded in Node.js as its largest dependency. It provides a runtime environment in which JavaScript code is parsed, executed and optimized and implements the ECMAScript language standard.

The V8 engine consists of numerous modules working towards parsing, executing and optimizing the JavaScript that is provided to it as an input by the process in which the V8 is embedded. The incoming source code is first parsed in order to produce an abstract syntax tree, which is later translated into bytecode by the Ignition module. During bytecode execution, various metrics are being collected based on which the V8 might decide to optimize a particular unit of code using the Turbofan module.

## 2.3 Hidden Classes

In a statically typed programming language, each object type has a fixed set of properties of a known size. As a consequence, accessing object properties can be done very efficiently by applying an appropriate offset to the object's pointer. This can be achieved thanks to the fact that the compiler is aware of the properties that exist within an object of a particular type and therefore can generate fixed offsets for each property at compile time, resulting in the values of properties (or pointers to said properties) being stored as a contiguous buffer.

By contrast, in a dynamically typed language like JavaScript, properties can be added to and removed from any object at runtime, which renders it impossible to access them via a fixed memory offset. In order to solve that problem, objects in a dynamically typed languages are often implemented as hashmaps, where the key is the name of the property and the value is the value is the value of that particular property. Such a solution introduces a significant performance overhead when accessing a given property (which is referred to as *dynamic lookup*) alongside resulting in an increased memory footprint.

To bypass the performance cost of dynamic property lookup at runtime, the V8 engine employs a technique called *hidden classes*, originally introduced in the Self programming language [2]. While unrelated to classes in OOP sense, they are attached to JavaScript objects and convey information about *object shape*, also referred to as *object layout*.

The main idea of hidden classes is to create a structure resembling a fixed layout of an object similar to that used in a statically typed language, except for doing it at runtime. Each hidden class contains information regarding at what offsets the properties of an object assigned to that hidden class are located. Additionally, a hidden class may contain class transition information, which keeps track of what other hidden classes shall be used if a given property was to be added to an existing object.

## 2.4 Inline Caching

Usage of hidden classes in the V8 JavaScript engine enables implementation of one of the most important optimization techniques called *inline caching*. This technique was first introduced in the Smalltalk-80 programming language [5] and is based on an observation that subsequent calls to a given function tend to have repeating object shapes in the set of parameters passed to that function. If such pattern is detected in the metrics collected at runtime, the compiler/interpreter can make speculative assumptions about a hidden class of a given parameter and cache the result of a relatively expensive operation that is going to be identical for every object with the same class (i.e., determining the offset of a particular property).

Inline caching in V8 identifies and monitors sites within the Ignition bytecode where object properties are accessed or modified. These sites, known as IC Slots or Object Access Sites, are tracked in the Feedback Vector or ICVector, which logs hidden class information observed during function executions. Each IC slot, categorized as LOAD (access) or STORE (modification), can exist in one of five states: uninitialised, pre-monomorphic, monomorphic, polymorphic, or megamorphic. When an IC slot reaches the monomorphic state, it caches the property offset from the object's hidden class. This cached information significantly speeds up subsequent property accesses or modifications for objects of the same hidden class, enhancing the efficiency of repeated object interactions.

## *2.5 Selective Machine Code Generation with Turbofan*

Turbofan is the optimizing compiler of the V8 JavaScript engine. Its main responsibility is to selectively compile Ignition bytecode into significantly more performant machine code. The V8's decision to optimize a given function is based on type feedback collected in the form of previously discussed feedback vectors alongside runtime profiler metrics. The latter are collected by recording the current code location during bytecode execution at a constant interval to estimate how much time is spent interpreting the unoptimized version of a given function, which is a good predictor of the potential savings resulting from compiling that function with Turbofan.

Due to the fact that JavaScript is an expressive language, its specification often allows multiple object types to use the same syntax. A good example of that would the plus (+) operator. Depending on the type of the arguments on both sides, it can be used for, among others, adding numbers, concatenating strings, converting a number to a string and concatenating it with another string, etc. These options, detailed in the ECMAScript specification, require runtime evaluation by the Ignition interpreter, involving numerous type checks and consequently incurring a performance cost. Turbofan optimizes functions using type feedback to make speculative assumptions about object shapes passed as parameters, leading to highly optimized machine code akin to a statically typed language's compilation. This machine code must validate the parameters to ensure their types match Turbofan's assumptions. If a mismatch occurs, the machine code is discarded, and the function resumes execution as Ignition bytecode, a process called *de-optimization*.

## *2.6 The Orinoco Garbage Collector*

JavaScript, being a dynamically typed language, relies on a garbage collector for memory management. This collector, known as Orinoco in the V8 JavaScript engine, uses advanced techniques like incremental, concurrent, and parallel garbage collection to enhance performance by minimizing runtime disruptions. Orinoco categorizes garbage collection into minor GC (scavenging) and major GC. Scavenging is a quick, frequent process targeting young objects, while major GC is more comprehensive and time-consuming.

The V8 heap is segmented into 3 age-based regions: nursery, intermediate, and old generation. Such design choice is justified by the *generational hypothesis*, which states that most objects in a garbage-collected language are short-lived and the small percentage of the ones that aren't tend to persist throughout the entire program execution [26]. Initially, objects are placed in the nursery; if they survive a scavenging phase, they move to the intermediate, and eventually to the old generation if they remain reachable.

This approach should result in the application performance improving over execution time, as long-lived objects are moved into the old-generation segment of the heap, reducing the load of minor GC cycles.

# 3 Related Work

## *3.1 Instrumentation and Collected Metrics*

Apache JMeter is among te most commonly used load testing tools [1, 32]. LoadRunner, another system of similar purpose, was also used in several load testing experiments [6, 12, 16, 27, 38].

Several metrics are in use for analyzing the performance of web applications. Response time, also referred to as *request latency* is the most commonly used. Due to possible measurement noise and resulting bias, the mean or median values are primarily concerned [21, 27, 29], but tail distribution metrics, such as 90th, 95th or 99th percentile, are also in use [11, 15, 16, 33]. Additionally, some works advocate the use of the average number of *requests completed per second* (RPS) as a less complex metric [18, 21, 31]. Apart from latency and RPS, various SUT resource usage metrics related to CPU, memory, or network throughput are also mentioned [12, 14, 16, 27].

## *3.2 Load Testing Environment*

Several works recommend conducting end-to-end load tests in public cloud environments [21] such as AWS EC2 [14] or Microsoft Azure VMs [18] (with VMs located in the same region to reduce latency), which are more representative of where the actual, production instances of a given application are deployed, whereas others use local hardware. Works that deploy the latter solution rely on two machines connected over a local network, one for load generation and another running the SUT [8, 9, 17, 27]. Two variations of that approach have been identified. The first one is *peer-to-peer load testing*, which involves multiple load generation machines targeting a single SUT machine [15, 23], and the other one relies on running the load testing software and the SUT on separate virtual machines within a single underlying hardware [31, 36]. Another option involves deploying the load driver and the SUT application on the same machine [12, 38].

### 3.3 *Good Practices for Load Testing*

The literature has proposed a few good practices regarding methods of executing the load tests and analyzing collected data to foster the reproducibility of performance experiments. Below, we outline the most relevant ones.

- **Model the generated load after real user traffic** [6, 9, 17, 34, 37] by extracting historical data about the past user behavior from web server logs [16, 28].
- **Eliminate noisy neighbors**. Since background processes running alongside SUT affect the results [8], all non-essential services in the VM should be disabled for the test duration [32].
- **Repeat test runs**. Performing multiple test runs strengthens the significance of the results and minimizes potential bias [22, 24].
- **Ensue a fixed CPU clock**. To ensure consistent hardware performance throughout the load test, Turbo Boost features should be disabled and CPU clock should be fixed [15].

## 4 Approach

### 4.1 *Research Questions and Hypothesis*

In this work, we aim to answer the following questions:

RQ 1. What are the performance differences among applications developed using various Node.js backend frameworks in different scenarios?
RQ 2. Do Node.js backend applications improve their performance characteristics over time under sustained load?

Given that various V8 optimization techniques presented in Sect. 2 are being incrementally applied by the Node.js runtime environment, we conjecture that the performance of subject SUTs may improve over time under sustained load. Still, individual characteristics would differ for specific frameworks.

### 4.2 *Experimental Setup*

To compare the relative performance of Node.js application frameworks, we used a *synthetic benchmarking* model. Instead of creating real-world applications with simulated workloads modeled after actual users' behavior, synthetic benchmarking tests various functions of the SUT independently, in isolation. In this paper, such an approach relied on identifying a set of functions shared by all the tested frameworks (e.g., sending HTTP responses, request validation, or error handling) and performing a series of load tests against SUTs implemented using each framework.

In the study, we used the following testing scenarios that included repeated calls of dedicated backend application HTTP endpoints:

- *Static JSON*—responding with a static JSON payload (measuring the framework's performance in request routing, response writing, and JSON serialization).
- *Fibonacci*—responding with a recursively computed value of the 23rd element of the Fibonacci sequence, simulating a computationally intensive request.
- *Redis*—retrieving a single key from a local Redis database instance over a TCP connection and sending it back to the client to simulate asynchronous I/O workload.
- *Error*—reading a parameter from the request path and performing a forced division-by-zero operation if the parameter value is 1 (resulting in HTTP response with code 500, thus testing framework-specific exception handling.
- *Validation*—checking if the query string contains two keys (integer and a string with a minimum length of 5 to test the framework's built-in request validation capabilities).

## *4.3 Subject Frameworks*

Due to a large variety of Node.js backend application frameworks being in use, we identified the most relevant ones by evaluating their *popularity*, measured via the number of GitHub stars and npm package downloads, *versatility*—by preferring general-purpose frameworks over domain-specific ones, and the *availability of documentation* and other resources helpful in developing of SUT applications.

Finally, we tested the following frameworks:

- Express.js—a popular, unopinionated, minimal, and flexible framework;
- hapi—which focuses on security, simplicity, and stability.
- Fastify—a relatively new (first released in late 2016) performance-first framework inspired by Express and hapi.
- NestJS—a framework built top of Express.js (with optional Fastify adapter) inspired by Spring and Angular.
- AdonisJS—an all-in-one web application framework that uses the Model-View-Controller pattern and relies on a custom HTTP server implementation.
- Feathers—a framework that combines Service-Oriented Architecture with Aspect-Oriented Programming.

Furthermore, to put the obtained performance metrics into perspective, we developed two additional SUT applications exposing the same HTTP API: one in the Go programming language (using the Gin framework) and another in Python (using the Flask framework).

## 4.4 Tooling

The choice of a tool may significantly impact results in performance-related analyses. Initially, we considered Apache JMeter for that purpose due to its popularity. However, a pilot experiment that allowed for comparing JMeter's metrics with those obtained via WRK [10] (another popular, low-overhead HTTP benchmarking utility) indicated that WRK delivered a 134% increase in the number of requests per second generated against the Go/Gin SUT in the static JSON load testing scenario compared with JMeter, which was a strong indication of its bottlenecking.

Unfortunately, WRK lacks a more robust statistics collection functionality. Upon each HTTP response received, the only data retained regarding that request is its latency, which is saved in a global latency histogram using an atomic increment operation to ensure thread safety. Consequently, it is not possible to track changes in SUT performance over time using WRK. In an effort to mitigate that functional limitation, we have decided to create a purpose-built load-testing tool from scratch.

Due to previously discussed performance limitations of JMeter as well as the functional limitations of WRK, Gocannon was created [19]. The programming language chosen for its implementation was Go, as goroutines allowed for relatively easy development of multi-threading features while relying on efficient, epoll-based I/O features delivered by the underlying runtime. On top of that, Go, being a lower-level, performance-focused language, was an additional factor motivating its choice.

One key design characteristic that differentiates Gocannon from other low-overhead HTTP load testing tools such as WRK, Autocannon [3] or Bombardier [7] is the fact that similarly to JMeter, it saves the complete data of each request (its starting and ending timestamps, HTTP code and identifier of the connection via which it was sent) in a *request log* instead of storing just the request latencies in a histogram. Numerous optimization techniques were used during the development of Gocannon to ensure adequate performance despite the introduction of extra functionality. Its core design relies on creating a separate goroutine for each connection (a total number of which can be specified by the user) at program startup. Each goroutine has its own *slice* representing the request log. A slice in Go is a lightweight abstraction over an array, somewhat similar to `std::vector` in C++. Whenever exceeding the capacity of the underlying array, a slice is copied to a different place on the heap with double its previous capacity in a process called *slice re-allocation*. Each spawned goroutine keeps sending a request to the specified HTTP endpoint in a loop until a pre-calculated load test end timestamp is reached. Storing completed request data in a goroutine-local slice allows for writing new responses synchronization-free, as no additional steps are needed to ensure thread safety. On top of that, request log slices can be pre-allocated with user-defined capacity using the `-preallocate` flag. This optimization technique ensures that slice re-allocation will not happen during the load test, potentially impairing performance. Additionally, instead of using the standard `net/http` package, `fasthttp` was used, as its HTTP client performance was demonstrated to be up to 10 times better [35]. One key optimization enabling such performance uplift comes from reusing the request objects between multiple requests to reduce the pressure on the Go's garbage collector.

When developing Gocannon, extensive testing was conducted, achieving an overall coverage of 78.3% of statements in all packages. Integration/system tests included the creation of a mock HTTP server, against which a Gocannon instance was conducting a load test while collecting performance metrics with three different methods simultaneously: the request log, latency histogram (similar to that of WRK or Autocannon), and atomic increment request counters. To pass the tests, all three methods had to obtain equal results.

The performance of Gocannon was then compared with that of WRK and Apache JMeter (version 5.4.1) by conducting load tests against selected endpoints of SUTs implemented in Go with the Gin framework and in Node.js using Fastify. To ensure a fair comparison, Gocannon was invoked with `GOMAXPROCS` environment variable set to 3, WRK was started with two worker threads (with a third one responsible for collecting statistics), and JMeter was limited to 3 logical CPUs using the Linux `taskset` command. The maximum number of concurrent connections in each load-testing tool was 100. Following the documentation's advice, JMeter was executed in CLI mode, and each test run was repeated 10 times. The results illustrated by Fig. 1 indicate that WRK and Gocannon achieved near-identical performance in all tests despite Gocannon's more elaborate request logging features. The number of requests per second generated by JMeter in less demanding tests was 5–10% lower than the corresponding rates obtained using Gocannon and WRK. The performance gap widens significantly in more demanding tests, in which the SUT applications achieved throughput exceeding 20k requests per second. The amount of HTTP load generated by JMeter flatlines at about 17k requests per second, indicating bottlenecking.

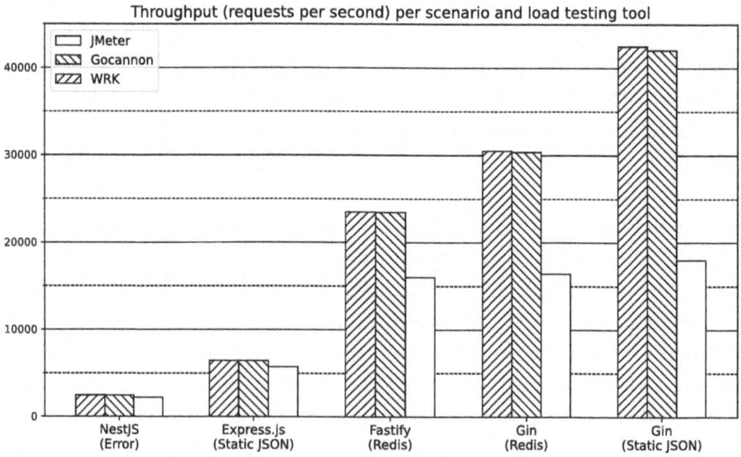


**Fig. 1** Comparison of JMeter load generation performance with WRK and Gocannon

### 4.5 *Testing Procedure*

The entire load-testing procedure was automated using a bash script. A series of previously described scenarios were carried out for each tested backend application (seven Node.js programs, one compiled Go binary, and one Python project). Each testing scenario (out of five total) was repeated ten times. During the test, Gocannon, the SUT, and a Redis database instance were running on a single machine.

Additional measures were undertaken to ensure constant hardware performance over the entire duration of the load test. These included disabling Intel Turbo Boost, Enhanced Intel SpeedStep Technology, and frequency scaling via Linux `cpupower` package (to ensure a constant CPU clock at 4 GHz). To confirm that the Redis instance is not becoming a bottleneck, we ran a verification test using the *redis-benchmark* utility, which showed that without instruction pipelining, the system could sustain 130K key lookups per second.

## 5 Results and Discussion

### 5.1 *Comparison of Node.js Backend Application Frameworks Performance*

Results showing the number of requests per second handled are presented in Table 1. Subject frameworks are given in rows, while test scenarios are in columns. Time is a mean value of 10 runs, as designed in Sect. 4. Additionally, the results are presented in Fig. 2, to facilitate comparisons between the frameworks and in different test scenarios. Based on that, we provide an answer to RQ1. Details and possible explanations for the observed results are further discussed in Sect. 5.2.

The examined application frameworks can be divided into two groups. The first one contains Express and two other frameworks that use it as a dependency, NestJS, and Feathers, which all had rather poor performance metrics compared to other

**Table 1** Mean number of requests per second by framework and load testing scenario

| Framework | Static JSON | Fibonacci | Redis | Validation | Error |
|---|---|---|---|---|---|
| Flask (Python) | 2159.78 | 148.79 | 1954.79 | 2047.19 | 1655.90 |
| Feathers | 3158.17 | 1469.11 | 3506.55 | 3056.99 | 2571.10 |
| NestJS (Express) | 5303.64 | 1788.35 | 5843.45 | 4342.29 | 2384.03 |
| Express | 5850.01 | 1858.43 | 6264.94 | 4284.94 | 5388.53 |
| AdonisJS | 19,395.50 | 2533.78 | 17,051.89 | 9820.35 | 6292.51 |
| Hapi | 21,782.20 | 2566.75 | 21,731.95 | 15,945.76 | 9314.06 |
| NestJS (Fastify) | 22,597.08 | 2432.39 | 22,348.36 | 15,721.51 | 4110.02 |
| Fastify | 25,737.06 | 2571.89 | 22,976.41 | 23,539.39 | 11,484.62 |
| Gin (Go) | 42,039.97 | 5743.55 | 29,731.90 | 34,242.94 | 1521.76 |

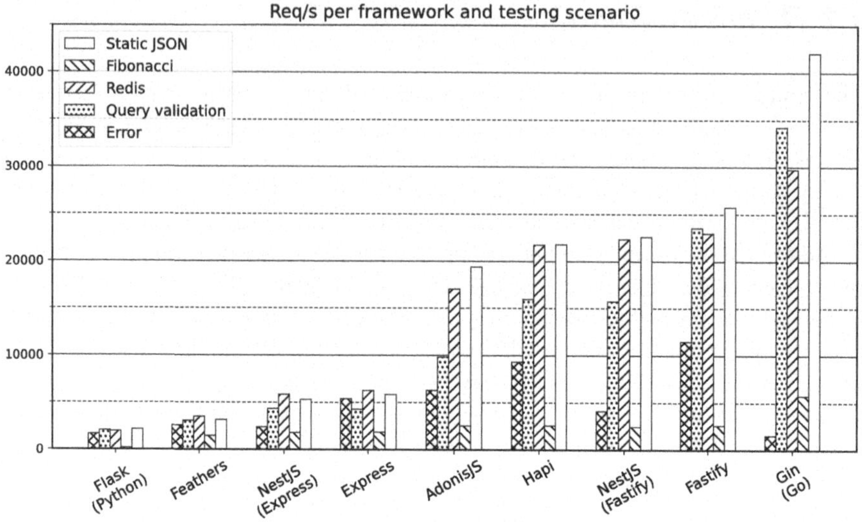


**Fig. 2** Mean number of completed requests per second by framework and load testing scenario

SUTs. As expected, both frameworks based on Express performed worse than that of pure Express SUT due to the additional overhead they introduced. The other group consists of frameworks, including AdonisJS, Hapi, NestJS (with the Fastify adapter), and Fastify itself, that have considerably better execution performance in all testing scenarios than the first group.

Despite JavaScript being a dynamically typed programming language, the most performant Node.js SUTs managed to sustain significant load even when compared to a backend application implemented in Go, a statically typed, compiled language. Most notably, the Fastify SUT in the Redis load testing scenario was only 23% behind Gin in the average number of served requests per second (22,976 vs. 29,731 requests per second). On the opposite side of the performance spectrum, Python with Flask achieved the worst performance out of all examined frameworks in four out of five load-testing scenarios.

## 5.2 *Framework Performance in Different Scenarios*

A majority of SUT implementations managed to serve the highest number of requests per second in the static JSON load testing scenario, with the Go/Gin backend application achieving just over 42 thousand req/s. In the Fibonacci load testing scenario, the performance gap between Node.js SUTs implemented in different frameworks shrinks, as the same CPU-intensive operations performed when handling that API endpoint across all frameworks outweigh the latency introduced by Express HTTP server implementation used by the previously identified, less performant group of frameworks. Differences in the number of requests per second served by the more performant Node.js SUTs are negligible, as the slowest framework from the group (AdonisJS) achieved results within 5% of the fastest one (Fastify). Following previously stated expectations, given the performance limitations of Python in CPU-intensive tasks, the baseline Flask SUT implementation achieved rather poor results in the discussed load testing scenario, with the average number of served requests per second 10 times lower than that of the slowest Node.js backend application implemented using Feathers. Conversely, the Gin implementation, considering that Go is a compiled, statically-typed programming language, served over 120% more requests in the Fibonacci load test than the most performant Node.js SUT implemented using the Fastify framework.

Particular attention shall be drawn to the results of the Redis test, as it is the only load-testing scenario that requires completing an asynchronous I/O operation before responding to the incoming request. The values of the requests per second metric achieved by each framework in that test are correlated with those obtained in the static JSON test. Surprisingly, all three slower Node.js frameworks (Express, Feathers, and NestJS with Express) achieved a greater number of req/s in the Redis test than in the static JSON test.

In the query string validation test, Fastify's built-in schema validation functionality based on `ajv` emerged as the most efficient among the tested Node.js backend frameworks. Despite employing different request validation libraries, Hapi and NestJS with Fastify adapter (using `joi` and `class-validator` respectively) produced similar results. NestJS's validation solution is not only more declarative but also outperforms AdonisJS. The built-in validator of AdonisJS achieved just over half the requests per second served by the same SUT in the static JSON load test, indicating significant overhead in the validation process.

The error handling load testing scenario results indicate that Express.js, despite its poor overall performance in comparison with other frameworks, doesn't appear to introduce significant overhead when handling errors, as the number of requests per second served in the error test was only 8% lower than that obtained in the static JSON test. On the other hand, NestJS appears to introduce significant overhead into error handling, as its performance in that test is significantly worse than that achieved in high-throughput load testing scenarios such as Redis test and static JSON test. Such performance degradation in the error handling test was observed when NestJS was used with Fastify and Express as the underlying HTTP server implementation. This indicates that the internal implementation of exception filter framework functionality causes it.

An intriguing finding is that the SUT implemented in Go with the Gin framework served the fewest requests per second in the error test despite outperforming the other four load-testing scenarios. Such difference may be attributed to Go's distinctive error-handling model. Unlike JavaScript, Java, and C#, which all use `try/catch` blocks for error handling, Go encourages returning errors instead of throwing them, leveraging the fact that the language supports multiple return values. Since some failures, such as division by zero, can still occur without an error value being returned, the Go runtime may also encounter a *panic*, which halts function execution. During a panic, a deferred recover call `recover()` may retrieve the error that caused the panic and prevent the process from terminating.

The Gin framework uses `recover()` in its error-handling middleware. If an error-causing panic is recovered, the stack trace is logged using a custom function that iterates over the stack frames and reads their content with `ioutil.ReadFile()`. Given the performance anomaly in the error handling test might be due to the panic/recover runtime behavior or Gin's unique error logging method, a modified Go SUT was created. This employed a custom recovery middleware responding only with an HTTP 500 code to error-inducing requests, bypassing stack trace printing. This revised application was performance-tested in the error-handling scenario. After 10 test runs, an average number of 42,381 requests per second served by the SUT was obtained, which is a strong indication that panic/recovery behavior does not introduce noticeable overhead in and of itself and that the observed performance anomaly of the initial SUT can be attributed to a rather resource-intensive traversal of the stack performed by Gin's error recovery middleware.

## 5.3 *Changes in Application Performance Over Time Under Sustained Load*

To investigate RQ 2 stated in Sect. 4.1, the data was processed to visualize changes in request latency throughout load test runs. As depicted in Fig. 3, during the load test, no substantial changes were observed in the request latency distribution in the Redis testing scenario executed against a Go/Gin SUT. Similar time characteristics were observed in other load tests performed on the Go/Gin SUT. We can conclude that in the case of the SUT implemented using the Gin framework, no noticeable fluctuations in request latency distribution over the load test duration were observed, and the application throughput remained stable.

The other baseline SUT implementation, implemented using Python in conjunction with the Flask microframework, exhibits similar behavior under load to that of the Go backend application, albeit with a considerable performance gap. While the

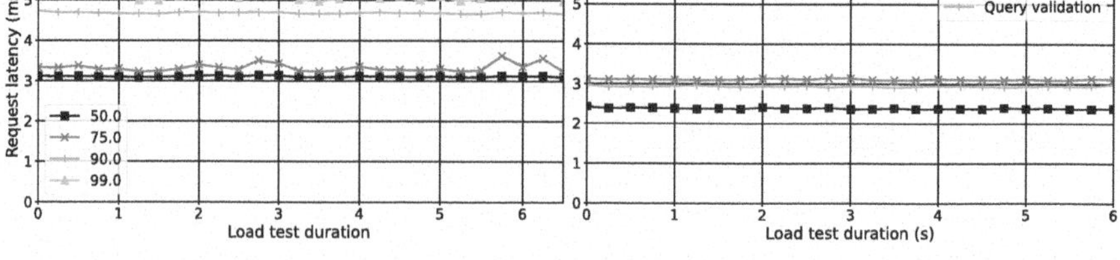


**Fig. 3** Performance metrics of the Go (Gin) SUT in selected testing scenarios

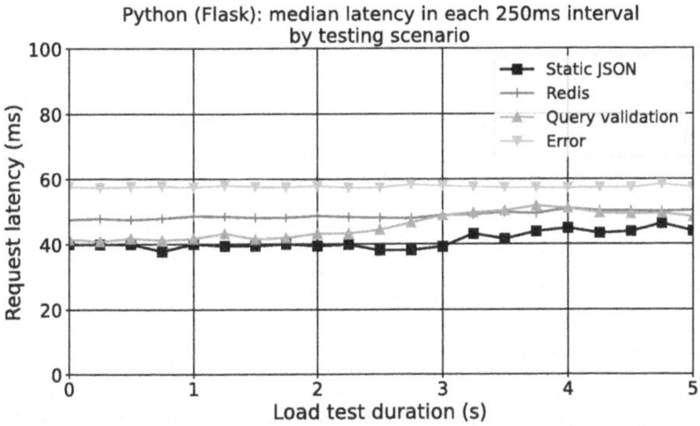


**Fig. 4** Median response time overload test duration of the Python/Flask SUT in four load testing scenarios

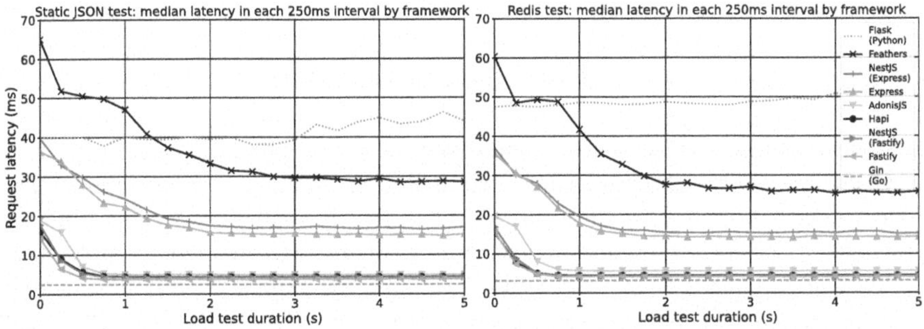


**Fig. 5** Median request latency over the Static JSON/Redis load test duration by Node.js framework

obtained request latencies visualized by Fig. 4 exhibit some minor fluctuations over the load test duration, especially when compared with near-perfectly straight graph lines of the Go/Gin SUT, these can be attributed to the fact the Python application served at least 15 times lower number of requests per second in all tests except for the error handling one as compared with the Go/Gin SUT. Consequently, there was a significantly lower number of requests completed in each 250 ms interval, distributions of which were calculated and visualized compared to the Go/Gin backend application.

Unlike SUTs implemented in Go and Python, the ones developed using Node.js frameworks exhibit a noticeable request latency decrease throughout the load test. In the Redis load testing scenario, results of which are presented in Fig. 5, all seven SUTs show a considerable decrease in median request latency since the beginning of the load test. It appears within a group of three frameworks previously categorized as delivering high performance (Fastify, Hapi and NestJS with Fastify adapter); their request latency stabilizes after about 750 milliseconds of the load test, whereas less performant frameworks based on Express.js take about 2.5 seconds

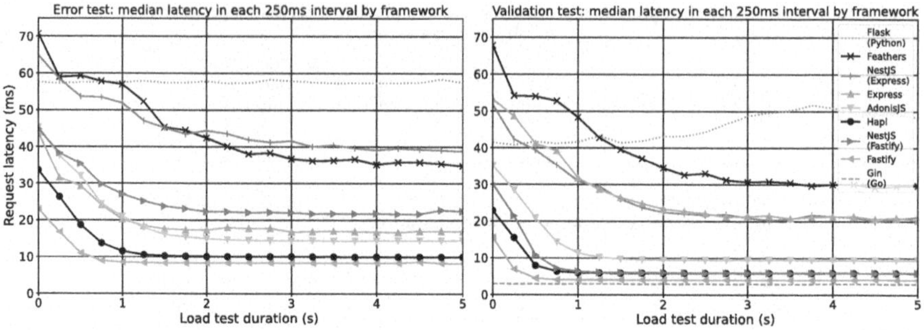


**Fig. 6** Median request latency over the error/validation load test duration by Node.js framework

before reaching stable latency throughout the remaining duration of the load test. A similar trend can be observed in the results of the static JSON load testing scenario (Fig. 6).

In the error handling load tests, Express.js showed minimal overhead, with an 8% drop in requests per second, compared to the static JSON test. However, NestJS exhibited significant performance drops in this scenario, regardless of whether it used Fastify or Express, pointing to the impact of its exception filters.

Given the observed performance anomalies of Node.js backend application frameworks, which confirm the previously stated hypothesis, we can formulate practical advice for server-side JavaScript developers. One area where application performance changes over time under load may be critical is high-throughput environments, in which numerous application instances are placed behind a load balancer to ensure horizontal scalability and high availability. Most load balancer implementations rely on one of two algorithms: Round-Robin and Least-Connections [25]. The former cycles through available instances in a set order, while the latter opts for the instance with the fewest in-flight requests. Since Node.js backends tend to improve performance under sustained load, new instances may initially struggle to handle incoming requests compared to warmed-up instances. Consequently, Least-Connections could be favored to prevent overloading new instances.

Another practical recommendation is related to the load-testing methodology of such applications when attempting to establish the maximum throughput they can sustain. Because for a certain amount of time, after the application starts to be hit with high HTTP load, its request latency appears to decrease before flat-lining, long-lasting load tests can be recommended over short ones to minimize the impact of such initial process warm-up period on the overall metrics.

Finally, for latency-critical applications requiring their time characteristics to remain stable over the entire process lifetime without allowing for any warm-up period just after its startup, choosing a different technology than Node.js for its implementation may be preferred over alternative solutions.

## 6 Threats to Validity

Some concerns in the area of *conclusion validity* arise from using Gocannon, as opposed to well-established load testing utilities. As discussed in Sect. 4.4, the decision to develop Gocannon was made after carefully evaluating the available alternatives and concluding that JMeter offers inadequate performance and is susceptible to bottlenecking the SUT applications in some scenarios. Given that low-overhead alternatives failed to track performance changes throughout load tests, they were unsuitable for testing the stated hypothesis. Extensive source code test coverage was achieved to mitigate validity threats from using Gocannon, and its load test results were compared with those from WRK. Additional steps were taken to minimize anomalies in the performance metrics, including hardware and software configuration adjustments to ensure consistent performance throughout each test run.

Concerning *internal validity*, the observed improvement in Node.js backend performance over the load test duration may not necessarily result from the V8 JavaScript engine's runtime optimizations. To address this issue, two additional systems under test (SUTs) were implemented in Go and Python and subjected to the same testing procedures as the Node.js systems. Given that neither the Go nor Python SUTs showed the hypothesized anomalies, the performance improvement in Node.js under sustained load can be attributed to V8's runtime optimization techniques, such as the selective machine code generation of the Turbofan module.

Multiple load testing scenarios were designed and conducted to generalize the results beyond the experimental settings and thus reduce study *external validity threats*. Since all of the examined Node.js frameworks exhibited a similar tendency to improve their performance metrics over the first seconds of the load test in every load testing scenario, such performance anomaly is likely inherent to Node.js backend applications.

Additional considerations need to be addressed regarding the *construct validity threats* of the study. During the development of the SUT applications, we adhered to best practices established by the framework's creators and primarily selected external libraries from within the framework's ecosystem. It is important to note that the SUT applications' resemblance to real-world backend programs was somewhat compromised by opting for a synthetic benchmarking approach. This choice helped eliminate potential variables that could skew results, as detailed in Sect. 4. However, we recognize performing similar experiments on real-world SUTs as a potential direction for future research.

## 7 Conclusions

In this study, we examined a number of JavaScript frameworks in several testing scenarios to evaluate their performance.

One of the key findings is that Express.js, despite its vast popularity, delivers poor performance in comparison to more modern, low-overhead alternatives. Express.js's under-performance has important ramifications for other Node.js application frameworks, which use it as an underlying dependency for network operations. As expected, both SUTs developed with frameworks built atop Express.js (NestJS and Feathers) in this study showed worse performance metrics than pure Express SUTs.

On the other hand, Fastify, Hapi, and AdonisJS demonstrated substantial load resistance, even against an equivalent SUT written in Go—a statically typed, compiled language. Interestingly, NestJS can optionally use Fastify instead of Express as an HTTP server. This choice significantly improved performance, placing NestJS SUT metrics within a single-digit percentage of pure Fastify application metrics in certain scenarios. This outcome is remarkable, considering NestJS's numerous abstractions aiming to facilitate backend application development through a convention-over-configuration approach. The only significant performance degradation caused by NestJS's functionality occurred in the error-handling scenario.

Another fully featured framework that has been shown to deliver good performance is AdonisJS. Unlike other MVC frameworks available within the Node.js ecosystem, which are often built on top of Express.js, AdonisJS uses its own HTTP server implementation, which allows it to outperform Express.js by a considerable margin.

The results also provide an answer to RQ 2: the performance of Node.js backend applications generally improves over time under sustained load. SUTs implemented in all of the examined frameworks exhibited this tendency in all load-testing scenarios. The fact that such performance anomalies were not observed in baseline Python and Go SUT implementations strongly indicates that the observed peculiarity is, as previously hypothesized, related to Node.js runtime optimization techniques used by the V8 JavaScript engine.

Based on the results, we formulated the following recommendations that could be used by Node.js backend application developers:

- If low request latency and high throughput is a strict requirement, the use of Express.js and other frameworks that use it as an underlying dependency in favor of Fastify, Hapi, AdonisJS, or NestJS (with the optional Fastify adapter) should be avoided;
- When developing a backend application in the NestJS framework, we advise using the Fastify adapter instead of the default Express HTTP server implementation.
- We also advise using the least-connections load balancing algorithm instead of the round-robin when deploying them behind a load balancer in an effort to prevent newly-spawned instances from becoming overloaded.
- When developing performance testing suites for Node.js applications, we recommend tracking changes in application performance metrics throughout the load test duration and not just their average values.
- Finally, we recommend avoiding Node.js for latency-critical applications that require consistent performance throughout the entire process lifetime, particularly those that cannot accommodate an initial warm-up period under reduced load after application startup.

## References


1. Abbas, R., Sultan, Z., & Bhatti, S. N. (2017). Comparative analysis of automated load testing tools: Apache JMeter, Microsoft Visual Studio (TFS), LoadRunner, Siege. In *2017 International Conference on Communication Technologies (ComTech)* (pp. 39–44).
2. Chambers, C., Ungar, D., & Lee, E. (1989). An efficient implementation of SELF a dynamically-typed object-oriented language based on prototypes. *ACM SIGPLAN Notice, 24*(10), 49–70. https://doi.org/10.1145/74878.74884
3. Collina, M., et al. (2021). AutoCannon - fast HTTP/1.1 benchmarking tool written in Node.js. https://github.com/mcollina/autocannonversion7.4.0
4. Contributors, Libuv. (2021). Libuv Documentation: Design Overview. Retrieved August 12, 2021, from http://docs.libuv.org/en/v1.x/design.html
5. Deutsch, L. P., & Schiffman, A. M. (1984). Efficient implementation of the smalltalk-80 system. In *Proceedings of the 11th ACM SIGACT-SIGPLAN Symposium on Principles of Programming Languages. POPL '84. Salt Lake City, Utah* (pp. 297–302). Association for Computing Machinery. https://doi.org/10.1145/800017.800542
6. Draheim, D., Grundy, J., Hosking, J., Lutteroth, C., & Weber, G. (2006). Realistic load testing of Web applications. In *Conference on Software Maintenance and Reengineering (CSMR'06)* (pp. 11–70).
7. Fedoseyev, M. (2020). Bombardier - fast cross-platform HTTP benchmarking tool written in Go, version 1.2.5. https://github.com/codesenberg/bombardier
8. Gao, R., & Jiang, Z. M. (2017). An exploratory study on assessing the impact of environment variations on the results of load tests. In *2017 IEEE/ACM 14th International Conference on Mining Software Repositories (MSR)* (pp. 379–390).
9. Gao, R., Jiang, Z. M., Barna, C., & Litoiu, M. (2016). A framework to evaluate the effectiveness of different load testing analysis techniques. In *2016 IEEE International Conference on Software Testing, Verification and Validation (ICST)* (pp. 22–32).
10. Glozer, W. (2018). WRK - modern HTTP benchmarking tool. Version 4.1.0. https://github.com/wg/wrk
11. Grossman, D., McCabe, M., Staton, C., Bailey, B., Frieder, O., & Roberts, D. (1996). Performance testing a large finance application. *IEEE Software, 13*(5), 50–54.
12. Hamed, O., & Kafri, N. (2009). Performance testing for web based application architectures (.NET vs. Java EE). In *2009 First International Conference on Networked Digital Technologies* (pp. 218–224).
13. Ihrig, C. (2019). Introduction to libuv: What's a Unicorn Velociraptor? In *Node.js Interactive Conference*. https://www.youtube.com/watch?v=_c51fcXRLGw
14. Imre, G., Charaf, H., & Lengyel, L. (2013). Performance analysis of a java web application running on amazon EC2. eng. *Acta Electrotechnica et Informatica, 13*(4), 32–39.
15. Kasture, H., & Sanchez, D. (2016). Tailbench: A benchmark suite and evaluation methodology for latency-critical applications. In *2016 IEEE International Symposium on Workload Characterization (IISWC)* (pp. 1–10).
16. Khan, R., & Amjad, M. (2016). Smoke testing of web application based on ALM tool. In *2016 International Conference on Computing, Communication and Automation (ICCCA)* (pp. 862–866).
17. Khan, R., & Amjad, M. (2016). Web application's performance testing using HP LoadRunner and CA Wily introscope tools. In *2016 International Conference on Computing, Communication and Automation (ICCCA)* (pp. 802–806).
18. Kolic, K., Gusev, M., & Ristov, S. (2015). Performance analysis of a new cloud e-Business solution. In: *2015 38th International Convention on Information and Communication Technology, Electronics and Microelectronics (MIPRO)* (pp. 263–268).
19. Kuffel, P. (2022). *Gocannon - Performance-focused HTTP benchmarking tool*, version 1.3.0. https://github.com/kffl/gocannon

20. Kuffel, P., & Walter, B. (2024). Performance of Node.Js backend application frameworks. An empirical evaluation. In B. Marcinkowski, A. Przybylek, A. Jarzebowicz, N. Iivari, E. Insfrán, M. Lang, H. Linger, & C. Schneider (Eds.), *Harnessing Opportunities: Reshaping ISD in the Post-COVID-19 and Generative AI Era (ISD2024 Proceedings), Gdańsk, Poland, August 26–28 2024*. University of Gdánsk/ Association for Information Systems. https://aisel.aisnet.org/isd2014/proceedings2024/managingdevops/7
21. Lenka, R. K., Rani Dey, M., Bhanse, P., & Barik, R. K. (2018). Performance and load testing: Tools and challenges. In *2018 International Conference on Recent Innovations in Electrical, Electronics Communication Engineering (ICRIEECE)* (pp. 2257–2261).
22. Malik, H., Hemmati, H., & Hassan, A. E. (2013). Automatic detection of performance deviations in the load testing of large scale systems. In *2013 35th International Conference on Software Engineering (ICSE)* (pp. 1012–1021).
23. Meira, J. A., Almeida, E. C. D., Le Traon, Y., & Sunye, G. (2012). Peer-to-peer load testing. In *2012 IEEE Fifth International Conference on Software Testing, Verification and Validation* (pp. 642–647).
24. Mukherjee, J., Wang, M., & Krishnamurthy, D. (2014). Performance testing web applications on the cloud. In *2014 IEEE Seventh International Conference on Software Testing, Verification and Validation Workshops* (pp. 363–369).
25. Mustafa, M. E. (2017). Load balancing algorithms round-robin (RR), least-connection, and least loaded efficiency. *Computer Science & Telecommunications, 51*(1), 255–257.
26. Paz, H., Petrank, E., & Blackburn, S. M. (2005). Age-oriented concurrent garbage collection. In *International Conference on Compiler Construction* (pp. 121–136). Springer.
27. Pu, Y., & Xu, M. (2009). Load testing for web applications. In *2009 First International Conference on Information Science and Engineering* (pp. 2954–2957).
28. Quan, X., & Lu, L. (2010). Session-based performance test case generation for Web applications. In *2010 8th International Conference on Supply Chain Management and Information* (pp. 1–7).
29. Singh, M., & Singh, R. (2012). Load testing of web frameworks. In *2012 2nd IEEE International Conference on Parallel, Distributed and Grid Computing* (pp. 592–596).
30. Stack Overflow Annual Developer Survey (2022). Retrieved April 18, 2023 from, https://insights.stackoverflow.com/survey/
31. Stamenov, D., Venov, D., & Gusev, M. (2018). Scalability performance evaluation of the E-Ambulance software service. In *2018 41st International Convention on Information and Communication Technology, Electronics and Microelectronics (MIPRO)* (pp. 0324–0329).
32. Suffian, M. D. M., & Fahrurazi, F. R. (2012). Performance testing: Analyzing differences of response time between performance testing tools. In *2012 International Conference on Computer Information Science (ICCIS)* (vol. 2, pp. 919–923).
33. Tran, P., Gosper, J., & Gorton, I. (2023). Evaluating the sustained performance of COTS-based messaging systems. *Software Testing, Verification and Reliability, 13*(4), 229–240.
34. Trubiani, C., Bran, A., van Hoorn, A., Avritzer, A., & Knoche, H. (2018). Exploiting load testing and profiling for performance antipattern detection. *Information and Software Technology, 95*, 329–345. https://www.sciencedirect.com/science/article/pii/S0950584917302276
35. Valialkin, A. (2021). Fasthttp package, version 1.26.0. https://github.com/valyala/fasthttp
36. Vögele, C., van Hoorn, A., Schulz, E., Hasselbring, W., & Krcmar, H. (2018). WESSBAS: Extraction of probabilistic workload specifications for load testing and performance prediction-a model-driven approach for session-based application systems. eng. *Software and Systems Modeling , 17*(2), 443–477.
37. Wang, X., Zhou, B., & Li, W. (2010). Model based load testing of web applications. In *International Symposium on Parallel and Distributed Processing with Applications* (pp. 483–490).
38. Zhu, L.-Z., & Li, F. (2011). The collection and analysis of performance parameters in web applications. In *Proceedings of 2011 International Conference on Electronics and Optoelectronics* (vol. 3, pp. V3-150–V3-154).